THE COMPLETE BOOK OF
TARTAN

THE COMPLETE BOOK OF
TARTAN

A heritage encyclopedia of over 400 tartans and the stories that shaped Scottish history

IAIN ZACZEK AND CHARLES PHILLIPS

HERMES HOUSE

This edition is published by Hermes House

Hermes House is an imprint of Anness Publishing Ltd
Hermes House, 88–89 Blackfriars Road, London SE1 8HA
tel. 020 7401 2077; fax 020 7633 9499; info@anness.com

© Anness Publishing Ltd 2004

A CIP catalogue record for this book is available from the British Library.

Publisher: Joanna Lorenz
Editorial Director: Helen Sudell
Executive Editor: Joanne Rippin
Picture Research: Bob Lawson
Designer: Nigel Partridge
Editorial Reader: Penelope Goodare
Production Controller: Stephen Lang

1 3 5 7 9 10 8 6 4 2

CONTENTS

INTRODUCTION

All over the world, tartan is immediately recognized as a symbol of the Scottish people and their culture. It is glamorous, colourful and conjures up a romantic set of associations – the sway of the kilt, the skirl of the pipes, and brave Highlanders fighting for their rights.

The history of tartan lives up to these expectations. Over the centuries, its fortunes have ebbed and flowed. It has been mocked as the attire of savages, who were too poor to afford trousers; it has been outlawed, as the uniform of dangerous rebels; but ultimately it has triumphed, becoming a badge of honour not only for native Scots, but for their descendants around the globe.

CELTIC ROOTS AND HIGHLAND CULTURE
From ancient times the Celts, early inhabitants of the Highlands, enjoyed a high reputation as weavers, and they did much to develop the clan system, which has become so closely associated with the wearing of tartan.

▼ *Scotland's most romantic hero, Bonnie Prince Charlie.*

▲ *Tartan is produced in large quantities and endless variety.*

Although Scotland had won its independence early on in the 14th century, it was still a divided land. The Lowlands were increasingly drawn into the orbit of English affairs, while the Highlands remained isolated. The language was Gaelic, different religious and political views were held and the economy was different and much poorer. In purely physical terms, both the climate and the terrain could be challenging, while transport links were virtually non-existent, deterring all but the most intrepid visitor.

This isolation helped to preserve Highland dress and tartan, but at the same time it heightened a sense of disaffection. While the Stuart kings were on the throne, these feelings were kept in check, but after James VII lost his crown, many clans felt alienated. Events such as the Massacre of Glencoe (1692) and the Act of Union (1707), through which Scotland lost both its Parliament and its independence, moved much of the Highlands to the brink of rebellion.

THE BAN ON TARTAN
Succeeding generations have romanticized the two Jacobite uprisings (1715 and 1745), in which the Highland chiefs sought to restore the Stuarts to the British throne. In reality, they were unmitigated disasters from the rebels' point of view; they hastened the demise of the clan system and almost brought about the destruction of tartan itself.

For the uncompromising British solution was to root out the entire cultural system that had spawned the rebels. Tartan and Highland dress were among the prime targets. The ban on wearing tartan remained in force for a generation, so before it had even evolved into a recognized system for identifying the clan of the wearer, tartan seemed to be threatened with extinction.

REVIVAL

Tartan was rescued from obscurity by its links with the army, however. In a bid to boost recruitment for the new Highland regiments, which were needed to protect the interests of the growing British empire, the English government exempted soldiers from the ban. At the same time, the Romantic movement cast Highlanders in a new light. Increasingly, they were no longer seen as a threat to national security, but as the colourful and exotic descendants of the mysterious ancient Celts.

This change of image was confirmed in 1822, when George IV paid a state visit to Edinburgh. The event was a glorious pageant, in which the Highland clans took centre stage. The success of this venture had instant impact, and many of the elements of Highland costume only date back as far as this influential period. The romantic image of the Highlands was perpetuated by Queen Victoria, who developed a deep love for the area. At the same time, historians and enthusiasts endeavoured to document what they could of Highland culture.

MODERN DEVELOPMENTS

A similar dichotomy was apparent during much of the 20th century. On the one hand, the old romantic image of the Highlands began to degenerate into tourist cliché. It seemed as if tartan was destined to become little more than a form of packaging, for use on tins of shortbread or other souvenirs of Scotland. Equally, though, the expansion of tartan into other areas gave new life to the tradition. The creation

▶ *The sword and shield of a traditional Scottish warrior.*

▲ *Iqbal Singh, owner of a Scottish castle and his own tartan.*

of modern tartans started to accelerate in the 1950s. New designs covered a much broader range of themes, including commemorative and corporate tartans. Many of a considerable number of foreign tartans reflected a growing interest in traditional activities, such as Scottish country dancing and Highland games. In the United States and Canada there has been mounting interest in the celebration of Tartan Day. In addition, tartan has attracted the attention of fashion designers, and wearing Highland attire remains in vogue at celebrity events. Alongside all this, tartan has lost none of its power as an emotive symbol, however, and it is still a regular feature of purely Scottish landmark events and state occasions.

Purists may have their doubts about a few of the innovations, but the truth is that tartan is part of a living and ever developing tradition and, as such, a certain amount of change is inevitable. Far from diluting its Scottish character, the international scope of new tartan designs helps to strengthen and promote Scottish culture around the world.

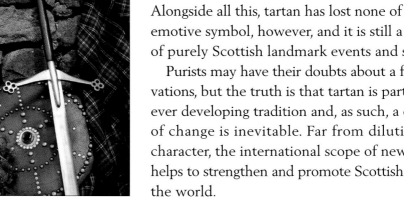

THE HISTORY OF TARTAN

TARTAN ORIGINS

THE STORY OF SCOTLAND'S NATIONAL DRESS IS BOUND UP
WITH THE COLOURFUL HISTORY OF THE HIGHLANDS.
THE CELTIC INHERITANCE AND THE UNIQUE COMPOSITION
OF THE HIGHLAND CLANS INSPIRED A LOVE OF THE BRIGHT
TARTAN CLOTHING THAT EVERY FAMILY WORE WITH PRIDE.

THE ORIGINS OF TARTAN

Although the origins of tartan extend far back into Scotland's past, the meaning of the term has changed over the centuries. Initially it referred to the type of cloth that was worn by Highlanders, rather than to its pattern, or to any notions of kinship. The word probably stemmed from the French *tiretaine* or *tertaine*, which described a coarse blend of linen and wool that is also known as linsey-woolsey.

THEORIES AND MYTHS

The derivation from the French is not universally accepted, but historical sources do offer some clues about the original purpose of tartan. It is apparent from the *Senchus Mor* ("Great Tradition"), an important anthology of documents relating to the legal system of the ancient Celts, that stripes were used as an indication of rank on early

▼ *Part of a series of Roman carvings found near the Antonine Wall offers clues to the ancient Celtic style of dress.*

clothing. Thus, a king's apparel would feature seven stripes, a druid's six, and so on down to the lowliest peasant, who was entitled to a single stripe. The colour of the stripes was also significant, and it seems possible that this symbolic form of attire may have provided inspiration for the initial development of tartan.

Alongside these perfectly feasible theories, there have been other, more speculative offerings. One scholar argued that the word emerged as a corruption of "Tartar", referring to the warlike people of central Asia. Another authority linked it with an Assyrian general named Tartan, who is mentioned fleetingly in the Bible (II Kings XVIII, 17 and Isaiah XX, 1) as the conqueror of the city of Ashdod. In both cases, the supposed link appears to have been based on little more than a perceived similarity between the exotic and colourful Highland garb and that of the inhabitants of those distant, eastern regions.

GAELIC TRADITION

Some authorities claim that the word tartan comes from the Gaelic *tuar* ("colour") and *tan* ("district"), arguing that this accords well with the theory that the design of individual tartans originally indicated a region, rather than a specific clan. The proposition is tempting, but largely unsupported by documentary evidence. Instead, the earliest references to tartan in Gaelic texts invariably made use of the word *breacan*, meaning "speckled".

CONTEMPORARY SOURCES

The earliest information we have about the Celts is from their enemies, the Romans. The latter acknowledged that the Celts were skilled at weaving and dyeing, and they often commented on their love of colourful clothing. A fragment of a stone carving, discovered near the Antonine Wall in southern Scotland, shows Celtic warriors (either Picts or Caledonians) wearing something akin to the *sagum*, a type of military cloak. Like the plaid, which developed later, this was fastened at the shoulder with a pin or brooch.

From Ireland, the Scoti, or Scots, brought a garment known as a *leine croich* – a saffron shirt or tunic, perhaps made of linen, that extended almost to the knee. This was probably the dress described in the *Saga of Magnus Barefoot* (1093), the earliest known reference to the Highlanders' clothing. The saga describes how the Norwegian king, Magnus III, led an expedition to the Western Isles to force the Scots king, Edgar, to acknowledge his claim to the Hebrides. The campaign proved so successful that Magnus and his followers decided to adopt the local style

of dress – "a short tunic and upper garments". Attempts have been made to interpret the tunic as an early version of the kilt; it is more likely that this was the *leine*, but the unclassified "upper garments" may well have been

▼ *Clansmen used a belt to gather up the long folds of their plaid and keep it in a manageable state.*

a precursor of the long woollen cloth known as a plaid. Either way, Magnus's new attire won him the nickname Barfod ("barefoot" or "barelegs").

This style of dress was slow to change, and more than four centuries later, the historian John Major described the garb of the Highlanders in similar terms. "From the middle of the thigh to the foot they have no covering for the leg, clothing themselves with a mantle instead of an upper garment, and a shirt dyed with saffron…"

THE POPULARITY OF PLAID
By the 16th century, there was growing evidence of the adoption of the plaid. In 1582, George Buchanan noted how some Highlanders were selecting the colours of their attire for camouflage rather than tribal allegiances: "They delight in variegated garments, especially stripes, and their favourite colours are purple and blue. Their ancestors wore plaids of many colours, and numbers still retain this custom, but the majority now in their dress prefer a dark brown, imitating nearly the leaves of the heather, that when lying upon the heath in the day, they may not be discovered…" Buchanan marvelled at their hardiness, facing the elements in their scanty apparel: "…in these [plaids], wrapped rather than covered, they brave the severest storms

◄ *Early Highlanders wore variants of the* leine croich, *a linen tunic that originated in Ireland.*

in the open air and sometimes lay themselves down to sleep, even in the midst of snow…"

Tartan had already received the official seal of approval, for the 1538 accounts of the Lord High Treasurer reveal that James V was the first member of the royal family to order a Highland outfit. The items included "two and a quarter ells [1 ell = 1.1m/3¾ft] of variously coloured velvet for a short Highland coat at £6 per ell; three and a quarter ells of green taffeta, to line the said coat…and three ells of Highland tartan for the hose." In other words, the king was ordering a pair of tartan trews (tight trousers) and a short, multicoloured jacket.

▼ *John Speed's map of Scotland of 1646 showed Highlanders in skimpy plaids, emphasizing their poverty.*

WHAT IS A TARTAN?

In its structure, a tartan is essentially a checked pattern. This type of design is common to many cultures and can be traced back to prehistoric times. In Scotland, the earliest surviving example is the so-called Falkirk sett, which dates from the 3rd century AD. Excavated from a site near the Antonine Wall (a boundary wall erected by the Romans in southern Scotland), this tiny piece of fabric had been used as a stopper in an earthenware pot containing a hoard of silver coins. The cloth itself had not been dyed: its checked pattern was formed from the natural colouring of woven wool from brown and white varieties of Soay sheep.

This kind of simple woven checked pattern was used for centuries, in both the Lowlands and the Highlands, by shepherds for their plaids and *mauds*

▲ *Found near Falkirk, this fragment of cloth is thought to be the oldest example of Scottish tartan.*

or wraps, and came to be known as "the shepherd's plaid". The design is distinct from the clan tartans that developed at a later stage, since no symbolic overtones linked it to a particular place or group of people. Significantly, the tartan that it most resembles is the Scott Black and White, designed by Sir Walter Scott in 1822.

PATTERNS AND COLOURS

The pattern of an individual tartan is often described as a "sett". This refers to its structure, which was originally defined by exactly measuring the width of each stripe. More recently this method has been replaced by a precise thread-count. Some weavers are said to have kept a record of the early setts by colour-coding and numbering the threads on pattern-sticks.

Most setts are symmetrical. Each series of stripes is reversed around a

◄ *The shepherd's plaid, worn here by the poet James Hogg, is the simplest of all tartans.*

central stripe, known as the pivot. The blocks of pattern are then repeated in a regular fashion throughout the entire design. In a few cases, the structure of the sett is asymmetrical. Instead of reversing around pivots, these patterns are simply repeated over and over again. Additionally, in some of the older tartans, the sequences of stripes on the warp and the weft are different, and this also affects the symmetrical appearance of the design.

The colouring of individual setts may be described as "ancient" or "modern", which rather confusingly does not necessarily indicate the age of the sett. The term ancient refers to the colours produced by natural vegetable dyes, which were used until the mid-18th century and were generally very mellow in appearance. It may also be used to describe newer colours that imitate this natural effect. Modern colours are those produced using chemical dyes, which became available from the 1860s. As the precise shade of each colour was governed by the availability of dyes and the taste of individual weavers, different versions of the same tartan may look quite different and yet still be correct.

▼ *On a loom, threads are stretched out lengthwise to create the warp, while those woven across it form the weft.*

FUNCTIONALITY OF TARTAN

From an early stage, tartans were classified according to their purpose. In addition to their standard setts, many clans also adopted their own "dress" and "hunting" tartans. The latter were devised for those families who normally sported very bright colours, which were deemed unsuitable for the chase. In hunting setts, earthy colours such as muted browns and greens usually predominated. This did not mean that the outfit itself was necessarily plain. One of the earliest depictions of a hunting tartan was featured in John Michael Wright's portrait of Lord Mungo Murray. Painted in the early 1680s, the wearer's costume can only be described as ostentatious, even if the colouring is restrained.

TARTAN WEAVE

The checked pattern of a tartan is formed by interweaving two bands of stripes at right angles. First, the weaver sets the warp (the lengthwise threads) on the loom. The weft, or crosswise threads, are then woven into the warp. Traditionally, the patterns of the warp and the weft are identical, although it was not uncommon for slightly different yarns to be used to form each of these. For practical purposes, the yarn used for the warp is the stronger of the two.

The style of weave is known as twill. This means that each thread passes first over two and then under two of its crosswise counterparts. This produces the ribbed, diagonal effect on the length of material, where two different colours are blended. The only exception to this is the selvedge (the narrow border at the edge of the tartan), where a different style of weaving is often employed to prevent the fabric from unravelling.

By contrast, dress tartans were designed to be showy. They were used on formal occasions and have become popular wear at Highland dances. Generally, the design is a variant of the clan's normal tartan, but with one of the background colours changed to white. In direct contrast to the positive mood that dress tartans were meant to evoke, some clans also had special wear for periods of mourning. These are now rare, and the two Stewart mourning setts are among the very few that are still registered.

▲ *Wright's portrait of Mungo Murray shows how elaborate Highland dress could be when worn by the aristocracy.*

The *earasaid*, usually anglicized as "arisaid", provided another category of tartan. This garment, which was worn by many women in the Highlands and islands until the 18th century, was a large shawl or plaid that could also be used to cover the head. Some clans adopted specific tartans for arisaids. The MacLeod and Perry arisaids are among the few registered examples.

EARLY TARTAN CLOTHING

During the years when clan tartans were developing, Highlanders wore the designs in three ways: the belted plaid, the kilt, and trews. The respective merits of each were keenly debated from the outset, and the topic was to grow more contentious in later years.

By the 18th century, enthusiasts were producing pamphlets on the subject. Typical of this was the lively correspondence between the antiquarian John Pinkerton and Sir John Sinclair of Ulbster. In 1795, after hearing how the latter was championing the cause of trews, Pinkerton wrote to congratulate him: "When I first saw in the papers that you had appeared at court in a new Highland dress, substituting trousers or pantaloons for the

▼ *By fastening their plaid at the left shoulder, warriors were able to wield a weapon effectively with their right arm.*

THE KILT'S ORIGINS

There are numerous theories about the origins of the kilt. A controversial one is that it was invented by an Englishman, Thomas Rawlinson, who worked in the Glengarry iron works. Finding the plaid impractical, he divided it into two parts. The chief of Glengarry copied the idea and the kilt spread rapidly. Rawlinson's views on Highland attire are documented, but the notion that he invented the kilt remains questionable.

philabeg [kilt], I was highly pleased… The Highland dress is, in fact, quite modern and any improvement may be made without violating antiquity. Nay, the trousers are far more ancient than the philabeg."

THE VERSATILITY OF PLAID

The word "plaid" is sometimes used as a synonym for tartan, but it refers more specifically to the long woollen cloth worn over the shoulder. Supposedly first adopted by the Picts, such a cloth was formerly a standard form of dress among the ancient Scoti. The term has been linked to the Gaelic *plaide* ("blanket"), although this may have been a borrowing from a Scottish word already in use.

As a garment, the plaid was both simple and versatile. Essentially, it was a long, rectangular strip of fabric that required no sewing or tailoring. In order to put it on, the wearer first placed it on the ground, on top of his belt, and arranged it into pleats. He then lay down on it, fixing the belt around his waist and ensuring that the material reached down almost to his knees. When he stood up, the lower half of the plaid resembled a kilt. After donning a coat or jacket, the surplus material could either be looped over one shoulder, where it was attached with a brooch, or else employed as a cloak. Even after the advent of the kilt, the plaid remained a popular choice for Highlanders when they were engaged on military activities because, if they needed to sleep outdoors, it could also serve as a blanket.

THE HISTORY OF TREWS

Triubhas, or trews, also have a long history, and have sometimes been linked with the *braccae* (breeches) of the Gauls. They were close fitting and, in many cases, elaborately tailored. On the most expensive examples, the seams were decorated with gold braid or lace. Even on less costly items, the seams had to be carefully sewn so that the pattern matched. The checks of the tartans used to make trews were usually smaller than those used for plaids.

▲ Raeburn's portrait of Niel Gow (c.1796) shows a combination of breeches and hose of similar pattern.

There has been some debate about the occasions on which trews were worn. In his book *The Scottish Gael* (1831), James Logan suggested they were mainly intended for use by sick, lame or old Highlanders. Other sources have claimed that they were used in bad weather, or by Highlanders travelling in the Lowlands, who felt that they would look too conspicuous in a kilt. It has also been claimed that the garments carried class overtones, since they were frequently worn by chiefs and gentlemen, particularly when they were out riding.

As with the plaid, early illustrations show that trews took on many different forms. One popular variant was the use of matching breeches and stockings, which met at the knee. This combination is evident in Sir Henry Raeburn's portrait of Niel Gow, the celebrated fiddler. At first glance, he appears to be wearing a pair of tartan trews. Upon examination, however, it can be seen that he is wearing breeches buttoned along the side of the thigh. These reach down almost to his stockings, which are of a similar design.

WOMEN'S TARTAN

The plaid was also worn by women, usually in the form of a long shawl. On a visit to Scotland in 1636, Sir William Brereton noted that these garments were draped over their heads, covering their faces, "and would reach almost to the ground, but that they pluck them up, and wear them cast under their arms." A century later, the traveller

Martin Martin observed that these plaids were predominantly white, with a few small coloured stripes, and that they were often fastened at the breast with a buckle. In the Highlands, the garment was usually known as an arisaid, or *tanac*. By the 18th century, tartan dresses had also become popular in some quarters. These were modelled on contemporary styles, with low-cut bodices and wide sleeves.

ARRIVAL OF THE KILT

The kilt was a comparatively late arrival in the tartan story, although there is considerable debate about the way it actually evolved. Initially, it was known as the *fèileadh beag* ("little plaid"), in order to distinguish it from the *fèileadh breacain* ("plaid of tartan") or the *fèileadh mor* ("big plaid"). It was commonly anglicized as "philabeg". The word "kilt" derives from Danish *kilte* ("to tuck up") and is related to the literal meaning of *fèileadh* ("folded").

▼ In the Highlands, the standard form of female attire was the arisaid. This example features the Sinclair tartan.

TRADITIONAL WEAVING

Travellers who toured the Highlands before the mid-18th-century ban on wearing tartan were much impressed by the standard of the weaving. Most were astonished that, in areas where many people lived on the poverty line, it was possible to produce clothing of such quality. In some communities there were professional weavers, but in the majority of cases everyday garments were produced at home by the women of the household.

By the end of the 1700s many commentators regretted the damage that had been done to Scotland's native weaving skills during the period of proscription. "The Act of 1746, discharging the Highland Dress, had the worst of consequences," lamented one citizen of Kincardine. "Prior to that period, the Highland women were remarked for their skill and success in spinning and dyeing wool, and clothing themselves and their households, each according to her fancy, in tartans, fine, beautiful and durable."

▼ *Weaving began on simple looms that were later modified for the Industrial Revolution.*

▲ *Female weavers often worked as a team, singing rhythmic "waulking" songs to ensure that they worked in unison.*

A HOME-BASED CRAFT

The preparation of the material was a lengthy process and involved a range of different skills – spinning and dyeing the wool, weaving, and fulling the lengths of cloth.

The wool had to be carded and spun into yarn before being dyed and woven. For the weaving, the women used small hand looms, throwing the shuttle from hand to hand, which placed limitations on the size of the items that could be produced. In many cases, it was necessary to sew two lengths of tartan together in order to create a standard plaid.

The most colourful process, however, was the fulling of the cloth, which was known as *luathadh*, or "waulking" the cloth. The purpose of this was to cleanse the wool of oil and shrink the cloth to thicken and felt it, making it

PATTERN-STICKS

According to the 17th-century observer Martin Martin, female weavers kept careful records of the patterns they used. In an account of his travels in the Western Isles, he noted that "the women are at great pains, first to give an exact pattern of the plad upon a piece of wood, having the number of every thred of the stripe on it."

Some authorities have cast doubt on the accuracy of this particular passage, however, since no original pattern-sticks have survived from the period prior to the ban on tartan.

▼ *Weavers were said to use pattern-sticks to help them remember the thread-counts of individual tartans.*

more hard-wearing. The cloth was washed in warm water and urine (used as a source of ammonia), then laid upon a board with a ribbed or uneven surface. A length of wattle-work was ideal for this but, if there was nothing else, a door would be taken off its hinges and placed on the ground. On the island of St Kilda, it was traditional to use a mat made of thick grass ropes. About a dozen women sat on either side of the cloth and kneaded it against the board. When their arms grew tired, they would waulk the material with their bare feet. They worked as a team, moving the cloth rhythmically and in unison. To help them co-ordinate their efforts, they would sing one of the many popular Highland waulking songs, which became louder and louder as the work progressed.

NATURAL DYES

The preparation of the dyes may have been equally picturesque, but details have long since been lost. Costume historians regret this, since the early Highland tartans were renowned for having colours that remained fast and did not fade. Many visitors reported having seen garments that were reputedly over a hundred years old but were still as brightly coloured as the day they came off the loom.

The dyes themselves mostly came from local vegetable sources. In the 19th century James Logan noted that although the Highlanders had little access to imported colours, "their native hills afforded articles with which they had found the art of dyeing brilliant, permanent and pleasing colours." He went on to say, "Every good farmer's wife was competent to dye blue, red, green, yellow, black, brown and their compounds. When we consider the care with which the Highlanders arranged and preserved the patterns of their different tartans, and the pride which they had in this manufacture, we must believe that the dyers spared no

pains to preserve and improve the excellence of their craft."

The most widely used dyes came from such items as bark, roots, moss, heather and bog-myrtle, but many Highlanders were evidently prepared to experiment. In the 1750s, Cuthbert Gordon of Banffshire produced a new purple dye, which he made out of a variety of lichens. He named this "cudbear" (after his first name) and marketed it with great success, after taking out advertisements in the *Scots' Magazine*. Similarly, when James Logan was researching for *The Scottish Gael*, he met a clansman who proudly declared: "Give me bullock's blood and lime, and I will produce you fine colours."

Perhaps the greatest accolade that these early dyeing techniques have received is the amount of time and effort that today's tartan manufacturers spend in trying to reproduce them. Synthetic dyes can appear harsh, and producers have taken great pains to mimic the "ancient" colours of the vegetable dyes. Significantly, the body that regulates the production of tartan has rejected suggestions that manufacturers should standardize their colours by adopting the international colour code.

▼ *Vegetable dyes could produce surprisingly bright, unfading colours.*

EARLY DISTRICT TARTANS

One of the main reasons why clansmen were able to develop their distinctive form of dress was the isolated nature of their homeland. Prior to the 18th century, travel in the Highlands was a difficult and dangerous affair. Transport links were virtually non-existent, some parts of the terrain were hard to cross, the climate could seem forbidding and, for southerners, the Gaelic-speaking areas presented language problems. None of these factors prevented a series of intrepid travellers from touring the northern regions, however, and the accounts they published have provided valuable information.

ASSOCIATIONS WITH LOCATION

Although accounts of this kind were often colourful and detailed, they shed very little light on the extent to which specific tartans were adopted by individual clans. Instead, the most telling account suggests that early tartans were a better indicator of place than of family. Martin Martin, who was himself a Gaelic-speaking Highlander, wrote the following in his *Description of the Western Isles of Scotland* (*c*.1695), one of the earliest books on the region: "The plad, worn only be the men, is made of fine wool, the thred as fine as can be made of that kind; it consists of

divers colours, so as to be agreable to the nicest fancy... Every Isle differs from each other in their fancy of making plads as to the stripes in breadth and colours. The humour is as different through the mainland of the Highlands, in so far that they who have seen those places are able, at the first view of a man's plad, to guess the place of his residence."

Martin's views have come under very close scrutiny, with experts seeking to iron out every possible ambiguity in his text. There has been discussion,

▲ *Since dyers used local materials, the colours of the landscape, as in this view of Ben Nevis and Inverlochy Castle, were echoed in many tartans.*

for example, of the precise meaning of "guess". Was this meant to convey any uncertainty on the author's part? Or was it simply an example of the narrower, 17th-century meaning of the word, roughly equivalent to "know"? Some commentators have argued that Martin's views are not incompatible with the idea that tartan grew out of

▼ *The Glen Orchy district tartan dates back to at least the early 1800s.*

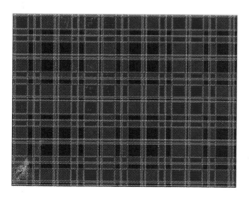

▼ *The 18th-century Huntly district tartan may have Jacobite overtones.*

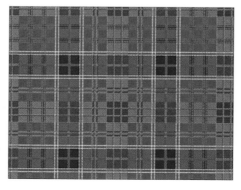

▼ *The Lennox is unusual in being both a district and a family tartan.*

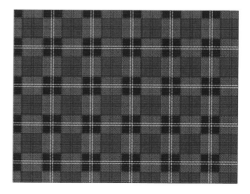

the clan system. Instead, they point out, his book underlines the close links that the clans had already forged with their ancestral territories.

LOCAL CLAN TARTANS

In spite of these reservations, the importance of the early district tartans is now readily acknowledged. In particular, historians have noted how some territorial setts – notably those of Old Lochaber, Lennox, Huntly and Glen Orchy – appear to have formed the basis of a number of local clan tartans.

The Huntly region, in north-east Scotland, provided one of the oldest known district tartans. Several clans were wearing it in the years leading up to the 1745 Jacobite uprising, among them the Gordons, the Forbes, the Munros, the MacRaes, the Rosses and the Brodies. Bonnie Prince Charlie is believed to have worn a variation of it while staying with the MacRaes, and his hosts appear to have employed it earlier in the century, when they fought at the battle of Sheriffmuir in 1715.

The prominent reds and greens of Huntly are reminiscent of several of the clan setts that were later introduced in this region, particularly those of the

▼ The Falls of Arkaig are in the region of Lochaber, which produced one of the earliest known tartans.

Munro, Ross and MacRae tartans. By contrast, the colour schemes that evolved in the Old Lochaber district, in the west Central Highlands, were far more muted and earthy. Lochaber lay in the heartlands of the Campbells and its tartan, which dates back to at least the 18th century, undoubtedly influenced their four main setts. It also has an affinity with the designs approved by the nearby MacDonald clan and with the principal military tartan, the Black Watch. The closest match, however, is with the Fergusson sett.

Situated in a picturesque stretch of Argyllshire, Glen Orchy is also in Campbell country. Its early district tartan appears to be one of the designs discovered by the agents of Wilson's of Bannockburn, the renowned tartan

▲ The Bridge of Orchy spans the River Dochard in the area that spawned the Glen Orchy sett.

manufacturers. Its structure, which features boxes within boxes with alternating light and dark squares, is reminiscent of several clan tartans of the area. These include the setts of the Stewarts of Appin, the MacGillivrays, the MacDonells of Keppoch, the MacIntyres and the MacColls.

The Lennox sett is actually a Lowland tartan, relating to a district north of Glasgow. Said to have been based on a lost 16th-century portrait, it can claim to considerable antiquity, and was certainly used as a source for some of the patterns introduced after the tartan revival of the 19th century.

HIGHLAND DRESS

Typical of 17th-century accounts of Highland clothing is the following extract from the writings of John Taylor, better known as the Water Poet. It describes the spectacle in 1618, when, at the invitation of the Earl of Mar, he joined a hunting party at Braemar.

"Their habit is shooes with but one sole apiece; stockings (which they call short hose) made of a warme stuff of divers colours, which they call tartane.

As for breeches, many of them, nor their forefathers, never wore any, but a jerkin of the same stuffe as their hose…with a plaed about their shoulders, which is a mantle of divers colours, much finer and lighter stuffe than their hose."

Taylor went on to stress that this form of dress was adopted by men of all classes, and was worn with a sense of pride.

THE CELTIC CONTEXT

The earliest tartans may have been notable for their geographical associations, but ultimately the links with the Highland clans were to prove far more significant. This extended family system traces its roots back to the nation's Celtic origins. The Celts spread their influence far and wide throughout Europe, and some elements of their social practices can be found elsewhere, particularly in Ireland, but it was the exceptional conditions in Scotland that enabled the clans to flourish.

CELTIC ANCESTRY

Initially an ancient people who flourished in central Europe, the Celts were mentioned in historical documents from the 6th century BC, but archaeologists have found hints that their culture may date back even further. In their heyday they were extremely powerful, even managing to sack the strongholds of Rome in 386 BC and Delphi in 279 BC. With the growth of the Roman Empire, however, their

▼ *Located in the heart of Dalriada, this stone footprint was used during the inauguration ceremonies of chieftains.*

▲ *This carving of Pictish warriors at Aberlemno may represent their victory over the Angles at Nechtansmere (685).*

influence declined and they were gradually pushed westwards, towards the fringes of the continent. Eventually, they were restricted to just a few areas beyond the confines of the empire. These included Scotland, Ireland, Wales, Cornwall and the region of Brittany in north-west France.

THE SCOTI

Rather than a single race, the Celts were a loose association of tribes. The Scoti, or Scots, were one such tribe, first

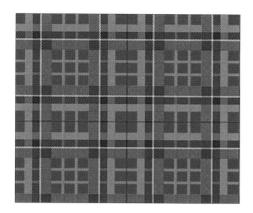

▲ *The name of the Caledonia tartan ultimately derives from a Celtic tribe based in the Tay valley area.*

recorded in the north-east of Ireland, where their principal sphere of influence was the tiny kingdom of Dál Riata, or Dalriada. Fierce intertribal conflicts prompted a group of Scoti to make the 19km/12-mile sea journey to the Argyll coast on the west side of Scotland, where they established a new settlement based on the rocky stronghold of Dunadd. This branch of Dalriada was founded in about AD 500. The kingdom remained divided for more than a century, but the Irish and Argyllshire Scoti maintained very close links. The latter gradually extended their influence in western Scotland, however, and severed ties with their homeland in Ireland.

THE PICTS

The Scoti were by no means the only Celtic tribe inhabiting the northern part of Britain. Their most illustrious rivals were the Picts.

Traditionally, these people were associated with the north-eastern areas of present-day Scotland, which was often described as Pictland. In common with the Scoti, however, they actually settled in a number of different regions in both Britain and Ireland. The Picts left no written records and, as a result, much of the information about their shadowy history is available only from Roman sources. Their name comes

from the Latin word for "the painted ones", alluding to their custom of painting or tattooing their bodies.

Very few Scottish families have managed to establish any link with this ancient people. Among the clans that claim Pictish descent are the Ogilvies, the Brodies, the Hendersons of Glencoe and the MacNaughtons. The latter have one of the stronger claims, given that their name derives from Nechtan, a celebrated Pictish king.

The Romans identified different tribes within the Picts. The most notable of these were the Venturiones, who were based in the tiny kingdom of Fortriu, which stretched from the Forth to the Tay, and the Caledonii, from whose name the Latin name for Scotland – Caledonia – is derived. In later years, it lost its precise historical meaning and came to be used as a poetic term for Scotland in its entirety. This trend peaked during the Romantic era, and the name's popularity at that time can be gauged by the fact that Caledonia was one of the very first fancy tartans produced by Wilson's of Bannockburn in 1819.

KENNETH MACALPIN'S ALBA

While the southern Celtic tribes wrestled for control with the Angles (the Germanic people who would eventually give their name to England) the Highlands were contested by the Scoti of Dalriada and the Picts. Their rivalry was eventually resolved in the mid-9th century by Kenneth MacAlpin, a Scot who gained the kingship of Dalriada in 840 but achieved real power only when he also acquired the Pictish throne seven years later.

This was not the first time that a single ruler had held both titles, but Kenneth managed to make the situation permanent. His own supporters claimed that his success was due to his mixed origins (his mother was a Pictish princess), though others believed it owed more to his brutal methods. The

rumours that he had murdered his Pictish rivals for the throne at a banquet persisted for generations.

Kenneth's enlarged kingdom was called Alba, or Albany, although by the end of the 9th century it was already better known as Scotland. Even though the territory did not include much of the Lowlands, the uniting of the two crowns is traditionally viewed as the first significant step in the creation of the Scottish nation. In the context of the clan system, this is reflected in the determination of many families to trace their lineage right back to MacAlpin himself. Alongside the more conventional dynasties, a group of clans define themselves as the Siol Alpin ("race of Alpin"), even though the true extent of their links with the ancient king is open to question. These clans include the MacNabs, the Grants, the MacKinnons and the MacAulays.

▼ *A medieval depiction of Kenneth MacAlpin, who managed to form a lasting union between Scots and Picts.*

SCOTTISH SURNAMES

Although most books about Highland clans and their tartans are structured around surnames, these were actually a comparatively late development. For centuries, most Europeans made use of patronymics, emphasizing the name of the individual's father: for example, Gregor, son of Donald. In Scotland, "son of" was conveyed by the Gaelic prefix *mac*, so he would be known as Gregor MacDonald. While this may have resembled a surname, it did of course change with each generation. Thus, Gregor MacDonald's son would be a MacGregor. This system proved confusing in written records and, in addition, made it hard to identify a person's clan from their name.

FIXED SURNAMES
In western Europe, the custom of using fixed surnames dates from around the 11th century. It developed initially in France, reaching some southern areas of Scotland in the following century. The Highlands were far more resistant to the idea, and the system did not really catch on until the 17th century.

Patronymics continued to be a common feature of fixed surnames. Increasingly though, the father in question was less likely to be the immediate parent. Instead, the patronymic usually referred to a distinguished ancestor, and within the context of a clan it was frequently applied to the dynasty's founder. In most cases, this ancestor was a genuine historical figure, but some surnames contained an aspirational element, as the genealogists of the clan strove to trace their descent from a legendary hero or ancient king, whose true lineage had long been lost.

The spelling of some names highlighted the differences between the Highlands and the Lowlands. The *mac* form, for example, was used in the former, while further south it was often anglicized as the suffix "son", as in Donaldson rather than MacDonald. The same meaning was also sometimes conveyed by adding "s" at the end of the forename; thus Andrews means "son of Andrew".

TERRITORIAL NAMES
While patronymics were the most ancient form of Scottish name, they were soon overtaken in popularity by territorial names. Most of these were based on the lands where the person lived, and this was certainly the system most favoured by the authorities. At the Council of Forfar in 1061, Malcolm III (r.1058–93) urged his subjects to adopt the practice. For a feudal ruler, the advantages were obvious, since it tied people to the land. However, territorial names were equally popular with clan chiefs, because they helped to bind their supporters to their ancestral homelands. Private landowners can often be identified through the uniquely Scottish phrase "of that Ilk". This means "of the same place", referring to the estate of the lord, or laird. A typical example of this form is the name of Sir Iain Moncreiffe, 24th of that Ilk, the genealogist and one of the foremost authorities on Scottish clans and tartans.

In many cases, territorial names indicated the origins of a person, rather than their place of residence. In Scotland, a high proportion of these were linked with locations in Normandy (such as Bruce, Cumming and Menzies). These ultimately stemmed from the aftermath of the Norman Conquest in 1066 for,

◄ *Many surnames reflect common medieval trades and pastimes. Hunting was an obvious source of names.*

although William I's followers settled in England, some of their descendants later began to migrate north in search of new opportunities.

In the same way, a few surnames offer clues to the nationality of a person. For obvious reasons, these names were applied to foreigners so that, although Scott is a common name in Scotland, it was more widely used south of the border. Instead, the most widely used national names were Inglis ("English"), Wallace (from a word that meant "foreigner", but was also linked to the root of Welsh) and Fleming ("Flemish"). As with the Norman names, these examples can sometimes be linked to specific historical events. It is no surprise, for instance, that the number of Flemings in Scotland increased after 1155, when Henry II expelled them from England.

OCCUPATIONAL NAMES

After territorial themes, the most common sources of Scottish surnames were occupations or trades. These were of particular relevance to the clans, since many of their ancestral leaders had acquired important hereditary posts. The most celebrated examples of this were the Stewarts, who derived their name from their role as high stewards

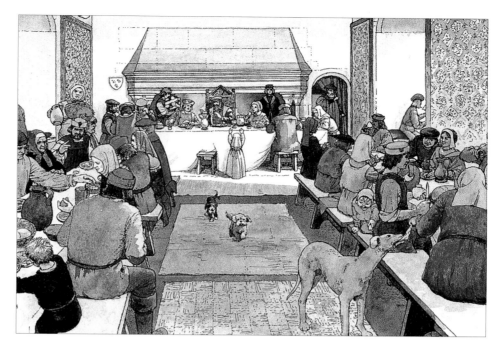

▼ *Scottish surnames often have religious links, as the Church was an extremely popular choice of profession.*

to the royal household. On a less exalted level, many names can be related to hunting (Hunter, Warren, Fletcher) or to trades related to clothing (Taylor, Glover, Dyer, Weaver) or cooking (Cook, Baker, Baxter). On a few occasions, records may even link some individuals with a specific job. Thus, one branch of the Porter family was so called after five generations had served as head gatekeeper at the abbey in Cupar Angus.

Many surnames have religious overtones. Here, the Scottish approach was markedly different from that in other Christian countries. For while, in most areas, children were simply given the name of a favourite saint, in Scotland

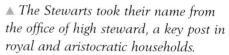

▲ *The Stewarts took their name from the office of high steward, a key post in royal and aristocratic households.*

this was often prefaced by a word that indicated they were a devotee of the holy man in question. The two most common forms were *maol* and *gille*, both of which denoted a servant. Thus the names Malcolm and MacCallum both indicated that the founder of the family was a follower of St Columba, while Gilchrist means "servant of Christ". Names of this kind usually indicated that the ancestor of the family had been a monk or a cleric. A few surnames specified this directly. Typical examples include MacNab ("son of the abbot"), MacTaggart ("son of the priest") and MacMillan ("son of the tonsured one").

NICKNAMES

Some Scottish surnames are based on nicknames. Often, these were colours that were used to describe the hair or complexion of the individual, while others were related to physical attributes. In addition, a number of surnames have Scandinavian origins, underlining the longstanding influence of the Vikings in northern and western Scotland.

THE CLAN SYSTEM

Due to their lack of political organization, throughout their long history the Celts failed to achieve any lasting territorial control. They compensated for this by developing tightly knit, extended family units that gave them cohesion at grass roots level and formed the basis of the clan system.

The Celts operated on a tribal basis, holding their land in common and owing their principal allegiance to a chief. Their basic territorial measurement was the *tuath*, or tribe, which was large enough to provide a fighting force of anything between 500 and 3000 men. Their simplest family grouping was the *derbfhine*, which spanned four generations, linking the descendants of a common great-grandfather. The word *clann* was used to describe a child or children, rather than having the broader sense of kinship that it came to acquire in Scotland.

THE CHIEF'S ROLE

At the heart of the system was the role of the chief. He offered protection to his clansmen, settled their disputes and led them in battle. In return, the clan members yielded to his authority on all

Though borders fluctuated, this map provides a rough guide to the spheres of influence of the major powers.

matters, granting him their unflinching loyalty. They also provided military service for him, as and when it was required. For their part, the chief's followers shared in a right of heritage known as *duthus*, which allowed them to settle and hunt on the clan lands held by their leader.

For these privileges, clan members paid a rent, which was collected and administered by the chief's "tacksmen", minor gentry who effectively acted as estate managers for their chiefs. Clansmen also benefited from a genuine feeling of equality. For, while the chief and his immediate entourage were held in high esteem, the main body of the clan was essentially classless. As the descendant of a distinguished ancestor, each member of the family could consider that they possessed a strain of gentility. "Though I am poor, I am noble," ran the motto of the MacLeans, while "As noble as a

A Victorian painting of Rob Roy paying his rent due to the chief, to his representative, or tacksman.

Scot" was a popular saying. Not surprisingly, perhaps, Scotland's southern neighbours were apt to poke fun at these attitudes. In the 18th century, in particular, English caricaturists frequently satirized the Scots for their obsession with their ancestry.

KEEPERS OF TRADITION

The clan's traditions were upheld by the "sennachie", one of the most important members of the chief's household. Learned in the clan's history, he maintained its records and genealogy, organized the inauguration of each new chief and addressed the host at clan gatherings. At times, the overriding emphasis on tradition could present problems. On more than one occasion, for example, an alliance between different clans was undermined by arguments over a family's customary right to occupy the most prestigious position in the battle formation.

FOSTERAGE AND ALLEGIANCE

Within the clan, family ties were strengthened by an elaborate system of fosterage. Children were often brought up in the household of the chief or a relative. These youngsters were not necessarily orphans; instead, the practice was designed to bind the individual *derbfhine*, or family units, closer together. Fosterage was often a more important link than marriage. The Celts recognized several different types of union – some permanent, others distinctly not. In Scotland, a form of trial marriage, known as "handfasting", was particularly popular, until it was outlawed during the Reformation.

On an economic level, social ties were cemented by the system of "manrent". This was a bond contracted between individual clansmen and their chief. It involved the payment of "calps", or death duties, as a mark of allegiance to the leader, and in return for his

protection. This was payable even if the person in question was not actually living on the clan's estates. Although the practice was outlawed in 1617, it continued on an unofficial basis for many years.

RULES OF SUCCESSION

The various Celtic societies also had a distinctive attitude to the question of succession. They did not insist on primogeniture (the automatic right of inheritance by the firstborn, male child), even if in practice this was often what happened. In many cases, the succession would instead be granted to the most able or the most suitable member of the family units. The heir was nominated during the life of the chief, and was known as the tanist ("second"). There was some variation within the different Celtic communities. The Picts, for example, were unusual in favouring matrilinear succession (that is, through the female line).

The strength of the Highland clan system can be gauged by the fact that it survived the advent of feudalism. On

the face of it, these two organizational structures might seem to be totally incompatible. The clans were essentially tribal in nature, while feudalism was strictly hierarchical, with all power and possessions deriving ultimately from the king. Alone among the Celtic nations, Scotland found a compromise between the two opposing forces. In its hierarchy, the king was recognized as a type of supreme chief, comparable with the high kings of ancient Ireland.

In effect, the early Scottish rulers had little choice but to accept this compromise, given that large parts of the country remained outside direct royal control until the later Middle Ages. This was particularly true in the western isles and the north, where the Scandinavian influence was very strong. Once the nation was genuinely unified, the dual loyalties of the clansmen – to their chief and to the king – became a potential problem. When these conflicted, as they did during the time of the Jacobite rebellions, the authority and independence of the clan chiefs became all too apparent.

▼ *Kinship was all-important in Scotland so paintings of weddings, like this one by John Phillip, were common.*

COMPOSITION OF THE CLANS

Many clans are described as "septs", but since the term covers a variety of different situations this is a highly contentious issue. In its loosest sense, it can suggest followers or dependants, and usually refers to those families who attached themselves to larger clans for reasons of protection, or else to branches within a clan that boasted a surname that was different from their kinfolk (for example the MacIans of clan Donald). However, it can also allude to the complications that arose when patronymic surnames were fixed. The person in question might "freeze" his name to include his father, or else he might choose to honour a more distant ancestor. Either way, this might make it difficult to assess which was his rightful clan.

ADOPTED NAMES

Alongside their "native men" (blood relations), many clans contained "broken men". These were Highlanders who, for one reason or another, could no longer use their own names. The most celebrated example of this was the MacGregor clan. After accusations

▲ *Cattle stealing was endemic in the Highlands; the authorities tried to curb it by outlawing the worst offenders.*

of violent conduct, the name of MacGregor was outlawed in 1603, forcing the clansmen to take other names. Failure to comply with this order amounted to a crime that was punishable by death. For more than a century, the MacGregors were persecuted in this way, living, in Sir Walter Scott's words, as "children of the mist" until the ordinance was repealed in 1774. The most famous of these shadowy figures was Rob Roy, whose career as an outlaw was romantically retold in one of the author's novels.

In order to enhance the power and prestige of their followers, clan chiefs did their utmost to swell clan numbers. Often, they would try to persuade families who were living on their land to adopt their surname. Indeed, some cases were also reported of payments being made to poorer tenants if they would agree to rename their children. In most instances, the families in question needed very little prompting. In an

◄ *One of Waitt's portraits of the Laird of Grant's retinue shows Alastair Grant Mor, the chief's champion.*

age when surnames were still very fluid, it was common for people to take their name from the place where they lived. Scott himself gained first-hand experience of the consequences of moving from one clan territory to the next, when he was travelling through the Highlands. His guide called himself a Gordon, but the writer was convinced that on a previous meeting he had known him by another name. "Yes, certainly," the fellow confirmed, "but that was when I was living on the other side of the hill."

CLAN TARTAN AS LIVERY

Like the clan name, tartan was not used exclusively as the badge of an individual's family or clan; it could also be employed as a form of livery. Throughout the Middle Ages, many chiefs maintained princely courts in the old Celtic fashion. Their retainers included poets and musicians, who held their posts on a hereditary basis

▲ *Music was important in Celtic courts; most chiefs employed a harpist and piper, both hereditary posts.*

and were often dressed in the livery of their masters, irrespective of their own family origins.

The practice of using a clan tartan as livery for retainers survived well into the 18th century, as is confirmed by a remarkable series of portraits belonging to the Grants. This mighty clan reached the peak of its influence in the late 17th century. Ludovic Grant, the 8th Lord of Freuchie, was so powerful that he earned the nickname of the Highland King. In 1694, William II (William III of England, r.1689–1702) rewarded him for his support by granting him the Regality of Freuchie, a rare honour that enabled him to rule like a monarch on his own lands.

In 1710, Ludovic resigned the regality, transferring power to his son Alexander. This took place at a ceremonial gathering of the clan, at Balintome in Strathspey. According to William Fraser, writing in the 19th century, on this grand occasion, "all the gentlemen and commons of his name" were commanded to appear, "wearing whiskers and making all their plaids and tartan of red and green". Determined to maintain the exalted reputation of his clan, Alexander decided to create a new portrait gallery at Castle Grant, containing pictures of

his immediate family as well as the leading members of his household. The artist Richard Waitt (d.1732) embarked upon the project in 1713.

Although some of the portraits are now dispersed, the Grant collection is notable for two reasons. First, it underlines how loosely the notion of a clan tartan was applied. Officially, the Grants were expected to wear a sett of dark green and red, but a precise design was not specified. This somewhat vague stipulation was enforced only during periods of conflict. In peacetime, clansmen were allowed to wear the

plaid of their choice. As a result, no two figures in the Grant portraits are wearing identical tartans. More significantly still, the collection includes paintings of members of the chief's retinue, dressed in livery. The most impressive of these is the picture of William Cumming, piper to the lord of Grant. Behind him is displayed the lord's standard, showing his arms and motto, together with a view of Castle Grant.

▼ *Richard Waitt's portrait of the piper, William Cumming, is unusually elaborate in its detail.*

FOREIGN INFLUENCES

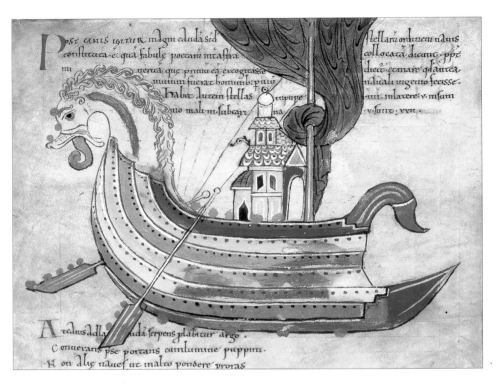

domains independently, until the Stewarts suppressed the Lordship of the Isles in 1494.

This Scandinavian influence did much to strengthen the development of the clans. Somerled, for instance, was an enthusiastic supporter of the Celtic traditions in his homeland, far preferring them to the process of anglicization that was being carried out by the Scottish kings. He even tried to revive the Celtic church, by creating a new foundation on Iona.

ANGLO-NORMAN REFORMS
In this respect Somerled was swimming against the tide. Celtic rule in Scotland had effectively come to an end with the reign of Macbeth (r.1040–57). Public perceptions of this monarch

Both tartans and the clan system had their roots in the customs of the ancient Celts, but these traditions did not survive in their purest forms. The early years of the Scottish nation were precarious in the extreme, as invaders threatened on every side.

VIKING RAIDERS
Even as Kenneth MacAlpin united the Picts and the Scots, the borders of his new kingdom were assailed by Viking raiders. The first record of attack on the boundaries of present-day Scotland dates from 794, when Vikings plundered some of the remote northern isles. Their raids increased in both frequency and ferocity through the 9th century. In 849, just two years after coming to the throne, Kenneth felt compelled to remove some of the relics of St Columba, Scotland's most important saint, from the island of Iona to a safer location in the east.

In the north, the Vikings eventually established the earldom of Orkney, which at times encompassed large

▲ *A Viking longship, pictured here in an 11th-century manuscript, would have struck fear into Scottish hearts.*

tracts of Caithness and Sutherland. In the west, they occupied the Hebrides, becoming Lords of the Isles. This dominance persisted for several centuries, and only with defeat at the battle of Largs in 1263 did the Vikings' influence begin to wane.

As a result, several of the major clans have Viking origins. The founder of the MacLeods, for example, is traditionally thought to have been a Viking prince called Leod, the younger son of King Olaf the Black, who ruled over Man and the North Isles. Olaf himself came from the distinguished royal line of Godred Crovan, who had ruled over Dublin and the Hebrides.

In the same way, the MacDonalds are said to stem from Reginald, the son of Somerled, most famous of the self-styled kings of the Isles. Subsequent MacDonald chiefs continued to style themselves by this title, ruling their

▼ *The actor William Macready presents the popular image of Macbeth in a scene from Shakespeare's play.*

▲ *Malcolm Canmore's pious wife Margaret (c.1046–93) is idealized in stained glass in Edinburgh Castle.*

have been given a very negative slant through Shakespeare's play, but in fact he was neither a murderer nor a tyrant. By the standards of the time he was a peaceable and popular ruler, who travelled to Rome as a pilgrim and donated money to the poor. On his death, Macbeth was accorded the ancient privilege of being buried with the old Celtic kings on Iona.

Macbeth was the last of the Scottish kings to rule from the Highlands. With the accession of Malcolm Canmore as Malcolm III in 1058, the country became increasingly prey to influences

▶ *David I (left) is enthroned beside his grandson and successor, Malcolm IV, in an elaborate example of Celtic calligraphy.*

from the south. Malcolm himself had been raised at the Saxon court of Edward the Confessor (r.1042–66), where he also learned much about Norman ways.

Crucially for the clans, Malcolm changed the law of succession, replacing the old Celtic system of tanistry with the primogeniture that was common in mainland Europe. English influences were pressed even further by Malcolm's wife, Margaret, who two centuries later, in 1249, was canonized as St Margaret. She introduced wide-ranging reforms to the church in Scotland, replacing the Celtic rites that had been championed by St Columba with practices advocated by the Papacy. As part of this reorganization she placed the Scottish church under the jurisdiction of the Archbishop of York.

THE NEW FEUDAL SYSTEM

With the coming of the Normans, Scotland was drawn still further into the European orbit of affairs. This gathered pace during the reign of David I (r.1124–53). More than any Scottish king before him, he had divided loyalties. He was the brother-in-law of the English king, Henry I (r.1100–35), and

had grown up at his court. Prior to his accession to the Scottish throne, he had also established himself as one of the most powerful barons south of the border. A judicious marriage brought him the earldom of Northampton and Huntingdon, and he also owned extensive lands in Northumberland.

Given this background, it is hardly surprising that David reshaped his new kingdom in the image of the Anglo-Norman world he had known since his youth. Feudalism was introduced, along with a new system of justice and a string of castles designed to bolster royal authority. The feudal structure cut across the old notion of ancestral clan estates. Instead, all land was owned by the king, who granted it through charters in return for loyal service. Often, the two systems co-existed quite happily, but the monarch's increased power offered scope for future conflict: by granting one chief a charter to land that had traditionally been held by a rival, it was possible for the king to weaken the clans by playing them off against each other.

Upon his accession, David made many grants of land in Scotland to his Norman followers. This provoked considerable discontent in the Highlands, where there was talk of an "invasion by invitation", and there were sporadic uprisings in some areas that were Gaelic-speaking. However, a substantial number of today's clansmen are descended from the Norman adventurers. The most significant newcomers were Robert de Brus and John de Bailleul, whose descendants – Robert the Bruce and John Balliol – were to play a crucial role in Scotland's struggle for independence.

THE WAR OF INDEPENDENCE

Scotland's increasing ties with England enabled it to develop an efficient government broadly in line with much of continental Europe, but raised concerns that the country might be swallowed up by its powerful southern neighbour.

A CRISIS OF SUCCESSION

The threat became a reality in 1286, when Alexander III suddenly died, causing a succession crisis that threw Scotland into turmoil. His heir was his infant granddaughter, the so-called Maid of Norway. The English king, Edward I (r.1272–1307), saw an opportunity and proposed that his son, Prince Edward, should marry the child. The implication – the union of England and Scotland – was very clear. However, the Maid died on the voyage from Norway to Britain, re-opening the succession debate. More than a dozen claimants to the throne came forward, the most realistic candidates being Robert Bruce

the Competitor (the grandfather of Robert the Bruce) and John Balliol. In a bid to prevent bloodshed, Edward was invited to preside over the court that decided between the two men. Robert claimed he had been nominated as tanist (heir apparent) by the previous monarch, Alexander II (r.1214–49), but Balliol, who had the stronger case under the law of primogeniture, won the decision and was duly made king in 1292.

The disadvantages of the feudal system now became all too apparent. Balliol owned land in England, which meant that he owed fealty to Edward as his overlord, and Edward exploited this loophole to rule Scotland in all but name. As a vassal, Balliol was commanded to render military service and help fund Edward's campaigns in France. The English king also encouraged disgruntled claimants in Scottish courts to appeal to the higher authority of the courts in the south.

▼ *Robert the Bruce is depicted as a courtly knight, with his second wife Elizabeth, daughter of the Earl of Ulster.*

▼ *John Balliol's act of subservience in paying homage to Edward I lost him the respect of most Scots.*

BALLIOL'S REBELLION

Not surprisingly, these measures provoked Balliol into rebellion. He forged an alliance with the French king and prepared to march on England. Edward had expected no less and, in 1296, launched a devastating response. His army swept through the Lowlands, plundering Berwick before defeating Balliol at Dunbar. To consolidate his victory, he seized the Stone of Scone – the inaugural stone of the Scottish kings – and carried it off to England. He also compelled the leaders of the defeated nation to assemble at Berwick and sign a declaration that recognized him as king of Scotland.

The speed and ease of Edward's victory had highlighted a weakness of the clan system: a tendency to place personal squabbles before national unity. Nothing illustrates this more forcibly than the rivalry between Balliol and

Bruce. For, when the former was trying to forge an alliance against Edward I, the Bruces deliberately snubbed him. In retaliation, Balliol seized their estates in Annandale and granted them to his relative, Red John Comyn. Robert the Bruce (the grandson of Balliol's rival) exacted his revenge several years later, when he stabbed Comyn during a quarrel in a Dumfries churchyard. This incident was all the more tragic, given that the pair had arranged to meet precisely to organize a plan of action against their English enemy.

WILLIAM WALLACE AND ROBERT THE BRUCE

Edward had knowingly exploited this kind of feuding in order to gain control of Scotland. However, the events of 1296 provoked a response that caught him unawares. First, in 1297, an uprising led by Sir William Wallace produced an unexpected victory over the English army at Stirling Bridge. Edward responded with his customary ferocity, inflicting a crushing defeat on

the rebels at Falkirk the following year. Wallace managed to evade capture for a time, but was eventually caught and executed in 1305.

Edward may have thought that he had extinguished all sparks of resistance, but Wallace's revolt was swiftly followed by a new rebellion. After Robert the Bruce stabbed Red John Comyn he needed to take decisive action. The fact that the killing had taken place on holy ground made it a

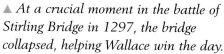

▲ *At a crucial moment in the battle of Stirling Bridge in 1297, the bridge collapsed, helping Wallace win the day.*

sacrilege, which laid Robert open to excommunication by the Church – a punishment that would snuff out any possible claim to the throne. So he marched straight to Scone and declared himself king of the Scots.

This daring act of defiance ultimately proved successful for two main reasons. First, Edward died suddenly of dysentery as he travelled north to lead a counterattack against the Scots. More importantly, Robert the Bruce's rebellion finally managed to unite the clans against a common enemy. The key victory took place at Bannockburn in 1314, when he mobilized a Celtic army composed of more than 20 clans. These included the Camerons, the Campbells, the Chisholms, the Frasers, the Gordons, the Grants, the Gunns, the Mackays, the Mackintoshes, the MacPhersons, the MacQuarries, the MacLeans, the MacDonalds, the MacFarlanes, the MacGregors, the Mackenzies, the Menzies, the Munros, the Robertsons, the Rosses, the Sinclairs and the Sutherlands. The reward for their unity was independence.

▼ *The stabbing of John Comyn was a pivotal event, prompting Robert the Bruce to make a bid for the throne.*

THE SUPPRESSION OF TARTAN

AS RIVALRY WITH ENGLAND TURNED TO OUTRIGHT REBELLION, TARTAN BECAME A SYMBOL OF SCOTS PATRIOTIC FERVOUR AND NATIONAL UNITY. RECOGNIZING THIS, THE GOVERNMENT DID ITS UTMOST TO SUPPRESS IT, BY BANNING THE WEARING OF HIGHLAND DRESS.

CAUSES OF DISSENT

The military successes of Robert the Bruce may have won independence for the Scots, but the close genealogical links between the royal families of England and Scotland ensured that the threat of new claimants from the south remained strong. This problem eventually resurfaced at the beginning of the 17th century.

Initial fears were mainly experienced by the English. For much of her reign, Elizabeth I (r.1558–1603) was concerned about the claim of her kinswoman Mary, Queen of Scots, to the English throne, and she eventually had her executed in 1587. In spite of this, after the death of Elizabeth Mary's son, James VI of Scotland, inherited the English throne as James I. This did not present an immediate cause for concern north of the border, where James had been king since 1567, as his outlook was undoubtedly Scottish. During his early years in London he was viewed with suspicion by the English. Significantly, when the idea of creating

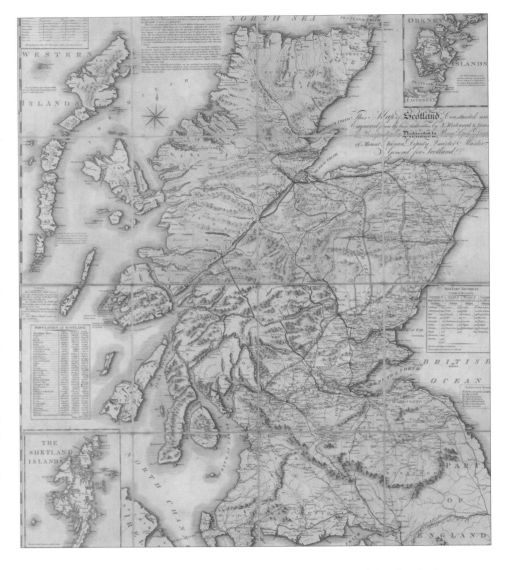

▼ *Mary, Queen of Scots, being led to execution in 1587, after long years of imprisonment by her cousin, Elizabeth.*

▲ *A 1804 map of Scotland, showing the Highland Line in green, running north-east from the Firth of Clyde.*

a permanent union of the two crowns was mooted in 1607, the English parliament dismissed the idea.

James's reign, however, did accentuate the growing gulf between the Highlands and the Lowlands. Although politically the two regions were both part of Scotland, their social, religious and linguistic differences were so deeply rooted that they remained separate countries in all but name. This

Previous pages: Ruthven Barracks.

concept of a divided land was widely accepted until early modern times. It was epitomized by the Highland Line, from Argyllshire in the west to Aberdeenshire in the east, which was set down as a boundary line for different rates of taxation in an Act of Parliament of 1784 dealing with whisky production.

With the accession of James VI to the English throne, the Lowlands were drawn increasingly into the orbit of English affairs, while the Highlands remained marginalized. The bonds between England and the Lowlands began to seem much stronger than the links between the two Scottish regions. To a large extent, this was deliberate government policy. James introduced a number of measures designed to "civilize" the Highlands by undermining the old Gaelic culture with its clan system. Many chiefs were ordered to prove their right to their long-held ancestral territories by presenting their charters, or else paying for new ones. The king was equally determined to cut the size and influence of their princely households, specifying in particular that the maintenance of bards "and other idlers" was forbidden, in a measure directed

▼ *After James VI's accession to the English throne in 1603, Scotland was increasingly ruled from the south.*

against the clan sennachies. In addition, members of the gentry were required to send their eldest sons to be educated in the Lowlands to ensure that they learned English.

THE FIFE ADVENTURERS

James also sought to weaken Celtic influence by introducing Lowland settlers into key areas of the country. The most infamous example of this policy took place in Ireland, where "plantations" of English and Lowland settlers were established at the expense of local families. Similar schemes were adopted in the Highlands, the most notorious instance occurring on the island of Lewis. In 1598, it was granted to a Lowland company known as the Fife Adventurers, headed by the Duke of Lennox, the king's cousin.

The Adventurers' charter authorized the company "to plant policy and civilization in the hitherto most barbarous Isle of Lewis...and to develop the extraordinarily rich resources of the same for the public good and the king's profit." In doing so, its representatives were given leave to carry out whatever "slaughter, mutilation, fyre-raising, or utheris inconvenities" were deemed necessary. Ultimately, this was to no avail, since there was stiff resistance from the inhabitants, mobilized by the dominant local clan, the MacLeods. The company's camps were looted and its livestock seized, and by 1610 it was bankrupt. But James had his revenge: the Adventurers sold their interests to the Mackenzies of Kintail, who ultimately supplanted the MacLeods.

THE RISE OF PRESBYTERIANISM

In the long term, religion was to prove an even greater source of discord. James was anxious to bring Scottish modes of worship into line with English practice, and he sought to put this policy into effect through the Five Articles of Perth in 1618. In the Lowlands, however, Calvinism (a strict

▲ *An influential Reformation figure, John Knox popularized the austere teachings of John Calvin in Scotland.*

form of Protestantism) had already taken root, largely through the efforts of John Knox (*c.*1513–72). This doctrine repudiated the hierarchical set-up of the Church, believing that it should be run by ministers (presbyters) of equal status, rather than bishops. As a result, Presbyterianism became the dominant religious force in Scotland. In general, these ideas were received less enthusiastically in the Highlands, where there was widespread support for more traditional forms of worship.

HIGHLAND UNITY

In spite of their growing isolation from the Lowlanders, the Highland clans remained as tightly knit as ever. One important example of this occurred in 1618, when Sir Robert Gordon of Gordonstoun wrote to Murray of Pulrossie, asking him "to remove the red and white lines from the plaids of his men, so as to bring their dress into harmony with that of the other septs". The original letter has not survived, and the surviving copy may be a forgery. If the message is genuine, however, it constitutes one of the earliest attempts to harmonize a tartan within a clan in order to promote a sense of unity.

THE END OF STUART RULE

By the reign of Charles I (r.1625–49), the Scots had become closely identified with the Stuart cause. This led them to take part in the king's religious conflicts, as well as the Civil War (1642–49), which ultimately cost him his life. For many Highlanders, the consequences of supporting the Stuarts were severe. After the execution of Charles I, his son made a determined attempt to recapture the throne, which ended in failure at the battles of Dunbar in 1650 and Worcester in 1651. These defeats were followed by the transportation of many clansmen to the Americas. After Dunbar, for example, some 900 Scottish prisoners were sent as bond-servants to Virginia, and a further 150 to New England. Similarly, over the next few years, around 270 men were deported to Boston, while others were taken to the new colony of Jamaica.

Following the restoration of the monarchy in 1660, the Scots maintained reasonable relations with the Stuart kings. Charles II (r.1660–85) was well disposed towards the country where he had first been crowned king (at Scone in 1651), although his rule there was marred by continuing religious divisions. The brief reign of Charles's brother, James VII (James II of England, r.1685–88), was more troubled. Prior to his accession, he had served successfully as viceroy in Scotland, working with the clan chiefs to pacify the Highlands. However, he never returned north after ascending the throne and, ominously perhaps, he was the first ruler of his country not to take the Scottish coronation oath or to be crowned in Scotland.

THE JACOBITE CAUSE

James was a Catholic, and his determination to remain true to his faith lost him support in both England and

▲ *This Dutch engraving shows the execution of Charles I, outside the Banqueting House, Whitehall, in 1649.*

▼ *A highland warrior, complete with tartan trews, bonnet and plaid, a mode of dress that astonished the English.*

Scotland. It was the birth of his son James, a Catholic heir, that finally galvanized his opponents into chasing him from the throne. In the aftermath, the Protestant William, Prince of Orange, the Dutch Stadtholder, and his wife Mary, James's daughter, were invited to rule jointly in his place.

This marked a decisive shift in Scottish politics. For, while the Scottish Convention of Estates followed their English counterparts and voted to offer the throne to William and Mary, the decision was by no means unanimous. There were many who felt that, even if James VII was deemed to have abdicated, his infant son James was the rightful heir to the Scottish throne.

They described themselves as Jacobites, taking their name from Jacobus, the Latin form of James. For the following 70 years, this faction presented a genuine threat to the authority of the government in London.

The first insurrection against the new order manifested itself at the battle of Killiecrankie in 1689, when the Jacobite clans massed against William's troops. The Highland army was raised in the traditional manner of the clans, with a fiery cross carried through the glens. The Scottish forces won the day, but their charismatic leader, John Graham, Viscount Dundee (better known as Bonnie Dundee), was killed, and without him the rebels were soon dispersed. During these campaigns, Highland warriors made some rare excursions outside their native region, when their "antique" style of dress astonished Lowlanders and Englishmen alike. The novelist and pamphleteer Daniel Defoe, for example, noted, "Their swords were extravagantly, and I think insignificantly long... These fellows looked when drawn out like a regiment of Merry-Andrews [buffoons] ready for Bartholomew Fair."

THE GLENCOE MASSACRE

Although the uprising was obviously a cause for concern, the majority of Scots were still open-minded about the new administration. This soon changed, however, following one of the most shameful episodes in Scottish history. In a bid to make peace, William offered the hostile Highland chiefs an olive branch by granting them an amnesty, provided that in return they swore a personal oath of allegiance to him.

The final date by which this oath had to be taken was 1 January 1692, but through a chapter of accidents, Alasdair MacIain, chief of the MacDonalds of Glencoe, missed the deadline by five days. William mistakenly interpreted this as an act of insubordination and decided to make

TARTANS OF THE *GRAMEID*

The first Jacobite uprising inspired the *Grameid*, an epic poem written in Latin, supposedly by a loyal standard-bearer. Modelled on Virgil's *Aeneid*, it features stirring descriptions of Highland dress. MacNeill of Barra sported a plaid that "rivalled the rainbow", while the multicoloured coat of Lochiel and the scarlet and purple outfits of Glengarry's men also gave rise to notable verses. For costume historians, the *Grameid* has proved something of a mixed blessing, since none of the patterns described bears any resemblance to existing tartans, and there are suspicions that they are colourful examples of poetic licence. Even if this is so, it is nonetheless significant that descriptions of tartan were being used as an expression of patriotic fervour.

an example of the MacDonald clan. Accordingly, the order went out "to fall upon the rebels...and put all to the sword." The instruments of the king's justice were the Campbells, who had been billeted with the MacDonalds for a fortnight. On the night of 13 February, they set upon their hosts while they lay in their beds, killing at least 38 men, and set fire to their homes. The casualties would have been higher, but for the fact that a violent snowstorm was raging and some of the intended victims escaped into the hills.

The Glencoe massacre proved to be a huge miscalculation on William's part: far from intimidating his Scottish subjects, it united them in outrage. The cowardly nature of the attack, the fact that many women and children died after being turned out into the snow, and the way that the Campbells had contravened the laws of hospitality combined to strengthen Jacobite sympathies throughout the country.

▼ *The Glencoe massacre, shown in this artist's impression, actually took place at night, in the middle of a snowstorm.*

THE ACT OF UNION

In the early years of the 18th century, a new menace began to cast a shadow over the Highland way of life. William II died in 1702 and was succeeded by Anne, the younger daughter of James VII. Though she had conceived 19 children, most of them were either stillborn or miscarried, and the only one to survive infancy had died in 1700, at the age of 11. It was clear that Anne's eventual death would be followed by a succession crisis.

Those with the strongest claim to the throne were the Stuarts. This delighted the Jacobites, of course, but appalled the English, since the Stuart family were still staunch Catholics. As a result, it was decided that the succession would eventually pass to George of Hanover, who was distantly related to James VI. This arrangement was acceptable to members of the English parliament, but it seemed unlikely that their Scottish counterparts would agree to it. The only

▼ *Women wore tartan to show their Jacobite sympathies, as in this portrait attributed to Cosmo Alexander.*

solution was to join the two countries on a permanent basis, uniting them under a single crown.

After much argument, the Act of Union was passed in 1707. Using a combination of bribery and blackmail, the English government eventually persuaded the Scottish parliament to vote itself out of existence in return for a number of economic benefits. Although the move was carried through quite legally, it attracted considerable opposition in Scotland. For many, it seemed that the nation's liberties had been sold off to its southern rival.

TARTAN AS A SYMBOL OF RESISTANCE

The Scottish public showed their discontent in a variety of ways and, for the first time, these included the use of tartan. Significantly, its use in this fashion was not limited to the Highlands. Even prosperous Edinburgh ladies registered their protest by wearing a tartan accessory or using it as a decorative material in their homes. Sir Walter Scott confirmed this many years later when he wrote: "I have been told, and believed until now, that the use of tartans was never general in Scotland until the Union, with the detestation of that measure, led it to be adopted as the National colour, and the ladies all affected tartan screens [scarves]…"

TARTAN IN PORTRAITS

The growing use of tartan in portraiture also dates from this period. Once again, the trend covered a broad spectrum of people. It was shortly after the Act of Union, for example, that the Grants decided to create a portrait gallery showing the family and their household attired in Highland dress. At the same time, an attempt was made to standardize the clan sett as a "tartane of red and green, set broad-spring'd".

▲ *In Waitt's portrait, Lord Duffus wears a belted plaid with loose folds of cloth gathered below the tunic.*

The Grants were firm government supporters and they went on to oppose the Jacobites in the 1715 rebellion. It is clear, therefore, that in the case of this clan the use of tartan held no political overtones. The same can also be said of the early 18th-century portrait of Sir Robert Dalrymple. Like the Grants, he had close connections with the Whig government of the day. Indeed, he was a relative of James Dalrymple, the royal Secretary of State in Scotland who had borne much of the blame for the Glencoe massacre. Robert Dalrymple's portrait is particularly interesting because it provides one of the earliest illustrations of a Lowlander wearing tartan. The sitter is not wearing an item of Highland dress; instead, his tartan adorns a long, loose-sleeved jacket.

In contrast to this pillar of the establishment, Richard Waitt's celebrated portrait of Kenneth Sutherland, Lord Duffus, depicts a prominent rebel who served as a naval officer during the rebellion of 1715. Painted in about 1712, the picture shows the nobleman in a belted plaid, wearing hunting colours. The pattern of the hose does not match the plaid and, in any case, neither can be linked with any certainty to a known sett. Typically for this period, tartan was more notable as a form of national dress than for its affiliation with specific clans.

THE 1715 REBELLION

Queen Anne died in 1714 and was succeeded by the Hanoverian George I. Immediately, Jacobites called for the return of the Old Pretender, James Francis Edward Stuart, the last son of James VII, who had already made one

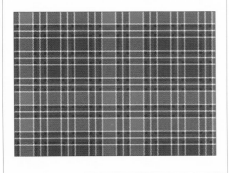

JACOBITE SETTS

For Jacobite supporters there was a tartan that they could wear as a badge of their protest. Over the years, at least six different Jacobite setts have been registered. The history of these tartans is difficult to gauge, as many of them are thought to date from a later era, when the Jacobite troubles were viewed with a sense of nostalgia. The one shown below, however, was created in 1707 and worn by particpants in the 1715 rebellion. It can still be worn as an alternative to a clan or district tartan.

abortive bid for the throne in 1708. There were considerable doubts about George, both north and south of the border, and many Scots who had supported the Act of Union were by now thoroughly disillusioned with it.

This should have been the Old Pretender's ideal opportunity, but the campaign proved a shambles. Sporadic, poorly co-ordinated Jacobite uprisings were easily suppressed. The main force, under the leadership of the Earl of Mar, achieved some early successes, capturing Perth and fighting with distinction at the battle of Sheriffmuir. But James's lacklustre approach undermined the impetus of the rebellion. Fighting had actually broken out in August 1715, but he did not land on Scottish soil

▲ *A rare depiction of a Lowlander wearing tartan. Dalrymple's elaborate, tailored garment is very different from normal Highland dress.*

until the end of December. Even then, his dour, fatalistic approach did little to inspire the Highlanders. Dubbed "old Mr Melancholy", in a speech to his officers he remarked: "It is no new thing to be unfortunate, since my whole life from my cradle has been a constant series of misfortunes." His army dwindled away and the rebellion petered out. Just six weeks after his arrival, the Old Pretender slunk back to France. He spent the rest of his life in exile, mainly in Rome, where the Pope continued to address him as the king of England.

AFTERMATH OF THE 1715 REBELLION

The government was not complacent about its success in quelling the 1715 rebellion. In many quarters it was readily accepted that the victory owed more to the incompetence of the enemy than to its own endeavours. As a result, attempts were made to pacify the Highlanders once and for all.

At this stage no measures were taken against the wearing of tartan, but efforts were made to undermine other aspects of the Highland way of life. There were renewed attempts to discourage the use of Gaelic. At the same time, religious bodies such as the Society for the Propagation of Christian Knowledge tried to persuade the clans to abandon their Catholic or Episcopalian beliefs in favour of the Presbyterianism that flourished in the Lowlands. The government also passed a Disarming Act although, in common with many other anti-Jacobite measures, it appears to have been enforced in a very half-hearted manner. Most of the Scots who handed over their weapons were loyal Lowlanders, while the rebels largely ignored the order.

▼ *Ruthven Barracks in Kingussie, built in 1718 to help suppress the Jacobites, were enlarged by George Wade in 1734.*

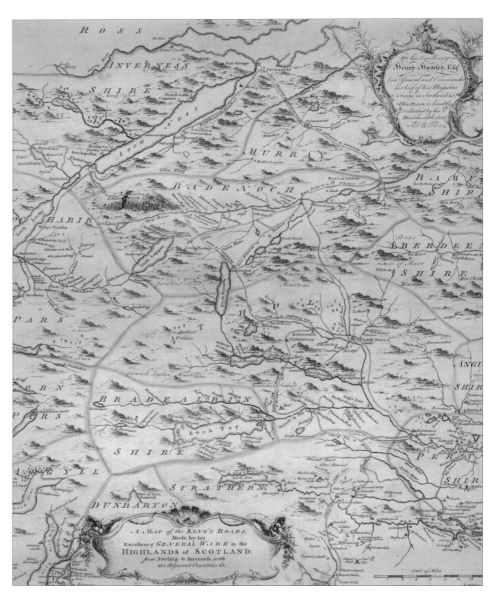

TRANSPORTATION TO THE COLONIES

Immediately after the 1715 rebellion, there were several executions and 19 peerages were forfeited. For other rebels, the standard penalty was transportation. There were fewer of these than is often supposed – probably no more than 800. The typical sentence was seven years, but many prisoners appear to have returned far sooner. James Mackintosh of Strathspey, for example, was indentured to serve a seven-year term in Virginia, but is known to have been back in Scotland

▲ *This map shows the roads and other improvements made by General Wade in the wake of the 1715 rebellion.*

less than two years after his departure. Nor was transportation always the terrible punishment it was designed to be. In 1717 Donald MacPherson, a Jacobite prisoner who had been taken to Maryland, sent back an optimistic message to his family in Inverness: "My master says to me, when I can speak like the folk here that I shall not be bidden to do nothing but make his blackamoors work; for decent folk here

ADOPTION OF THE KILT

Between the rebellions of 1715 and 1745, the kilt seems to have become established as the chief item of Highland dress. Before this, the belted plaid had been the preferred form of attire, particularly among soldiers and travellers, who used the garment as a blanket at night. Many theories have been put forward for the change in fashion, but the most likely reason was a military one.

The Earl Marischal began his account of the Jacobite rising by noting the flexibility of the plaid, "which the Highlanders tie about them in such a manner that it covers their thighs, and all their body when they please, but commonly it is fixed on their left shoulder, and leaves their right arm free." He went on to observe, however, how the clansmen tended to discard the plaid in battle. This was not necessarily a problem if a warrior was on the winning side. If he lost or was forced to retreat, on the other hand, then he had lost a vital piece of his equipment.

▲ *Rob Roy, immortalized by Sir Walter Scott's romanticized version of his exploits, ambushes government troops.*

do not use to work but the first year after they come into the country; they speak all like the soldiers in Inverness."

Many Scottish prisoners fared even better. In the 1720s, Daniel Defoe noted: "So many of the Scots servants which go over to Virginia settle and thrive there, more than of the English…that if it goes on for many more years, Virginia may be rather called a Scots than an English plantation." Once such views became common, the deterrent value of transportation was somewhat reduced.

MILITARY ROADS

In fact, the only really effective measure taken by the English government in the wake of the 1715 rebellion lay in the field of communications. In 1725 George Wade, Commander-in-Chief in Scotland, embarked on a massive building programme in the Highlands. Military roads were constructed in strategically important areas, most notably between Inverness and Fort William, from Inverness to Dunkeld, and between Crieff and Fort Augustus. Wade also built more than 40 bridges and transformed the royal barracks at Fort William, Fort Augustus and Fort George. These improved facilities enabled the English to police the Highlands far more effectively when the next rebellion occurred.

A ROMANTICIZED HERO

The Old Pretender was nowhere near colourful enough as a character to inspire the mythmakers of later generations, so instead the plaudits went to an outlaw named Rob Roy. His story is now mainly associated with the eponymous novel by Sir Walter Scott published in 1817, but Rob was earlier brought to the public's attention by Daniel Defoe's *Highland Rogue*, which appeared in 1729.

Rob belonged to the outlawed MacGregor clan, but spent much of his career masquerading as a Campbell. He operated at times as a *bona fide* livestock dealer and at other times as a cattle thief. His days as a Jacobite were equally ambiguous. He openly espoused the cause, acting as a guide for the rebels' army as they moved towards Sheriffmuir, but he took no part in the actual fighting. In spite of this, he was charged with treason and spent his later years as a fugitive.

THE JACOBITE REBELLION OF 1745

Thirty years after the first main rebellion, the Jacobites rose again, making their final bid to place a Stuart on the throne. Technically, their candidate was still the Old Pretender, who had failed in the previous revolt, but he took no part in the campaign. Instead, it was his charismatic young son, Charles Edward Stuart, better known as Bonnie Prince Charlie or the Young Pretender, who championed the cause.

BONNIE PRINCE CHARLIE

Charles was born in exile in Rome, but travelled to France in 1744 in the hope of finding an ally. This was a logical move, since the French were involved in a major conflict against the English (the War of the Austrian Succession had broken out in 1740), and were rumoured to be planning an invasion. The French king was supportive at first, but abandoned the project when his fleet was dispersed by bad weather.

Undeterred, Charles made his own way to Scotland, landing initially at Eriskay in the Outer Hebrides before

▲ *Bonnie Prince Charlie's triumphant entry into Edinburgh, where the Old Pretender was proclaimed king.*

proceeding to Glenfinnan on the mainland, where he raised his father's standard. The early response was unpromising. After previous failures, many of the Highland chiefs were understandably reluctant to commit themselves, particularly as the Young Pretender did not have the backing of any foreign troops. However, Charles's great passion and commitment gradually convinced the western clans, most notably the Camerons and the MacDonalds, to rally behind him.

The initial signs were encouraging. The Jacobite army captured Perth and entered Edinburgh without opposition. This was swiftly followed by a significant victory over government forces at the battle of Prestonpans.

Buoyed by his early successes, Charles was anxious to press on into England, but already divisions were appearing within his own council. For

some of the clansmen, the main object of the exercise had been achieved: the rightful Scottish king had been restored to his throne. The priority now was to defend it, until the French could launch their attack on England.

INVASION OF ENGLAND

This cautious approach was ignored, however, and in November 1745 Charles's army crossed the border. For a time, it seemed that the right decision had been made. The Scots encountered little resistance, and there was a mounting sense of panic further south. In London, one of the king's leading ministers, the Duke of Newcastle, admitted, "I look upon Scotland as gone," while George II (r.1727–60) gave orders for his most precious belongings to be transferred to the royal yacht in case he was forced to flee from his capital. Elsewhere, shops closed down as the city's inhabitants sought refuge in the countryside,

▼ *A highlight of the Jacobite campaign was the victory at Prestonpans, where the enemy commander was killed.*

and the Bank of England was almost ruined by a massive run on its funds.

In spite of this, there were growing concerns within the Scottish camp. As they marched south, they were gathering virtually no new recruits and some of their supporters were drifting away and heading back to Scotland. Increasingly, the realization dawned that they would be hopelessly outnumbered in England, where their dwindling force of around 5000 men would be pitted against as many as 30,000 Hanoverian troops. The army reached as far south as Derby, just 210km/130 miles from London, before these fears prompted them to halt their advance and turn around.

Charles was distraught at this decision, and historians have speculated ever since on what might have been. The retreat from Derby took much of the sting out of the Jacobites' campaign. The rebels did enjoy some further successes, particularly a minor victory over government troops in Falkirk, but once the threat of a genuine coup was removed the English were able to muster their forces and launch a decisive counterattack.

THE BATTLE OF CULLODEN

While the Jacobites were returning north, government ministers recalled some of their most experienced troops from the war in Flanders and placed them under the command of the king's ruthlessly efficient son, the Duke of Cumberland. He led them to Inverness, where the final encounter would take place. On nearby Culloden Moor the Jacobite forces were cut to pieces in a battle that lasted less than an hour. The barbaric behaviour of the Hanoverians, who slaughtered the wounded and anyone else in the vicinity in Highland dress, earned their commander the nickname "Butcher" Cumberland.

Charles made his escape from the battlefield, but spent the next five months living as a desperate fugitive, while royalist troops tried to hunt him down. In spite of the sizeable reward that was offered for his capture, none of his Highlanders betrayed him and he was eventually able to board a frigate bound for France. For the clansmen he left behind, the outlook was far bleaker. The authorities in London had been given a genuine scare by the Jacobite rising and were determined that the danger should never be repeated. Their solution was brutally simple – the destruction of the Highland clans and their entire way of life.

▼ *After the rout at Culloden, Prince Charles was forced into hiding, taking shelter wherever he could find it.*

A VOGUE FOR TARTAN

Amid the euphoria that followed Bonnie Prince Charlie's initial successes, there was a patriotic fashion for tartan clothes and artefacts. In Edinburgh, for example, merchants rushed to publicize their stocks of tartans "of the newest patterns". There was some irony in this, since Charles had not worn Highland dress thus far and had made his entry into the capital wearing red breeches and a green bonnet. Nevertheless, he did wear a kilt later in the campaign, as did his Lieutenant-General, Lord George Murray.

▼ *During his stay in Edinburgh, Charles held court at Holyrood.*

THE JACOBITE ROMANCE

No one knew it at the time, but the rebellion of 1745 was the swansong of the Jacobite movement. After the defeat at Culloden in 1746, Bonnie Prince Charlie spent his remaining years living as an exile, mainly in France and Italy. Eventually he became a disillusioned and embittered drunk, often confessing to his friends that he wished he had died on the battlefield alongside his loyal Highlanders.

In a later age, when the threat of Jacobitism was a distant memory, Scots looked back on this episode with an almost masochistic sense of nostalgia. It became a focus for national pride and as such inspired the creation of

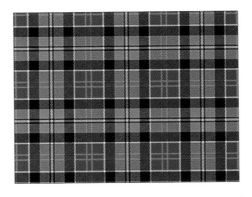

▲ *This Culloden is said to be based on a tartan worn by one of the prince's men.*

▼ *Bonnie Prince Charlie raised his standard at Glenfinnan, calling on all Highlanders to join the Jacobite cause.*

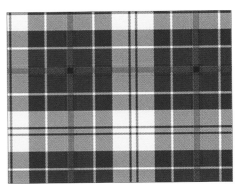

▲ *Culloden Red (dress) tartan is usually worn for dancing.*

numerous tartans. The designs relating to Bonnie Prince Charlie and Flora MacDonald, who aided his escape, fall into a similar category. Both have several setts named after them, and they were extremely popular during the revival period, when the careers of these two people were heavily romanticized. The designs were ostensibly based on historical artefacts, either old portraits or clothing that they were thought to have worn, but it is often hard to verify their authenticity.

CULLODEN TARTANS

Over the years, no fewer than 11 different Culloden tartans have been registered. Several of these are based, or purport to be based, on designs that were found on historical objects, such as clothing, portraits or furnishings. One is based on a set of bed-hangings found at Culloden House, which Charles had been using as his headquarters; the battle was fought just in front of the building. The most poignant example was apparently worn by one of the Highlanders who died on the field at Culloden. His identity is uncertain and the pattern is unlike any of the traditional clan setts, so it might almost be described as a tartan for the unknown soldier. Culloden tartans come into their own during events

▲ *As Bonnie Prince Charlie's saviour, Flora MacDonald – portrayed here by Richard Wilson – became the focal point of the Jacobite legend.*

staged on 16 April, the anniversary of the battle. This date is increasingly being chosen for celebrations as an alternative to St Andrew's Day (30 November) or Burns' Night (25 January), particularly for outdoor events, which are not well suited to winter weather. In Britain, for example, the National Tartan Day of 2000 (the so-called Maclennium) was held on the anniversary of Culloden.

BONNIE PRINCE CHARLIE AND TARTAN

In Charles's case there are signs that tartan was something of an after-thought. When he arrived in Scotland in 1745, he was dressed so soberly that one of his supporters mistook him for a minister, describing him as "a tall youth…in a plain black coat with a plain shirt not very clean and a cambrick stock fixed with a plain silver buckle…" It is likely, however, that the

prince soon realized the propaganda value of wearing Highland dress, particularly when his Jacobite supporters presented him with a tartan outfit.

During his stay in the Highlands, Charles made further enquiries about this attire. The poet Alexander MacDonald, Flora MacDonald's cousin, later recalled how Charles had asked him if he found the garb chilly and if, when he was wrapped up tightly in his plaid at night, he was not concerned about being ambushed by an enemy. To the latter question, Alexander replied that "in such times of danger or during a war, we had a different method of using the plaid, that with one spring I could start to my feet with drawn sword and cock'd pistol in my hand, without being in the least encumber'd with my bedclothes."

The prince must have been convinced of the benefits, for he is on record as having worn Highland dress at various times during the 1745 rebellion. When he was hiding on Uist, for example, a certain Hugh MacDonald noted, "His dress was then a tartan short coat and vest of the same… a short kilt, tartan hose and Highland brogues, his upper coat being English cloth." Charles had been given this outfit by Lady Clanranald, but during the months that he lived as a fugitive his attire would normally have been far less conspicuous.

FLORA MACDONALD

Charles also spent some time dressed as a woman when he was aided in his escape from the English by Flora MacDonald, who disguised him as her Irish maid, Betty Burke. This was a hazardous undertaking, particularly since the prince seems to have been less than convincing in his part; one observer described him as "a very odd, muckle, ill-shapen up wife".

Flora's own life was every bit as colourful as that of her leader. After Charles's escape, she was arrested and

taken to London where, even in captivity, she became something of a celebrity. Fanciful accounts were already circulating about her flight with the prince. In 1746, for example, an anonymous novel called *The Young Adventurer* created a great stir. This described how Alexis, "a shepherd of the first rank" (that is, Charlie), was defeated at the battle of Lachrymania, but was rescued by a beautiful girl called Heroica (Flora), who helped him escape to the island of Aetheria (Skye).

Flora was eventually released during an amnesty. She married and later emigrated to Wilmington, North Carolina, with her husband. There, she was greeted with great enthusiasm, as her fame had preceded her. Even so, a happy ending eluded her, for Flora's adopted homeland was soon caught up in its own struggle for independence. The couple were obliged to flee once again, taking refuge in Nova Scotia. There, they experienced a bleak, lonely winter, before returning home to Skye.

▼ *Later generations imagined a romance between Charles and Flora, though there is no evidence of this.*

AFTER CULLODEN

In England, the removal of the Jacobite threat was greeted with a mixture of elation and relief. The celebrations were extravagant. In London, a ballet called *Culloden*, which featured a deafening cannonade, was performed to packed houses at Sadler's Wells, while the Culloden Reel became the most popular dance of the day. For costume historians, though, the most intriguing contribution was a painting commissioned to mark the event – David Morier's *An Incident at Culloden*.

THE DISARMING ACT OF 1746

Away from the celebrations, the government showed a firm resolve to bring the Jacobite menace to an end. The Duke of Cumberland favoured a policy of transporting entire clans to the colonies, but in the end the authorities opted to tackle the problem at its roots. The Disarming Act of 1746 was the first of several decrees that struck at the very heart of Highland life. Along with a ban on the ownership of weapons, the heritable jurisdiction of the chiefs was abolished: Highland landowners

▲ *After Culloden*, the authorities outlawed the wearing of tartan and all the accessories of Highland dress.

▼ *Lucas' painting*, After Culloden: Rebel Hunting, *shows English soldiers arriving to arrest Jacobite supporters.*

HIGHLAND DRESS DURING THE JACOBITE ERA

An Incident at Culloden by the Swiss artist David Morier seems to confirm that no firm rules about the wearing of Highland dress had yet been established in the mid-18th century. Through the grace of his patron, the Duke of Cumberland, Morier was able to lend authenticity to his work by having a number of Jacobite prisoners brought to his studio to pose for him. They came from Southwark jail and the floating prison ships at Tilbury. Examples of plaids, kilts and trews are all pictured; no two men are dressed exactly alike and the eight principal clansmen in the painting wear 23 different tartans.

From other sources, it is clear that tartan was not used for identification purposes in battles of the period. Instead, Highlanders would usually rely on clan badges, often small plants, traditionally worn in their bonnets. Sometimes even this was insufficient, as members of the same clan might be fighting on different sides. Accordingly, at Culloden, clansmen wore a cockade in their hats – white for Charles, black for the English king.

had to accept English jurisdiction or forfeit their lands. This was a direct attack on clan loyalty, and many estates were forfeited.

HIGHLAND DRESS BANNED

Punitive restrictions on the wearing of Highland dress were introduced. "No man or boy shall, on any pretext whatever, wear or put on...the Plaid, Philabeg, or little Kilt, Trowse, Shoulder-belts, or any part whatever of

▲ *John Campbell, of the Royal Bank of Scotland, was painted by William Mosman. His government connections enabled him to flout the ban on tartan.*

men tried to exploit loopholes in the legislation. One youth, for instance, was held by soldiers for wearing a garment that resembled a kilt. He was later released, however, when it transpired that the offending article was stitched up the middle, in the manner of "the trousers worn by Dutch skippers".

CONTINUING PRIDE IN HIGHLAND DRESS

When the wearer was a known government supporter, the authorities would turn a blind eye, and as a result the practice of commissioning official portraits in Highland dress was unaffected. This trend was exemplified by William Mosman's striking depiction of John Campbell. Widely known as John Campbell of the Bank, he was a familiar figure in Edinburgh society. He enjoyed a long association with the Royal Bank of Scotland, which had been founded in 1727, serving as assistant secretary from 1732 and cashier from 1745, when he saved the bank's assets from the approaching Jacobite army by transferring them to the safety of Edinburgh Castle.

In spite of his firm allegiance to the Hanoverian cause, however, Campbell was proud of his Highland roots and, in particular, his descent from the house of Argyll. So, even though his portrait was commissioned from Mosman in 1749, not long after the new restrictions had come into force, he chose to be depicted in traditional Highland attire, in a belted plaid with a decorated cross-belt. He was also shown in the guise of a warrior, wearing both a claymore (a large double-edged broadsword) and a dagger, while a targe (a light shield) was displayed on the wall behind him.

The restrictions on Highland dress remained on the statute book for 35 years, until the law was eventually repealed in 1781. By this stage, the situation in the Highlands had been radically transformed.

what peculiarly belongs to the Highland Garb; and no tartan or parti-coloured plaid or stuff shall be used for Great Coats or upper coats…" Bagpipes were also banned as "instruments of war". The penalties for ignoring these restrictions were severe. A first offence was punishable with six months' imprisonment, and any repeat entailed transportation to the colonies for a period of seven years.

ENFORCING THE ACT

The measures proved difficult to enforce, although the authorities certainly tried their best. A typical record states that, in 1749, Duncan Campbell and his son "were apprehended in Highland Cloaths by the moving Patrole and were confined in the Tolbooth [town jail] of Killin." Sometimes the letter of the law was applied to an absurd degree. On one occasion, for example, a black servant employed by Stewart of Appin was arrested and imprisoned, simply because his master had kitted him out in tartan livery. Inevitably, some clans-

THE START OF SCOTTISH EMIGRATION

The punitive measures introduced in the wake of Culloden helped to bring about lasting change in the Highlands. For many clansmen, it seemed that life in their native land was no longer a viable option and they decided to try their fortunes elsewhere. In doing so, they were following in a long tradition.

Scottish emigration had begun long before the Jacobite problem arose. The overwhelming reason for this was poverty. In the Highlands, in particular, many people lived barely at subsistence level, rearing livestock or growing meagre crops. When the latter failed, as they did in 1572, 1587 and 1595, there were severe famines. From the early years of the 17th century many Scots also decided to leave their homeland due to the religious divisions that were starting to tear their country apart.

SOLDIERS OF FORTUNE AND SCHOLARS

From the outset, emigrant Scots distinguished themselves in a variety of fields. They were probably best known as soldiers: Scottish mercenaries became renowned for their courage and dependability throughout Europe. Their most common destinations were Scandinavia and France, with which Scots maintained the "auld alliance" against their common enemy, the English. These connections can be seen in the evolution of French names such as De Gaulle (from Dougal), De Lisle (Leslie), or Le Clerc (Clark).

Other Scots made their mark in Europe as scholars or clerics. The most celebrated examples of the former are probably the philosophers Duns Scotus (*c*.1266–1308), who taught at Oxford, Paris and Cologne, and Michael Scott the Wizard (*c*.1160–*c*.1235), who worked in Paris, Padua and Rome. In later years, so many Scots chose this route out of their native land that, in

the 16th century, the Collège d'Ecosse at the University of Paris catered for 400 Scottish scholars.

COMMERCIAL TRAVELLERS IN EASTERN EUROPE

In Poland, meanwhile, the Scots became better known in the field of commerce. They ranged from bankers and merchants to the *kramers*, or pedlars, who set up booths in many Polish towns, selling knives, scissors and woollen goods. In 1616 the traveller William Lithgow noted that 30,000 Scots families were living in Poland. It is hard to gauge the accuracy of this figure, although it is certainly true that the Polish authorities were concerned

▲ *Many Highlanders sought their fortune as mercenaries, acquiring a reputation for courage and ferocity.*

about the number of Scottish youths who resorted to begging. As in France, the trend can be confirmed from the prevalence of names such as Czamer (from Chalmers), Zutter (Soutar), Zlot (Scott) and Grim (Graham).

NOVA SCOTIA

After James VI's accession to the English throne as James I in 1603, Scots became more involved in the process of colonization. The king extended the policy of creating "plantations" in Ireland, although many colonists preferred to look further afield, to the opportunities opening up in the Americas.

The first Scottish venture of note in the New World was launched by Sir William Alexander, Earl of Stirling. In 1621, he acquired large tracts of land in Canada and hatched the scheme of creating a new Scotland, imitating the settlements of New Holland and New England. The colony was accordingly named Nova Scotia. Early attempts at establishing the settlement proved disappointing, however, even after Alexander penned a pamphlet entitled *An Encouragement to Colonies*.

Gradually, the project degenerated into little more than a money-making scheme, for in 1625 Alexander created his Nova Scotia baronetcies. This enabled Scottish entrepreneurs to purchase a title for cash and a promise to provide a certain number of settlers. Most of the investors had no intention of travelling to Nova Scotia, however, and in due course the undertaking to provide new settlers was replaced by an additional fee. In all, 64 baronetcies

▼ *Followers of the philosopher Duns Scotus were labelled "dunces" by critics of their unorthodox views.*

were created, many of them held by the chiefs of major clans. The colony itself soon passed to the French, and it was only in the 18th century that Scottish settlers began to arrive there in significant numbers.

THE EXPEDITION TO PANAMA

The driving force behind another, disastrous, enterprise was the financier William Paterson (1658–1719). As the founder of the Bank of England, he readily found backers for his project – a settlement on the Darien Isthmus in Panama that could serve as a trading base for both the Atlantic and the Pacific. Paterson's scheme was set up in 1695 as a joint venture between English and Scottish investors. However, the project was effectively sabotaged by William II, who had his own reasons for wishing to undermine any Scottish enterprise, and by the wealthy East India Company.

Following the intervention of these parties, the English investors withdrew, leaving the Scots to finance the entire risk on their own. Undeterred, Paterson pressed ahead, sailing out with the first batch of settlers in 1698. They grandly renamed the area New Caledonia and founded a base at Fort St Andrew. Unaware of the malarial conditions, many of the settlers succumbed to fever, while the remainder were soon overrun by Spanish forces. By 1700 the

▲ *This wooden church was erected in the 18th century by Scottish settlers at Pictou, in Nova Scotia.*

entire project had been abandoned, with considerable loss of life and money. The failure of the expedition was blamed on the English, although ironically it also increased calls for the union of the two countries, since it was evident that Scotland had more to gain by co-operating, rather than competing, with its powerful neighbour.

▼ *Herman Moll's 1699 map of New Caledonia relates to the attempt to found a Scottish colony in Panama.*

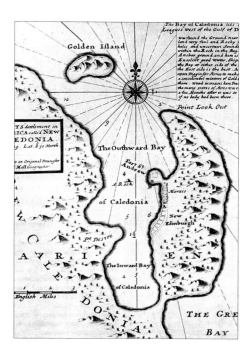

EMIGRATION IN THE 18TH CENTURY

The rate of emigration from the Highlands increased dramatically in the 18th century. Many of the expatriates eventually made new homes for themselves in the New World, taking with them the most important elements of their native culture.

POLITICAL DEPORTATIONS

Many of these emigrants were sent abroad under compulsion. Exile "beyond the seas" had been a standard punishment since the 17th century, particularly for those Scots who rebelled against the government. This form of transportation was usually for a fixed period (seven or 14 years were common terms), but many of the deportees remained in America after their release, and went on to become valued citizens. In Boston, for example, some of the Scots who had been expelled during the Civil War were responsible for setting up the Scots Charitable Society, which was founded in the city in 1657 and was the first organization of its kind in America.

TRANSPORTATION OF CONVICTED CRIMINALS

Certain types of criminal were also candidates for transportation. This kind of punishment was operated in a very

▼ The Scots Charitable Society held many of its meetings at the historic Green Dragon Inn in Boston.

▲ An engraving of 1770 shows Scottish convicts shackled together, awaiting transportation to North America.

haphazard fashion by the English, until the government introduced the Transportation Act of 1718, which regulated the system and made it far more profitable. Similar penalties were meted out in Scottish courts, although technically the latter had no legal right to send convicts to English colonies prior to the Act of Union of 1707. Instead, felons were banished "furth [outside] of the kingdom".

In Scotland, transportation was mainly reserved for capital offences, although prisoners could also petition for this sentence if they feared that the alternative might be worse. As a result, surviving records of Scottish transports indicate a wide variety of criminals, ranging from murderers and rapists to horse-thieves and counterfeiters. The system was open to abuse. Until heritable jurisdictions were abolished in 1748, after the battle of Culloden, clan chiefs enjoyed the right to banish certain offenders. Sometimes, however, prisoners were allowed to escape, if this suited clan interests; conversely, troublesome tenants were evicted from their land and transported purely on the basis of trumped-up charges.

Scotland deported considerably fewer of its criminals than either England or Ireland and, for this reason, the actual

process of transportation worked less efficiently. There were fewer ships dealing with this kind of cargo, and most captains were interested only in taking able-bodied young men who could readily be sold on as indentured servants. Many women and elderly people faced the prospect of lengthy delays, confined in prison, before they could actually begin their sentence. In 1734, for example, a female convict, Janet Jamieson, complained that "no merchants that traded to America would undertake to Transport her, unless she could pay her passage". Similarly, in 1729, a William Lauder bemoaned the fact that he had been held for three years in a tolbooth (jail), since he was old and "not fit for any Service in the Plantations".

A NEW LIFE

There was far greater Scottish participation in the more conventional forms of emigration, which mushroomed after 1700. New Jersey, which became a Crown Colony in 1702, was a popular destination for Scots, most notably in 1684, when almost 300 set sail from

WEARING HIGHLAND DRESS

Wherever they ventured, the clansmen made a point of displaying their Highland dress. In 1736, when Governor Oglethorpe of Georgia came to meet the Scots defending the frontier against the Spanish, he found them dressed in plaids and kilts and, in a diplomatic show of solidarity, agreed to try the outfit himself. Native Americans were fascinated by the bright colours of the tartans, which were so different from most European attire. Writing in the 1750s, David Stuart of Garth noted, "When the Highlanders landed, they were caressed by all ranks and orders of men, but more particularly by the Indians. On the march to Albany, the Indians flocked from all quarters to see the strangers who, they believed, were of the same extraction as themselves, and therefore received them as brothers."

▲ *Sentimental emigration scenes, such as John Watson Nicol's* Lochaber No More, *were a popular Victorian theme.*

▼ *The* Hector *is a replica of the ship that carried many Scots to Canada. It was launched at Pictou in 2000.*

home. The new settlement of Georgia, founded in 1732, attracted many Highlanders, as did the Cape Fear River area of North Carolina. In the latter, in particular, emigrant Scotsmen swiftly made their mark. There were also substantial Scottish settlements in the Mohawk and Upper Hudson Valleys in New York, and further north at Prince Edward Island and Pictou in Nova Scotia.

Even though the idea of a new start may have been tempting, the decision to emigrate was always a momentous step. Quite apart from the uncertainties surrounding their new home, the travellers were often exploited by unscrupulous speculators and ships' captains, and the voyage itself could be hazardous. The hazards were typified by the terrible journey endured by some 200 Scots who in 1773 set out from Ullapool aboard the *Hector*. The ship, which belonged to two Englishmen, departed with insufficient provisions, so that after two months at sea the drinking water was green and the only food was mouldy oatcakes. During the trip, 18 children died of smallpox or dysentery. At Newfoundland, the ship was driven back by gales, adding a further two weeks to the journey, so when the settlers finally arrived in Nova Scotia it was too late in the season to prepare the land or plant crops for the following year. Despite all this, they went ashore proudly, led by their piper and wearing the plaids and tartans that were still banned in their native land.

TARTAN REVIVAL

THE BAN WAS REPEALED IN 1782, BUT IT WAS GEORGE IV'S
STATE VISIT TO SCOTLAND THAT REALLY SIGNALLED A
CHANGE IN PUBLIC OPINION. ALMOST OVERNIGHT,
HIGHLAND DRESS BECAME HUGELY FASHIONABLE, AS EVERY
CLAN RUSHED TO VERIFY THEIR TARTAN.

THE REPEAL OF THE BAN

In the summer of 1782, the restrictions that had been placed on the wearing of tartan after the battle of Culloden in 1746 were finally removed. Once the bill had gained royal assent, a proclamation went out around the Highlands affirming "to every man, young and old...that they may after this put on and wear the Trews, the little Kilt, the Doublet and Hose, along with the Tartan Kilt, without fear of the Law of the Land or the jealousy of enemies..."

Earlier in the year, a delegation from the Highland Society of London had approached James Graham, the future 3rd Duke of Montrose, to ask if he might raise the matter in official circles. This was a shrewd choice. Graham was a member of parliament in England, but he came from a family that had a proud tradition of supporting the Stuart cause, and he duly introduced a bill calling for the repeal of the old Disarming Act. This provoked little controversy and the legislation was swiftly passed.

News of the lifting of the ban was greeted warmly by many Scots. The Gaelic poet Duncan MacIntyre, for example, composed a "Song to the Highland Garb", rejoicing in the occasion. Nevertheless, the overall response was surprisingly muted. In many quarters, there was a feeling that it was no longer an issue of major significance.

There were several reasons for this. In England, the most important factor was that the threat of another Jacobite rebellion had long since receded. After Culloden Prince Charles, the Young Pretender, had travelled around France and Spain before eventually settling in Italy. He gained no promises of support during the course of his wanderings in these Catholic countries, and gradually his own followers began to lose faith in

Previous pages: Inverlochy Castle.

▲ *David Wilkie's* Distraining for Rent *(1815) illustrates the plight of many crofters as rents rose dramatically.*

him. He was also heavily criticized in 1752, when he took Clementina Walkinshaw as his mistress. Her sister was a lady-in-waiting at the Hanoverian court, and there were many who regarded her as a spy.

The final turning point for the Jacobite movement occurred in 1766, with the death of the Old Pretender, Charles's father. Significantly, neither the Pope nor the king of France acknowledged Charles's right to the British throne. Instead, he remained in exile and, by the 1780s, was a forgotten man. When he died in 1788, his brother, Henry Benedict (1725–1807), last male heir of the Stuart line, made no claim to the throne. He had already pursued a successful career in the Church, becoming a cardinal in 1747.

A LOST CRAFT

Among the Scots themselves there was a more poignant reason for the mixed response to the repeal of the ban, namely that the measures drawn up in the Disarming Act had worked only

too well. Although there had been some notable attempts to evade the regulations, most people had simply conformed. This situation could not easily be reversed in 1782, because most Highlanders had more pressing problems to deal with. As Dr Johnson noted, "The same poverty that made it difficult for them to change their clothing, hinders them now from changing it back." Sir John Sinclair's *Old Statistical Account* (1799) included an entry from Kincardine that lamented the loss of the old cloth-making skills: "Deprived of the pleasure of seeing their husbands, sons, and favourites, in that elegant drapery, emulation died, and they became contented with manufacturing the wool in the coarsest and clumsiest manner..."

The truth of this account is confirmed by the problems that later researchers encountered when they were trying to trace the early development of tartan. They discovered that the old dyeing methods had largely been forgotten, and that the pattern-sticks described by the historian Martin Martin at the end of the 17th century had all been lost. At the time of the tartan revival, both chiefs and clansmen found it hard to establish which designs their ancestors had actually worn.

SHIFTING RELATIONSHIPS

One of the key strategies of the Hanoverian government had been to undermine the strength of the Highland clan system by weakening the links between the chief and his followers. They tried to do this by confiscating traditional clan lands and revoking heritable jurisdiction. Some of the estates were later restored but, even so, the parental nature of the relationship between the chief and his

▼ *In* The Last of the Clan *(1865), by Thomas Faed, a forlorn old clansman watches his family leave home forever.*

clansmen had begun to wane. In its place, there was a growing sense of commercialism, in which the chief assumed the status of a landlord rather than a patriarch.

LAND CLEARANCES

This subtle shift of attitudes became significant as the prevailing economic conditions deteriorated. From the

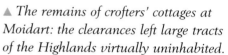 ▲ *The remains of crofters' cottages at Moidart: the clearances left large tracts of the Highlands virtually uninhabited.*

1760s, rents began to rise dramatically and landowners looked for more profitable ways of managing their assets. In practical terms, this often meant clearing the land of its tenants and sub-tenants, in order to exploit its full commercial value. The earliest attempts to do this, dating back to the 1730s, had been greeted with horror and threats of prosecution. As the 18th century went on, however, increasing numbers of landlords began to adopt this solution.

In many cases, the small crofting communities, with their scattered strips of arable land, were replaced by huge sheep farms. The industry was scarcely new in Scotland, but it underwent great changes in the 18th century. Different breeds, such as the black-faced Linton and the Cheviot, were introduced. These were hardy enough to survive the rigours of a Highland winter, and the combined value of their meat and their wool made them more profitable than cattle. The drawback was that they required a great deal of grazing land and, in many parts of the Highlands, they gradually began to displace the poorer clansmen.

A NEW IMAGE FOR THE HIGHLANDS

While the plight of many Highlanders grew steadily worse during the course of the 18th century, their public image began to change out of all recognition. As the threat of a Jacobite invasion faded, the history of the movement was rewritten, presenting a sanitized and romantic view of events.

Fictionalized versions of the 1745 rebellion soon began to captivate the public. The most popular of these was *The Young Adventurer* or, to give it its cumbersome full title, *The Young Adventurer, containing a particular account of all that happened to a certain person during his wanderings in the North, from his memorable defeat in April 1746 to his final escape on the 19th of September in the same year.* This was

▶ Bonnie Prince Charlie enters Edinburgh, *by John Leigh Pemberton, focuses on the glamour of the '45.*

Tartan featured heavily among the popular songs of the 18th century, largely, possibly, because "tartan plaidie" offered a convenient rhyme for "Highland Laddie". Even so, it soon came to acquire romantic connotations, which made it preferable to more costly materials, as the narrator of the following verse confirms:

A painted Room and Silken Bed
May please a Lawland Laird and Lady,
But I can kiss and be as glad
Behind a Bush in's Highland Plaidy.

Many songs took this a stage further, using the conceit of a lady exchanging her costly garments for the more romantic attire of the Highlands as a symbol of a passionate love affair:

TARTANA

Now She's cast off her silken Gowns
that she wear'd in the Lowland,
And she's up to the Highland Hills
to wear Gowns of Tartain.

Allan Ramsay (1686–1758), the poet who had done so much to popularize the Highland Laddie songs, wrote a lyric in praise of "Tartana". In it, he described how the warriors and shepherds throughout old Caledonia had decked themselves out in colourful plaids. Similarly, it is significant that one of the many accounts of the Young Pretender's adventures gave the prince the pseudonym of "Young Tartan".

▶ Tartana *(c.1845) by J.C. Armytage: the craze for all things tartan lasted well into the 19th century.*

fashionable reading not just in Britain but throughout much of western Europe, following its translation into French, Spanish and Italian.

POPULAR SONGS

The trend was not confined to novels, but was also evident in the popular songs of the period. Both the Jacobites and the Whigs (supporters of the Hanoverians) had produced songs that reflected their very different viewpoints. Alongside these were songs about the contemporary Highlander stereotype – the so-called "Highland Laddie" – who displayed very contradictory qualities. On the one hand, he was a violent and uncouth figure, yet at the same time his primitive qualities earned him a great reputation as a lover, who was more attractive to the English or Lowland ladies than their own refined menfolk.

After the Jacobite uprising, the political and romantic themes of such songs gradually merged, as Prince Charles, the Young Pretender, became increasingly associated with the Highland Laddie. In effect, he embarked upon his transformation into the romanticized figure of Bonnie Prince Charlie. As the memory of the rebellion receded and Jacobite sympathies became a picturesque reminder of the past, the underlying message of these songs began to change. Increasingly, the rebels seemed to conjure up a national spirit that could be appreciated by all Scots, whether Lowlanders or Highlanders. Tartan was tied in with this trend.

HEROIC BESTSELLERS

In 1760, James Macpherson (1736–96) published his *Fragments of Ancient Poetry Collected in the Highlands of Scotland and Translated from the Gaelic or Erse Language*. According to the author, these verses were part of a heroic epic that had been composed in the 3rd century AD by a Caledonian bard called Ossian. The *Fragments* aroused considerable interest in Edinburgh literary circles, and Macpherson was provided with the funds to continue his research into this field. The author duly travelled around some of the remoter parts of the Highlands and the Western Isles, returning with sufficient material for two further collections of verse – *Fingal, An Ancient Epic Poem...composed by Ossian, the Son of Fingal* (1761) and *Temora, An Ancient Epic Poem in Eight Books* (1763).

The response to Macpherson's books was phenomenal. They were bestsellers, both in Britain and throughout much

▼ *The Ossian poems inspired romantic visions of a Celtic past such as Ingres'* Dream of Ossian *(1813).*

of Europe. Goethe, Schubert and Schiller all sang their praises, while Napoleon owned an edition. The narrative was adapted into plays, operas and paintings.

Macpherson's verses recounted the adventures of a legendary race of giant warriors who had once ruled over the wilds of Caledonia, but the stories themselves were less important than the image they represented. The picture of a noble race of savages appealed to the sensibilities of the budding Romantic movement, and helped to promote a revival of interest in Celtic matters. From a Scottish standpoint, the poems, if genuine, meant that the country could lay claim to an ancient cultural tradition; a tradition that, very pointedly, England could not match.

THE HIGHLAND SOCIETIES

The Jacobite songs and the poems ascribed to Ossian presented a romantic view of the Highlands, mysterious and glamorous, which became known as "Highlandism". For all its attractions, though, it was in many respects a false vision, and one that the area has been slow to shake off. Yet, at the very time that Highlandism was emerging, attempts were also being made to define and preserve the true origins of Highland culture.

The pioneers in this field were the Highland Society of London, founded in 1778, and its sister organization, the Highland Society of Scotland, established six years later. The structure of these bodies was most unusual. In part, they were economic think-tanks that aimed to improve the financial state of the Highlands by promoting modernization. Among other things, they called for improvements in the fishing and farming industries, the upgrading of transport links, and the establishment of new towns and villages.

PROMOTING HIGHLAND CULTURE

Alongside these commercial activities, the societies also took a keen interest in the language and the arts of the Highlands. Their most illustrious achievement in this respect, perhaps, was the creation of a long-running piping competition, which the London branch established in 1781. In addition, both societies took a keen interest in the state of the Gaelic language. Their prognosis was hardly encouraging, for they believed it had "found a refuge in the Highlands of Scotland as a sanctuary in which it might expire". Even so, they commissioned a Gaelic dictionary, which was published in 1828.

The societies' other main task in this field was to organize an enquiry into the authenticity of James Macpherson's

Ossianic verses. This had remained a controversial issue, largely because the author had been so coy about revealing the Gaelic sources he had used. For many, it seemed suspicious that the material was so close to the stories in the Irish Fenian cycle, which featured several of the same characters. The investigating committee of the Highland Society considered the matter for several years before eventually producing a 300-page report, which was published in 1805. Its conclusions were disappointingly non-committal: it found that Macpherson had used some material of genuine antiquity, but had altered it dramatically, changing the names, places and mood of his Gaelic source and filling in the gaps with long passages of his own invention. Significantly, the committee's report had no effect whatsoever on the popularity of the books.

TARTAN SURVEY

In 1815, the Highland Society of London embarked on one of the earliest and most valuable surveys of tartan. Anxious to discover just how many named clan tartans were in circulation, they asked the chief of each clan for a

▲ *As Highland travel became easier, artists sought out picturesque sights such as this view of Inverness (1779).*

sample of their traditional sett. The chiefs were also encouraged to authenticate the sample by adding their seal and signature to it.

The project went ahead smoothly and, by 1816, 74 different specimens had been collected and identified. In some cases, they are the earliest known examples of the tartan in question. The Galbraith, Gow and Mackinnon setts all fall within this category. The survey often highlighted the inconsistent manner in which tartans were still being used. The Galbraith design, for example, is identical to that used by the Russells, the Hunters and the Mitchells, and it is not clear who first adopted the pattern. Similarly, the Highland Society's sample of the Mackinnon tartan features a light blue stripe that distinguishes it from other early versions of the sett. Most revealing of all, perhaps, was the comment that came back from many of the chiefs, confessing that they did not know their clan tartan and asking for help in ascertaining what it should be.

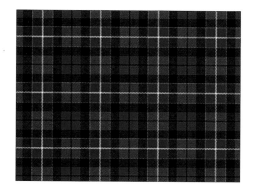

▲ *The Galbraith tartan is identical to the Russells, Hunters and Mitchells.*

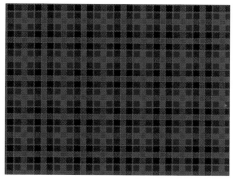

▲ *The Gow tartan, one of the earliest identified setts.*

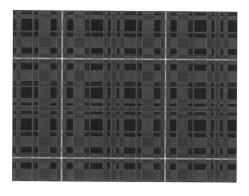

▲ *The Mackinnon tartan, with its distinguishing blue stripe.*

EARLY TOURISTS

While bodies such as the Highland Society were analysing the living conditions of the far north for the benefit of their learned members, the area was also becoming more familiar to the public at large. The road links that General Wade had constructed in the 1720s along the main arteries of the Highlands meant that travel through the region, while still hazardous, was considerably easier than in the past.

▼ *Fingal's Cave, discovered in 1772, rapidly became a source of inspiration for Romantic musicians and artists.*

This encouraged more outsiders to visit the area, many of whom published accounts of their journeys.

Prominent among these tourists was the naturalist Sir Joseph Banks, who travelled to see the geological wonders on the isle of Staffa. The highlight here was Fingal's Cave, which took its name from a hero in Macpherson's *Ossian*. A Welshman, Thomas Pennant, found the Highlands "almost as little known to its southern brethren as Kamchatka".

The most celebrated visitors were Dr Johnson and James Boswell. They travelled through the Highlands and islands in 1773, later recording their impressions in two famous books. Johnson's *Journey to the Western Isles* appeared in 1775, and Boswell's *Journal of a Tour to the Hebrides* a decade later. The doctor's notorious dislike of the Scots hardly presented a balanced view of the local culture. Nevertheless, his colourful descriptions of the Highlanders and their customs brought the region to life for many British people, who had regarded it as a wild and savage place.

▼ *Despite Dr Johnson's forebodings, he and Boswell were treated hospitably during their tour of the Highlands.*

GEORGE IV'S VISIT TO SCOTLAND

Although tartan was being worn again by the early years of the 19th century, a full-scale revival had not yet begun. This occurred almost overnight following George IV's official visit to Edinburgh in 1822, which was of considerable political significance as it marked the first occasion on which a Hanoverian monarch had set foot on Scottish soil. It was also an important moment for advocates of Highland dress, since tartan featured heavily in the proceedings and the king himself donned a kilt during the celebrations.

After years of living in the shadow of his father, George III, and having spent almost ten years as regent (1811–20) after he was deemed insane, George IV (r.1820–30) finally became king at the age of 42. Already notorious for his extravagance and dandyism, he spent a year planning his summer coronation in 1821 and, having developed a taste for lavish ceremonial,

▼ *George IV travelled to Scotland on his yacht the* Royal George, *this painting depicts his arrival at Leith.*

decided to follow this up with a royal progress through his kingdom. The focal point of his visit to Scotland was to be an affirmation of the union between England and Scotland, a symbolic reconciliation between the two countries, following the Jacobite uprisings in the previous century.

SIR WALTER SCOTT'S PAGEANT

The details of the visit were put in the hands of the Lord Provost of Edinburgh, who in turn invited the novelist and poet Sir Walter Scott to manage the affair. Scott's love of pageantry and tradition made him the ideal choice. He had already attended George's coronation and conducted detailed research into the subject of royal progresses for his latest novel, *Kenilworth*, which had been published in 1821. Once preparations got under way, Scott's house in Castle Street, Edinburgh, became a hive of activity, prompting the author himself to remark, "This town has been a scene of such giddy tumult...I am astonished that I did not fever in the midst of it."

TARTAN AS A SYMBOL OF UNITY

The amount of tartan on show during King George IV's visit to Scotland impressed most people. One observer noted, "It seemed that the Highland clans with sword and pistol at their belts, bagpipes playing, and tartans waving, had come to re-occupy the capital, as in the '45...a tartan fit had come upon the city and...marched out to welcome the royal visitor." Scott would not have been pleased at this mention of the Jacobite uprising of 1745, since these were the very associations that he wished to dispel. In the past, tartan had been a mark of rebellion, but now it was to be a symbol of unity and lineage.

Scott wanted the royal visit to stress the cultural independence of his nation and to make the recently rediscovered Honours of Scotland – the royal regalia consisting of the crown, sceptre and

▲ The royal regalia, known as the Honours of Scotland, were the focal point of many celebrations during George IV's state visit to Edinburgh.

sword of state – a centrepiece of the event. They had been locked away in Edinburgh Castle after the Act of Union in 1707 and forgotten until Scott had made an official enquiry as to their whereabouts. Scott was present at their rediscovery in a padlocked oak chest in 1818.

TARTAN TAKES CENTRE STAGE

Walter Scott also insisted that kilts, tartans and pipes should play a prominent role and invited many of the leading clan chiefs to play a part in the proceedings. Not all of them came but a steady stream of "wild Highlanders" thronged to see him, often "completely armed so that the house rang with broadswords and targets and pipes from daybreak to sunset".

The response was also sufficient to create a genuine shortage in the supply of tartan, which led some of the guests to take drastic measures. The Sutherland Highlanders, for example, even persuaded a weaving firm to part with an entire batch of uniforms destined for the Black Watch.

The twin notions of ancestry and tradition were emphasized at every juncture during George's visit. After disembarking at the port of Leith, the king was led on a triumphal procession through the streets of Edinburgh, where banners proclaimed: "Welcome to the land of your ancestors," and "Descendant of the immortal Bruce, thrice Welcome." When the king appeared dressed in a kilt of Royal Stewart tartan at a sumptuous levée in Holyrood Palace, a deliberate link was forged between the Jacobite Pretenders of the past and the present-day legitimate monarch.

The clans played an even greater role during a second procession, in which George paraded, accompanied by the royal regalia, from Holyrood to Edinburgh Castle. On this occasion, the king was attended by the Drummonds, the MacDonells, the Sutherland Highlanders, the Breadalbane Men and the MacGregors, who were all attired in their tartan finery. The ceremony was marred by a heavy downpour, but the king was sufficiently impressed to remark to one of the organizers: "What a fine sight. I had no conception there was such a scene in the world...and the people are as beautiful and extraordinary as the scene."

During the remainder of his stay, George reviewed his Scottish troops, attended a service at St Giles's Cathedral and was guest of honour at several balls. One of his final and most enjoyable duties was a visit to the Theatre Royal, to see a dramatized version of *Rob Roy*, one of Sir Walter Scott's most popular novels. This was a fitting tribute to the man who, more than any other, had ensured the success of the royal visit and who, in the process, had almost single-handedly revived the fortunes of tartan.

▼ Painted by John Ewbank, this panoramic view illustrates the pageantry of the reception that greeted the king in 1822.

SIR WALTER SCOTT

man even met a few of the conflict's survivors. Inevitably, this stirred his imagination, giving him much of the material that he would later recycle into his stories.

POET AND NOVELIST

As he embarked on his literary pursuits, Scott initially made his mark as a poet. *The Lay of the Last Minstrel* (1805) brought him his first real taste of success, and was swiftly followed by a number of other verse romances. Scott ploughed this furrow for almost a decade, until the rise of Byron persuaded him to try his hand at other genres, culminating in the publication of the novel *Waverley* (1814), his ground-breaking venture into prose. The book was published under a pseudonym – because Scott was worried about jeopardizing his legal career – and was an immediate success, going through four editions in its first year.

Waverley tells the story of a naive young English soldier, who comes from a Hanoverian background but also has an uncle with Jacobite sympathies. When he is posted to Scotland during the rebellion, he comes into contact with some of his uncle's friends and rapidly becomes embroiled in the rising itself. These political complications are mirrored in the hero's private life: he falls in love with the sister of a Jacobite leader, but is eventually saved by a devoted admirer, who comes from a far less dangerous background.

The underlying theme of *Waverley* is one that Scott returned to again and again – a divided Scotland. This division centred on the choice between the emotional pull of the country's Celtic past and the modernizing influences that appeared to be its future. The dichotomy was apparent in Scott's own nature. In his heart, he was a Jacobite, captivated by the old culture of the

George IV's visit to Scotland in 1822 produced a mixed response from Scottish commentators. Most were impressed by the sheer spectacle of the occasion, though a few dismissed it as a masquerade. One pundit, for example, summed up the entire event as "Sir Walter's Celtified Pageantry". Even Scott's sternest critics, however, could hardly deny that the author had done much to foster a new public image for his country. This image was built up over the course of his career, and should not be linked exclusively to the royal visit.

Walter Scott was born in Edinburgh, but spent many of his formative years in the Borders, where he became entranced by the area's history and developed a fascination with the past

▲ *As the self-appointed guardian of Scottish tradition, no one did more to promote the revival of tartan than Sir Walter Scott.*

that would dominate his entire life. As a youth, he had hoped to become a soldier, but a childhood illness left him with a permanent limp and effectively ended this ambition. Instead, he followed his father into the law. The work seemed like pure drudgery to him, although it was not without relevance to his writing career. The Jacobite rebellion was still a living memory for the older generation and many of Scott's cases dealt with the lingering effects of the uprising – issues such as forfeited estates and disputed inheritances. As part of his job, the young

Highlands, but in his head he was a Unionist, aware that the links with England were likely to bring his country prosperity and influence.

In part, the book's impact was due to the sheer originality of the form, for with *Waverley* Scott effectively invented the historical novel. The combination of the colourful setting, the adventure and the love interest captured the spirit of the times, appealing to devotees of the Romantic movement then in full flood. The author wasted no time in exploiting this trend, producing a series of novels that dealt with evocative periods in Scottish history. Prominent among them were *Rob Roy* (1817), which revolves around the escapades of a famous outlaw, and *Redgauntlet* (1824), which focuses on an imaginary third Jacobite rebellion, in which Bonnie Prince Charlie returns to take up the struggle once more.

PRESERVING HIGHLAND CULTURE

Scott's attachment to the past led him to try to preserve its most important features. His determination to revive the popularity of tartan is a memorable example of this, but the same instincts

also prompted him to record the old ballads and folk tales of the Borders before they disappeared. When he became rich, he also felt driven to build up a collection of historical knick-knacks. Among the relics preserved in his home at Abbotsford are a lock of Bonnie Prince Charlie's hair, a purse and *skean dhu* (stocking dagger) that belonged to Rob Roy and, most poignant of all, a piece of oatcake found on the body of a Highlander killed at Culloden.

THE SCOTTISH FASHION

Through the medium of his books, Scott managed to transmit his enthusiasm for the traditional culture to the rest of Europe. His novels were enormously popular throughout the continent, and they inspired a vogue

◀ *A passion for Scottish styles swept Europe, and this tartan dress appeared on a French fashion plate in 1826.*

▲ *Jeanie Deans wears a tartan shawl in a scene from Scott's novel,* The Heart of Midlothian *(1818).*

for all things Scottish. The most visible evidence of this influence was the craze for tartan, which extended far beyond the borders of Scotland. In France, for example, fashion designers incorporated strips of tartan into their latest creations and there was a veritable passion for *la mode écossaise*.

In later years, this was sometimes seen as a cause for regret. Scott has often been described as the architect of Highlandism; more than anyone else, he was responsible for the way that Highland culture and history was reinvented and repackaged for the popular market. This gave Scotland a much higher profile within Europe, as well as a heightened sense of national identity, but it also laid the foundations of a stereotyped view of the country that persisted into modern times.

TARTAN AS A COSTUME

In its original form, Highland dress had developed as a simple and practical outfit, which was perfectly adapted to the needs of the people who wore it. During the period of the tartan revival, however, this approach no longer prevailed. Many of the people who donned kilts or plaids regarded them either as examples of national costume, or else as items of fashionable wear. Accordingly, the appearance of the garments seemed far more important than any notions of historical accuracy.

FANCY DRESS

The most extreme example of this attitude was provided by George IV. In his youth, he acquired a reputation as a dandy and, long before he ever set foot in Scotland, he had developed a fondness for Highland dress. In 1789, when he was 27 years old, he and his two brothers were given Scottish outfits and received instruction in the wearing of

▼ *While surveying Highland roads in the 1720s, Edward Burt recorded a very varied array of tartan outfits.*

the "tartan plaid, philibeg [kilt], purse and other appendages" from Colonel John Small. Shortly afterwards, the prince appeared at a fashionable London masquerade wearing a kilt. At this stage it is quite evident that he regarded Highland attire as a form of fancy dress.

◄ *George IV relished the imposing, theatrical air Highland dress gave him, as in this portrait by David Wilkie.*

GEORGE IV'S STATE OUTFIT

The official visit to Scotland in 1822 provided George with a genuine pretext for wearing tartan on a state occasion, and he seized the opportunity eagerly. His outfit for the reception at Holyrood, procured from George Hunter & Company at exorbitant cost, was made with the finest materials, which included 56m/61yd of satin, 28m/31yd of velvet and almost 18m/20yd of cashmere. The sporran was made of soft, silk-lined, white goatskin and adorned with clusters of gems; the leather brogues were topped with golden rosettes, surrounded with gold filigree; and the belts were decorated with golden buckles, bearing the figure of St Andrew on a saltaire of garnets. The weapons were particularly costly, and included a broadsword, a pair of pistols and an emerald-hilted dirk encased in a scabbard covered in crimson velvet, but the most expensive item was a gold badge on the king's bonnet, which was set with rubies, pearls, diamonds and emeralds.

Ironically, most commentators did not focus on the opulent finery of the costume, preferring to concentrate instead on the extraordinary flesh-coloured pantaloons that the king chose to wear beneath his kilt. George's intention, undoubtedly, was to conceal his unsightly legs, but some believed that it made a travesty of the entire outfit. There was a precedent, however, for this sartorial concoction. On the stage, actors had taken to wearing flesh-coloured tights beneath their kilts when appearing in Scottish productions, such as *Macbeth* or *Rob Roy*. Unconsciously the king was emphasizing the theatricality of Highland dress.

► *Alasdair Ranaldson MacDonell of Glengarry was a passionate advocate of Highland dress, as this striking portrait by Raeburn confirms.*

FULL HIGHLAND DRESS

The extravagance of George's costume for his Scottish visit was without parallel in the history of Highland dress, but it did typify a general trend. Among the Highland worthies who attended the royal visit there was a strong competitive element, as each tried to ensure that they created a more striking impression than their rivals in other clans. In many cases, this had less to do with the quality of the materials used than with the quantity of the accessories. For the first time, efforts were made to compile a complete inventory of the items that ought to be included in full Highland dress. The results were a very far cry from the kind of outfit originally worn by penniless Highlanders.

The most exhaustive list of clothes and accessories was provided by Alasdair Ranaldson MacDonell of Glengarry. In common with many of the Highland chiefs, MacDonell commissioned a portrait to show off his tartan finery and, in this, he displayed many of the items specified in his list. He may have intended the painting as the embodiment of an old tradition, but the effect was undermined by two main features. First, the outfit was elaborately tailored, unlike the early forms of Highland attire, which had become popular precisely because their manufacture was so simple. Second, the profusion of guns, swords and knives underlines the fact that MacDonell and many of his contemporaries chose to be portrayed as Highland warriors, even though this bore very little relation to their actual lifestyle. Instead, they were participating in a colourful form of role-playing, inspired by the romantic image that was now evoked by the Jacobites of old.

MACDONELL'S INVENTORY

A Belted Plaid and waist Belt

A Tartan Jacket with True Highlander Buttons and Shoulder Buckles

A Scarlet Vest with True Highlander Buttons

A Cocked Bonnet with Clan Badge and Cockade

A Purse and Belt

A Pair of Highland Garters

A Pair of Hose

A Pair of Highland Brogues

A Gun (or Fusee) with a sling

A Broad Sword and Shoulder Belt

A Target and Slinging Belt

A Brace of Highland Pistols and Belt

A "Chore Dubh" or Hose Knife [*skean dhu*]

A Powder Horn with Chain and Cord

A short Pouch and cross shoulder Belt

THE TARTAN CRAZE

The growing passion for tartan in the 19th century resulted in the creation of a host of societies and clubs devoted to the study and preservation of ancient Scottish culture. The Highland Society of London had already set the benchmark for the other organizations that now sprang up.

THE CELTIC SOCIETY

Originally devised by William Mackenzie of Gruinard, a captain of the Inverness Militia, this Edinburgh-based group was not limited exclusively to Highlanders and was less aristocratic in its composition than some of the other societies. Instead, there was a strong showing from the

▼ *Traditional music was important to the Highland societies: John Mackenzie was piper to the True Highlanders.*

mercantile class, along with a number of lawyers, doctors and bankers. Sir Walter Scott became the Celtic Society's president and, through his influence, it played a major part in the ceremonial aspects of King George's 1822 visit to Scotland.

Its mixed membership attracted criticism from some quarters, however. Alasdair Ranaldson MacDonell, for example, wrote a stinging letter on the subject to the *Edinburgh Observer*: "I dined one day with them...and I never saw so much tartan before in my life, with so little Highland material...There may be some very good and respectable men amongst them, but their general appearance is assumed and fictitious, and they have no right to burlesque the national character or dress of the Highlands…"

To some degree, MacDonell's remarks stemmed from the rivalry that existed between the Celtic Society and his own group – the True Highlanders.

▲ *The inaugural meeting of the Society of True Highlanders was held by the ruins of Inverlochy Castle.*

However, it did also reflect a genuine concern among some Highlanders that their traditions were being hijacked by Lowlanders. In a sense their fears were justified. When in 1804 Sir John Sinclair proposed a motion that tartan should be worn at all future meetings of the society, he stressed that there was an urgent need to assert the unique qualities of Scottish culture, before "Scotland becomes completely confounded in England". This underlined the real value of the tartan revival to Lowland Scots. As the latter's economic ties with England grew ever closer there was a danger that the region would be swallowed up by its southern neighbour. Only by adopting the very distinctive culture of the Highlands as its own could it retain its Scottish national identity.

THE TRUE HIGHLANDERS

The Lowlanders' view cut very little ice with the exclusive membership of the Society of True Highlanders. Founded in 1815, its supporters were drawn entirely from "Highlanders of property and birth", and its declared aims were to promote "the Dress, Language, Music, and Characteristics of our Illustrious and Ancient Race in the Highlands and Islands of Scotland". Many of its activities were actually lavish social events, such as the balls held in the grounds of Inverlochy Castle.

ALASDAIR RANALDSON MacDONELL OF GLENGARRY

The driving force behind the Society of True Highlanders was Alasdair Ranaldson MacDonell, 15th Chief of Glengarry. He was a firm advocate of tradition, even if some of his views belonged to another era. Walter Scott

▼ *Hunting became a popular pastime. This picture by Sir Edwin Landseer depicts a deer-stalking expedition in the Highlands.*

called him "a kind of Quixote in our age, having retained... the whole feelings of clanship and chieftainship, elsewhere so long abandoned. He seems to have lived a century too late…"

MacDonell's commitment to the old ways led him to maintain elements of a traditional Highland court, employing a clan bard and often appearing in public with a piper and servants carrying his weapons. He also liked to go out hunting in the manner of his ancestors, dressed in his plaid and sleeping under the stars. In other respects, however, he was all too modern. Stewart of Garth, for example, accused him of hypocrisy, for playing the role of an old-fashioned Highland chief while at the same time removing many of his tenants from their lands in order to make way for sheep. Ironically for a man who was so dedicated to the past, MacDonell's name is associated with one of the

◄ *The distinctive Glengarry bonnet, linked to the name of MacDonnell, was adopted by several Scottish regiments.*

more recent items of Highland dress – the Glengarry bonnet, which he may have devised.

HIGHLAND SOCIETIES

The rivalry between the Celtic Society and the True Highlanders gave them a high profile during the revival period, but they were by no means unique. New branches of the Highland Society were established in a number of Scottish cities. One of them was founded in Aberdeen where, in common with their London counterparts, members were expected to appear in their clan tartan at every meeting. The society's principal aim was to "promote the general use of the ancient Highland dress," but it also lent support to Gaelic schools, studied the "relics" of Celtic literature, and provided relief for poor Highlanders.

SOCIAL CLUBS

The revival of tartan was also linked with a variety of local social clubs, such as the Highland Mountain Club of Lochgoilhead, formed in 1815. The club espoused the lofty desire to "adopt the dress, cultivate the language, and perpetuate the manners and refined sentiments of our remote ancestors". In practice, this entailed a combination of mountaineering, drinking and musketry, with the members attired in Highland dress. A typical outing would consist of a bracing climb up a local peak, where various songs and toasts were made in Gaelic, each of which was followed by a celebratory burst of gunfire. After this, the members would return downhill "to the reverberating sounds of bagpipes and musquetry".

EARLY HISTORICAL RESEARCH

The numerous Highland organizations that sprang up during the revival period in the 19th century achieved very mixed results. Some were genuinely distinguished bodies that did much to preserve and promote the cause of Highland culture, while others effectively reduced the function of tartan to the level of fancy dress. Outside the clubs and societies, there were also an increasing number of individuals who added their own contributions to the study of the subject.

PRESERVING TRADITIONAL TARTANS

The initiative taken by the Highland Society of London in instituting its tartan survey in 1815 was invaluable, even if the results were not widely publicized. The chief aims of the survey had been to record the old patterns, to prevent them being lost, and to encourage some degree of consistency in the use of tartan. At the time, this was still the exception rather than the rule. When,

---

TRADITIONAL GARB

In the Highland dress section of *The Scottish Gael*, published in 1831, James Logan was keen to refute the idea that tartan was a comparatively recent development. "It will be proved that this primitive costume, so well suited to the warrior, so well adapted for the avocations of the hunter and shepherd," he wrote, "has not only been the invariable dress of the Highlanders from time immemorial, but is to be derived from the most remote antiquity... Their country and pursuits rendering the belted plaid and kilt the most convenient apparel, they were not likely to lay it aside for any other."

---

for example, Alexander Robertson of Struan wished to discover the traditional sett for his family, he made enquiries among the elders of his clan. Many of them claimed to know the true design, but the descriptions they supplied were quite different from each other. Accordingly, Robertson was forced to make his own choice and, as he felt that the suggested patterns were "all very vulgar and gaudy", he decided to adopt the Atholl tartan instead.

A UNIQUE ARCHIVE

The Highland Society's survey resulted in the creation of a unique archive, and its efforts were supplemented by a number of enthusiastic tartan collectors. The most notable of these was General Sir William Cockburn, who was a member of the society. Between 1810 and 1820, he built up a collection of 56 specimen tartans, which he catalogued and mounted in a large, leather-bound volume.

The samples Cockburn included in his collection are thought to have been woven by the tartan manufacturers Wilson's of Bannockburn. This is of particular interest, since the results can be compared with the thread-counts and colours specified in the company's own pattern book of 1819. Wilson's went out of business in 1924 and none of their original stock has survived. Most of the specimens they made for Cockburn were of "hard" tartan (a densely woven, coarse wool variety that went out of fashion after the mid-19th century) and they were identified with Cockburn's hand-written labels. These are not without controversy. The Cockburn tartan, for example, was later discovered to be a Mackenzie sett, even though Sir William had confirmed the identification himself. The Cockburn Collection is now housed in Glasgow's Mitchell Library.

▲ *James Logan drew this Highland piper from the 42nd Regiment for his book* The Scottish Gael *(1831).*

THE SCOTTISH GAEL

The first book to include a detailed listing of clan tartans appeared in 1831. This was James Logan's seminal study, *The Scottish Gael or Celtic Manners, as Preserved among the Highlanders.* Logan was born in Aberdeen around 1794, the son of a merchant. He studied at Marischal College with the intention of becoming a lawyer, but following an unfortunate accident – he is said to have been struck on the head by a hammer at an athletics competition – he was unable to complete the course. During his recuperation he became fascinated by early Scottish history and archaeology, and his interest led him to devote much of his career to antiquarian research.

For most of the 1820s Logan earned his living writing articles for newspapers and magazines, while also working on his most important book. The research for this was spread across five years, during which time, in his own words, "with staff in hand and knapsack on his shoulders, he wandered leisurely over all of Scotland, from the Mull of Galloway to John O'Groats...carefully examining and sketching its antiquities of every kind."

When compiling his list of tartans, Logan received assistance from both the Highland Society of London and Wilson's of Bannockburn. The former allowed him to consult their archive of certified tartans, while the latter sent him a summary of the "patterns of all the clan and family tartans". This was annotated with a series of useful comments, such as "MacDougall, as we make it" or, regarding the Douglas sett, that they had been selling it for "a considerable time". Logan published a collection of 55 tartans that he believed to be "as correct as the most laborious personal investigations, and the able assistance of some valued friends, could make it".

▲ *An array of clan shields from Robert McIan's seminal two-volume study,* The Clans of the Scottish Highlands.

After completing *The Scottish Gael*, Logan gained the post of secretary of the Highland Society of London, largely through the good offices of his friend Sir John Sinclair. He subsequently became involved in the Gaelic Society of London, channelling his energies into the promotion of the Gaelic language and its literature. His interest in tartan persisted, however, and he later wrote the text for *The Clans of the Scottish Highlands* (1845–47), which contained an attractive series of 74 engravings by the actor and illustrator Robert Ranald McIan. *The Clans* proved to be one of the most popular books on the subject during the Victorian period. Through it, Logan made the acquaintance of Prince Albert, who helped him to gain lodgings in the Charterhouse to offset the genteel poverty of his declining years.

▼ *McIan's lively pictures of clansmen were the finest of the period. Here, the Lord of the Isles delivers judgment.*

▼ *A barefooted Highland warrior, with his plaid folded around his body, wields a traditional Scottish longsword.*

▼ *Another illustration from McIan shows how women wore the arisaid, the female equivalent of the plaid.*

THE TARTAN FORGERIES

At the height of the 19th-century tartan craze new patterns were created at an alarming rate, and many were passed off as traditional designs. The Sobieski brothers appeared on the scene at this time, claiming access to ancient manuscripts that would end all disputes about who had a right to wear what.

The brothers' mysterious origins seemed as romantic as one of Sir Walter Scott's plots. John (1795–1872) and Charles (1797–1880) were the sons of Thomas Allen. The latter believed that he was related to the earls of Errol and adopted their family name

▼ *Jan Sobieski, king of Poland, a name with romantic associations in Scotland because of its links with Prince Charles.*

(Hay), while also changing the spelling of Allen to its Scottish form, Allan. John and Charles Hay Allan went much further, intimating that Thomas Allen had been the legitimate son of Bonnie Prince Charlie and his wife, Louisa of Stolberg-Gedern. Officially, no such child had existed, but a story circulated that a boy had been born in secret and was raised away from court, under an assumed identity, lest the Hanoverians should try to murder him. As well as hinting that they were the offspring of this Stuart heir, the Allen brothers adopted the name of a Polish royal dynasty, Sobieski, since Charlie had been related to this family through his mother. When they made their entrée into Scottish society, they were

calling themselves John Sobieski Stolberg Stuart, Count d'Albanie, and Charles Sobieski Stuart.

The brothers spent their early years in Europe, where they claimed to have served with Napoleon's army, and lived for a time in London, where they learned some Gaelic. They arrived in Scotland around 1817, and their charm and cultivated manners soon won them friends in the highest circles. Their chief patron was Lord Lovat, who gave them a house on his estates, on a small island in the Beauly river.

ANCIENT MANUSCRIPTS

Once firmly established in Edinburgh, the brothers gradually revealed the existence of three tartan manuscripts in their possession. The oldest dated back to about 1571 and had apparently been preserved in the Scots College in the French town of Douai. They said it had been presented to Bonnie Prince Charlie and had thus been inherited by Thomas Allen. The Cromarty manuscript, so called because it had been acquired from an old Highlander in that region, was dated 1721, while a third text, supposedly found at the

▼ *The Sobieski brothers became the darlings of Scottish society.*

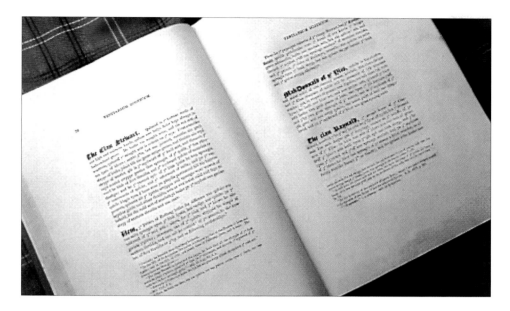

▲ *The* Vestiarium Scoticum *was hugely successful because it suggested that clan tartans had a long pedigree.*

Monastery of St Augustine in Cadiz, in southern Spain, was said to have been written in 1608.

If genuine, these manuscripts would have revolutionized the history of tartan, giving some of the clan setts a pedigree that stretched back to Tudor times. For this very reason, many historians were sceptical, particularly since the Sobieskis seemed so reluctant to let anyone examine the documents. A few privileged individuals were allowed to peruse the Cromarty manuscript, but the other two remained unseen. Sir Walter Scott was even more suspicious when he learned that many of the tartans in the various texts related to the Lowlands, for he had always been convinced that clan tartans had been the sole preserve of the Highlands.

THE *VESTIARIUM SCOTICUM*
The brothers revealed the existence of one of the documents in 1829 to Dick Lauder, a friend of Sir Walter Scott, and, after years of prevaricating, they eventually published its contents in *Vestiarium Scoticum* (1842). This contained colour illustrations of 75 tartans, many of them hitherto unknown. From the outset, the *Vestiarium* proved highly controversial. Nevertheless, when the book was finally published, it won many supporters. Several clans adopted, and indeed are still wearing, patterns that first appeared in its pages. A proper, scientific analysis of the manuscripts has never been possible, since none of them have ever been found, if indeed they ever existed. The only evidence has come from a series of photographs of the Cromarty manuscript, taken around 1895. These suggest that the documents had been artificially aged, and probably only dated from the early 19th century. On the internal evidence of the manuscript, too, there was one key finding. The text included an accurate description of the Gordon regimental tartan, even though it is clear from surviving correspondence that this was chosen much later, in 1793.

Undeterred by the controversy, the Sobieski brothers continued to produce books on Scottish traditions. They included the *Lays of the Deer Forest*, as well as another, less contentious book about tartan, *The Costume of the Clans*. In later years, the Sobieskis moved to Austria, then finally settled in England.

INVENTED SETTS

Serious scholars sometimes despaired at the proliferation of tartans making the rounds. Thomas Dick Lauder complained to his friend Sir Walter Scott: "In these times of rage for tartans...the most uncouth coats of many colours are every day invented, manufactured, christened after particular names and worn as genuine... At present, a woeful want of knowledge in the subject prevails. Some of the clans are at this moment ignorantly disputing for the right to the same tartans, which in fact belong to none of them, but are merely modern inventions for clothing Regimental Highlanders. Hardly does one of the clans now wear its tartan with its legitimate setts."

▶ *An officer of the 92nd Regiment, also known as the Gordon Highlanders.*

QUEEN VICTORIA'S SEAL OF APPROVAL

The gimmickry of George IV's state visit to Scotland kick-started the tartan revival, but did not guarantee its survival. After 1822, the king never again demonstrated the same level of interest in his northern kingdom. Instead, it was his niece, Queen Victoria, who developed a genuine fondness for the Highlands and did much to ensure the lasting popularity of tartan.

Victoria and her husband Prince Albert paid their first visit to the area in 1842, two years after they were married. They were received with due pomp and pageantry, but without the element of fancy dress that had attended George's trip. At Dunkeld, they were greeted by a spectacular gathering of the Atholl clans. Shortly afterwards, they were given an even grander reception at Taymouth Castle, which the queen recorded enthusiastically in her journal: "The *coup d'oeil* was

indescribable. There were a number of Lord Breadalbane's Highlanders, all in the Campbell tartan, drawn up in front of the house, with Lord Breadalbane himself in a Highland dress at their head...a number of pipers playing, and a company of the 92nd Highlanders, also in kilts. The firing of the guns, the cheering of the great crowd, the picturesqueness of the country... altogether formed one of the finest scenes imaginable. It seemed as if a great chieftain in olden feudal times was receiving his sovereign. It was princely and romantic."

The trip was such a success that the royal couple were eager to return and, in 1844, they stayed for several weeks at Blair Castle. Three years later, they toured the Hebrides in the royal yacht and enjoyed an extended break at Ardverikie by Loch Laggan.

BALMORAL

In 1848, Victoria and Albert leased Balmoral for the first time, swiftly realizing that this was the ideal place for them. Four years later, they bought the

▲ *Queen Victoria described Balmoral, built in the Scottish baronial style, as "this dear Paradise".*

estate and set about remodelling it to suit their own needs. A local architect, William Smith of Aberdeen, rebuilt part of the structure in the Scottish baronial style. The interior was very largely designed by Prince Albert and included a series of "cheerful and un-palace-like rooms" that conjured up the atmosphere of a cosy but elegant hunting lodge, enlivened with chintzes and tartans. Once the improvements were in place, it became a favourite retreat for the couple. For both Victoria and Albert, and indeed for many of their successors, Balmoral represented a genuine sanctuary, where they could escape from the rigours and formality of court life. The relaxing atmosphere was confirmed by an outside observer, Charles Greville, who noted of the royal family, "They live there without any state whatever: they live not merely like private gentlefolks, but like very small gentlefolks…"

COMMERCIAL HIGHLANDISM

Queen Victoria's growing fondness for spending time in the far north of Britain coincided with rapid improvements in communications. New railway lines and shipping routes, together with the blossoming of the tourist industry, brought visitors flocking to Scotland. This in turn generated a demand for suitable souvenirs and memorabilia. Suddenly, tartan designs were no longer confined to woven materials, but could be found on every imaginable form of knick-knack – from tea caddies and spectacle cases to cheap jewellery and plates. "Highlandism" had found a powerful commercial outlet: one that has continued to thrive to the present day.

BALMORAL TARTANS

Prince Albert's interior design for Balmoral included many tartans. The Royal Stewart and Hunting Stewart patterns were used for the carpets, while the curtains and upholstery mainly featured the Dress Stewart sett. In addition, two new tartans were created to add variety to the decor. The queen herself was fond of the design called Victoria, a subtle variant of Royal Stewart, while Prince Albert devised an entirely new sett for the project. Known as Balmoral, this tartan is still popular, although its use is restricted solely to members of the royal family.

▼ *The Balmoral tartan, devised by Albert for use at the castle.*

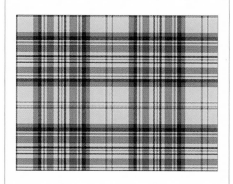

Victoria was the first reigning monarch for several centuries to choose to spend a significant amount of time in Scotland. In doing so, she tacitly gave the royal seal of approval to an entire range of Highland activities. It was no longer unusual for the British public to hear or read of the queen being attended by pipers, or the royal children playing in kilts, or Prince Albert watching the Highland games. Victoria's links with the Highlands

▼ *This depiction of Queen Victoria's personal sitting room at Balmoral appeared in an early edition of her Highland journals.*

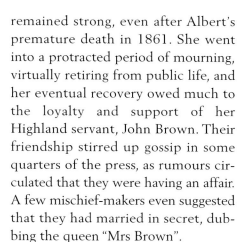

▲ *Returning from the hunt at night, Prince Albert proudly displays to Victoria the game that has been killed.*

remained strong, even after Albert's premature death in 1861. She went into a protracted period of mourning, virtually retiring from public life, and her eventual recovery owed much to the loyalty and support of her Highland servant, John Brown. Their friendship stirred up gossip in some quarters of the press, as rumours circulated that they were having an affair. A few mischief-makers even suggested that they had married in secret, dubbing the queen "Mrs Brown".

On a less contentious level, Victoria also maintained the high profile of the Highlands through two influential publications. In 1868, a carefully edited version of her journal, entitled *Leaves from the Journal of Our Life in the Highlands*, appeared in print and became an instant bestseller. This was followed two years later by *The Highlanders of Scotland*, the preparation of which Victoria supervised closely. She commissioned for it a lavish set of illustrations from the watercolourist Kenneth MacLeay. These consisted of a series of portraits of individual Highlanders in full costume, which must rank among the very finest images of tartan ever produced.

TARTAN IN ART

Initially, the portrayal of tartan in the visual arts was largely confined to costume prints and commissioned portraits. With both of these, there was a tendency to emphasize the exotic nature of Highland dress, as a form of attire entirely distinct from that of other European nations. Accordingly, some artists were encouraged to exaggerate the complexity of the garb, by combining it with a gaudy jacket or hat, or by adding a profusion of accessories. There is some irony in this, given that the plaid owed its longevity to the simplicity of its design and to the fact that even a modest crofter could afford it. Despite this, the extravagance of some portraits was noticeable from an early stage. The 17th-century outfit depicted in John Michael Wright's *Lord Mungo Murray*, for example, was spectacular, if hardly convincing as typical hunting attire.

▼ *Raeburn's portrait of the MacNab exudes pride and resilience, typifying the Romantic view of the Highlander.*

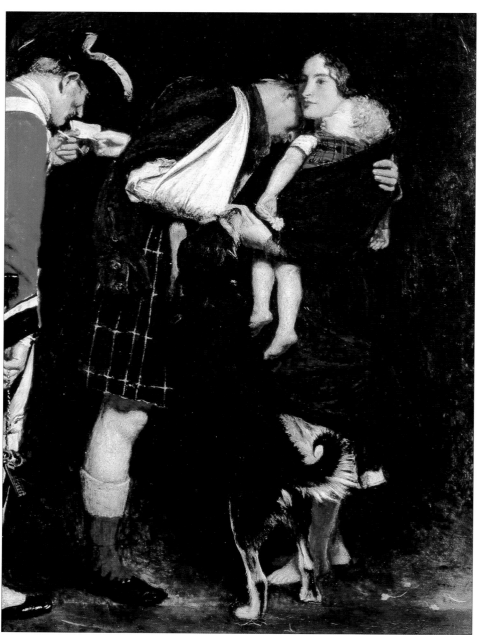

TARTAN IN PORTRAITS

The vogue for tartan portraits reached a peak in the 18th and early 19th centuries. Some were commissioned as statements of national or political identity, although in many cases patrons and artists were simply seduced by the glamour of the costume. This was particularly true of the Neoclassical painters who flourished in the 18th century. They were interested in recapturing the spirit and grandeur of the

▲ *Millais's* The Order of Release *was a trial for the artist, as the child and the dog proved restless models.*

ancient world in their pictures, and Highland dress proved eminently suitable for this. Both the kilt and the belted plaid bore a passing resemblance to a toga, while the sweep of tartan material over the shoulder carried echoes of classical drapery. This enabled artists to endow Highland figures with the nobility of an ancient warrior or the dignity of a classical philosopher. Pompeo Batoni's portrait of William Gordon is an example of the former, while Allan Ramsay's elegant depiction of the 22nd chief of the MacLeods typifies the latter.

ROMANTICISM

Highland subjects were equally popular with Romantic portraitists, who were attracted by the Celtic origins of the costume, its associations with a rebellious and independent people, and the tragic overtones of its history. The pictures were often composed in a very theatrical manner, with a low viewpoint to heighten the sense of drama and a spectacular background. Typical of this was Henry Raeburn's vivid portrait, *The MacNab*, which showed a stern-faced old man kitted out in the guise of a young warrior and posing on a bleak mountain-top, while storm-clouds gathered in the distance. Evidently, portraits of this kind were designed to create a strong, emotional impact. In part, this was due to the fact that they were normally sent to London to be exhibited at the Royal Academy – a factor that the artist would have taken into account when designing his composition.

SENTIMENTAL SCENES

The taste for extravagant Highland portraits began to wane after 1822, surfeited perhaps by the pageantry of George IV's visit. Tartan featured increasingly in other types of painting, however, notably in the narrative and sentimental scenes so beloved by the Victorians. The most celebrated was John Millais's *The Order of Release*, which managed to combine a dog, a child and a fallen woman in a single composition. The picture shows a Highland soldier gaining his freedom, presumably after Culloden. He is greeted by his family but, overcome with emotion, fails to notice the

solemn expression of his wife. This, coupled with the trampled blooms at her feet, suggests that she has paid for his liberty with her virtue.

With typical thoroughness, Millais researched the tartans in Robert Ranald McIan's *Clans of the Scottish Highlands*, opting for the Gordon and Drummond setts. The model for the wife was Effie Ruskin, a Scot, and she approved of the theme, describing it as "quite Jacobite and after my own heart". The painting was exhibited at the Royal Academy in 1853, where it met with huge acclaim. One newspaper reported that the artist had attracted "a larger crowd of admirers in his little corner...than all the Academicians put together," and eventually the organizers had to station a policeman beside the painting to chivvy the spectators along.

Jacobite themes proved a popular subject for many Victorian painters. John Pettie, for example, earned considerable praise for *Disbanded*, which showed a Jacobite soldier heading home, with a sack full of Hanoverian loot slung over his shoulder. There was

also a market for more contemporary illustrations of the Highland way of life. These touched on some very thorny issues, such as emigration and the clearances, though the artists rarely adopted a critical stance and most seemed content to focus on the picturesque qualities of their chosen scene.

Several painters depicted the shooting parties that were becoming commonplace in the Highlands, on land that had formerly been occupied by crofters. Typical examples include Carl Haag's *Morning in the Highlands* and Richard Ansdell's *A Shooting Party in the Highlands*. Rosa Bonheur's charming animal studies hinted at changes in the farming world. In *Changing Pastures*, she painted a boat, crammed full of sheep, being rowed across a loch. The scene appears faintly whimsical until one remembers that the sheep, like the shooting parties, had displaced many Highland families.

▼ *Rosa Bonheur's painting has poignant overtones, as the rise of sheep-farming led to many evictions.*

MASS EMIGRATION

By the middle years of Queen Victoria's reign, tartan and the ancient culture of the Highlands were firmly established as symbols of Scotland's national identity. There was a cruel irony about this, given that the Highlands themselves were in crisis. As a succession of economic disasters hit home, many Scots were forced to emigrate, turning the romantic image of Highlandism into a hollow myth.

Owing to the precarious nature of Highland agrarian economy, emigration had always been a fact of life, but the situation deteriorated considerably in the 19th century. The clearances had begun in the closing years of the previous century, as entire townships were evicted to make way for huge sheep farms. On the Sutherland estates alone, more than 7,000 people were moved out between 1807 and 1821.

▼ *Relatives on the quayside wave goodbye, as an emigrant ship is towed out of a Scottish harbour to begin its journey to Sydney.*

ECONOMIC PROBLEMS

The initial phase of the clearances had peaked by 1820, but the Highlands were soon affected by other problems. After the end of the Napoleonic wars, the region lost some of its export markets and faced stiffer competition from cheap imports. The herring industry went into a steep decline and the processing of kelp (a type of seaweed) for use in the glass and soap industries was no longer profitable. On top of this, there was an influx of demobilized and unemployed soldiers from the Highland regiments.

These economic woes placed added pressure on Highland landowners, many of whose estates were already mortgaged to the hilt. As a result, most were forced to sell up or place their lands in trust. It has been estimated that in the first half of the 19th century, more than two-thirds of Highland properties changed hands. Many of the new owners were Lowlanders or Englishmen, who had few inhibitions about taking the drastic measures that

were deemed necessary in order to restore the viability of the large estates. Sheep farming remained the most popular choice, but it was not the only option. Some areas were turned into sporting playgrounds for the rich, with facilities for hunting, shooting and fishing. In 1835, this led a correspondent from the *Inverness Courier* to comment, "Even unconquerable barrenness is now turned to good account. At the present moment, we believe, many Highland proprietors derive a greater revenue from their moors alone, for grouse shooting, than their whole rental amounted to sixty years since."

THE POTATO FAMINE

For those who had survived the worst of the economic difficulties, a new horror awaited. In 1846, the potato crops failed, destroyed by the *Phytophthora infestans* fungus, which had already caused devastation in many parts of Europe. The Hebrides and the western mainland were the worst affected areas of Scotland, but nowhere was immune to the problem. Throughout the Highlands, every community became all too familiar with the sickly stench of rotting potatoes.

The effects were catastrophic. A standard cereal crop might fail one year and recover the next, but the potato blight lingered for over a decade. This was particularly serious given that the poorest districts relied heavily on the potato for their survival.

Once the scale of the problem became apparent, efforts were made to provide famine relief. Committees were set up in Glasgow and Edinburgh to raise money for the purchase of oatmeal, and by 1847 their work was co-ordinated by the Central Board of Management for Highland Relief. In addition to supplying food, some local authorities initiated new construction

projects in order to provide work for the destitute. Money and food also came in from Scottish expatriates in Canada and the United States, as well as from charitable appeals throughout Britain. Even some of the least prosperous members of society were keen to contribute – servants at Cramond House, the inmates of the asylum at Dumfries and workers at Dalkeith Colliery all managed to donate hard-earned cash.

THE LONG-TERM SOLUTION

In spite of these efforts, it was clear that emigration offered the only genuine long-term solution to the problem, and this occurred on a massive scale. In the immediate aftermath of the famine, the islands of Barra and Jura lost a third of their population, for example, and this type of figure was by no means exceptional. Many of those who left took advantage of assisted emigration

schemes run by such organizations as the Highlands and Islands Emigration Society, or by the government's Colonial Land and Emigration Department. These were ostensibly concerned with helping the destitute to leave the country, although it became increasingly clear that they had a second agenda – namely, to provide able-bodied labour for the colonies. In their own words, they preferred to help those who were "a burden to the British community in the Mother Country" to become "a support to it when transferred to the Colonies."

Concerns about emigration were mirrored in the work of many Scottish artists, although, in true Victorian fashion, they were generally interested in the pathos rather than the politics of the situation. This was particularly evident in the paintings of Thomas Faed. He produced touching portrayals of homesick emigrants yearning for their

▲ *Thomas Faed won plaudits for his touching domestic scenes. Here he depicts a group of Scottish settlers in North America.*

native land, as well as tender scenes of families bidding farewell to their loved ones. His most famous picture in this vein was *The Last of the Clan*, which depicted an aged Highlander, too old to make the journey, watching his children sail away from Scotland forever. When the painting was exhibited at the Royal Academy, Faed added an explanatory note, which might have served equally well as an epitaph for many of the Highland clans: "When the steamer had slowly backed out...we began to feel that our once powerful clan was now represented by a feeble old man and his grand-daughter who, together with some outlying kith and kin, owned not a single blade of grass in the glen that was once all our own."

REGIMENTAL TARTANS

WHEN HIGHLAND DRESS WAS BANNED IN CIVILIAN CIRCLES, IT COULD STILL BE WORN BY THOSE WHO JOINED ONE OF THE SCOTTISH REGIMENTS WITHIN THE BRITISH ARMY. THROUGH THEIR EXPLOITS AROUND THE WORLD, THE REPUTATION OF TARTAN REACHED NEW HEIGHTS.

EARLY MILITARY TARTANS

It has been suggested that tartan owes its survival to the Scots' reputation as soldiers. For, when the Hanoverian government decided to outlaw Highland dress in 1746, it allowed certain exceptions. The most important of these concerned a number of Scottish regiments, which were given permission to retain their traditional attire.

The reasoning behind this was simple. The Jacobite rebellions had occurred at a period when the British Empire was expanding at a prodigious rate, and more troops than ever were required to protect national interests. By encouraging Highlanders to enlist,

the authorities meant to meet this need while also ensuring that some of their most troublesome subjects were removed from their homeland.

SCOTTISH MERCENARIES

The Scots had long been renowned for their military prowess, a reputation dating back to early periods of emigration, when Highlanders often hired themselves out as mercenaries. The links with France were particularly strong, and the Scots formed the core of two elite corps: *Les Gardes du Corps Ecossaises* (the Scottish Guard of Archers), who served as bodyguards to

▲ *The district tartan from Romsdal, Norway, where Scots landed in 1612.*

▼ *The Gudbrandsdalen is based on a jacket worn by a fallen Scottish soldier.*

the French king, and *Les Gens d'Armes Ecossaises* (Scottish Men-At-Arms).

Not all exploits of the Highlanders were as distinguished as this. Two modern tartans – Gudbrandsdalen and Romsdal – commemorate a military disaster from 1612. Colonel George Sinclair raised a contingent of his clansmen in Caithness, and led them into action as mercenaries in Sweden. Sinclair landed his men at Romsdal, on the coast of Norway, and took them through the narrow pass of Gudbrandsdal. Here, the clansmen were ambushed by local peasants, who hurled down rocks from the heights, bringing their campaign to a premature end. The Gudbrandsdalen tartan is said

SOLDIERS IN TARTAN

While they were stationed at Stettin (now Szczecin, in Poland), the colourful dress of Mackay's Regiment attracted the attention of an anonymous local artist, who produced a woodcut of the costumes. Although the men were described as Irish, there is little doubt that this represents the earliest image of Scottish soldiers wearing tartan. Three of the figures are shown in plaids, while the fourth is wearing

baggy breeches and matching hose. All the men have bonnets. The depictions of the plaids illustrate the different ways that the garment could be worn: one soldier wears it belted at the waist; the second has it draped around him, like a cloak or blanket; while the third wears it looped over his right shoulder.

▼ *Soldiers from Mackay's Regiment in Stettin in 1631.*

Previous pages: Eilean Donan Castle.

▲ Gustavus Adolphus of Sweden employed Scots soldiers in his lengthy wars against the Catholic powers.

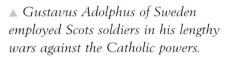

▶ A soldier of Mackay's Regiment, which was dubbed the "right hand" of Gustavus Adolphus.

to be based on a jacket worn by one of the fallen men.

Many other Scots travelled to Sweden and Germany to enlist as mercenaries in the Thirty Years' War. Thousands of Highlanders are said to have served under Gustavus Adolphus (r.1611–1632), the so-called Lion of the North, including no fewer than three field marshals, 14 generals, 41 colonels and 20 captains.

MACKAY'S REGIMENT

For the student of tartan the most significant of these may have been Donald, Chief of Mackay, who was created Lord Reay in 1628. Two years prior to this, he obtained permission from Charles I to raise a force of 3000 men to serve in Germany.

Around a third came from his own clan, while the remainder were recruited from other Highland families. This force became known as Mackay's Regiment.

The regiment fought for the Protestant cause, and their numerous feats were publicized in Robert Monro's personal chronicle of the war, published in 1637. The author heaped fulsome praise upon the soldiers' deeds, declaring, "The memory thereof shall never be forgotten, but shall live in spite of time."

THE ROYAL COMPANY OF ARCHERS

Some military bodies adopted tartan in an official capacity long before the Disarming Act of 1746 was put in place. Ironically, the earliest example relates to a

▲ The charter of the Royal Company of Archers provided for public butts to be set up for annual competitions.

Lowland force, rather than a Highland one. For in 1713, the Royal Company of Archers, the Queen's Bodyguard in Scotland, adopted a bright red sett as their new uniform. There has been speculation that tartan was chosen as a form of protest against the Act of Union, but this seems highly unlikely as contemporaneous medals suggest that most archers of the period wore tartan. More tellingly still, the royal family commissioned a portrait of the young Prince George wearing the outfit in question. This rare image of a Hanoverian dressed in tartan underlines the fact that, in the early part of the 18th century at least, the influence of Highland costume did not seem remotely threatening.

The Royal Company of Archers was not a standard regiment. Instead it was more akin to the civic militia of Holland, drawing its membership from prominent local citizens and mainly performing ceremonial duties. The Archers later changed their colours to a predominantly green sett, which can be seen in the portraits of Sir James Pringle and Dr Nathaniel Spens, commissioned in 1791 from David Martin and Henry Raeburn respectively.

THE BLACK WATCH

In 1667, Charles II authorized the 2nd Earl of Atholl to raise an independent company of Highlanders to keep a "watch upon the braes [upland areas]", to counter widespread lawlessness in the area. The company proved a considerable success as a form of police force and by the end of the century several others, generally known as the Watch, had been established. According to a contemporary observer, each was composed of "Highlanders cloathed in their ancient, proper, Caledonian Dress and armed all with Broad Swords, Targets [shields], Guns, Side-pistols and Durks, alias Daggers".

For all its merits, the Watch did nothing to prevent the Jacobite rebellion of 1715 and, indeed, some of their men took part in it. As a result, it was disbanded two years later, and replaced with garrisons of English or Lowland troops. But the usefulness of the independent companies was not forgotten, and when Major-General Wade was entrusted with the task of pacifying the Highlands, he revived the idea. In 1725, six independent companies were established. Three were placed under the command of Campbell chiefs, while the remainder were led by Lord Lovat, Colonel Grant of Ballindalloch and George Munro of Culcairn.

THE GOVERNMENT TARTAN
The Black Watch tartan became instantly recognizable as the badge of the Highland companies and, for most of the 18th century, it was commonly

▶ *Black Watch uniforms through the ages (top to bottom, left to right): officer, piper and sergeant (1739); private (1742); officer (1770); piper (1840); private and officer at the battle of Alexandria (1801); corporal, drummer and private (1845); officer in full dress (1830).*

described as "the Government tartan". It also became the basis for several other regimental tartans, which were usually distinguished from the original design by the addition of one or more coloured over-stripes. In some cases, the pattern was retained without alteration, which could have unforeseen benefits.

The "new" Sutherland tartan, for example, which was worn by the Argyll and Sutherland Highlanders, was identical to the Black Watch design. When the unprecedented demand for tartan prior to George IV's 1822 visit to Scotland caused it to be in very short supply, the Sutherland commander managed to

▶ *Military uniforms were simplified in the 19th century. Some regiments adopted shakos (caps) in place of bearskins, or trews instead of plaids.*

persuade Wilson's of Bannockburn to send them a batch of plaids that had actually been promised to a Black Watch garrison in Ireland.

REGIMENTAL STATUS

Meanwhile, the Black Watch performed its duties well and four new companies were added in 1739, bringing it up to full regiment strength. This was placed under the command of the Earl of Crawford and, following a muster at Aberfeldy in 1740, it was numbered the 43rd Regiment.

As long as they were stationed in the

BLACK WATCH TARTAN

When six new companies were formed in 1725, Wade was anxious to impose a degree of uniformity on his forces, so he gave orders for "the plaid of each Company to be as near as they can to the same Sort and Colour". The resulting pattern, dominated by blues and greens, had the subdued tones of a hunting sett. From an early stage it earned the soldiers the nickname Am Freiceadan Dubh (the Black Watch). This referred not only to the dark colouring of the tartan, but also to the fact that one of the force's principal functions was to suppress cattle theft, known as the "black trade".

Highlands, the soldiers of the new regiment acquitted themselves well. However, a lingering mistrust, both on the part of the clansmen and the government, surfaced during the 1740s, when Britain was becoming increasingly embroiled in the War of the Austrian Succession and required more troops for service in Europe. The war coincided with growing fears of another Jacobite uprising, so the authorities in London deemed it prudent to remove the Highlanders from their homeland, lest they join the cause. Accordingly, in 1743, the order was given for the Black Watch to march south.

A SHORT-LIVED MUTINY

This caused consternation among the Gaelic-speaking Highlanders, many of whom had enlisted in the firm belief that they were to be used as peacekeepers in Scotland. However, they were given assurances that the only reason for the journey was to take part in a review, staged for the benefit of the king, and that they would afterwards be allowed to return to the Highlands.

Having marched to London, the Black Watch discovered that the king was absent and their review was to be supervised by Major-General Wade. Their suspicions immediately revived amid rumours that they were about to be sent to the West Indies. By reputa-

tion, this was one of the most unwelcome postings, partly because of its ignominious association with transportation and partly because of its fever-ridden conditions. The resulting short-lived mutiny, during which many of the soldiers tried to march back to Scotland, was swiftly suppressed and three of the ringleaders were executed.

▼ *As one of the ringleaders of a mutiny of the Black Watch in 1743, Corporal Samuel Macpherson was executed in the Tower of London.*

THE HIGHLAND REGIMENTS

After the Jacobite defeat at Culloden in 1746, a series of new Highland regiments was rapidly formed. As soldiers were exempt from the ban on wearing tartan it is tempting to believe that many recruits enlisted as a means of preserving a vestige of their traditional way of life, but this may be too romantic a view. In reality, the Highland economy had already been in decline prior to the 1745 rebellion, and the ruling Hanoverians' punitive measures after the uprising simply aggravated this further. As a result, many ordinary clansmen simply faced a bleak choice between joining the army or starving.

FRASER'S HIGHLANDERS

In fact, the main incentives were directed at the nobility. For those whose lands had been forfeited after the uprising, or who feared the threat of future reprisals, the offer of raising

THE GORDON TARTAN

In 1793, William Forsythe of Huntly, acting as an agent of Wilson's of Bannockburn, wrote to the Duke of Gordon regarding the choice of regimental tartan, enclosing three separate tartan samples. These featured different versions of the Black Watch pattern, showing how it would look with one, two or three yellow over-stripes. "When the plaids are worn, the yellow stripes will be square and regular," Forsythe assured his client. "I imagine the yellow stripes will appear very lively." In the end, the Duke selected the single-stripe design for the Gordon Highlanders, while the Gordon-Cummings adopted two stripes and the Gordons of Esslemont chose the remaining option.

a regiment provided a convenient way to curry official favour. The Frasers of Lovat epitomized this approach. Simon Fraser, 11th Lord Lovat, had been a prominent Jacobite and was executed in 1747. His son had also taken part in the rebellion, but he was pardoned and, in 1757, was given permission to raise a regiment (the 78th or Fraser's Highlanders). This was a difficult task, given that the family estates had been forfeited, but the loyalty of the clan soon brought him sufficient recruits. Fraser's Highlanders served with distinction both in Canada and, as the

▲ *A soldier from the 79th Cameron Highlanders, pictured in 1853.*

71st Regiment, in the United States. Arguably their finest hour came in 1759, when they played a major part in Wolfe's victory at Quebec. At first light, they had the unenviable task of clambering up a precipitous cliff, disposing of a French battery at the summit, and then guarding the cliff path, while their comrades made their ascent. Feats such as these eventually enabled Fraser to buy back the forfeited Lovat estates.

▲ *Many Highlanders took part in the American War of Independence, which began with this confrontation at Lexington in 1775.*

LAND GRANTS IN THE NEW WORLD

Many of the newly formed Highland regiments followed a similar path and went to fight in the Americas. Between 1756 and 1763, several took part in the Seven Years' War, in which Britain competed with France for control of the New World. Prominent among these were Montgomery's Highlanders (the 77th Regiment), which was composed of volunteers from a number of the Jacobite clans, including the Camerons, the MacLeans, the Frasers and the MacDonalds.

Once peace had been concluded through the Treaty of Paris, most of the forces were disbanded. Some were brought back to Scotland, while others were given the option of receiving a grant of land in proportion to their rank and making a new home for themselves where they had been fighting. In the case of Fraser's Highlanders, more than 300 of the men decided to settle in Canada, forming a strong clan presence that remains to this day.

THE WAR OF AMERICAN INDEPENDENCE

The recruiting campaigns started all over again just a few years later, when troops were needed by the government to fight in the War of Independence (1775–81). On this occasion, the new regiments included the Fraser Highlanders (now the 71st Regiment), the Argyll Highlanders, and the Highland Light Infantry (MacLeod's Highlanders). Remarkably, the government also persuaded many of those clansmen who had already settled in America to take up arms in their cause. Most of these joined the 84th Royal Highland Emigrant Regiment, which was based in Canada. Included in their number was Allan MacDonald of Kingsburgh, the husband of Flora MacDonald. He was captured at the battle of Moore's Creek and held prisoner for over a year. Once peace had been agreed the regiment was disbanded and Allan received a grant of 700 acres of land in Nova Scotia.

REGIMENTAL TARTANS

Most of the Highland regiments adopted a tartan that was closely based on the Black Watch sett, although individual commanders had a say in the matter. In the case of the Gordon tartan, for example, the surviving correspondence has shed an interesting light on the way the system worked.

The chief exception was the 79th Cameron Highlanders (The Queen's Own Cameron Highlanders). Raised in 1793, this was one of the last regiments to be recruited through family influence. The driving force was Alan Cameron of Erracht, who had served in America with the 84th Royal Highland Emigrant Regiment and had been a prisoner-of-war for two years.

Upon Alan Cameron's return to Scotland, he obtained permission to raise a regiment, together with Ranald MacDonell of Keppoch. The two men wanted a regimental sett that combined elements from both their clan tartans, but this proved difficult, since both had red grounds, which did not suit the scarlet of the military doublet. Ultimately, the solution was found by Lady Erracht, Alan's mother, who created a pattern that merged details of the Cameron sett with those of one of the darker tartans belonging to the Clan Donald.

▲ *These sergeants from the 78th Highlanders, also known as the Ross-shire Buffs, were photographed during their service in Canada.*

THE FENCIBLE REGIMENTS

In addition to the regiments that served Britain's interests overseas, the country required a domestic military force to protect its own shores. This need was fulfilled by the various fencible regiments. The term originated as a diminutive of "defensible", referring to those men who were deemed suitable for defensive duties, and dated from the 16th century, when it was applied to part-timers fit only for militia duties. During the 18th century, and particularly in the Napoleonic era when the threat of invasion was very real, the authorities saw the advantage of using a more professional, full-time force.

For reasons of economy, the government wanted the services of the

▼ *A contemporary engraving of 1743 illustrates different types of highland uniform and dress.*

fencibles for fairly brief periods only. The earliest examples, the Argyll and the Sutherland Fencibles, were in existence for a mere four years (1759–63). The next three companies lasted just one year longer (1778–83). When Henry Dundas, as Home Secretary, decided to revive the policy at the outbreak of war in 1793, the fencible system mushroomed. Within six years more than 20 regiments had been founded, although most were disbanded by 1802.

TERMS OF CONTRACT

In theory at least, most of the Highland troops recruited for the fencible regiments were meant to serve within the nation's frontiers. More specifically, the soldiers were not to be garrisoned outside Scotland "except in the event of a landing by the enemy upon the coast of England". As with the Black Watch, however, the government wasted no time in breaking its promises when deemed expedient. Accordingly, several regiments were stationed in southern England or sent to deal with a rebellion in Ireland. A few were posted further afield. The Argylls, for example, were despatched to Gibraltar.

These contract changes caused discontent and, in the most extreme cases, outright mutiny. The worst example occurred in 1804, when attempts were being made to raise a regiment of Canadian Fencibles, that is, a regiment of Highlanders prepared to serve in Canada. Initial recruiting had gone well, apparently because the volunteers had been chosen from one of the clearance areas. It soon transpired, however, that the recruiters had overstepped the mark. As the investigating officer later reported: "The men of this corps were ordered to assemble in Glasgow, where it was discovered that the most scandalous deceptions had been practised upon them and that terms had been promised that Government would not, and could not, sanction. The persons who had deceived these poor men... obtained a great number of recruits without any, or for a very small bounty." When the truth was revealed to the recruits, there was uproar and the entire project had to be abandoned.

THE GLENGARRY FENCIBLES

By contrast, the experience of the Glengarry Fencibles was far more encouraging. This regiment was raised from a community of Catholic emigrants who had been shipwrecked off the Scottish coast, not far from Glasgow. Destitute and unable to continue their journey, their future looked bleak until a local priest, Father MacDonell, came up with a solution. He persuaded the men to enlist as

▶ *Sir John Sinclair of Ulbster, portrayed here by Henry Raeburn, designed the distinctive uniform worn by his own fencible regiment.*

soldiers, under his kinsman Alexander MacDonell, Chief of Glengarry. As the Glengarry Fencibles the troops remained in service for eight years (1794–1802), stationed on the islands of Jersey and Guernsey.

When the regiment was disbanded, along with the other fencibles, Father MacDonell petitioned for assistance in helping the men and their families emigrate to Canada. This was eventually granted and 200 acres of land in Ontario were allotted to each of the former soldiers. They named their new settlement Glengarry County and revived the Glengarry Fencibles when trouble erupted during the American War of 1812, which was fought between Britain and the USA along the Canadian border.

SIR JOHN SINCLAIR OF ULBSTER

The fencible regiments adopted a variety of costumes. The most eye-catching, perhaps, belonged to the Rothesay and Caithness Fencibles, which had been raised in 1794. Their colonel was the flamboyant Sir John Sinclair of Ulbster, who had recruited the regiment at the request of the Prime Minister, William Pitt.

Sinclair had wide-ranging interests: he was a maverick politician, an "improving" agriculturalist, the founder of the British Wool Society, and a tireless pamphleteer who produced more than 300 tracts, including several on the origins of Highland dress. This led him to design the uniform for his own regiment, along with an elaborate dress version for the officers. Sinclair was delighted with the results and commissioned a portrait from Henry Raeburn, which showed him wearing the outfit. Others were less impressed,

however, and a friend remarked: "One day he treated us with a sight of him in the Uniform of his Rothesay and Caithness Regiment, and a more curious figure I never saw. The Coat was the only part of his Dress not perfectly outlandish. Scarlet turned up with yellow, a large silk Plaid, partaking of the

Nature of a Spanish Cloak crossed before and was flung over one shoulder. Trousers of the same Silk halfway down the leg and checked Red and White Stockings. He was not quite compleat, as he had not his Scotch bonnet, which would have added a foot or so to his Stature."

REGIMENTAL WEAVERS

Prior to the battle of Culloden in 1746, most tartans were woven either at home or by independent weavers, but the coming of the Highland regiments had a profound effect on both the form and the production of tartan. As the traditional sources were no longer sufficient, specialized firms emerged, which dealt specifically with the army. The need for a standardized military uniform resulted in a consistency of design that had not materialized under the clan system, while the sheer volume of kilts and plaids required by the regiments prompted a change in production methods.

WILSON'S OF BANNOCKBURN

The most influential of the new companies was William Wilson & Sons (commonly referred to as Wilson's), based in Bannockburn, close to the city of Stirling. Wilson founded his firm in about 1770 to service the needs of the growing number of regiments, and his two sons, James and William, later expanded the business. They provided uniforms for the wars in America and for the lengthy Napoleonic campaigns. When peace was finally achieved, Wilson's successfully exploited the new market that was opening up in fashionable circles. In 1822, the year of

▲ *The Royal George, Wilson's original mill, is the distant white building in the middle of this view of Bannockburn.*

George IV's visit to Scotland, the company installed 40 new looms at their works to meet demand.

For historians, the most crucial legacy of Wilson's operations is their pattern books. Although these date from a comparatively late stage in the firm's history (1819 and 1847), they provide a unique insight into the way that the tartan industry was changing. Notes in the books make it clear that Wilson went to some trouble to acquire early, authentic designs. He employed agents to travel through the Highlands, seeking out the "true"

▼ *Wilson tartan was named after Janet Wilson, the wife of the founder.*

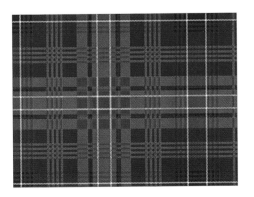

examples that handloom weavers were still producing in small quantities for their local areas. Many clan tartans that are now regarded as traditional were originally identified in this way.

Wilson's longevity also owed much to their forward-looking commercial instincts. During the 19th-century revival period, when tartans were very much in vogue, they created their own designs, advertising the "newest" or "latest" setts for individual clans. Their pattern books also contain scores of unidentified designs, which were intended as "off-the-peg" tartans for customers who wanted to wear a "traditional" family tartan.

FANCY TARTANS

Wilson's seem to have invented the notion of "fancy" tartans for purely decorative purposes. Among the designs in their pattern books are several that clearly had nothing to do with either clans or regiments. Titles such as Robin Hood, Caledonia and Wellington were chosen for their commercial appeal, and were changed or adapted as the situation demanded. Prior to 1820, for example, Wilson's marketed a tartan called Regent, which was obviously inspired by the Prince Regent (the future George IV). Once he had ascended the throne, this name no

▼ *Caledonia was one of Wilson's evocatively named "fancy" tartans.*

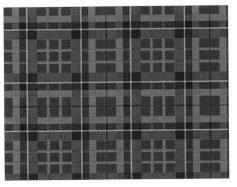

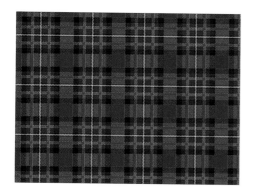

▲ *The Regent tartan was popular during the Regency period (1811–20).*

longer had a topical ring and was soon withdrawn. Despite this, the pattern itself remained in production and was eventually adopted as one of the MacLaren tartans.

Wilson's fancy tartans were often used to adorn such items as domestic furnishings or shawls. The latter were already becoming popular before the repeal of the ban on wearing tartan, largely because women were excluded from the ban. Wilson's made further attempts to capture the female market by producing tartan garments in a softer material made from the finest merino wool.

OTHER TARTAN MANUFACTURERS

Wilson's enjoyed a virtual monopoly in their field for many years. During the revival period, however, they faced competition from several other tartan manufacturers, perhaps the most notable being John Callander & Company of Stirling, who received commissions from no less a figure than George IV.

The city of Stirling itself gained a reputation as a weaving centre, and many workers joined the Incorporation of Weavers within the city, or the association of Country Weavers in the surrounding villages. For, as a commentator noted in the *Stirling Journal*: "Almost all the persons formerly engaged in the weaving of muslins...

have commenced the weaving of tartan, in consequence of its affording a better return for their labour."

ECONOMY TARTAN

Writing in the 1790s, John Lane Buchanan bemoaned the fact that, during the period of proscription, many Highlanders had lost the art of making their own tartan and had taken to buying cheap "Stirling plaids" instead. Sometimes, though, the weavers were not to blame for the quality of their goods. In army circles, it was not unusual for commanders to try to make a profit from the clothing they supplied to their regiment. For example, while the first colonel of the Black Watch, the Earl of Crawford, provided his men with two shirts and two pairs of hose each year, his successor, Lord Sempill, halved this allowance and made the plaids narrower to save on material. These penny-pinching ways may explain why English caricaturists of the period depicted Highlanders wearing ludicrously short kilts.

The most common form of economy when producing army uniforms was to use the cheapest and coarsest material available. This attitude was to

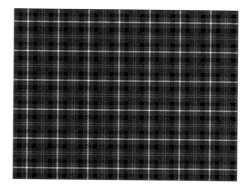

▲ *Wellington tartan honoured the achievements of the famous Duke.*

prove a long-running source of discontent that was only addressed in the 19th century through the intervention of Queen Victoria. In 1872, she noticed that the plaids of her Guard of Honour at Ballater were manufactured from a hard material and that "after a march in wind and rain the men's knees were much scratched and cut by the sharp edge of the tartan". Accordingly, she gave orders that "soft instead of hard tartan be in future supplied to Highland regiments".

▼ *A French print entitled* Female Curiosity: the revealing nature of the kilt *proved a popular comic theme.*

HIGHLAND UNIFORMS

The uniforms worn by Scottish soldiers made a significant contribution to the development of Highland dress. The standardization of setts was a new phenomenon, which exerted a great influence over clan tartans when they became fashionable during the revival period. Some elements of military attire also became popular in civilian circles, eventually becoming a routine feature of tartan outfits.

In spite of this, the English authorities made periodic attempts to change the Highland dress. From the outset, many pundits expressed doubts about its suitability for overseas campaigns. When Fraser's Highlanders embarked for North America in 1757, for example, it was suggested that the climate would prove too cold for the clansmen, and there were calls for the kilts to be replaced with something more practical. Colonel Fraser overruled these objections, much to the relief of his men. "Thanks to our generous chief," one veteran later recalled, "we were allowed to wear the garb of our fathers and, in the course of six winters,

showed the doctors that they did not understand our constitutions; for in the coldest winters, our men were more healthy than those regiments who wore breeches and warm clothing."

THE KILT REPLACES THE PLAID

For civil servants in London, the kilt was certainly preferable to the belted plaid. This was largely a matter of cost, for once it became clear that the manufacture of a kilt required far less material than the older plaid, most regiments were obliged to accept it. Surprisingly perhaps, the garment did not prove a deterrent to recruits from other countries. When describing the Seaforth Highlanders in 1802, for instance, a commentator noted, "One-fourth of the men and officers were English and Irish, and three-fourths Scotch Highlanders and, singular as it may seem, the former were as fond of the kilt and the pipes as the latter, and many of them entered completely into the spirit of the national feeling."

It often seemed that the only exceptions to this rule were some of the

THE CHILDERS TARTAN
Pressure was put on the Highland regiments to accept a single, universal tartan. This reached a peak in the 1880s, when Hugh Childers, Secretary of State for War, commissioned a sett that he hoped would fulfil this function. Inevitably, this design (the Childers tartan) was strongly resisted, although it was eventually adopted by one of the Gurkha battalions. It was only in the 20th century that most elements of Highland dress were removed from the battlefield uniform and reserved for use on ceremonial occasions.

officers. Many of them preferred to wear trews, since they were more comfortable for riding, and used the kilt only on ceremonial occasions.

▼ *The 72nd Regiment was ordered to discard Highland dress in 1809, but was directed to resume it again in 1823.*

ACCESSORIES

The sporran evolved from a rather mundane civilian accessory. In essence, it was nothing more than a leather pouch, as can be seen in Waitt's portrait of Lord Duffus. In the hands of the military outfitters, however, this simple accessory was transformed into a flamboyant adornment that has since become an essential element of Highland dress. In some cases, sporrans were decorated with embroidered tassels or richly engraved clasps; at other times, they were decked out with tufts of badger fur. In certain parts of the world they were made of more exotic materials, locally sourced. In Canada, for example, the Frasers used raccoon skins to make their sporrans.

Headgear, too, changed dramatically. The old-fashioned flat bonnet was lined with a diced band of various colours. This design is thought to have been inspired by two coloured ribbons threaded in and out of slits in the cap, in order to make it fit more tightly on the head. In a very different vein, some Highland regiments began to wear much larger feather bonnets, similar to bearskins, and these were often adorned with a "heckle" (a plume) on the side. In most cases the heckle was white, but the Black Watch were entitled to wear a red heckle as one of their battle honours.

THE *CLOATHING BOOK*

Other details of military dress were set down in the *Cloathing Book*, which was first produced in 1742. This manual defined the minutiae of each uniform, right down to the spacing between the buttons, the style of the buttonholes, and the shape of pockets and cuffs.

The only omissions from the book were descriptions of the uniforms of officers. The main distinctions between their dress and that of the lower ranks were that their coats were scarlet, rather than red; they displayed decorative knots or aiguillettes on their shoulders; and they still wore a symbolic piece of armour in the form of a small, crescent-shaped gorget.

CEREMONIAL DRESS

As the threat of Highland rebellions receded, the bureaucrats in London lost interest in retaining the individualism of Highland dress. Instead, there were increasing attempts to bring the Scots into line with other regiments. Most criticism focused on the kilt, which was repeatedly described as too impractical a garment for use in some parts of the empire. In 1809, this resulted in seven regiments abandoning their kilts for trews or trousers, although the arguments still rumbled on.

▼ *The Kilmarnock bonnet was worn by soldiers serving with the Royal Scots between 1903 and 1939.*

▼ *This suit, in Ross tartan, is finished off by a sporran that was made from a complete animal pelt.*

▼ *Initially, sporrans were simple money-pouches, but military versions became increasingly large and ornate.*

▼ *The feather bonnet that was worn by the officers of 92nd Gordon Highlanders, around 1865.*

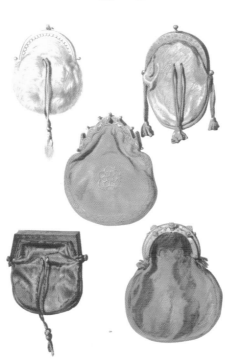

MILITARY PIPES

Nothing has been guaranteed to raise troops' spirits more effectively than the sound of bagpipes, and, in a way, this tradition can be traced back to the ancient Celts, whose warriors marched into battle accompanied by musicians carrying huge, animal-headed war horns. These would have emitted an ear-splitting noise when blown and the Celts probably hoped that the blaring din, which appeared to come from the mouths of monstrous creatures, would terrify their enemies.

THE FIRST BAGPIPES

Instruments similar to bagpipes were known in the ancient world, but it is unclear how they first developed in the Highlands. Some people believe that they evolved from the Roman *tibia* (mouth-blown double pipes), while others suggest that the Celts brought

▼ *The pipes were thought to date from Roman times, and are shown in this 15th-century miniature of Caesar crossing the Rubicon.*

them from their original homeland in the east. Either way, the pipes do not appear to have been combined with a bag until the Middle Ages, in an instrument known as a chorus.

There are early records of pipers at court, but the links with war do not seem to have occurred until the late medieval period. One of the earliest references relates to James IV's defeat at Flodden in 1513 where, according to tradition, the town piper of Jedburgh played his pipes on the battlefield. In spite of the carnage, he survived the conflict and handed the instrument down to his son; it was still in the family's possession in the late 18th century.

By the 17th century, references to bagpipes were more common. In 1645, for example, a piper tried to rally the Marquis of Montrose's royalist troops at the battle of Philiphaugh after they had been taken by surprise. Standing by the edge of a stream, the musician played until he was silenced by an enemy bullet. The spot has since become known as the Piper's Pool.

▲ *The Highland piper in this engraving by George Bickham plays an instrument with only two drones, while modern pipes have three.*

THE PIPER'S ROLE

The piper's role within the army was largely unofficial in the early days. The military authorities in the south regarded the drums, the fife (a high-pitched flute) and the bugle as instruments of war, but were slow to acknowledge the value of the bagpipes. The piper in one of the units of Mackay's Highlanders even had to hide his instrument on inspection days, while in many of the early regiments the piper was listed as a drummer on official records.

The first piper to gain proper recognition appears to have been Alexander Wallace, who became pipe-major of Dumbarton's Regiment in 1679. The standing of this rank has fluctuated over the years. Wallace himself was an officer, but in later years a pipe-major

was the equivalent of a sergeant (as indeed was a drum-major).

All regiments regarded their piper as an essential member of their team, building the morale of the troops on every occasion. The ruling Hanoverians came to realize this, so in the aftermath of Culloden they banned bagpipes, along with tartan. This was emphasized by the fate of James Reid, a piper in Ogilvie's Regiment, who was captured during the 1745 rebellion. At his trial, Reid pointed out that he had not wielded any arms during battle, but the judge dismissed his defence, pointing out that "a Highland regiment never marched without a piper…therefore his bagpipe, in the eye of the law, was an instrument of war". Reid was convicted and executed.

POPULAR TUNES

The music played by the regimental piper was very different from that of his civilian counterpart, who mostly played dance music. The army piper specialized in the *píobaireachd*, or pibroch, which assumed three main forms: these were stirring martial airs suitable for the

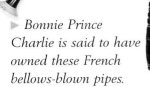

▶ *Bonnie Prince Charlie is said to have owned these French bellows-blown pipes.*

▲ *At the battle of Vimeiro in 1808, during the Peninsular War, George Clark continued to play his pipes, even though he was badly wounded.*

battlefield; marches to lift the spirits of soldiers on the move; and long, slow laments for funerals and other solemn occasions. For all of these, the piper frequently drew inspiration from historical events, so many pibrochs refer to battles. *The Desperate Battle* is thought to commemorate a clash at the North Inch of Perth in 1396, while *Black Donald's March to the Isles* relates to the battle of Inverlochy in 1431.

The greatest source of inspiration proved to be the Jacobite Rebellions, and a popular proverb of the time declared, "Twelve Highlanders and a bagpipe make a rebellion." The hopeful mood of the 1745 uprising was typified by *My King has Landed at Moidart*, a reference to Bonnie Prince Charlie's arrival in Scotland, while its sad aftermath was echoed in *Prince Charles' Lament*. Accounts of the uprising also make it clear that pipers accompanied the Young Pretender throughout much of the campaign. One source, for instance, described how "His Royal Highness made his entry into Carlisle seated on a

white charger and preceded by no less than a hundred pipers." This episode was later immortalized in the words of a popular song.

Over time, certain tunes became associated with individual clans and regiments. The Camerons, for example, liked to go into battle playing *Sons of Dogs, Come and I will give you Flesh*, while the Breadalbane Fencibles made use of *Lord Breadalbane's March*. Similarly, most units had their own tale of heroism, adding lustre to the honour of the regiment. At the siege of Badajos in 1812, for example, Piper MacLaughlan was in the forefront of an assault on the ramparts, playing a spirited rendition of *The Campbells are Coming*, when a shot tore through his bag and halted his playing. Undaunted, the piper calmly sat down on the nearest gun carriage and proceeded to repair his instrument, while the bullets fizzed around his head. Once this was done, he raised the pipes to his mouth and resumed playing.

MODERN TARTANS

WHILE RESEARCH INTO THE OLDER TARTANS CONTINUED IN THE 20TH CENTURY, THERE WAS ALSO AN UPSURGE OF INTEREST IN NEWER DESIGNS. EXPATRIATE SCOTS AND OFFICIAL BODIES RUSHED TO ADOPT THEIR OWN TARTANS, USING THEM TO STRENGTHEN TIES WITHIN THE GLOBAL SCOTTISH COMMUNITY.

THE KILT SOCIETY AND LORD LYON

By the start of the 20th century, the future of tartan was assured. Its history and traditions had been exhaustively researched and moves were afoot to formalize its role within society.

PRINCIPAL TARTANS

On the research side, the dubious impact of the *Vestiarium Scoticum* had been superseded by a swathe of less romantic, but ultimately more reliable

Previous pages: The Grampian mountain range

▼ *Queen Victoria commissioned a series of portraits of her staff, dressed in Highland attire. Kenneth MacLeay's pictures, are perhaps the most lavish of all tartan illustrations. A surviving photograph of one of the models – Willie Duff – suggests that MacLeay romanticized his material considerably.*

publications on the subject of tartan. These included the *Authenticated Tartans of the Clans and Families of Scotland* by William and Andrew Smith, published in 1850, and the monumental, two-volume *Tartans of the Clans and Septs of Scotland* by W. and A.K. Johnston, first published in 1891. The latter featured more than 200 setts, many of which had never been illustrated before.

D.W. Stewart's *Old and Rare Scottish Tartans* appeared in 1893. It was far less comprehensive than the Johnston book, but has become a collector's item itself on account of its unique format. Instead of traditional illustrations it contained 45 miniature samples of actual woven-silk tartan. In complete contrast, Frank Adam's *Clans, Septs and Regiments of the Scottish Highlands,* which was first published in 1908, adopted a conventional format. It

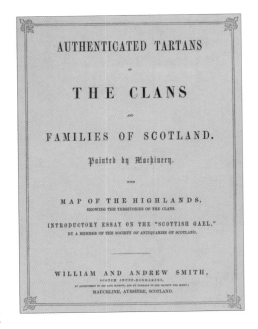

▲ *Each new publication added extra tartans. The snuffbox makers William and Andrew Smith used setts from the pattern books of Meyer and Mortimer, and Wilson's of Bannockburn.*

proved the most comprehensive source book of the period, however, and was later updated by Sir Thomas Innes of Learney, the Lord Lyon King of Arms.

THE KILT SOCIETY

While various publications recorded the principal designs in use, other bodies sought to regulate the way the tartans were worn and who was entitled to wear each pattern. The Kilt Society (Comunn an Fheilidh) was founded in Inverness around 1902 to "encourage and perpetuate the wearing of Highland dress" and to this end members promoted their ideas during Wool Market Week – one of the busiest events in the city's calendar.

THE LORD LYON

Meanwhile, a system of registration was put in place under the auspices of the Court of the Lord Lyon King of Arms, the supreme authority on all matters relating to Scottish heraldry. The Lord Lyon is a minister of the Crown and a judge and, in many ways, his court operates like a normal court of law. He has considerable jurisdiction covering all aspects of ceremonial procedure

▼ *A badge with St Andrew, his cross, and the royal arms, which is associated with a Lord Lyon of the 1700s.*

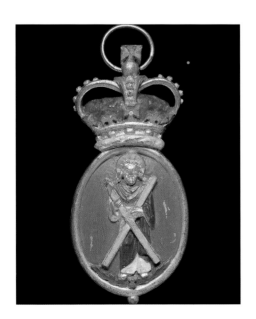

during state occasions. His post dates back to the Middle Ages: the office of Lord Lyon was mentioned in records from 1318 and played a significant role in the coronation of Robert II in 1371.

The Lord Lyon holds his post directly from the Crown, although his precise powers were not set down until a statute of 1592 granted him full authority on the question of armorial bearings, enabling him to inspect and register the arms of the nobility. At the same time, he was also given the power "to put inhibition to all the common sort of people not worthy by the law of arms to bear any signs armorial".

The actual title of Lord Lyon King of Arms dates from 1662, and stems from the device of the lion that appears on the national coat of arms. Lord Lyon's post gained added powers in a statute of 1672, but these were short-lived, for in the wake of the Act of Union of 1707 the office went into a decline, becoming little more than a sinecure. The situation was eventually reversed following George IV's visit to Edinburgh in 1822, and the Lyon Court was reorganized by an Act of Parliament in 1867.

REGULATIONS FOR BADGES AND TARTANS

The Lord Lyon had close links with the Highland clans on account of the regulations governing crested badges, which were usually based on the arms of the chief. It was customary for the latter to give his followers a silver plate of the crest, which was traditionally worn as a bonnet badge. The badges took a number of different forms, in each case with the crest and motto displayed in a plain circlet. On the chief's badge, this would be surmounted by three tiny silver feathers. For a peer, a miniature coronet would be added. For untitled followers, the crest and motto would be depicted within a plain strap and buckle, showing that they were designated members of the clan.

▲ *The Lord Lyon precedes the Duke of Kent and Lord Provost in a procession in Edinburgh on Armistice Day 1934.*

The authority of the Lord Lyon over tartan developed as an offshoot of the regulations governing the style of badges. During the revival period, many clansmen had rushed to adopt their own tartan without establishing its pedigree. This resulted in considerable confusion and, in a few cases, different clans laid claim to the same tartan. By the time the tartans were recorded in print, it was often difficult to determine which clan had the best claim to a particular sett. Wherever possible, the Lord Lyon made a ruling on these cases and sought to avoid the problem occurring in the future by setting up a proper system of registration.

To enforce his authority, the Lord Lyon declared that only designs with the official approval of his court were in future to be known as tartans; the rest could be described only as "plaids". A list of all the registered tartans was included in Adam's *Clans, Septs and Regiments of the Scottish Highlands*.

Some of the registration duties were later passed to the Scottish Tartans Society, which was founded under the auspices of the Lord Lyon in 1963. This society also maintains its own cloth archive, which was based on the sizeable collection built up between 1930 and 1950 by two enthusiasts, James Cant and John MacGregor Hastie.

CLAN SOCIETIES

Just as tartans were being placed on a more formal footing with registration, the internal organization of the clans was being strengthened through the formation of clan associations and societies, which multiplied rapidly at the end of the 19th century. The idea was not new. The first clan societies dated back to the opening years of the 18th century, but their purpose and structure altered considerably over the years.

THE BUCHANAN SOCIETY
The first recorded club, the Buchanan Society, was founded in Glasgow in 1725. The initial stimulus appears to

have been the publication of a book, *The History of the Ancient Surname Buchanan*, but, like a number of other early associations, the society became deeply involved in charitable works. A fund was set up to assist impoverished clansmen and to pay for the education or apprenticeship of their children. The members were also anxious to celebrate their most distinguished ancestors. In 1788 they raised funds to erect an obelisk to the memory of George Buchanan (1506–82), a former Keeper of the Privy Seal, who had been the tutor of the future James VI. The society was later granted its own coat

of arms by the Lord Lyon in recognition of its achievements. It remains proud of its long tradition and still makes donations to worthy causes. Each new member is given a handbook, containing the names of every member since 1725 – some 2000 in all.

CLAN CHATTAN
The clan Chattan established its association in 1727. In this case, its primary concern was with the organization of the clan itself. Clan Chattan's unique structure – as a confederation of separate clans – led to ongoing fears about its dispersal. As a result, the leaders of the group engaged a number of lawyers "to watch and defend the interests of the clan against all who would seek the injury of any of the subscribers".

THE CLAN MACKAY SOCIETY
Following the foundation in 1759 of the Graham Charitable Society, which devoted most of its energies to the care of the needy, no further associations were formed until 1806, by which time the situation in Scotland had altered dramatically. The creation of McKay's Society (later renamed the Clan Mackay Society) was set against the looming shadow of the clearances. The first evictions had already taken place on Lord Reay's estates and there were fears about the clan's future. The aim of the Mackay Society was "to raise a fund for the mutual help of each of us in the time of afflictive dispensations".

One of the most significant aspects of the Mackay Society was the composition of its membership. In contrast with most Highland societies, which were often effectively clubs for the aristocracy or affluent professionals, the

◄ *The success of the 1888 Glasgow International Exhibition stimulated renewed interest in Highland tartans.*

▲ *A military review during George IV's stay in Edinburgh, which prompted many clans to found their own societies.*

Mackay association was dominated by tradesmen. The Preses, or chairman, was an undertaker, and his fellow directors included a grocer, a weaver, a vintner, a plasterer and a piper. In essence, they were ordinary clansmen struggling to provide the mutual protection that in former times they would have expected from their chief.

THE CLAN GREGOR SOCIETY

Formed under happier circumstances than the Mackay Society, the Clan Gregor Society was the next association to materialize, in 1822. The MacGregors had suffered greatly during the 18th century, when the whole clan was outlawed and their very name was proscribed. Once these measures had been repealed in 1775, the family were determined to recover their former prestige. Their good reputation

was largely restored at the time of George IV's visit to Edinburgh in 1822, when the MacGregors played a major role in the proceedings. Among other things, they provided the guard of honour when the Honours of Scotland, the royal regalia, were paraded from Edinburgh Castle to Holyrood Palace, and they formed part of the king's entourage during his subsequent processions through the city.

The Clan Gregor Society was founded in the euphoric aftermath of King George's visit. Ostensibly, the group's main aim was to generate and provide funds for the education of the children of needy clansmen. However, there was also a determination finally to lay to rest any vestiges of the stigma that had been associated with the MacGregor name for so long. Among the society's rules there was a significant passage stressing that "no person…who does not bear or will not resume the name of the clan…should be admissible as a candidate".

THE CLAN FRASER SOCIETY OF CANADA

A further innovation occurred in 1868, when the Clan Fraser Society of Canada was founded, long before its counterpart in Scotland. This was a reminder, if it were needed, that clanship matters were no longer exclusively a Scottish preserve. The Fraser association did not prosper at the time of its foundation, but was successfully relaunched in 1894. Invitations to its inaugural dinner were sent out as far afield as New York and Detroit and received around 300 replies.

The Clan Fraser Society of Canada was effectively the last of the early clan associations, which had developed sporadically over more than a century. The next phase was ushered in by the International Exhibition of 1888, staged in Glasgow. This influential show produced a surge of enthusiasm for Scottish traditions. As a result, almost 20 new clan societies were formed within the space of a decade.

HIGHLAND DRESS ACCESSORIES

As the identification and registration of tartans became more organized, so did other aspects of Highland dress. Members of the clan and Highland societies, who took such an interest in the minutest details of their traditional sett, found that there were a host of other items that required their attention. With the current growth in popularity of costume hire and specialist tartan shops, there is an ever-expanding list of accessories that may be worn.

CRESTS AND BADGES

The most traditional items of dress were, like tartan itself, concerned with the identification of the wearer. The clan crest, which is worn in the guise of a cap badge, enabled any observer to recognize not only the clan of the wearer but also his status within that body. In a similar vein, each clan was associated with a particular plant, a tiny sprig of which was attached to the cap behind the crest badge.

It is said that the sprig was intended to allow clansmen to identify their allies in battle, although in reality this theory hardly seems likely. Many of the plants chosen by the clans were very similar in appearance and were available for only a limited season each year, and in any event most clans used flags or banners as their rallying points in times of conflict. Nevertheless, the plant badge has given rise to an intriguing theory about one of the witches' prophecies in Shakespeare's *Macbeth* – when they assure him that he is safe until Birnam Wood comes to Dunsinane. In the play, the prophecy is fulfilled when Malcolm's troops cut down branches to use as camouflage. In fact, this could not have happened, since the battle took place in an open

▲ *The most elaborate sporrans were usually made of sealskin, with engraved decoration on the metal cantle.*

◀ *Military accessories adapted for civilian wear include the sporran, dirk, plaid brooch and belt plate.*

▼ *A silver shoulder-belt plate, worn by soldiers from the 1770s onwards. This one belonged to a Peterhead Volunteer.*

field, but it has been suggested that Malcolm's soldiers, as men of Atholl, might well have been wearing sprigs of rowan in their caps. In this sense, a "forest" of rowan could be said to have moved towards Dunsinane, giving rise to the legend.

THE SPORRAN

Among the accessories of Highland dress, the most celebrated item is the sporran. This started out as a simple leather pouch, and developed into the *sporan molach* ("hair sporran") in the 18th century. It was normally made out of goat, seal or badger skin (in Henry Raeburn's portrait of *The MacNab*, the gruesome sporran is formed out of the skin and fur of a badger's head). Fortunately, more environmentally friendly versions are now available. The metal mounting, or cantle, may be decorated with the clan crest.

In modern times the variety of sporrans has increased enormously, although they generally fall into three main categories – everyday wear (normally made out of leather and similar in many ways to the original sporran), semi-dress and dress.

▼ *The traditional black handle of this* Highland sgian dubh *includes the clan crest badge of the wearer.*

▲ *This 17th-century annular brooch from Tomintoul was used to fasten the plaid at the shoulder.*

DAGGERS AND DIRKS

The skean dhu, or *sgian dubh* ("black dagger"), is regarded as a traditional item, although it was not worn with any regularity before the 19th century. Its name probably stems from the fact that the handle was normally carved from black bog oak, although it may also refer to the implicit menace of the knife. In the past, it was usually carried as a concealed weapon and placed on show – frequently in the top of the stocking – only as a courtesy to a host. The original versions were often quite plain, but modern equivalents are frequently very showy. There may be a semi-precious stone set at the end of the hilt and the clan crest may be featured on a metal plaque.

Longer than the skean dhu, the dirk is and was always openly displayed. It became an accepted part of a military officer's uniform and can still be included in Highland wear today, but only on the most formal of occasions.

BROOCHES, KILT PINS AND OTHER FASTENINGS

If a plaid is worn, it can be attached at the shoulder with a brooch. The favourite format was the penannular brooch, which has a small gap in its hoop that is covered in interlacing and Celtic knotwork patterns. Brooches are

▲ *Queen Victoria gave this magnificent cairngorm brooch to John Brown, her controversial Highland manservant.*

now mostly worn by women, although they were originally used by men. Worn only by soldiers, shoulder-belt plates were first introduced into the British Army around 1770. They were metal badges displaying the regiment's name or number and were worn on the shoulder-belt, which was used to carry a sword, pouch or carbine.

According to tradition, the kilt pin which is fastened to the top apron of the kilt, was introduced by Queen Victoria, who ordered that her soldiers should be supplied with a fastening for their kilts after seeing a young recruit discomfited by a high wind. Kilt pins are worn decoratively, and can also be used for the display of a clan badge.

WAR SLOGANS

In addition to crests and plant badges, each clan had its own distinctive slogan or war-cry. The MacNeils, for example, adopted *Buaidh no Bas* ("Victory or death") as their battle-cry, while the MacDonells used *Dia's Naomh Aindrea* ("God and St Andrew"). Some of these slogans were registered with the Lord Lyon as part of a coat of arms.

THE DEVELOPMENT OF DISTRICT TARTANS

The decision to introduce a system of registration may have brought a sense of order to Highland dress, but it also left some people feeling excluded. Inevitably, many Scots no longer had a tartan that they could officially call their own. This was particularly true of those Lowlanders who had adopted a sett during the revival period and now regarded it as a symbol of their national identity. For Scots in this situation, district tartans offered a solution.

There is considerable evidence that the first district tartans developed at a very early stage and probably pre-dated clan tartans. It is unlikely, though, that there was any deliberate intention to create a sense of unity within a particular area. The patterns probably just reflected the personal preference of the weaver and his customers, and were to some extent governed by the locally available dyes and materials.

THE ARGYLL SETT

As clan tartans became more popular, the older district patterns fell out of use or were adapted into family setts. However, as Scottish surnames were frequently based on land, the two systems occasionally overlapped, as in the tortuous history of the Argyll tartan. This was included in Wilson's pattern book of 1819 and may be identical to

the Argyll sett mentioned in their accounts in 1798. In later 19th-century sources, however, the pattern was identified as Campbell of Cawdor. This connection was logical, given that the Duke of Argyll was the Campbell chief. During the period between 1865 and 1881, the design was used as a regimental tartan, worn by the 91st Argyllshire Highlanders. Following their amalgamation with the 93rd Sutherland Highlanders, however, the tartan returned to its original function

▲ *The rugged Grampian mountains cover much of the area of Argyll, in the western Highlands.*

as a district tartan. Once again, this was perfectly logical, since this was the area where the regiment had been raised.

IRISH DISTRICT PATTERNS

Prior to the modern period, a few district tartans had also been linked with places outside Scotland although, in each case, their precise origins are

▼ *The Argyll sett has served as both a district and a regimental tartan.*

▼ *Named after the seat of the Irish high kings, Tara dates to about 1880.*

▼ *The oldest Irish tartan, Ulster, was based on a historic garment.*

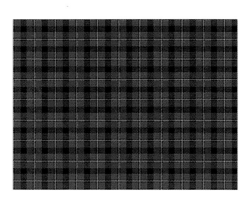

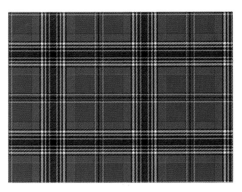

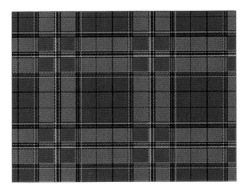

▲ *The Durham tartan was recorded in Wilson's pattern book of 1819.*

▲ *The Earl of St Andrews, initially a royal sett, is now a district tartan.*

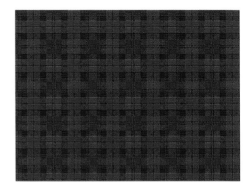

▲ *The Tyneside district tartan was originally meant for army use.*

unclear. There are, for example, three Irish district tartans that appear to be of some antiquity – Ulster, Tara and Clodagh. The Ulster pattern was based on fragments of clothing discovered in 1956 in a peaty ditch near Dungiven, in County Londonderry. Experts believe that the cloth scraps date back to the late 16th or early 17th century, and once formed part of a woollen cloak and a pair of trews. Their origins have remained a puzzle, however, since there is nothing to indicate how the clothing came to be there, or how it fits into the framework of Irish dress of the period. This has given rise to suggestions that the garments may have belonged to a Scotsman.

TRANSFERRED USAGE

The origins of the Durham tartan are equally mysterious. This design was recorded by Wilson's of Bannockburn in their pattern book of 1819. Wilson's were not averse to giving their patterns English names if they thought these might have a commercial or topical appeal, but there is no obvious reason why this should apply here. Instead, the general assumption is that the design was commissioned by a resident of the city or by someone bearing the surname. Either way, it has since been adopted as a district tartan.

This type of transferred usage was quite common. The St Andrews design, for example, was originally produced

for the Earl of St Andrews, but is now widely used by citizens of the Scottish town. Similarly, the Tyneside pattern was initially conceived as a regimental tartan, ordered by Lord Kitchener in 1914 for a new battalion, the Tyneside Scottish. The proximity of this English region to the Scottish border also made it suitable for use as a district tartan, however, and in recent years this has been its principal function.

MODERN CELTIC TARTANS

Within the British Isles, the number of new district tartans increased dramatically in the 20th century. One of the chief stimuli came from the growing ties between the various Celtic communities in western Europe. These have become increasingly determined to preserve the distinctive elements of their cultural heritage – in particular, their various tongues – while also

▼ *East Kilbride, a new town just south of Glasgow, uses this district tartan.*

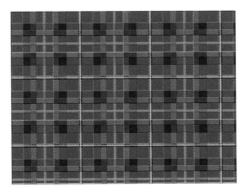

emphasizing their links with the broader Celtic community. As one of the most instantly recognizable symbols of Celtic culture, tartan was seen as the ideal means of cementing these bonds. Accordingly, setts have now been designed for Wales, Cornwall, the Isle of Man, Brittany and the Spanish region of Galicia.

The creation of the Welsh National tartan, using the colours from the Welsh flag, typified this trend. It was designed in 1967 by the Welsh Society in the hope that it would help the organization fulfil its stated aims – to be fully united with other Celtic countries, while retaining the individual character of Welsh culture, language and dress.

RECENTLY CREATED SCOTTISH DISTRICTS

In complete contrast, some Scottish authorities have decided that tartan may be an effective way of promoting a sense of community spirit in areas that have no inherited traditions. It is notable, for example, that the development corporations of the new towns of Cumbernauld and East Kilbride wasted little time in commissioning tartans for their areas, hoping that these might produce a ready-made feeling of civic pride. Queen Elizabeth was presented with a rug bearing the East Kilbride tartan when she made an official visit to the town in 1990.

LINKS WITH THE NEW WORLD

Emigrant Scots played a significant role in the history of both Canada and the United States, and political and cultural ties with both countries remain very strong. In recent years, they have been reinforced by the creation of dozens of new tartans, re-emphasizing Scotland's ancestral links with the New World.

The waves of Scottish emigration were most evident in the 18th and 19th centuries and reached a peak in the middle years of Queen Victoria's reign. Upon their arrival in the Americas, most Scots tended to settle in communities alongside their fellow

▼ *Louis Dodd's painting shows the* Columbia *fur-trading in Nootka Sound, Vancouver, in 1787.*

countrymen. They also tried to join forces with their kinsmen and help each other wherever possible. The bonds of loyalty and clanship remained in force, even though the people in question were far away from their native land.

ST ANDREW'S SOCIETIES

Co-operation between emigrant Scots in America was channelled through a number of Scottish clubs that were generally known as St Andrew's Societies, although names such as Caledonian Society or Burns' Club can also be found. The organizations were similar in structure and function to the clan societies, although they were not restricted to a single clan.

Some of these bodies have a very long history. As early as 1657, a group of expatriates founded a Scots Charitable Society in Boston, modelled on a similar organization in London. This remained an isolated case until the 18th century, when such clubs began to proliferate. The first St Andrew's Society was formed in Charleston, South Carolina, in 1729, and a member of this group is said to have created the next, the St Andrew's Society of Philadelphia, in 1749. Similar bodies were founded in New York and Savannah, Georgia, in the 1750s.

With a few notable exceptions – an earlier Scotch Club in Savannah had been closely involved in politics – the groups were charitable organizations.

Most were restricted to Scots, though not all: the Charleston Society, for example, had some English members and pledged to "assist all People in Distress, of whatsoever Nation or Profession they may be."

As their membership became more prosperous, the societies functioned as dining clubs in addition to their fundraising activities. St Andrew's Day was a major event in the social calendar before it was superseded by Independence Day. Annual dinners were attended by many prominent citizens, including the governor, the chief justice and leading councillors.

AFTER INDEPENDENCE

The War of American Independence changed the fortunes of many Scottish emigrants. In spite of the difficulties they had experienced at home, many

---

THE DEMAND FOR TARTAN

The maintenance of strong links across the Atlantic ensured a ready demand for tartan. In the 1820s a shipping firm offered to help Wilson's of Bannockburn export their goods, noting, "Tartans are much worn in America, and seen at all seasons, tho' best in the Fall; the patterns best adapted are large clan patterns…" The source of the pattern was less important. One New York retailer wrote to his supplier: "Never mind whether they are any known tartan exactly – that is not cared for here." This attitude would soon change. The International Exhibitions in Glasgow attracted over 5 million visitors in 1888 and more than 11 million in 1901, among them many Americans. The tartan warehouses' impressive exhibits prompted the creation of new clan associations and rekindled the enthusiasm of their counterparts in America.

---

remained loyal to the British crown and, as a result, settled in Canada after the war – playing a major role in the fur trade, opening up new frontiers in the west, and assisting in the creation of the Canadian Pacific Railway.

The continuing strength of Scottish ties was echoed in regimental affairs. In the late 19th century, two new Highland units were raised in Nova Scotia – the Pictou Highlanders and the Cape Breton Highlanders – and both wore tartan uniforms. Even in the 1920s and 1930s, when several numbered regiments were reorganized, some were given very Scottish names

▲ *A lavish banquet was held in New York in 1856 to celebrate the centenary of the local St Andrew's Society.*

▲ *A print from* The Canadian Pacific *shows Scottish settlers heading west on the Canadian Pacific railway in 1915.*

– among them, the Canadian Scottish, the Cameron Highlanders of Canada, and the Lanark and Renfrew Scottish. All sported either kilts or trews.

A number of new initiatives have been taken to reinforce the ties. The Fraoch Eilean Canadian Foundation is a government-sponsored body that aims to promote "schemes and undertakings...for fostering and/or preserving Canadian and Scottish history and culture, in Canada and elsewhere", while Cassoc (Clans and Scottish Societies of Canada), set up in 1975, preserves clan traditions. Links have been forged through *The Clansman*, an Ontario-based magazine for all expatriate Scots, and the early inspiration for Tartan Day came from Canada. As a result, many Scots feel a closer kinship with Canada than with any other country.

AMERICAN AND CANADIAN TARTANS

Since 1831, when James Logan listed just 55 patterns in *The Scottish Gael*, the number of new tartans has steadily increased. Around 200 setts were identified by W. and A.K. Johnston in their *Tartans of the Clans and Septs of Scotland*, published in 1906, and close to 3000 tartans had been registered by the start of the new millennium.

A major reason for this increase has been the growing internationalism of tartan, as the diaspora of the Scottish clans has led to the creation of new

▼ *Prince Edward Island tartan was designed for an important anniversary.*

▲ *Many US tartans were created for public service departments, such as the New York Police Pipe Band.*

patterns around the globe. Inevitably, a high proportion of these have come from North America, where many Scots chose to settle.

DESIGNING MODERN TARTANS
The process began in earnest in Canada in the 1950s. Initially, most of the patterns were designed to commemorate

▼ *The British Columbia tartan was designed in 1966 by Eric Ward.*

a landmark in the nation's history. The Prince Edward Island tartan, for example, marked the centenary of the Confederation Conference in 1964; the British Columbia celebrated the union with Vancouver Island in 1966; and the Canadian Centennial was one of several new tartans produced to coincide with the centenary of the Dominion of Canada in 1967. Several American tartans were introduced to mark the bicentenary of the USA in 1976.

The initial impetus behind the creation of many of these new tartans came from the scores of St Andrew's Societies that, over the years, had helped to bring together the descendants of expatriate Scots. The Illinois tartan, for instance, was commissioned by the local St Andrew's Society to mark the 150th anniversary of their foundation in 1840.

SYMBOLIC UNDERTONES
The creation of modern tartans offers considerable scope for innovation. During the revival period, clan chiefs had looked to the past for their setts, trying to restore a lost tradition. With a new tartan, however, designers can enjoy the freedom of working with a blank canvas. As a result, the patterns of many modern tartans have symbolic undertones, as weavers opt for colours

▼ *The colours of Canadian Centennial symbolize Canada's natural resources.*

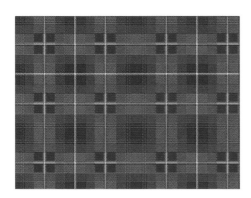

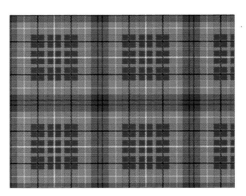

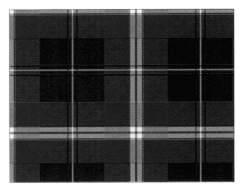

that have a particular relevance to their client. This symbolism takes many forms. Frequently, the heraldic aspect of tartan is maintained by merging the colours of flags and coats of arms. In American district tartans it is common to find the colours of the Stars and Stripes mingling with those of the St Andrew's Cross. At a local level, the US flag may be replaced by the state flag or the coat of arms of a city.

The topographical approach is almost as popular. Here, the colours represent local landmarks. Blue may stand for a river or a lake, green for a forest of pines, and yellow for a vast expanse of cornfields. In a few instances, the creators of the tartan have shown a great deal more imagination. When the District Fire Hall of the Caribou Islands in Canada was registering its design, for example, the inspiration for the colour scheme was outlined as follows: "Red for our sunsets, our lobsters and our fire trucks; white for our boats and our little white church; grey for the herring and the

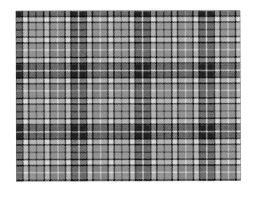

▲ *Caribou relates to an area strongly linked with Scottish emigration.*

▼ *This is one of five tartans that have been dedicated to Nova Scotia.*

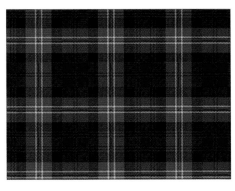

▲ *The Polaris tartan was designed for the US submarine base at Holy Loch.*

▼ *Designed for a naval base, the Edzell sett was later adopted by the US navy.*

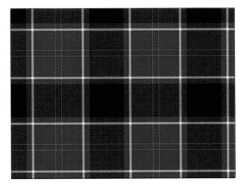

seagulls." Similarly, the community of Sydney, Nova Scotia, chose to pay tribute to its leading industries. Thus the grey lines relate to the local steel plant; the orange refers to red-hot ingots; black stands for the coal in the furnaces; off-white for the limestone used in the production process.

OFFICIAL RECOGNITION

Whatever the size of the area linked with a tartan, American organizations are usually scrupulous about obtaining official recognition of their design. Perhaps conscious of the confusion that has sometimes arisen in Scotland, they take stringent measures to avoid any duplication. When a new state tartan is created, confirmation of its validity will often be sought through the state legislature. If more than one pattern is in circulation, the matter is occasionally resolved in the courts. A few tartan

designs have been copyrighted, though this can be counterproductive, since the retailers who have been excluded from using it will often seek an alternative tartan, which, through its greater availability, will eventually become the more popular design.

REGIMENTAL AND PUBLIC SERVICE TARTANS

Not all the new American tartans relate to states, provinces or cities. A high proportion have regimental overtones. Some were created for long-established services or military academies, which have a strong sense of tradition, while others are linked with newer forces that have a specific link with Scotland. The Polaris and Edzell tartans, for example, both relate to American naval bases. The Edzell base closed some time ago, but the tartan itself has now been adopted by the US navy.

TARTANS FOR PIPE BANDS

In modern times, many public authorities, notably police and fire departments, have commissioned their own regimental tartans, with the aim of promoting a sense of brotherhood within the service. In most cases, the setts have been created for the use of the departmental pipe band. These groups often take part in public parades, such as those held on Tartan Day.

It is significant that many of the American pipe bands have Irish origins. The tartans of the New York Fireman's Pipe Band and the Metropolitan Atlanta Police were both commissioned by Emerald (Irish) Societies, rather than their Scottish equivalents.

A NEW APPROACH TO TARTAN

Traditionally, most tartans were associated with a clan, a district or a regiment. Beside these, "fancy" or trade tartans were used for decorative or commercial purposes. They gained very little coverage in the tartan surveys of the 1800s, but they had been in circulation since the previous century, when they were marketed by Wilson's of Bannockburn. In the 20th century the image and purpose of tartan were reinvented. Some of the older categories were expanded dramatically while, alongside them, entirely new concepts were introduced.

NEW THEMES

After World War II, when new patterns began to proliferate, other concepts appeared. The most common was the commemorative tartan, celebrating the anniversary of an event or body. Corporate tartans were used to promote firms or institutions, and charity tartans were used for fundraising. In addition, there was a veritable glut of other popular themes, among which were novelty tartans, sporting tartans, setts for non-military pipe bands and Highland games, and universal tartans.

There is a considerable degree of overlap between the various categories. Many trade tartans are named after places, so that they sound like district

tartans, while some designs that carry the names of corporations or institutions are actually used only by their pipe bands. To complicate matters further, some tartans go through changes of name or function. Many commemorative tartans, for example, have a fairly limited shelf-life, so once the immediate anniversary for which they were created has passed they may be reassigned as district or universal tartans. This process is typified by a tartan that was produced for the Queen's Silver Jubilee in 1977. After the festivities were over, it lost its topical appeal and was renamed Holyrood.

FAMILY TARTANS

Some of the older categories of tartan have also been modified to reflect the changing times. For instance, some tartan enthusiasts who do not belong to any clan or sept have chosen to provide a sett for themselves and their family. Most of these relate to long-established Scottish names, but a few reflect more recent patterns of immigration. They include a number of Italian names, underlining the fact that many Italians – often former prisoners-of-war – settled in Scotland after 1945.

ASIAN TARTANS

A popular Sikh design was created in 1999, partly to mark the millennium and partly to celebrate the 300th anniversary of the Khalsa order. Its colours are drawn from the Scottish and Indian flags, while the structure of the design was inspired by one of the Campbell setts, which has been worn by several Sikh regiments. The pattern can be worn not only on kilts and trews, but also on turbans.

In the same year, the Singh tartan was commissioned by Sirdar Iqbal Singh, a retired businessman and the owner of a castle in Lesmahagow. He commissioned several portraits of himself proudly wearing his new tartan from his twin daughters, Amrit and

▼ *The Holyrood tartan was named after the royal palace in Edinburgh.*

▼ *The Italian tartan was designed for the use of Italians living in Scotland.*

▼ *The Singh tartan was commissioned in 1999 by Sirdar Iqbal Singh.*

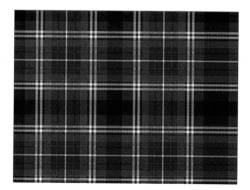

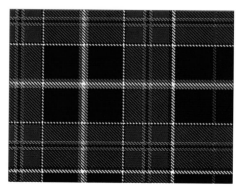

Scottish. Robin Hood was designed to cash in on the vogue for outlaws, as was Gipsy, which was reputedly inspired by James Macpherson, a Scottish free-booter who was the illegitimate son of a gipsy woman. Meg Merrilies was also named after a gipsy – a character in Sir Walter Scott's *Guy Mannering*. By the early 20th century, however, this reference had become so obscure that the pattern was listed as a conventional family sett.

In order to avoid this fate, most modern trade tartans are given much more general titles, such as Loch Ness, Niagara Falls, Harmony and Cavalier. Topical references are usually avoided, although there are some exceptions. The obvious example is the Stone of Destiny tartan, designed in 1996 after the Coronation Stone of Scone had been returned to Scotland having languished in England for 700 years.

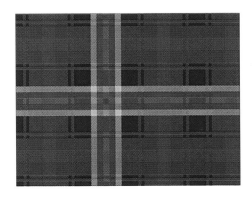

▲ *The fancy tartan Meg Merrilies was produced by Wilson's of Bannockburn.*

▼ *Despite its name, Niagara Falls is a trade rather than a district tartan.*

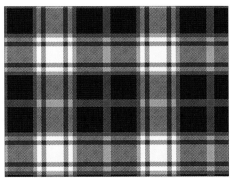

▲ *In this portrait of Sirdar Iqbal Singh by his daughters, Scottish-Asian links are wittily reinforced by the traditional weavers at the foot of the picture.*

Rabindra. Stylistically, these pictures resemble Indian miniatures, but as tartan portraits they belong to the same tradition as the canvases by Henry Raeburn and Richard Waitt.

The Singh tartan may be worn by anyone bearing the name, as well as any Asian with Scottish connections. As such, it has the same broad appeal as many of the older clan tartans. By contrast, however, a growing number of modern family tartans are highly restricted in their use. These are private tartans, designed to celebrate a specific domestic occasion, such as a golden wedding anniversary or the union of two families through marriage.

TRADE TARTANS

The function of trade tartans has changed very little since Wilson's day, although the numbers involved have multiplied rapidly. The early examples often have a very romantic flavour, even if they do not always sound very

COMMEMORATIVE AND NOVELTY TARTANS

Among the newer categories of tartan, commemorative designs are probably the most common. The desire to celebrate an anniversary or an event has become one of the prime reasons for commissioning a new tartan.

ROYAL CELEBRATIONS

Some of the oldest commemorative designs are linked to royal events, such as coronations, jubilees and weddings. They were not always officially sanctioned; sometimes, private firms produced them to help sell merchandise relating to the event. One of the Coronation tartans, for example, was made at the time of George VI's coronation in 1936. It is known only from a sample in the MacGregor Hastie Collection, and there is no evidence to suggest that it ever gained royal approval. Technically, it is probably a trade tartan, although its origins remain a mystery.

SPECIAL OCCASIONS

Whether genuine or not, the existence of designs to mark royal events encouraged other institutions to follow suit. The celebrations for the Canadian centenary and the American bicentenary both spawned a number of commemorative tartan designs, which in turn paved the way for similar moves from individual American states and Canadian provinces.

Some tartans commemorate specific events such as the Olympics or the Commonwealth Games. For example, the Clanedin tartan was commissioned in 1970 to mark the fact that the Commonwealth Games were being held in Edinburgh. Tartans have also been produced for games staged outside the British Isles, although in such cases attempts are made to give the pattern a more lasting purpose. When the Olympic Games were staged in Barcelona, the authorities introduced a Catalan tartan. After the games, the sett became a straightforward district tartan – a practical response, although some might question whether there is any demand for such a tartan in Spain.

As commemorative tartans have proliferated, the links with Scotland are sometimes rather tenuous. There is, for example, a tartan commemorating the 400th anniversary of the sinking of the Armada in 1588. Here, the main

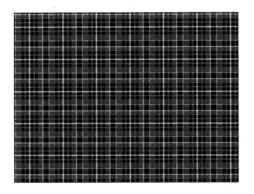

▲ *Coronation tartan appeared when George VI came to the throne in 1936.*

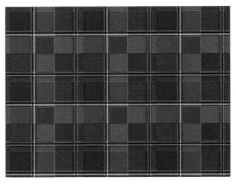

▲ *The Olympic tartan bears the games' emblem on each red block (not shown).*

▲ *Hogmanay Plaid was designed to mark the millennial New Year.*

▼ *Clanedin commemorates the 1970 Commonwealth Games in Edinburgh.*

▼ *The red stripes of the Catalan tartan represent the blood of a local martyr.*

▼ *Scotland 2000 is one of a host of new designs for the millennium.*

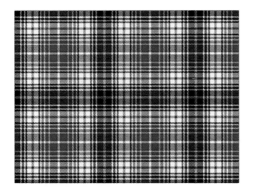

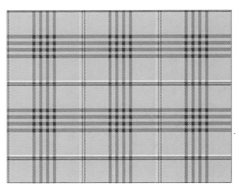

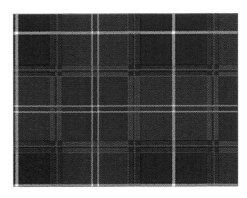

link is an old legend that some of the ships from the defeated Spanish fleet foundered in the Western Isles of Scotland, and that the shipwrecked sailors made a new home there.

On rare occasions, there is nothing more than a date to commemorate. A number of new tartans were introduced at the time of the millennium celebrations, among them the Hogmanay Plaid and Scotland 2000 setts. In cases such as these, where there is no obvious link with a district or a corporation, the design will probably either fall out of use or else become a universal tartan.

UNIVERSAL TARTANS

Tartans that can be used generally have grown in popularity largely because of their adaptability. Clothes-hire firms find them useful for customers who need to borrow Highland wear for a function, but have no particular links with Scotland. The same is true of film-makers, photographers and advertisers who want to convey a Scottish setting, while avoiding any specific clan associations. When the 1995 film *Braveheart* was being made, the producers took great pains to avoid using any recognizable clan tartans. Ironically, a Braveheart tartan already existed. It had been designed a few years earlier for a Japanese martial arts expert, who competed under this name.

The Scots have long had their own universal tartans: the Royal Stewart and Black Watch designs. However, these are appropriate only for people with UK connections and, even among Scots themselves, there are some who would prefer to avoid their royal or military overtones. A broader range of choice enables the wearer to find a design that has some relevance to their background. For example, when the boxer Mike Tyson was promoting a forthcoming bout in Scotland, he posed for the press wearing the American Bicentennial tartan.

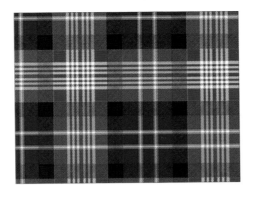

▲ *This US Bicentennial sett was renamed American (St Andrew's).*

▼ *A true novelty, the MacMedic sett was created for a first aid post.*

NOVELTY TARTANS

Many purists resent the use of tartan on occasions such as these, believing that it is undermining a key part of Scotland's heritage. Their real ire, however, is reserved for novelty tartans, which are currently on the increase. Some of these do, at least, display a laudable sense of humour. The MacMedic tartan, which is worn at the first aid post at the Stone Mountain Highland Games, adds a lighthearted touch that may well be appreciated by those who require medical help. At the games themselves, which are staged near Atlanta, the Georgia tartan is the favourite choice.

The sheer diversity of novelty tartans is extraordinary. The Balmaha tartan, for example, relates to a series of children's books about the Caledonian brown bear. It was produced for the clothing of the cuddly

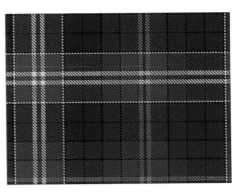

▲ *Produced for a range of teddy bears, Balmaha is based on the local scenery.*

▼ *Originally called Madonna, this sett is now known as Romantic Scotland.*

toys that accompany the books. The colours of the design represent the geography around Balmaha, which is a genuine place in the Loch Lomond region. In a very different vein, the Madonna tartan was commissioned as a tribute to the singer, who raised Scotland's tourist profile with her marriage to Guy Ritchie in Dornoch Cathedral in 2001. It has since been renamed Romantic Scotland.

Perhaps the least successful forms of innovation are those that attempt to team a tartan pattern with other motifs. The two most notable examples of this are the Olympic and the American with Eagle designs. The former has miniature versions of the Olympic emblem superimposed on each red block, while the latter features the United States heraldic emblem – a white-headed sea eagle – on every blue square of the design.

COMMERCIAL TARTANS

In recent years, the most significant development in the design and use of tartan has been the rapid growth of the corporate tartan. This is an enormously diverse field, which encompasses a wide variety of institutions, ranging from business concerns to government departments, from charitable organizations to pipe bands.

The motivation behind the development of the new corporate tartans is almost as varied as the bodies themselves, although it is fair to say that commercial instincts play a major role in their use. The new designs may be intended to promote a form of corporate branding, to create a clan-like cohesion between different departments of the same company, or to raise funds for a specific project.

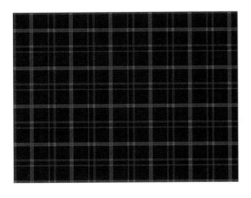

▲ *Highland Spring use two setts: one for still water, the other for sparkling.*

▼ *Irn Bru's tartan uses its packaging colours in a form of corporate branding.*

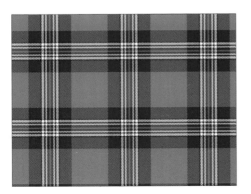

EARLY ADVERTISING

The rise of corporate tartans is a logical development from early forms of advertising. As long ago as the 18th century, images of Scotsmen in full Highland dress were already being used to market certain goods. Both in America and Britain, for example, the Scots were closely associated with tobacco and snuff. As a result, it was common to find wooden carvings of Highlanders serving as shop signs. These figures were invariably portrayed as soldiers, mainly because the kilt was chiefly a regimental garment during the proscription period, but also to avoid linking the product with any specific clan. The use of clan tartans remained a constant concern in later years, when Scots began to appear in illustrated advertisements, promoting a growing selection of goods.

BRANDING

It was always possible to keep the pattern vague, of course, but once the bandwagon of modern tartans gathered speed, it made more sense to jump on it. Accordingly, in the second half of the 20th century, many Scottish companies adopted their own tartans. For obvious reasons, the trend is most prevalent in industries that have a high Scottish profile. In international terms, the nation's most famous product is probably whisky. It comes as no surprise, therefore, to find that most, if not all, whisky manufacturers now have their own tartans. The makers of liqueurs and soft drinks have also followed suit.

As with other types of modern tartan, companies usually try to pick a design that has

▲ *Nairn's use of tartan underlines the firm's traditional values, century-long history and reputation for fine baking.*

◀ *In the 18th century, wooden images of Highland soldiers were often used to advertise snuff or tobacco.*

a special relevance to their product. Thus, in common with many district setts, the choice of colours in the design often has a symbolic association with the merchandise. In many cases, it is linked to the firm's packaging livery or its logo. For example, when the soft drinks company, Irn Bru, decided to launch their own tartan, they used the same shades of orange and blue that were already familiar to customers from the labels on their bottles.

MARKETING CAMPAIGNS

If a business does have a close connection with a particular clan, this will often be reflected in their choice of tartan. The history of Drambuie liqueur provides a case in point. According to the company literature, the recipe for this drink was handed down to the family who first produced it by Bonnie Prince Charlie. After his defeat at the battle of Culloden in 1746, the prince was sheltered on Skye by Captain John MacKinnon of Strathaird. When he escaped to France, Charles rewarded the captain for his protection by giving him the private recipe. As a result, the design of the Drambuie corporate tartan is closely modelled on the MacKinnon sett.

The pattern itself is mainly used for promotional purposes to emphasize the product's Scottish origins. This strategy is clearly aimed at overseas markets. Significantly, when Drambuie introduced its last series of "tartan" advertisements in 2001, the campaign was launched in Spain. The tartan was displayed in a humorous, modern context – the days of using images of Scotsmen in kilts have long gone. This emphasizes how, in global marketing terms, tartan is becoming increasingly detached from its links with Highland dress. The pattern alone, rather than its traditional applications, is now an instantly recognizable symbol of Scottishness worldwide.

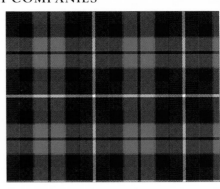

NON-SCOTTISH COMPANIES

The use of tartan is not confined to UK companies. For, just as Scottish firms have employed their tartans when marketing their goods overseas, so foreign companies operating in Scotland have commissioned their own designs, to emphasize the strength of their commitment to the host nation and its workforce. Thus, the Swiss firm Forbo Nairn adopted a tartan when it opened up two factories in Scotland. Similarly, American Express produced a corporate tartan for use in its Scottish offices.

▲ *The American Express tartan is based on the MacWilliam sett.*

THE FASHION INDUSTRY

Corporate tartans are closely associated with clothing firms. Almost all the companies that make, sell or hire Highland dress have introduced their own designs. Familiar names such as Burberry, Aquascutum, Barbour and Pringle have all registered the checks and tartans that are uniquely associated with their products.

In some instances, clothiers have used their tartans to raise money for good causes. In January 2003, for example, Pringle joined forces with Amnesty International to raise money for the human rights organization. To mark Amnesty's 40th anniversary, Pringle launched a new range of fashion garments, designed by the couturier Russell Sage and featuring the Amnesty tartan. A percentage of the proceeds was donated to the charity.

Links between tartan and fashion have existed since the Romantic era, when French couturiers in particular used tartan in their designs, but they have increased dramatically since the boom in modern tartans took hold. The most celebrated examples are perhaps found in the work of Vivienne Westwood. Her 1993/4 Anglomania range included a tartan wedding gown, and her tartan bondage suits appear to have been inspired by the uniforms of Scottish regiments. With Jimmy Choo and Pringle, she took part in the "Tartan Fair" held at Isetan, a leading Tokyo department store, in 2003.

▼ *The three Drambuie designs are based on the MacKinnon tartan.*

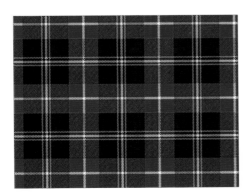

▼ *The distinctive Burberry check was introduced in 1924, as a coat lining.*

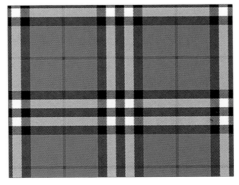

▼ *Aquascutum, founded in the 1850s, employs this familiar check.*

TARTANS OF CHARITIES AND INSTITUTIONS

The promotional value of tartan has become apparent to a broad spectrum of organizations, both in the public and the private sector, and they have helped to swell the ever-growing list of corporate tartans.

TOURISM AND HERITAGE
One of the most obvious applications for tartan is in the heritage-related industries. Several Scottish tourist boards have adopted their own designs, especially when they are launching joint projects. The United States tartan, for example, was produced by the tourist authorities in a bid to encourage more Americans to visit Scotland. The design features the colours from the flags of both nations. Similarly, the Chattahoochee tartan was commissioned by Scottish Border Enterprise in 1993 to mark the twinning of the Tweed and Chattahoochee rivers for tourism purposes. The Culture tartan was introduced in 1990, to coincide with Glasgow's status as the European City of Culture.

▼ *Gleneagles, opened in 1924, is one of Scotland's most famous hotels, renowned for its golfing facilities.*

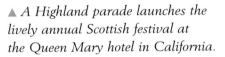

Corporate tartans have been linked with many popular tourist locations. The tartan of the National Galleries of Scotland underlines its official status by adapting the Black Watch or Government tartan, adding colours based on the architect William Playfair's original colour scheme for the gallery in Edinburgh. At the Gleneagles Hotel, the corporate tartan can be found on banners in the ballroom, as well as on a variety of merchandising. Its colours are even repeated on the hotel's distinctive fishing flies. But not

▲ *A Highland parade launches the lively annual Scottish festival at the Queen Mary hotel in California.*

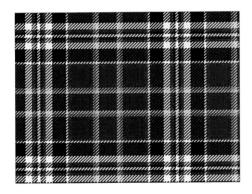

▲ *Queen Mary tartan was created for the old royal liner.*

▼ *Gleneagles tartan is one of two designs commissioned by the hotel.*

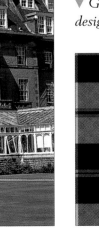

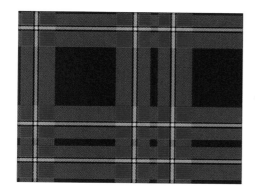

▲ *The Salvation Army tartan was commissioned by the Perth branch.*

▲ *The Diana Memorial tartan was launched in 1997 to aid her charities.*

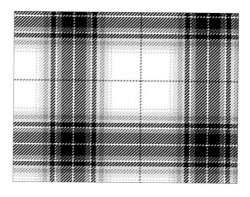

▲ *The Antarctica tartan raises funds for the British Antarctic Survey.*

all tourist attractions with tartans are in Scotland. In 1967, the liner *Queen Mary* was relocated permanently to Long Beach, California, and transformed into a tourist centre. It stages an annual Scottish festival to commemorate the land where it was built. The event is little short of a Highland games. There are sheep-herding demonstrations, whisky-tasting sessions, historical re-enactments and pipe-band competitions. The climax of the festivities is the Grand Tartan Ball, where the Queen Mary tartan may be worn.

TARTAN LIVERIES

The Historic Scotland tartan is used in a very different way. This is essentially a livery tartan, which can be worn by the custodians of various heritage properties, among them the guards in Edinburgh Castle. The notion of using tartan as a form of livery is very old, dating back to the days of the old Celtic courts, but it underwent a revival in the 19th century. When the great estates were rented out for hunting or shooting parties, staff were generally provided and some of these wore a set uniform. This could take the form of an estate check or tweed, or else the local tartan.

In the modern era, livery tartans are not confined to historical properties. They have also been used by airlines, such as Loganair and Business Air, and hotel chains such as Holiday Inn.

OFFICIAL BODIES

The popularity of corporate tartans has spread to official bodies such as local councils, churches and schools. Councils in Scottish have used new tartans as a way of forging links with councils in other countries through the twinning system. The Berwick Friendship and Elgin-Landshut tartans were both created for this purpose. Unlike most organizations, councils often choose the design of their tartans through an open competition, rather than by commissioning a professional designer.

Religious tartans are produced for a variety of bodies, ranging from specific churches, such as the Kirk in the Hills (a Michigan church modelled on Scotland's Melrose Abbey), to organizations such as the Salvation Army and the Baptist Union. The designs of these tartans often carry elaborate symbolic overtones. In the Salvation Army sett, for example, the red stripes symbolize the blood of Christ, blue represents the Heavenly Father, and yellow refers to the Holy Spirit at Pentecost.

Many universities and schools have acquired corporate tartans, although their reasons for doing so are very diverse. At Queens University in Ontario, the tartan represents the entire establishment, which was founded by Scottish Presbyterians, and its design has a precise, heraldic significance – it is based on the colours of the academic hoods of the six major

disciplines. In contrast, the Oxford University tartan was produced specifically for the use of the students' Scottish Dance Society.

In many schools, the real impetus for adopting a new tartan comes from former pupils, who sometimes produce the design themselves. In one instance, however, Newton Primary, the tartan was actually created by the children as part of a project. At Hydesville Tower, an English school with Scottish owners, the tartan has been incorporated into part of the uniform.

MONEY-RAISING ACTIVITIES

In the modern era, the creation of new tartans has often been seen as a good way of raising money for worthy causes. Usually, this is achieved by selling a range of merchandise in the relevant pattern and then donating part of the proceeds to charity. Corporate, commemorative and district tartans have all been used for this purpose, and the range of charities is virtually endless. The most celebrated example, perhaps, is the memorial tartan created in memory of Princess Diana, which continues to raise funds for her favourite charities. In stark contrast, the Antarctic tartan was produced for the benefit of the British Antarctic Survey, which sponsors scientific studies in the region, and the UK Antarctic Heritage Trust, which aims to preserve the bases of early British explorers.

SPORTING TARTANS

One of the most remarkable modern developments of tartan has been its expansion into areas that are far removed from the traditional themes of clanship or the land. Sports-related tartans have proved particularly successful, perhaps because, in some eyes, the bonding between fans is as close and passionate as any family ties.

FOOTBALL

In the UK, anyone who starts a search for "tartan" on the internet will find that more than half the sites are devoted to the Tartan Army. This term dates from the 1970s and describes the supporters of Scotland's sporting activities, although it is most associated with the national football team.

The Tartan Army sett was an immediate success in 1997, and has been in evidence at World Cup events ever since. It features on traditional items, such as scarves, but has also been used to good effect on some outlandish

▲ Part of the course at St Andrews, the home of golf, with the Royal and Ancient clubhouse in the background.

▼ A happy football fan wears a "See you Jimmy" hat and wig, with the Scottish flag painted on his face.

accessories, which were playful parodies of Highland dress. These include the "See you Jimmy" hat (a type of cap attached to a bright orange wig) and giant "bunnets" (huge bonnets or "tammies", adorned with pheasant feathers).

Predictably, many individual football teams have acquired their own tartans. The two biggest Scottish clubs – Rangers and Celtic – took this step in the late 1980s, and most of their rivals followed suit. In most cases, the design is loosely based on the team's playing colours. In keeping with the growing internationalism of tartan, there is even an overseas team with its own sett – Hammarby IF, which won the Swedish Championship in 2001.

GOLF

While football is Scotland's national game, the country is probably better known in many quarters for its association with golf. The Scots are said to have invented the game in the 14th or 15th century. It soon became immensely popular. Indeed, in 1457 James II of Scotland banned the game, because he felt it was distracting too many of his subjects from their archery practice. The first organization, founded

▲ *The tartan of The St Andrews Old Golf Course Hotel and golf resort.*

▼ *The similar Royal and Ancient sett is restricted to members of the golf club.*

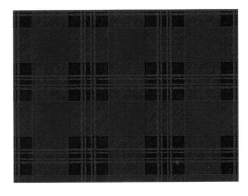

in 1735, was the Edinburgh Golfing Society (now the Royal Burgess Golfing Society of Edinburgh), but its fame was eventually eclipsed by the Society of St Andrews. Formed in 1754, this body encountered some early problems, notably when the links were sold off to a rabbit farmer in 1799. It was responsible for reducing the standard golf course from 22 to 18 holes and went on to become world famous after gaining the king's permission to change its name to the Royal and Ancient Golf Club of St Andrews in 1834. Its reputation was further enhanced in 1897, when it was recognized as the principal authority on the rules of the game.

Given Scotland's prominent role in the sport, it is hardly surprising that

THE TARTAN ARMY

Keith Lumsden, of the Scottish Tartans Society, designed the Tartan Army sett in 1997 by incorporating elements from the Royal Stewart and Black Watch designs. These were chosen because both are universal tartans, that is, tartans that can be worn by any Scot. As the sovereign's tartan, Royal Stewart can be worn by any of the Queen's subjects, while the Black Watch design was early on classified as the Government sett.

▼ *Although mainly associated with football, Tartan Army can be worn by supporters of any Scottish team.*

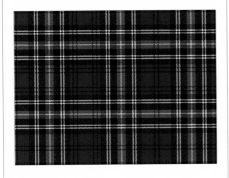

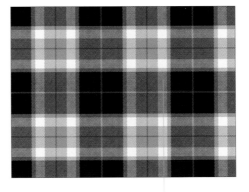

▲ *The Callaway tartan is a modern design for a golf course in California.*

there are many golf-related tartans. The emphasis is very different to football, however, since most golfing tournaments revolve around individual competitors, so the wearing of team colours is not appropriate. The commercial purpose, too, is often quite dissimilar. The Royal and Ancient tartan, for example, was introduced in 1993 as part of a fundraising project to help restore some of the club's historic buildings. The design proved such a success that it is now used on a bewildering range of accessories, from jackets and baseball caps to tee bags and visors.

Often, the tartan is linked to a specific tournament, rather than a club or a course. The Hilton Champion design, for example, was commissioned specifically for the MCI Classic – the Heritage of Golf tournament (recently renamed the WorldCom Classic – the Heritage of Golf), which has been running for more than 30 years at Hilton Head Island in South Carolina. The tournament organizers have always been keen to stress their affinity with the old country: the competition is played on a Scottish-style links, and it raises money for charitable causes through membership of the prestigious Tartan Club. The most visible connection with Scotland, however, is the prize awarded to the winner of the tournament – a tartan jacket.

Among other golfing designs, there are tartans for the Kingsbarns golf club,

which is connected to St Andrews, and the Callaway sett, which was produced for a course in Carlsbad, California. One of the most widely used patterns is the Golfers tartan, for anyone with an interest in the game.

OTHER SPORTS

There is a scattering of tartans relating to sports other than football and golf. The London Scottish Rugby Club design is self-explanatory. Bowlers is both a sporting and a commemorative tartan: it can be used by anyone involved in the sport of bowls, although it was specifically designed to celebrate the 700th anniversary of the game, which coincided with the 2004 World Bowls Championships.

Most tartans relating to athletics fall into a similar category, since they can usually be linked with a particular Olympics or Commonwealth Games.

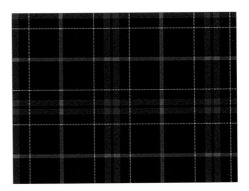

▲ *London Scottish Rugby Club tartan is for club members and employees.*

▼ *The Bowlers tartan commemorates the 700th anniversary of the sport.*

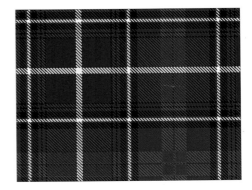

HIGHLAND GAMES

Once to be found only in Scotland, Highland games are now enjoyed in many parts of the world, and these colourful competitions have contributed to the growth of the international interest in tartan.

Numerous attempts have been made to find historical precedents for these contests. In ancient times, the Celts staged funeral games in honour of their gods. The most famous of these were held at Tailtiu (Teltown) in Ireland, where the main events appear to have been horse-racing and martial arts, although the festival also had religious overtones. In Scotland itself, Malcolm Canmore (who took the throne as Malcolm III, r.1058–93) used to summon clansmen to the Braes of Mar, where "by keen and fair" contest they could demonstrate who would make the best soldiers in his army.

The modern Highland games can be traced back to the 18th century. In 1781, the Falkland Tryst held the first Highland Society Gathering, although the main focus of the event was a piping competition rather than athletics. A more conventional programme was introduced at St Fillans in Perthshire in 1819. The idea of the Highland games really took off in the 1820s, however, following the success of George IV's state visit to Scotland.

THE BRAEMAR GATHERING

The most famous of the early games, the Braemar Gathering has its roots in the Braemar Wright's Friendly Society, formed in 1816. A decade later, this was reorganized as the Braemar Highland Society, which staged the first competitive events in 1832. They came to real prominence through the patronage of Queen Victoria. At Laggan in 1847, she had enjoyed watching the games that were arranged in honour of Prince Albert's birthday, and she paid her first visit to

◄ Tossing the caber is always the most popular of the "heavy" events at Highland games.

Braemar the following year. Before long, she was a regular visitor and became the games' chief patron, donating money for prizes and occasionally hosting the event at Balmoral Castle.

By the end of Victoria's reign, similar events were being staged in other parts of the country, and their popularity grew during the 20th century. In 2003, there were no fewer than 92 gatherings held in Scotland.

TOSSING THE CABER

The programme of activities at individual gatherings varies, although the main focus of attention is usually on the so-called "heavy" events. The most famous of these is tossing the caber. The origins of this contest are not

▼ The Illustrated London News *showed Victoria and Albert enjoying the Laggan Games in 1847.*

► *Initially, a sledgehammer or smith's hammer was probably used for throwing the hammer.*

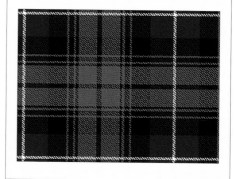

entirely clear, although most authorities believe that it was invented by foresters, who sometimes had to throw felled pieces of timber across small streams. The caber itself is a natural tree trunk and, as such, its dimensions vary. In *The Guinness Book of Records*, a maximum length of 7.6m/25ft and a weight of 127kg/280lb have been cited, but more realistic average dimensions would be 5.1–6.1m/17–20ft, at a weight of 59–68kg/130–150lb. In some places, the caber is left to soak in a loch or has molten lead poured into tiny boreholes prior to the contest, in order to keep the weight at a suitable level,

▼ *A shot putter hurls his shot at the Orange County Fair in California, one of America's many highland gatherings.*

since timber becomes lighter as it dries out. Contrary to popular belief, the contest is not decided on the length of the throw. Rather, the feat is meant to test the control of the competitor, and the winner is the man who manages to hurl the caber in the straightest line.

POPULAR EVENTS

Among the other trials of strength, the tug-of-war and the hammer-throwing competition are generally major attractions. Originally, the shot was a large stone and varied in size at different venues: at Tomintoul, for example, it weighed 5.9kg/13lb, while that used at Braemar was a massive 12.7kg/28lb. These power contests became popular because they often pitted local blacksmiths and farriers against trained soldiers. Alongside the athletic events, most gatherings also feature competitions and displays of pipe bands and Highland dancing.

WORLDWIDE GAMES

In recent years, Highland games have been staged in other parts of the world, most notably in North America and the Far East. In the USA, the trend was pioneered by North Carolina's Grandfather Mountain Games, which were founded in 1956. The initial impetus came from Donald MacDonald, who had attended the 1954 Braemar Gathering and determined to recreate its spirit in his homeland. "Armed with my Braemar souvenir programme and set of rules," he wrote, "we set about designing and staging 'an American Braemar'. I selected 19 August as the date, because it commemorated Glenfinnan and the raising of the Prince's standard, which was primarily the start of the downfall of the Highlands, and caused our people to go to North Carolina in the first place." To emphasize this connection

THE COWAL GATHERING TARTAN

Most Highland games do not have their own tartan, but in 1994 the Cowal Gathering commissioned a new tartan to mark its centenary. The gathering takes place at the end of August, and is held at Dunoon. The colour scheme of the design is dominated by blues, representing the neighbouring lochs, and greens symbolizing the mountains of Argyll.

▼ *The Cowal tartan features on merchandise ranging from kilts and scarves to ties, shawls and rugs.*

with the Jacobite rebellion even further, the prizes at the inaugural games were presented by the guest of honour, the great-great-grandson of the Scottish heroine Flora MacDonald.

In the overseas games the programme of events is often slightly different from those in Scotland. At many gatherings there is an "avenue of the clans", where visitors can learn more about their Scottish ancestors. In addition, there may be cattle shows, storytelling areas, parades of vintage cars, sheep-dog demonstrations and historical re-enactments. The most spectacular innovation of all, perhaps, is the finale at the Highlands of Durham Games in Canada, where – inspired by the traditional festivities of Up-Helly-Aa in Shetland – they burn a replica Viking longship.

SCOTTISH DANCING

In recent years dancing has provided one of the most obvious reasons for donning kilts and tartans. In competitions, demonstrations or at social events, the wearing of Highland costume has become an essential element of traditional Scottish dancing, whether it is Highland dancing or Scottish country dancing.

HIGHLAND DANCING

According to some authorities, Highland dances are ultimately derived from the ritual mime dances of the Picts. Today, these traditional dances are mainly seen only in the competitions or demonstrations at gatherings for Highland games.

There are four principal dances, each with its own colourful set of associations. The *Sean Triubhas* (Old Trews) is meant to portray a Highlander shaking off his English trousers in disgust during the period when the wearing of the kilt was outlawed. The Reel of Tulloch is said to have been created by accident

▼ In this photograph of around 1900, dancers stage a Reel of Tulloch for the benefit of the cameraman.

▲ Dancing competitions can be seen at most Highland games. These dancers are performing in Fort William.

by the villagers of Tulloch in Inverness-shire. One Sunday morning, when the weather was particularly cold, they were waiting outside the church for their minister to arrive from the next parish. He was delayed, however, and so, in order to keep warm, the congregation started to clap their hands and stamp their feet on the ground. This eventually developed into the frantic dance that is performed today.

THE HIGHLAND FLING

Probably the most famous of the Highland dances is the Highland Fling. According to one story, it was created in 1792 in honour of Jean, Duchess of Gordon, for the part she played in raising the Gordon Highlanders. More prosaically, it has also been said that the dance originated when a shepherd boy tried to mimic the graceful movements of a stag's antlers with his arms. Unusually, the Highland Fling is performed on a single spot. This is said to have occurred because Highlanders liked to show off their skill by performing the entire dance on the surface of their targe, or shield, without allowing their feet to touch the ground.

THE SWORD DANCE

Performers require equally nimble feet when attempting the Sword Dance, or *Gille Calum*. According to legend, the dance was invented by Malcolm Canmore (eventually Malcolm III),

after his victory over Macbeth at either the battle of Dunsinane in 1054 or at Lumphanan in 1057. After the conflict, Malcolm is said to have placed two swords on the ground, to form the sign of the cross, and then danced for joy in between the blades. As an extension of this apocryphal tale, clansmen were said to have repeated his feat prior to other encounters, as a form of war-dance. If they managed to complete the dance without touching the blades, this was seen as a good omen for the coming battle.

SCOTTISH COUNTRY DANCING

Also to be seen at Highland games, Scottish country dancing has developed into an independent pastime that can be enjoyed all the year round. It has strong links with folk dancing, even if the "country" tag should be used with caution. In some ways, it might be more accurately described as "contra-dancing", from the formation that is adopted in many of the numbers, where the dancers line up facing each

▲ *A vignette on the sheet music for* Danses Calédoniennes *shows children performing for Queen Victoria.*

other. It would also be wrong to assume that the current repertoire stems purely from the kind of dances that were once enjoyed by peasants. On the contrary, many elements appear to have come from courtly dances, and in the past, Scottish country dancing was enjoyed by all levels of society.

The dances themselves have an international flavour. When they were employed as mercenaries, Scottish soldiers took them to many parts of Europe, where they were modified by local influences. Indeed, one of the basic steps in many Scottish dances is the *pas de Basque*, which originated in the Pyrenees region.

TELEVISION PHENOMENON

In the UK, Scottish country dancing was popularized by a television show, *The White Heather Club*, produced by the BBC for over a decade at its Glasgow studio. The winning combination of song and dance in full tartan attire lasted for over 285 editions between 1958 and 1968, gaining impressive audience ratings and undoubtedly introducing many people to the activity. Eventually, the show's

unvarying format staled, however, and may have helped to give tartan an old-fashioned image in Britain.

A WORLDWIDE FOLLOWING

The most important contribution to Scottish dance has come from its governing body, the Royal Scottish Country Dance Society, which was founded in 1923 and has spread the gospel about Scotland's traditional dances to an international audience. Above all, this has been done through the medium of the society's summer schools, which are held at St Andrews and attract students from all over the world. The schools were organized for many years by a co-founder of the society, Jean Milligan, who was nicknamed "the First Lady of the Dance". After her death, a Strathspey (a dance with gliding steps, slower than a reel) was named after her, in honour of her inspirational achievements. The society has encouraged the foundation of many overseas branches and centres now flourish as far afield as Toronto, San Francisco, Tokyo, Sydney, Nairobi and the Hague.

▼ *With their competition numbers on their kilts, these women are performing a nimble version of the sword dance.*

DANCE SETTS

If dancers belong to a recognized clan, they will normally wear their traditional dress tartan. Many dance enthusiasts fall outside this category, however, and a number of modern tartans have been created for their benefit. For example, the Katsushika Scottish Country Dancers of Japan have registered their own tartan, as have the Scottish Dance Club at Leeds University and the dancers at the Aboyne Highland Games. In some places, new tartans have been shared by dancing and piping associations, as is the case with both the New Zealand and the South Canterbury Centre setts.

FAR EAST ENTHUSIASM

The use of tartan and the creation of new designs have increased dramatically in areas affected by past waves of Scottish emigration – notably North America and the Commonwealth countries. A more surprising development, though, has been the surging popularity of tartan and Scottish dance in the Far East, where the influence of the Highland clans was very limited.

TAIWAN AND SOUTH KOREA

This popularity can be discerned from the number of retail outlets and franchises that tartan suppliers have opened up in places such as Taiwan, Japan and South Korea. The trend began in Japan in the 1990s and has mushroomed. Previously, Scottish firms tended to market their goods in Asia under a "Best of British" umbrella, but the marketing now has a distinctly Scottish flavour, with the emphasis on Highland culture. A spokesman for Kinloch Anderson, a leading Scottish company in this field, recently commented on their expansion into Korea: "Of course, we are majoring on the heritage behind Scottish dress, but it is not a clan-affiliated push, such as you might employ in the US or the Commonwealth."

SCOTTISH DANCE IN JAPAN

The profile of Scotland's heritage has been raised by the spread of such activities as Highland

▶ *The Java St Andrews Society holds a ceilidh in the run-up to the Jakarta Highland Gathering.*

games and Scottish country dancing. The latter, in particular, has become extremely popular, leading to the creation of several overseas branches of the Royal Scottish Country Dance Society (RSCDS).

In the 1950s, two members of Japan's Folk Dance Federation – Mr Shimada and Mr Nakayama – became the first Japanese visitors to attend the summer school in St Andrews. Their lead was followed by Mr Hiroyuki Ikema, who has played a major role in popularizing Scottish country

▲ *A piper at the Jakarta Highland Gathering, where there are solo competitions for pipers and drummers.*

dancing in Japan. Educated in Tokyo and New York, Mr Ikema is a gymnast, teacher and the author of *Folk Dance in Japan*. During a visit to the USA in the late 1960s, he met Jean Milligan, a co-founder of the RSCDS, and rapidly developed a fascination for Scottish dance. After returning home to Japan he became the driving force within the Tokyo Metropolitan SCDS and ran a highly successful series of classes. The

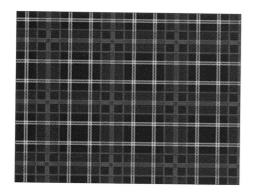

▲ *This sett was designed for a Tokyo-based country dancing team, the Katsushika Club, in 1995.*

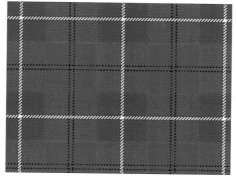

▲ *The Kansai Highland Games tartan was registered by the games' organization in 1999.*

group met several times a month and hosted an end-of-year party, which attracted over a hundred performers, with all the male dancers attired in traditional kilts.

Mr Ikema founded the official Tokyo Branch of the RSCDS in 1984, and his local group, the Katsushika Scottish Country Dance Club, was established two years later. The club's members take their dancing seriously and many attend RSCDS summer schools at St Andrews or in Canada. With so much enthusiasm, it is hardly surprising that the Katsushika Club has performed well in competition. In 1993, it won 3rd prize in the Scottish Country Dance section of the Mikasa-no-miya (Royal Family) Competition and, four years later, it gained 1st prize in the contest at the Tokyo Highland Games.

HIGHLAND GAMES

Many Far East Scottish country dancing clubs enjoy competing in locally held Highland games. At present, only two of these events have secured their own tartan – the Kansai Games in Japan and the Jakarta Highland Gathering in Indonesia – but the taste for these contests is spreading fast and there is little doubt that others will follow in the future.

Jakarta has two tartans, both of which come under the aegis of the Java St Andrews Society. The hunting sett

is used by the society itself, while the dress tartan is reserved for the dancers performing at the local Highland gathering held in September. Scottish country dancing forms a major part of the group's social activities.

THE KANSAI GAMES

As in Jakarta, the Kansai Games, which were founded in 1989 by Maud Robertson Ramsay, have separate tartans for the games and the local St Andrews Society. The games themselves feature most of the standard contests, along with homelier items such as beetle drives, egg-and-spoon races and a "wellie" toss. The organiz-

ers also try to bring over performers from Scotland. At the 2003 games, for example, the Kirkwall City Pipe Band was invited to make the 27-hour journey from the Orkneys to take part in the festivities.

KIRKIN O' THE TARTAN

An unusual aspect of some of the highland games around the world, including the Kansai Games, is the continuation of the old custom of a Kirkin o' the Tartan church service. This was a tradition originally established for the families of Scottish soldiers serving overseas, and perhaps dates as far back as the 1500s. While he was away fighting, a soldier's wife would take a sample of the family tartan to the kirk, or church, to have it blessed by the minister, and would pray for his safe return. The custom of kirking the tartan is still maintained by certain Scottish communities around the world, in particular North America, where it is seen as a way of blessing the clan or family. Ironically, it is no longer practised in Scotland itself.

▼ *The annual Jakarta Highland Gathering includes a display of massed pipes and drums.*

TARTAN'S FUTURE

If there were ever any doubts that tartan could maintain the same high levels of interest that it inspired in the past, these were dispelled during the resurgent period after the Second World War. At the Festival of Britain, which was staged in 1951, the nation shook off the despondency of the war years and celebrated in style. Tartan played a major part in these festivities.

In Scotland, the main focus of the 1951 festival was a huge Gathering of the Clans, which took place in Edinburgh over a period of four days. The events included grand balls, Highland games and pipe-band competitions but, for many people, the highlight was a spectacular parade down Princes Street, in which 1000 pipers took part.

THE EDINBURGH FESTIVAL
The taste for this kind of display had already been created by the recently established Edinburgh Festival. Its earliest events date back to 1947, but the Edinburgh Tattoo was introduced in 1950, under the auspices of Brigadier Alasdair MacLean of the Queen's Own Cameron Highlanders. The Tattoo forms the climax to the festival. It features some dramatic elements

▲ The grand finale of the military tattoo in Edinburgh in 1952 took place on the floodlit Castle Esplanade.

interspersed with folk dancing, gymnastic displays and musical interludes by military bands from around the world. The most impressive sight of all, however, is presented by the massed pipes and drums, in full Highland regalia, parading under the ramparts of the castle.

TARTAN DAY CELEBRATIONS
Spectacles similar to the Edinburgh tattoo have been seen at various Highland games, where there is usually a pipe-band competition. In recent years, however, these have been upstaged by the growing popularity of the Tartan Day celebrations. In just a few years, this event has grown into a genuine phenomenon that threatens to become the most significant date in the Scottish calendar. Like "kirking the tartan", it is a tradition that has developed outside Scotland rather than within it.

The initial impetus came from Canada. In 1987, Nova Scotia held its first Tartan Day as a tribute to the achievements of those of its citizens who had Scottish roots. The event proved a success and there were moves to extend it to other parts of the country. Then in December 1991, at the instigation of the Clans and Scottish Societies of Canada, Ontario followed

▼ With the castle as a magnificent backdrop, the tattoo is a spectacular climax to the Edinburgh Festival.

suit. Soon all the provinces had become involved, with the exception of Quebec and Newfoundland.

It did not take long for a similar momentum to build up south of the border. In March 1998, the US Senate passed a resolution confirming 6 April as National Tartan Day. The date was

NEW YORK'S TARTAN DAY PARADE

In 2002 around 7800 pipers and drummers took part in the Tunes of Glory procession down Manhattan's 6th Avenue – not far short of a world record. The chief guests of honour were Sean Connery and Scotland's First Minister, Jack McConnell. A new tartan – New York City – was specially produced for the occasion. Its colour scheme included a pale blue for the Hudson River; a deeper blue for Scotland's flag; green for the Scottish countryside; red for a local charity (Gilda's Club Worldwide); and black for the victims who lost their lives on September 11.

▲ *On Tartan Day 2002 nearly 8000 musicians took part in New York's Tunes of Glory parade on 6th Avenue.*

chosen because it marked the anniversary of the Declaration of Arbroath, which was signed on 6 April 1320. In effect, this was Scotland's declaration of independence, which Robert the Bruce and his followers sent to Pope John XXII, asserting their right to be free of the "yoke of English domination". It ended with the memorable sentiment: "For it is not for glory, riches or honour that we fight, but for freedom alone, that which no man of worth yields up, save with his life." The Arbroath document holds a particular resonance for all Americans, since their own Declaration of Independence was modelled on it. It is significant, too, that nearly half of the signatories on the American declaration had Scottish roots while, out of the 13 original United States, 9 had governors with Scottish ancestry.

Since its inception, there have been Tartan Day celebrations in Washington, New York, Boston and Chicago, and it seems certain that other cities will copy

this example. The tone of the festivities is similar to those of St Patrick's Day. In particular, the focal point of the event is usually a spectacular parade.

SCOTTISH PARLIAMENT

Tartan Day is not celebrated in the same way within Scotland, but politicians have been swift to recognize its value as a means of creating closer ties across the Atlantic. In 2003, Sir David Steel commented: "Tartan Day is hugely important... It captures the essence of the special links enjoyed by Scotland, Canada and America. I have no doubt Tartan Day...will reinforce this and help us gain a deeper mutual understanding."

In Scotland itself, the most important event of recent years has been the restoration of a Scottish parliament, after a gap of almost 300 years. This has done much to instil a renewed sense of national pride and confidence, which in turn has boosted the image of tartan. At the opening ceremony in 1999, the Queen wore a sample of a modern tartan – the Isle of Skye design. Shortly afterwards, a Scottish Parliament tartan came on the market, and this can now be purchased on a wide range of products – from braces to earrings. There could be no clearer sign that tartan is still flourishing, and will doubtless continue to do so for the foreseeable future.

▼ *The new Scottish parliament was officially opened in July 1999, in the presence of Queen Elizabeth.*

TARTAN
DIRECTORY

THE MAJOR CLANS

THIS SECTION OF THE BOOK IS A DIRECTORY OF TARTANS. THE FIRST CHAPTER CONCERNS THE MAJOR CLANS, THE SECOND DEALS WITH THE TARTANS OF THE MAIN FAMILIES AND ASSOCIATED CLANS, WHILE THE THIRD CHAPTER IS AN ECLECTIC SELECTION OF SOME OF THE TARTANS THAT HAVE APPEARED AROUND THE WORLD IN RECENT DECADES. THE DEEDS OF THE MAJOR CLANS LIGHT UP THE PAGES OF SCOTTISH HISTORY. MANY TARTANS HAVE BEEN WOVEN IN HONOUR OF THESE GREAT FAMILIES, WHO INCLUDE THE ROYAL STEWARTS, THE PROUD MACDONALD LORDS OF THE ISLES AND THE FEARLESS BRUCES.

BRUCE

The name of clan Bruce is forever associated with the exploits of the patriotic hero, Robert the Bruce, who battles with the English in the 14th century. Through Robert's daughter Marjory, the Bruces were ancestors of the Stewart dynasty.

The Bruces are descended from Robert de Bruis, a Norman knight in William the Conqueror's company who was granted lands in Yorkshire. One of his sons, also Robert de Bruis, was a companion of Prince David, who made him Lord of Annandale when he bcame king of Scotland (r.1124–53). Robert's loyalties remained with England, however, for when David invaded England in support of his niece Matilda's claim to the English throne, Robert handed his title to his son, a third Robert, and lined up with the English forces. In 1138 the Scottish were defeated, and the elder Robert de Bruis took his own son, who had fought with the Scots, prisoner.

pp128-129: Dunure Castle.
Previous pages: Sound of Islay.

▼ *The chiefly sett is the earliest of the six Bruce clan tartans; according to Lord Bruce it can be dated to 1571.*

▲ *"Good King Robert" wields a sceptre-like axe in this 19th-century engraving.*

▼ *This variant of the family sett is the Bruce Hunting tartan.*

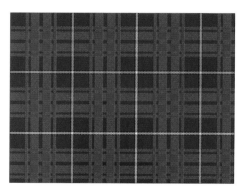

CLAIM TO THE SCOTTISH THRONE

The 2nd Lord of Annandale was freed and allowed to return to Scotland. In due course his grandson, another Robert, married Isobel, niece of William I of Scotland (r.1165–1214). Their son, yet another Robert, laid claim to the Scottish throne in 1290, but England's Edward I, who had been invited to arbitrate among rival claimants, ruled in favour of John Balliol (r.1292–96).

When Balliol entered a pact with the king of France against England, Edward invaded Scotland, defeating its army at Dunbar. Balliol abdicated, leaving the succession to the Scottish throne between the Bruces and the Comyn (Cumming) family.

In February 1306 Robert the Bruce arranged to meet his rival, John Comyn, in the church of the Minorite Friars at Dumfries; the two men quarrelled and Robert stabbed Comyn before the altar. He was excommunicated by the Pope for this act, but the throne was his.

▼ *This Bruce of Kinnaird tartan, reserved for that branch of the family, was authorized around 1950.*

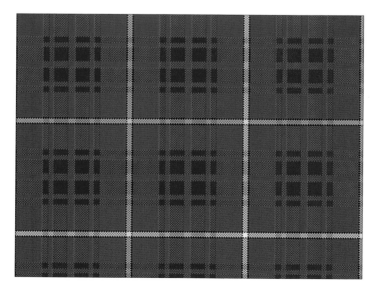

▲ *Clackmannan Tower was built in the 14th century on land granted to the family by their kinsman King David II.*

THE TRIUMPH AND LEGACY OF ROBERT THE BRUCE

In 1306 Robert the Bruce was crowned Robert I of Scotland at Scone and immediately embarked on a campaign to quell resistance in Scotland. His triumphs won him a reputation for courage and tactical skill. He overcame the Comyns and the MacDougalls, and one by one captured English strongholds in Scotland. Although he defeated a powerful English army led by Edward II at Bannockburn in 1314, his struggle to win freedom from English rule continued until 1328, when the Treaty of Edinburgh recognized an independent Scotland.

Robert the Bruce died at Cardross on 7 June 1329, aged 55, after extracting from his friend, Good Sir James Douglas, a promise to carry his embalmed heart to the Holy Land. He was buried in Dunfermline Abbey.

Robert was succeeded on the throne by his son David II (r. 1329–71), who died without offspring. The crown therefore passed to Robert Stewart, the eldest son of Robert's daughter Marjory, who ruled as Robert II from 1371 to 1390, and founded the Scottish royal house of Stewart.

Sir Edward Bruce accompanied James VI (r. 1567–1625) south when he became king of England and Ireland as James I in 1603, on the death of Elizabeth I. Sir Edward was appointed Master of the Rolls, and in 1633 his son Thomas was made Earl of Elgin.

THE BRUCES OF CLACKMANNAN

One of Robert the Bruce's cousins was ancestor to the Bruces of Clackmannan. In the 16th century, the son of a branch of this family from Airth, Stirlingshire, became a Calvinist minister. Also named Robert Bruce, he succeeded John Knox, founder of the Church of Scotland, as minister at St Giles in Edinburgh in 1572. His cousin James VI regularly listened to his sermons and appointed him to anoint his Danish bride, Anne, at her coronation in Holyrood in 1590. The cousins later had a disagreement, however, and Robert was banished to Inverness.

Robert's great-grandson, James Bruce, was an explorer, and located the source of the Blue Nile in Africa. He published his five-volume *Travels to Discover the Sources of the Nile* in 1790. The reports of his travels in Abyssinia (Ethiopia) were so astonishing that many of his contemporaries, including the poet and lexicographer Dr Johnson, dismissed them as invention.

THE ELGIN MARBLES

Another famous son of the Clackmannan Bruces was the soldier and diplomat Thomas Bruce, 7th Earl of Elgin. In the early 19th century he transported the ancient marble frieze of the Parthenon temple in Athens to London. Faced with controversy surrounding the marbles' removal from Greece, the Earl claimed he was saving them from destruction and decay. The sculptures, now known as the Elgin Marbles, were bought by the British Museum in 1816.

Thomas's son, James, the 8th Earl of Elgin, served as Governor of Jamaica, Governor-General of Canada and Viceroy of India. James's brother, Frederick William Adolphus Bruce, was a British minister to the Imperial Chinese Court in Beijing and British Representative in Washington, DC, at the end of the US Civil War.

▼ *James Bruce was an astronomer and linguist as well as a celebrated explorer.*

CAMERON

Clan Cameron has a proud military tradition. Its clansmen fought bravely for the Royalist cause during the English Civil War and the Jacobite rebellions, and founded the Cameron Highlanders regiment. The Cameron family name may suggest descent from a son of the Danish king Camchron, or derive from the Gaelic *cam-brun* ("crooked hill"). Cameron lands lie in Lochaber, in the West Highlands, and the clan is split into two branches – the Camerons of Lochiel and those of Erracht.

The first recorded chief was the warrior Donald Dhu (b.*c.*1400), who became the leader of a confederation of three tribes – the MacMartins of

▲ *The Nevis mountains dominate the Cameron lands of Lochaber.*

Letterfinlay, the MacGillonies of Strone and the MacSorlies of Glennevis – after marrying the MacMartins' chief's daughter. In about 1461 Donald was succeeded by his son Allan, who led so many raids on Mackintosh lands that he became known as Allan nan Creach ("Allan of the forays").

LOCHIEL AND ERRACHT

From 1528, when the Cameron lands were collected in the barony of Lochiel, the clan chief took the title Cameron of Lochiel. Allan's son Ewen, 13th chief, was involved in bloody and lucrative raids on Grant and Fraser lands, but after the death of his eldest son, Donald, he embarked on a pilgrimage to Rome, where he built six chapels as a mark of repentance.

Ewen was married twice, first to the daughter of Celestine of Lochalsh, then to Marjory, daughter of the Mackintosh chief Duncan. His second marriage failed to end the long-running and bitter conflict between the Camerons and

◀ *The Cameron Highlanders were said to be "fiercer than fierceness itself".*

THE CAMERONS OF ERRACHT

This branch of the family was founded by Ewen Cameron, son of Ewen, 13th chief of the Camerons. They were known as Sliochd Eoghain'ic Eoghain ("children of Ewen, son of Ewen").

Sir Allan Cameron of Erracht raised the 79th, or Cameron Highlanders, in 1793 and led them in Flanders during the French Revolutionary War. According to tradition, Sir Allan and his mother, Lady Erracht, designed the tartan now known as Cameron of Erracht, which was worn by members of the regiment and is now used by clan Cameron members as hunting dress.

When the 79th was disbanded in 1797, Cameron returned to the Highlands and raised a second regiment. Between the years 1792–95 Sir Allan was recognized by the Lord Lyon as the true Cameron chief, but following a petition from the Lochiel branch of the family the decision was overturned and Lochiel was established as the chief.

▼ *Donald, the 24th clan chief, poses for the camera in 1901.*

the Mackintoshes, but it did produce two sons – Ewen and John. This Ewen went on to found the Camerons of Erracht branch of the clan.

BLACK TAILOR OF THE AXE
Ewen was succeeded by his grandson known as Ewen Beag ("little Ewen"), the 14th chief, who fell in love with the daughter of the Lord of MacDonald. When she became pregnant Ewen was ambushed, captured and imprisoned by her vengeful father. Cameron clansmen attempted to free him but Ewen was fatally injured. His son by the Lord's daughter was nursed by a tailor's wife and grew up to be a brave soldier who, unequalled in his skill with the Lochaber axe, was nicknamed the Black Tailor of the Axe. He took control of the clan (1569–78), while the clan chief proper, Allan, was a child. Many tales were told of the Black Tailor's conflicts with, and triumphs over, the Mackintosh clan.

The 17th Cameron chief, another Ewen, was a great soldier and military strategist. He fought for the Royalist cause during the Civil War, for which he was knighted in 1682. During his chiefship, in 1665, the feud with the Mackintosh clan ended: clan leaders

▼ *The Cameron of Lochiel tartan is the personal tartan of the clan chief.*

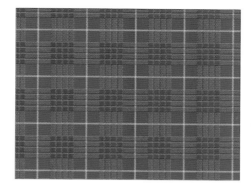

▲ *The Sobieskis'* Vestiarum Scoticum *(1842) reproduced this Cameron sett.*

drank a toast, exchanged swords and agreed that the Mackintoshes would sell certain lands to Lochiel.

The clan castle that Ewen built at Achnacarry was burned down in 1746 as part of the reprisals against the Highlanders following the battle of Culloden, which marked the crushing of the 1745 Jacobite rebellion. Achnacarry was rebuilt in the 19th century and is once more the seat of the Cameron chiefs.

GENTLE LOCHIEL
Ewen's grandson Donald, the 19th chief, dedicated himself to improving the living conditions of his clansmen and was nicknamed Gentle Lochiel. He supported Bonnie Prince Charlie in the Jacobite rebellion, taking Edinburgh with about 650 of his clansmen and

defeating an English army at the battle of Prestonpans. But after the Highlanders' defeat at Culloden, Lochiel fled to France, where he died on 28 October 1748, aged 53.

The design of the Cameron of Lochiel tartan is derived from the one worn by Gentle Lochiel in a posthumous portrait painted by George Chalmers in 1764.

Gentle Lochiel's brother, Archibald Cameron, was arrested in 1753 and taken to London. He was hanged, drawn and quartered at Tyburn, the last victim in Britain of this gruesome form of execution. The Lochiel estate was annexed by the Crown, but subject to a large fine it was returned to Donald Cameron, 22nd chief, in 1784.

MILITARY PROWESS
Donald Cameron, 23rd chief, fought with the Grenadier Guards at Waterloo in 1815. Donald Cameron, 24th chief, was Conservative MP for Invernessshire (1868–85). During the First World War, Donald Cameron, 25th chief, raised four battalions of Cameron Highlanders and led his men into battle in 1915. He was invalided home in 1916 following the battle of Loos, and was knighted in 1934.

▼ *This Cameron Hunting clan tartan was designed in the 1940s or 1950s.*

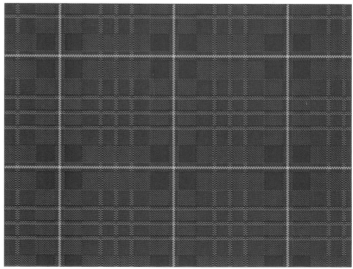

CAMPBELL

Campbell is one of the oldest names in the Highlands and for long periods the Campbells were Scotland's most powerful clan. It is famous for its military prowess and 16 British regiments have been drawn from its ranks.

Many Campbells claim descent from Diarmid O'Duine, a mythical Irish warrior-hero, whose lopsided mouth gave rise to the name Campbell, from the Gaelic *cam* ("bent") and *beul* ("mouth"). An alternative theory names de Campo Bello, a Norman knight who came with William the Conqueror's 1066 invasion of England, as the Campbell ancestor.

According to a 1368 Crown charter, the forefather of the Campbell lords of Loch Awe was Duncan MacDuibhne, who early in the 13th century married Eva O'Duibhne, heiress of Paul, Lord of Loch Awe. Duncan's warrior descendant Colin was knighted by Alexander III in 1280. He was killed in 1294 during a campaign against MacDougall, Lord of Lorne, and from this day on the clan chief was always known as MacCailean Mor ("son of Colin the Great").

▼ *This Campbell clan tartan has been approved by the Duke of Argyll.*

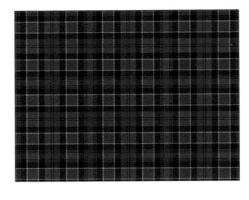

▲ *This tartan is reserved for the use of the Campbells of Breadalbane.*

Colin's eldest son, Sir Neil Campbell, fought alongside Robert the Bruce to free Scotland from English rule. His reward was the hand in marriage of the Bruce's sister, Mary, and the lands of the Earl of Atholl. His eldest son, Sir Colin, held the lands of Loch Awe and Artornish and was appointed hereditary governor of Dunoon Castle in Cowal. Another son, John, was created Earl of Atholl, but when he was killed at the battle of Halidon Hill in 1333 the title passed out of the family.

Sir Colin's grandson, Sir Duncan Campbell of Loch Awe, was appointed to the Privy Council of James I of Scotland and later, in 1445, made Lord Campbell. He married Lady Marjory

Stewart and one of their sons, Colin of Glenorchy, was the ancestor of the Campbells of Breadalbane. Sir Duncan was succeeded by his grandson, Colin, who was created Earl of Argyll in 1457, Lord Chancellor and Master of the Royal Household in 1464, and Baron of Lorne in 1470.

THE BEHEADED EARLS

In the 16th century, rivalry between the Cawdor, Breadalbane and Argyll Campbells threatened to split the clan, but Archibald, 7th Earl of Argyll, survived plots and murder attempts to restore order. His son Archibald, the 8th Earl and 1st Marquis of Argyll, led Scotland's anti-Royalist cause in the English Civil War. After the Restoration of the monarchy in 1660, Charles II ordered the beheading of Argyll for treason. His Protestant son, the 9th Earl of Argyll, fled to Holland in 1681 but returned in 1685 to gather 1500 Campbell clansmen in support of the Duke of Monmouth (Charles II's illegitimate son) in his claim to the throne. The Earl was captured at Inchinnan and beheaded in Edinburgh in 1685.

▼ *This Campbell of Argyll tartan dates at least to the early 19th century.*

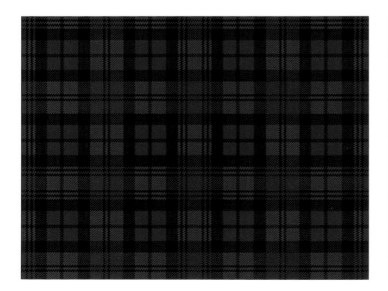

▲ *Princess Louise, Duchess of Argyll, had a tartan designed for her.*

▲ *John, Earl of Breadalbane in the early 1700s, wears the tartan as a child.*

Dowart, husband of Sir John's sister Elizabeth, left his wife stranded on a rock exposed only at low tide, in an attempt on her life. She was rescued by a passing boat and delivered to her brother. Sir John tracked Dowart down and killed him as he slept.

The family home, Cawdor (formerly Calder) Castle, was built in 1454. According to tradition, one of the Thanes of Cawdor learned in a dream that to find the right location for his fortified tower he should send out an ass laden with gold and build wherever the animal lay down to rest. The ass stopped next to a hawthorn tree and Cawdor built his castle around it. Today, an ash tree grows in the guard-room of the castle's great tower. It has been radiocarbon-dated to 1372.

BACK IN ROYAL FAVOUR

The 9th Earl's son Archibald, 10th Earl and 1st Duke of Argyll, was one of the Scottish Parliament representatives who offered the Scottish crown to William of Orange. He was created Marquis of Lorne and Kintyre and Viscount of Loch Awe and Glenila. A colonel in the Scots Horseguards, he led a regiment of Campbells, which won great honour, in battle in Flanders.

Archibald's son John, 2nd Duke of Argyll and Greenwich, was one of the commissioners who in 1706 negotiated the Union of Scotland and England. Under George I (r.1714–27) he was General and Commander-in-Chief of the King's Forces in Scotland. In the 1715 Jacobite rebellion he defeated the rebel army under the Earl of Mar at Sheriffmuir. He served as Lord High Treasurer of Scotland and was created Viscount and Earl of Isla. He also rebuilt the Campbell family seat at Inverary. When he died childless in 1743, his brother Archibald, 3rd Duke of Argyll, inherited his titles and estate.

The descendants in the Argyll line kept up the proud military traditions.

John, 4th Duke of Argyll, served in the armies of France and Holland and com-manded troops and garrisons in western Scotland, countering the 1745 Jacobite rebellion. His eldest son John, 5th Duke of Argyll, also served in the British Army and was the first president of the Highland Society of Scotland. In 1871 John, 9th Duke of Argyll, mar-ried Queen Victoria's daughter Louise.

CAMPBELLS OF CAWDOR

Sir John Campbell founded the Cawdor branch of the family by mar-rying Muriel, heiress of the 7th Thane of Cawdor, upon which he became Sir John Campbell of Calder (Cawdor). He is said to have captured Muriel as a girl while she was travelling with her nurse. Muriel's uncles, Alexander and Hugh Calder, gave chase, so Campbell overturned a large camp pot and ordered his seven sons to defend it to the death, while he escaped with his prize. Presuming the girl was under the pot, the Calders attacked Sir John's sons, and killed all of them before find-ing there was no one under the pot. Lauchlan Cattanach Maclean of

CAMPBELLS OF BREADALBANE

The Breadalbane Campbells, also known as Ma-Chailein Mhic Dhonnachaidh ("son of Colin son of Duncan"), are second only to the Argyll branch in the family hierarchy and were once one of Scotland's great land-owning families, with pos-sessions stretching from Aberfeldy in Perthshire to the coast.

In the 16th century the Breadal-bane Campbells' ancestor, Sir Colin of Glenorchy, built Kilchurn Castle on Loch Awe and Balloch Castle at the east end of Loch Tay, near Pitlochry and Aberfeldy. In the late 17th century Sir John Campbell, 11th Lord of Glenorchy, was created Earl of Breadalbane and restored his family's fortunes after difficult times. In his lifetime he was said to be "as cunning as a fox, as wise as a serpent and as slippery as an eel." Taymouth Castle, built in the 19th century on the site of Balloch Castle, is the main Breadalbane residence.

CHATTAN

Clan Chattan was a powerful confederation of smaller Highland families who from the 14th century onwards grouped together for protection. The families largely supported the Jacobite uprisings of the 18th century, but when these failed the confederation began to disintegrate.

Like other clans, the Chattan confederation probably began as a blood grouping, and many fanciful theories for its origins are based on the name. Some say that they were descended from the Catti, a tribe of Gauls who fled from Roman rule. Others claim they were tribesmen from Sutherland and the name comes from Catav, another name for that region. Yet others say they hailed from Caithness and took their name from the wild cats of that area. The most popular tradition claims descent from Gille Chattan Mor ("great servant of Cathan"), a 13th-century sheriff's officer at Ardchattan Priory; Cathan was a Celtic saint.

By the time of Malcolm II (r.1005–34), the Chattan chieftain held

▼ *Ardchattan Priory, perhaps home to the great Chattan ancestor Gille Chattan Mor, was established in 1230.*

land at Glenloy and Loch Arkaig in Lochaber, and had established his seat at Torcastle. The early chiefs are not known for certain, but records show that in 1291 Eva, daughter of the 6th clan chief Dougall Dall, married Angus, 6th Lord of Mackintosh, who through her claim became the 7th Captain of clan Chattan.

Angus fought alongside Robert the Bruce for Scottish independence, and in 1319 the new king rewarded him with lands in Badenoch taken from the Comyns (Cummings). Angus moved the clan seat from Torcastle to Rothiemurchus in Badenoch.

FAMILY FEUDS

In September 1396 Robert III decided to use judicial combat to resolve a feud between clan Chattan and the Camerons. Bloodlust drew a vast crowd to specially erected stands on the North Inch of Perth, a flat meadow by the river Tay. The king, queen and courtiers were in attendance and Prince David was chosen as umpire. When the Chattan warriors found themselves a man short Hal Gow of the Wynd, a local blacksmith, volunteered to join them. Each warrior carried a sword, a

▲ *Loch an Eilean Castle was held for some time by Mackintosh lords but passed to the Grants in 1567.*

dagger, an axe and a crossbow. Armour was forbidden, but each man held a leather shield.

At the start signal the men fired their crossbows, then hurled themselves at one another. They fought until just one Cameron warrior was left alive to face 11 Chattan men. Bloodied but still standing, he took to his heels and leaped into the Tay to escape. Victory was awarded to clan Chattan but it came at a price, as only one of their warriors, the brave Perth blacksmith, stood uninjured. This celebrated conflict was the inspiration for a scene in the final pages of Sir Walter Scott's 1828 novel *The Fair Maid of Perth*.

The Mackintosh and Chattan feud with the Cumming family was equally bloody. Early in the 15th century, Malcolm, 10th Mackintosh chief, avenged a Cumming attack on some of his men by capturing the Cumming castle in Nairn. When the Cummings counterattacked, the Mackintoshes ambushed them at Loch Moy and put them to the sword. The Cummings

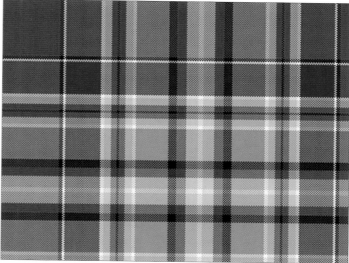

▲ *This Chattan tartan is reserved for the use of the clan chief and his family.*

▲ *This "Mackintosh tartan" was made by Wilson's of Bannockburn in 1852.*

expressed a wish to end the enmity and invited the Mackintosh men to a feast, though their plan was to slaughter their unsuspecting guests at the moment a stuffed boar's head was carried into the hall. However, a Cumming youth revealed the plan to a Mackintosh girl he was courting and she warned her kinsmen. When the boar's head arrived the Mackintoshes attacked first and slaughtered their Cumming enemies.

THE CHATTAN CONFEDERATION

The alliance of the Chattan and Mackintosh families evolved into a wider confederation that contained three main groups. The first were descendants of the Great Servant of Cathan, including MacBains, Cattanachs and MacPhersons. The second were the Mackintoshes and their dependent family branches, which included the MacThomases, the Ritchies, the Farquharsons and the Shaws. The third consisted of unrelated clans who wanted clan protection, including the MacLeans, the Davidsons, the MacAndrews, the MacIntyres, the MacQueens and the MacGillivrays.

Clan Chattan families fought in the Jacobite cause in the 1715 and 1745

rebellions. MacGillivray of Dunmaglas, a member of the third group, led an 800-strong Chattan regiment into the battle of Falkirk in 1746, in driving wind and rain. Although the Jacobite army won this confused conflict, the rebellion was eventually defeated and the importance of the Chattan confederation diminished as its member families followed their own destinies.

MACKINTOSH PRE-EMINENT

Over the centuries the Mackintosh chiefs came to be recognized as captains of clan Chattan. In 1672 the MacPherson chief briefly established

▼ *The Tay witnessed the Chattans' famous battle of North Inch in 1396.*

himself as head of the clan, but Lachlan Mackintosh, 20th chief of clan Chattan and 19th of Mackintosh, established his right to the title on appeal before the Court of Lord Lyon, the chief herald in Scotland. In 1938 the two chiefships were split when Alfred Donald Mackintosh, the 29th Chattan chief and 28th Mackintosh chief, died without any heirs. The Lyon Court ruled in 1947 that Duncan Alexander Elliot Mackintosh, head of the Mackintoshes of Daviot, should be accepted as head of clan Chattan. Malcolm Kenneth Mackintosh is the current chief of clan Chattan; he lives in Zimbabwe.

DOUGLAS

The Douglas clan from the Borders rose to become one of Scotland's most powerful families. Good Sir James Douglas was one of Robert the Bruce's trusted friends, and his Douglas descendants played a prominent role in many of the central events of Scottish history.

The name Douglas derives from the Gaelic *dubh glas* ("dark water") – perhaps a reference to a stream on one of the family estates. The first documented clan member was Sir William de Douglas, who witnessed an agreement between the Bishop of Glasgow and the monks of Kelso between 1175 and 1199. Two of his sons fought in the Scottish army that drove off the Norwegians under King Hakon at the battle of Largs in 1263. His great-grandson, William Douglas the Hardy, was governor of Berwick when it was sacked by English troops under Edward I in 1296. The English king had come north to confront the Scottish king John Balliol after he entered an alliance with the French. In a savage assault the English killed more than

▼ *Archibald, 3rd Earl of Douglas, built Threave Castle in the late 1300s.*

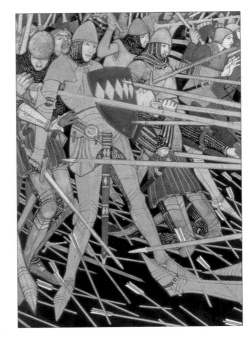

half the town's population of 12,500 but were for a long time unable to capture the castle. When promised safe escort from the town the defenders gave themselves up, but Douglas was taken prisoner. Although he was released upon accepting Edward as Scotland's overlord, Douglas later fought with the patriot William Wallace. Captured a second time, he died in the Tower of London in 1302.

▲ *The battle of Otterburn in 1388 was a proud victory for the Scots – despite the death of James, Earl of Douglas.*

GOOD SIR JAMES

Douglas's son James inherited his father's commitment to a free Scotland and fought alongside Robert the Bruce. His considerable bravery and prowess established him as the greatest of Robert the Bruce's military leaders. Nicknamed the Black Douglas because of his dark colouring, he was also celebrated in Scotland as Good Sir James.

On his deathbed Robert the Bruce made Good Sir James promise to take his heart to the Holy Land. Sir James set off with the embalmed heart in a silver casket but was killed at Tebas de Ardales in 1330. Tradition recalls that as he charged into battle for the final time he flung the casket ahead of him, shouting "Lead on, braveheart!" He was cut down, but his compatriot Borthwick carried both Sir James's body and the Bruce's heart back to Scotland. Sir James was buried in St Bride's Church, Douglas, and the heart was interred at Melrose Abbey.

▲ *The Douglas (Ancient) dress tartan is a 20th-century design.*

▲ *The Douglas (Green) was sold by Wilson's of Bannockburn c.1830.*

Good Sir James's nephew, Sir William, was made 1st Earl of Douglas in 1357 and became Earl of Mar through marriage. On his death in 1384 he was succeeded by his son James, 2nd Earl of Douglas and Mar. In August 1388 James led a raid into northern England, attacked Newcastle and took the standard of its garrison commander, Henry Percy. Percy gave chase: when he caught up with Douglas night was falling, but he still attacked, and the battle of Otterburn raged under moonlight across open country. The Scots at last prevailed, but their leader was mortally wounded.

James was succeeded by Archibald, Good Sir James's illegitimate son, who became 3rd Earl of Douglas. He acquired the lands of Bothwell and the title Lord of Bothwell through his marriage to Joanna, daughter of Thomas Murray, 5th Lord of Bothwell.

A POWERFUL CLAN
The Douglases were now in a position of great power, and in 1400 Archibald's daughter Mary married David, Duke of Rothesay, the son and heir of Robert III. David was to die in mysterious circumstances two years later, but the clan remained close to royal power and

Archibald, 5th Earl, was appointed Lieutenant General of Scotland in 1437. Two branches of the clan were now prominent – the Black Douglases and the Red Douglases. The first group were descended from Good Sir James, the original Black Douglas. The Red Douglases, so called because of their red hair, were descendants of George Douglas, an illegitimate son of the 2nd Earl of Douglas and Mar, and were earls of Angus.

THE PRICE OF POWER
The power of the Douglas clan made them a target. In 1440 William, 6th Earl of Douglas, was invited to dine with the ten-year-old James II at Edinburgh Castle by Sir Alexander Livingstone and Sir William Crichton. William and his brother David

▼ *The clan tartan, Douglas (Grey), was recorded by the Sobieskis in 1842.*

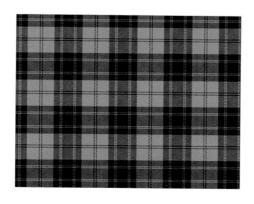

attended the banquet, but at the end of the meal, despite the king's protests, they were seized and beheaded.

Their great-uncle, James Douglas of Balvenie and Abercorn, known as James the Gross because of his corpulence, became the 7th Earl. He further extended the clan's territories and power base in central Scotland. His successor, William Douglas, the 8th Earl, was fatally stabbed by James II in 1452 when they quarrelled over an alliance that William had made.

RED DOUGLASES ASCENDANT
The Black Douglas line of the earls of Douglas ended with the 9th Earl, who died in England in 1491, and power passed to the Red Douglas branch of the clan. William, 11th Earl of Angus, was created 1st Marquis of Douglas in 1633 and fought on the Royalist side in the Civil War. His brother William, 2nd Marquis of Douglas, became Duke of Hamilton through his marriage in 1660. The Douglas and Angus titles passed to the dukes of Hamilton, while by complex descent the Douglas lands passed to the earls of Home. Sir Alec Douglas-Home, British politician and Prime Minister in 1963–64, was descended from this line.

FERGUSSON

The tribes of clan Fergusson fought as bravely as any of their contemporaries in Robert the Bruce's fight for an independent Scotland and in later conflicts, but they also won great distinction as statesmen and as men of letters.

The many families in clan Fergusson traditionally claim a common descent as "sons of Fergus". However, the Gaelic name Fhaerghuis (Fergus), which means "bold", "proud" or "angry", was very common in early Scotland and the Fergussons are certainly descended from multiple ancestors.

KILKERRAN – THE SENIOR BRANCH

The senior family in the clan are the Fergussons of Kilkerran, Ayrshire, who were landowners in the region from the 12th century onward. They are descended from Fergus MacFergus, who was granted lands in Ayrshire by Robert the Bruce (r.1306–29). John Fergusson was recorded as a witness to a 1314 agreement made by Edward Bruce, Robert's brother. The first documented clan chief, in 1464, was his descendant John Fergusson.

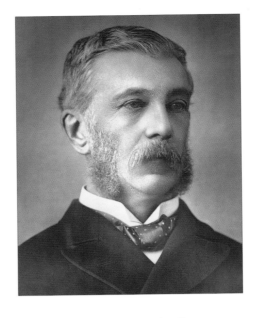

▲ *Sir James Fergusson of Kilkerran, 6th Baronet, served his family and his country with great distinction.*

In the Civil War Sir John Fergusson of Kilkerran fought on the Royalist side. His grandson, another Sir John, was created 1st Baronet of Nova Scotia in 1703. Sir James, 3rd Baronet, was made a judge of the Court of Session and Court of Justiciary in 1749, under the name Lord Kilkerran. In the late 19th and early 20th centuries, Sir James Fergusson of Kilkerran, 6th Baronet, was MP for Ayrshire and had a distinguished career as a statesman, during which he was Governor of Bombay and Under-Secretary of State for India and the Home Department. He was killed in an earthquake in Jamaica in 1907 while working on a commission to promote cotton growing in the British colonies. General Sir Charles Fergusson of Kilkerran, 7th Baronet, was a celebrated soldier and statesman who served in the Sudan and was a major-general in the First World War. He was appointed Governor-General of New Zealand (1924–30) and his son, Sir Bernard Fergusson, later held the same position in New Zealand from 1962–66.

In 1950 the Lyon Court ruled that Fergusson of Kilkerran should be regarded as chief of the clan. The current clan chief is Sir Charles Fergusson of Kilkerran, 9th Baronet, who lives in the clan's ancestral home at Kilkerran.

OTHER BRANCHES

The Fergussons of Argyll claim descent from Fergus Mor MacErc, a king of the Scoti tribe – the original "Scots" who left their ancestral Antrim territory in

▼ *The Fergusson of Balquhidder tartan is often confused with the clan tartan.*

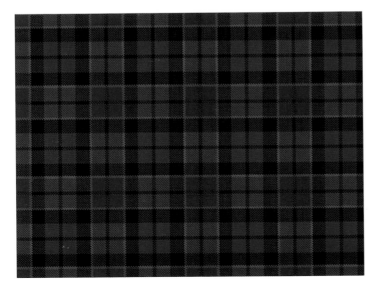

▼ *The Fergusson of Athol clan tartan is very similar to the MacLaren sett.*

▲ *Loch Fyne, whose shores were the homeland of the Argyll Fergussons, is the longest sea loch in Scotland.*

northern Ireland to settle in the Argyll mountains, where they founded the kingdom of Dalriada. Medieval historians claimed Fergus was ancestor of all the kings of Scotland. The Argyll Fergussons held lands on Loch Fyne.

The Fergussons of Craigdarroch, in Dumfries and Galloway, are said to be descended from Fergus, Prince of Galloway, founder of the Abbey of Dundrennan in the 12th century and great-great-grandfather of Robert the Bruce. Fergus became a monk at Holyrood, where he died in 1161.

The Fergussons of Dunfallandy in Perthshire are a junior branch of the Kilkerran line. In the 18th century they fought in the Jacobite cause in both rebellions, and an 80-year-old Fergusson who fought at the battle of Prestonpans in 1745 was recorded as the oldest Jacobite soldier. General Archibald Fergusson of Dunfallandy fought with the East India Company's troops. He was wounded at the battle of Seringapatam in 1799, where he survived a battlefield encounter with Tipu Sultan, the Muslim raja, and thereafter bore a sabre-slash scar on his forehead. In 1812 he rebuilt Dunfallandy House, near Pitlochry, on the site of the family's 14th-century ancestral home. Members of the Perthshire family would have worn the well-known Fergusson of Balquhidder tartan. The design appeared in James Logan's 1831 book, *The Scottish Gael or Celtic Manners, as Preserved among the Highlanders.*

The Fergussons of Aberdeenshire, the most notable families being Pitfour, Kinmundy and Baddifurrow, included distinguished lawyers and politicians.

FERGUSSON MEN OF LETTERS

Adam Fergusson, of the Perthshire branch of the clan, was professor of philosophy at Edinburgh University and wrote *An Essay on the History of Civil Society*, published in 1767. Widely regarded as the father of sociology, he died in 1816.

The poet Robert Fergusson, whose parents hailed from Aberdeenshire, grew up in Edinburgh and attended St Andrews University but took a clerk's job in order to support his widowed mother. Fergusson's work won many admirers, not least Robert Burns, who referred to Robert Fergusson as "my elder brother in misfortune, by far my elder brother in the muse." Despite the success of his poems Robert Fergusson suffered from depression and in 1773 was admitted to the Edinburgh public asylum, where he died the following year aged just 24.

James Fergusson, of the Ayrshire branch of the family, was a distinguished architectural historian who published *The History of Modern Architecture* (1862), *The History of Architecture* (1865) and *The History of Indian and Eastern Architecture* (1876).

FORBES

The position of power and prestige achieved by the Forbes of Aberdeenshire is reflected in the magnificence of Castle Forbes, the clan seat, which overlooks the river Don amid 7000 acres of land.

The Forbes take their name from the Braes o'Forbes region on the banks of the river Don in Aberdeenshire. By tradition the clan is descended from Ochonachar, a Celtic warrior who, having killed a bear or wild boar terrorizing the area, claimed possession of the land. John of Forbes was in possession of Forbes lands during the reign of

▼ *The Forbes Dress clan tartan is worn for dances and formal social events.*

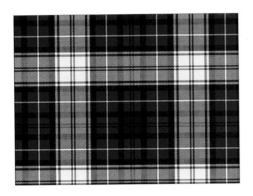

▼ *This Forbes sett was created in 1822 for the family's Pitsligo branch.*

William I (r.1165–1214) but the territories were only formally granted by charter in 1271, when Alexander III (r.1249–86) handed them over to Duncan of Forbes.

In 1303 Alexander of Forbes, Governor of Urquhart Castle near Inverness, was forced to surrender with his garrison to an English expeditionary force who then killed him with all his men. His pregnant wife escaped to Ireland, where she gave birth to a son, also named Alexander. He supported

▲ *The Forbes' striking Castle Craigievar has seven storeys and fairy-tale towers.*

Robert the Bruce who, once king, gave the Forbes clan further territories in Aberdeenshire. Alexander was killed at the battle of Dupplin Moor in 1322, fighting alongside David II, the Bruce's son, against an army led by Edward Balliol, son of John Balliol.

▼ *This tartan, Forbes Ancient, has been approved by the clan chief.*

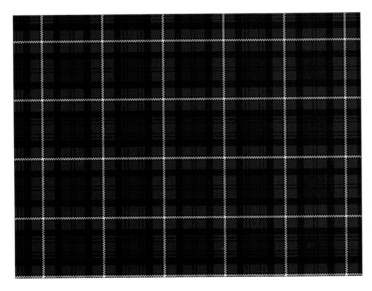

Alexander's grandson, Sir John Forbes of the Black Lip, consolidated the Forbes' position of power before his death in 1406. His four sons gave rise to the clan's main branches. William founded the Forbes of Pitsligo, Alistair those of both Skellater and Inverernan, and John those of Tolquhoun. Alexander, the eldest son and Lord Forbes (1436–42), married Lady Elizabeth Douglas, Robert II's granddaughter. Their son James, 2nd Lord Forbes, built the Castle of Druminner in the Forbes region sometime after 1456 and was knighted by James III. James's son Duncan founded the Forbes of Monymusk, while another son, Patrick of Corse, who was armour-bearer to James III, was ancestor of the Forbes who became baronets of Craigievar.

Alexander, 4th Lord Forbes, supported James III in his struggles with rebel nobles. When the young king was assassinated, Alexander attempted to raise an avenging army, riding through his lands with James's bloodstained shirt fluttering on the end of his spear. In the end he disbanded the army and paid homage to the dead king's son, James IV (r.1488–1513).

CLASHES WITH THE GORDONS

The Forbes were drawn into feuding with their neighbours, the powerful Gordon clan, partly due to religious differences – the Forbes were Protestants and the Gordons were Catholics.

The 8th Lord Forbes had married Lady Margaret Gordon, but the couple became estranged when their son entered a Catholic monastery. Lord Forbes disowned his wife and the quarrel eventually led to a pitched battle between the two clans at Clatt, Aberdeenshire, in which the Forbes were defeated and Lord Forbes's brother lost his life. In 1582, however, James VI (r.1567–1625) issued a charter confirming the Forbes in possession of their lands.

FOR AND AGAINST THE STUARTS

The Jacobite uprisings of the 18th century divided the clan. On the one hand Lord Forbes of the Culloden branch is said to have influenced many clans not to join the rebellion and so significantly limited its chances of success. On the other hand the Pitsligo Forbes fought on the Jacobite side. Alexander, 4th Lord Forbes of Pitsligo, forfeited his estates for his part in the uprising. Immediately after the battle of Culloden in 1746 he escaped with Lord Ogilvy and Hunter of Burnside to Scandinavia. He later returned to live undiscovered among his people on Forbes lands until his death in 1764, aged 85. Robert Forbes, episcopalian bishop of Ross and Caithness, survived arrest in 1745 to write a history of the uprising, *The Lyon in Mourning*.

Famous modern Forbes include James Ochoncar, 17th Lord Forbes, a British Army general who commanded the Cork and Eastern districts in Ireland in the early 19th century. Nigel, 22nd Lord Forbes, was Minister of State for Scotland (1958–59).

▼ *While some of their kinsmen held back, the Pitsligo Forbes threw in their lot with the Jacobites at Culloden.*

CASTLES

The imposing Castle Forbes, which overlooks the river Don, was built by James, 17th Lord Forbes, in 1815. His great-great-great-grandson Malcolm, Master of Forbes and Deputy Lieutenant of Aberdeenshire, still lives in the castle. Tolquhoun Castle, near the Aberdeenshire village of Tarves, was built in the 1580s by the Forbes of Tolquhoun, ancestors of Lord Forbes of Culloden who played a significant role in the 1745 Jacobite rebellion. It can be visited today as a ruin. Castle Craigievar was built in 1626 by William Forbes of the Craigievar, descendant of Patrick of Corse, son of James, 2nd Lord Forbes. Pitsligo Castle, near Fraserburgh in north-eastern Scotland, was built in 1424 by the Frasers of Philorth but in the 16th century it came into the possession of the Forbes of Drumminor. Clan descendant Malcolm Forbes, the US publisher, bought and partially renovated the castle in 1989.

The most popular Forbes tartan is said to have been designed for the family's Pitsligo branch in 1822. It appeared in the pattern book of Wilson's of Bannockburn. A different tartan, the Forbes Ancient, has been registered with the Lord Lyon.

FRASER

Clan Fraser has two tribes. The Lovat, or Highland, Frasers hail from Inverness-shire, while the Philorth, or Lowland, Frasers established themselves in north-eastern Aberdeenshire. The Frasers left an enduring legacy in the town of Fraserburgh, which was founded in the 16th century by the 8th Lord of Philorth.

The Frasers came to Scotland from Anjou or Normandy in the 12th century, and there are a number of fanciful explanations for the origin of their name. One of these stories dates from 916, when King Charles of France is said to have so enjoyed Julius de Berry's strawberries that he ordered the Frenchman to change his name to Fraise ("strawberry" in French) and

▶ *The Fraser badge bears three strawberry flowers – honouring the origins of the clan's name.*

▼ *Kelso Abbey, built with Fraser help, was one of Scotland's richest churches in the Middle Ages.*

adopt strawberry plants as a device on his coat-of-arms. Early Frasers went by the name of de Freselière or de Frisselle and later changed to Fraissier ("strawberry-bearer") in a reference to their coat-of-arms.

The clan's first documented ancestor is Simon Fraser, who left the church of Keith to the monks of Kelso Abbey in 1160. His descendant Sir Simon the Patriot fought alongside William Wallace and Robert the Bruce, but was captured in 1306 and executed in London, where his head was impaled on a spike next to that of Wallace.

Sir Simon's cousin's son, Sir Alexander Fraser of Cowie, was appointed Lord Chamberlain and married Mary, the sister of Robert the Bruce. He was the ancestor of the Philorth Frasers, who became the Lords Saltoun. His brother, another Sir Simon, was ancestor to the Lovat Frasers. He fought in the battle of Bannockburn in 1314 and was killed at Halidon Hill in 1333.

FRASERS OF PHILORTH

Sir Alexander Fraser of Cowie's grandson, Sir Alexander Fraser of Cowie and Durris, gained possession of Philorth, in north-eastern Aberdeenshire, through his marriage in 1375 to Joanna, daughter of William, Earl of Ross. Their descendant, Sir Alexander, 8th Lord of Philorth, developed the fishing village of Faithlee on Kinnaird Head into the port of Fraserburgh and built Fraserburgh Castle. His grandson, also Alexander, became 10th Lord Saltoun in 1669. He took the Royalist side in the Civil War and was severely wounded at the battle of Worcester in 1651. He was rescued and nursed by his servant, James Cardno, who helped him return to his Scottish lands, where he built Philorth House, near Fraserburgh, in 1666. The family lived there until it burned down in 1915, when they moved into Cairnbulg Castle. The Frasers of Philorth did not take part in the Jacobite rebellions of the 18th century.

The current clan chief is Flora Fraser, 20th Lady Saltoun, who sits in the House of Lords.

FRASERS OF LOVAT

The Lovat Frasers gained possession of lands in Stratherrick and around Beauly Firth, both in Inverness-shire, largely through marriage into the local Bisset family. As descendants of Sir Simon Fraser they had the Gaelic title MacShimidh ("sons of Simon"). Hugh Fraser, 6th Lord of Lovat and Sheriff of Inverness, was made 1st Lord Fraser of Lovat in about 1464.

Simon, 11th Lord Lovat, earned the nickname "the Fox" and a reputation for double-dealing in a long and colourful career that included charges of treason and rape. He switched sides several times between the Jacobites and the House of Hanover, as his own and

▲ *Some authorities date the Fraser of Altyre tartan to around 1850.*

▶ *This Fraser tartan is said to have been worn by the 78th Highlanders.*

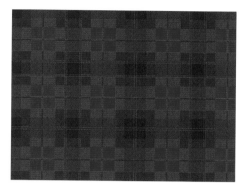

▲ *Unusually, the Frasers have a tartan that is reserved for use at weddings.*

his clan's interests dictated. He was not personally involved in the battle of Culloden but sent his clansmen to fight in the Jacobite cause. When the rebellion failed, Simon was captured by the English and was the last person to be beheaded on Tower Hill in London, on 9 April 1747.

Simon's son, also Simon, raised the 78th Fraser Highlanders, who fought in the British Army in Canada from 1758 under General Wolfe. When the regiment was disbanded in 1763, many of its soldiers remained in Canada and spread out across North America.

The Lovat estates were inherited by Thomas Fraser of Strichen, Aberdeenshire, who was made Baron Lovat in 1837. The title of Lord Lovat had been cancelled on the execution of Simon the Fox but this decision was reversed in 1857, when Thomas Fraser was made 14th Lord Lovat. His son Simon Fraser, 15th Lord Lovat, began building Beaufort Castle overlooking Beauly river. His son, yet another Simon, 16th Lord Lovat, raised the Lovat Scouts, who fought in the Boer War as part of the Highland Division.

▼ *The notoriously slippery Simon Fraser, Lord Lovat, sat for the English artist William Hogarth.*

FRASER CASTLES

Cairnbulg Castle, originally a Cumming stronghold, was given to the Ross clan in 1316 by Robert the Bruce, and became Sir Alexander Fraser's when he married the daughter of the Earl of Ross in 1375. Debt forced its sale in 1666. The Gordons reconstructed it and sold it back to the Frasers in 1934.

Fraserburgh Castle, which had been built in the 1500s by Sir Alexander, 8th Lord of Philorth, became Kinnaird Head lighthouse in the 18th century.

▼ *Fraserburgh Castle was converted into Scotland's first lighthouse in 1787.*

GORDON

Originally from the Borders, the proud Gordon family rose to a position of great power and influence in the 15th and 16th centuries. Their name is glorified by the exploits of the Gordon Highlanders, heroes of Waterloo and many other battles.

The Gordons take their name from the parish of Gordon, south of Edinburgh, where they first settled in the 11th or 12th century. Richard, Baron of Gordon (d.*c*.1200), gave land to the monks at Kelso. According to some accounts, his nephew Sir Adam rode with Louis IX of France on the 8th Crusade (1270–72). A later Sir Adam of Gordon, who fought alongside Robert the Bruce, gained territories in Aberdeenshire when he was granted the lordship of Strathbogie. The Gordons named the estate Huntly and made Huntly Castle their home from about 1376.

FRIENDS TO THE CROWN

Sir Adam's great-great-grandson, Sir Alexander, was created Earl of Huntly in 1449. As loyal servants of the Scottish Crown, the Gordons made enemies among other noble families, especially clan Douglas and the Mackintoshes of clan Chattan.

In 1498 James IV appointed George, 2nd Earl Huntly, High Chancellor of Scotland and in 1518 Alexander, 3rd Earl Huntly, was made Royal Lieutenant over all Scotland except the West Highlands. The family gained such a position of power in northeastern Scotland that their chief was nicknamed "Cock of the North".

George, 4th Earl Huntly, was captured by the English at the battle of Pinkie in 1547. He was imprisoned in England but made a dramatic escape on horseback the following year. On his return to Scotland he uncovered an assassination plot against him led by

▲ *William Gordon of Fyvie (d.1816) cut a dashing figure in Gordon tartan.*

the Mackintosh chief of clan Chattan. Huntly arranged for Mackintosh's capture and had him executed. The most powerful nobleman of his day, Huntly was drawn into a rebellion against Mary, Queen of Scots, and died of apoplexy in battle at Corrichie, west of Aberdeen, in 1562. His embalmed body was carried to Edinburgh, where Parliament declared him a traitor.

THE DEATH OF MORAY

In 1599 George, 6th Earl Huntly, was made 1st Marquis of Huntly. When James VI became alarmed by an alliance of James Stewart, 2nd Earl of Moray, with the Earl of Bothwell he commissioned Huntly to bring Moray to trial. Huntly arrived with his men at Moray's castle, Dunnibrissle on the Firth of Forth, at around midnight. When Moray refused to come out Huntly set fire to the house, forcing Moray and his house guests to flee. Huntly's men chased the earl on to the seashore where they stabbed him to death. The events are commemorated in the ballad *Bonnie Earl o'Moray*.

During the Civil War George, 2nd Marquis of Huntly and a staunch Royalist, was made Lieutenant in the

North for Charles I. In 1647 he was captured by Covenanter troops at Dalnabo, Strathdon, and imprisoned in Edinburgh, where he was beheaded for treason on 22 March 1649. The Huntly estates and title were withdrawn, but were restored in 1651 to Lord Lewis Gordon, 3rd Marquis of Huntly. His son George was made the 1st Duke of Gordon by Charles II in 1684.

BROTHER AGAINST BROTHER

During the Jacobite rebellions of 1715 and 1745 Gordons fought on both sides. Alexander, 2nd Duke of Gordon, fought for the Jacobites at the battle of Sheriffmuir in 1715. In 1745, Cosmo George, 3rd Duke of Gordon, took the side of the Government, while his brother Lord Lewis Gordon raised a Gordon regiment to fight in the Jacobite cause. The 3rd Duke's son, Lord George Gordon, was a staunch Protestant and MP. He precipitated the Gordon Riots of 1780 in London, when one of his speeches condemning Parliament's plans to extend the Catholic Relief Act – which lifted restrictions on Roman Catholics – inflamed Londoners and led to a six-day running riot in which 235 people were killed and 135 arrested.

▼ *The Red Gordon, also called "Old Huntly", is worn as a district tartan.*

GORDON REGIMENTS

In 1778 Alexander, 4th Duke of Gordon, raised the Gordon Fencibles regiment to fight in the American War of Independence. His son, George, Marquis of Huntly, raised the 92nd Gordon Highlanders in 1794. He was helped by his mother, who is said to have accompanied him around the Gordon estates holding the enlistment money between her teeth and greeting each recruit with a kiss. George subsequently became 5th Duke of Gordon but when he died childless in 1836 the dukedom became extinct. The chiefship of the Gordon clan passed to George, 5th Earl of Aboyne, a descendant of the fourth son of George, 2nd Marquis of Huntly. He became the 9th Marquis of Huntly. Aboyne Castle in Aberdeenshire is the clan's seat.

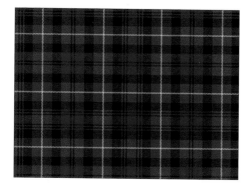

▲ *The Gordon family tartan is also identified as a regimental sett.*

OTHER BRANCHES OF THE GORDON FAMILY

Descendants of Patrick Gordon of Methlic were earls of Aberdeen from 1682. George Hamilton Gordon, 4th Earl of Aberdeen, was British Prime Minister (1852–55). The English poet Lord Byron was the son of a Gordon – his mother was Catherine Gordon of the family's Gight branch.

General Charles Gordon of Khartoum became a hero of the British Empire in 1884 when he was sent to relieve British garrisons under attack from rebels in the Sudan. He held Khartoum, the Sudanese capital, for ten months; it was captured and Gordon killed in January 1885, two days before British relief troops arrived.

TARTANS

The Gordons of Abergeldie are the source of the popular red and green Gordon tartan. The design is based on a 1723 portrait of Rachael Gordon wearing a scarf with this pattern. The Gordon regimental tartan was designed in 1794 by adding a yellow line to the familiar pattern worn by the Black Watch Regiment, which had been created by the Government to control the trade in stolen cattle.

▼ *The Gordon of Abergeldie is based on an early 18th-century original.*

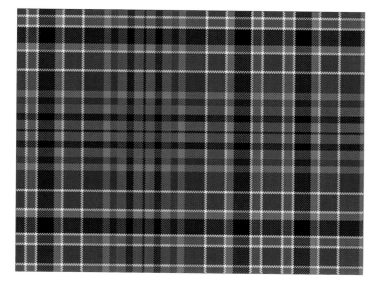

GRAHAM

The gallant Grahams served Scotland faithfully and proudly over nine centuries. Among their many great men figure James, 1st Marquis of Montrose, the Royalist general of the Civil War, and Bonnie Dundee, the Jacobite hero.

According to legend, the Grahams are descended from Greme, or Gramus, a Pictish warrior-chieftain. In about AD183, he breached the Antonine Wall built by the Romans between the Forth and Clyde rivers, hence the wall's popular name of Graeme's Dyke. In fact the family probably descended from Anglo-Norman knights who travelled north with Prince David when he claimed the Scottish throne as David I (r.1124–53). Some accounts say the first Grahams took their name from Graeg Ham in Lincolnshire.

The first documented ancestor is William de Graham, who received lands in Abercorn and Dalkeith from David I in 1127. The following year he was witness to the charter founding the Abbey of Holyrood. From his elder son, Peter, came the Grahams of Dalkeith and Eskdale; from the younger, Alan, came the Grahams of Montrose. In the 13th century a Graham chief married the Earl of Strathearn's daughter,

▲ *A Graham witnessed the founding of Holyrood Abbey, Edinburgh, as an Augustinian monastery in 1128.*

receiving the lands of Kincardine in the district of Strathearn, and established Kincardine Castle as the family's principal seat. The Graham clansmen were staunch in the struggle for an independent Scotland. Sir John Graham of Dundaff fought with William Wallace and died at the battle of Falkirk in 1298, while his son Sir David fought with Robert the Bruce.

A ROYAL WEDDING

Sir David's great-grandson, Sir William Graham of Kincardine, married Mary Stewart, daughter of Robert II (r.1371–90). Their eldest son, Sir Robert Graham of Strathcarron, was ancestor of the Grahams of Claverhouse, Fintry and Duntrune. His brother William gave rise to the Grahams of Garvoch. Their younger brother, Walter, was ancestor to the Grahams of Knockdolian in Carrick.

In 1405 the Grahams acquired the lands of Old Montrose in Angus. Patrick Graham of Kincardine was made Lord Graham in 1451. His

grandson William, 3rd Lord Graham, fought with great valour at the battle of Sauchieburn in 1488 and was made Earl of Montrose in 1504. He was killed at the battle of Flodden in 1513.

THE MARQUIS OF MONTROSE

Without doubt the foremost Graham of the clan was James Graham, 5th Earl and 1st Marquis of Montrose, the great general of Charles I (r.1625–49) during the English Civil War. With a makeshift force that included the Graham clansmen and a contingent of Highlanders he won victories over the Covenanter army at Tippermuir, Aberdeen, Inverlochy, Auldearn, Alford and Kilsyth (1644–45). But in September 1645 his dwindling force was taken by surprise by Covenant troops at Philiphaugh and suffered a heavy defeat. Montrose escaped to Norway, but returned to Scotland after Charles's execution at the head of an army. His troops were shipwrecked and with just 200 men he was overwhelmed at Carbisdale and later captured. When he was executed in Edinburgh on 21 May 1650 the parts of his body were put on display, but in 1661, after the Restoration, he was given a magnificent state funeral and interred in St Giles' Cathedral, Edinburgh, beneath a marble effigy.

In the time of Montrose's son, the 2nd Marquis, the Grahams' castle at Kincardine was attacked and destroyed by an army of Campbells. In 1682 the 3rd Marquis of Montrose acquired Loch Lomond territories that had been the possession of Buchanan chiefs, and Buchanan Castle became the seat of the clan chiefs. The 4th Marquis was created Duke of Montrose in 1707. His descendant James, Marquis of Graham and later 3rd Duke of Montrose, was the toast of Highlanders for his part in lifting the 1747 ban on wearing tartan.

▲ *The Graham of Menteith tartan also comes in a design with a green ground.*

▼ *John Graham ("Bonnie Dundee") proved his battle prowess as a volunteer in William of Orange's army.*

▲ *This Graham of Montrose tartan has been dated to 1815.*

BONNIE DUNDEE

Another Graham military hero was John Graham of Claverhouse, 1st Viscount Dundee. He fought hard against the Covenanters and later led Jacobite Highlanders in support of the deposed king James VII of Scotland and James II of England (r.1685–88). This dashing, charismatic figure, a skilful horseman, led the Jacobites to great victories at Inverlochy (1645) and Killiecrankie (1689). The Covenanters reviled him as Bloody Claverse, but the Jacobites hailed him as Bonnie Dundee. He died from a musket wound after the battle of Killiecrankie and such was his importance to the cause that Jacobite hopes died with him.

GRAHAMS OF MENTEITH AND OF THE DEBATABLE LAND

In the late 14th century Sir Patrick Graham Dundaff acquired the earldom of Strathearn by marrying Euphemia, daughter and heiress of Robert II's son Prince David. When Sir Patrick died in 1413 Scotland's James I (r.1406–37) seized his opportunity and deprived the infant heir, Malise, of most of his valuable inheritance. James bestowed on Malise the title of Earl of Menteith. Among his descendants were the earls of Menteith and Airth and the Grahams of the Debatable Land, who under James VI (r.1567–1625) were deported because of their troublesome activities, an event commemorated in the song *Sweet Ennerdale*.

GRANT

The Grant chief had such power and influence in the 17th and 18th centuries that he was referred to as the Highland king. The clan's tartan and proud traditions have been an inspiration to many of his descendants, including, some say, Ulysses S. Grant, the American Civil War general and 18th President of the United States.

Some clan members claim descent from Kenneth MacAlpin, the first king of both the Scots and the Picts in the mid-9th century, but others argue that the clan name derives from the French *grand* ("large", "great") and believe the Grants are descended from Norman knights. By the end of the 13th century the Grants were significant Highland chiefs. The first to be mentioned in historical records of the 1260s was Sir Laurence le Grand, Sheriff of Inverness. John and Randolph de Grant, supporters of the Scottish patriot Robert the Bruce, may have been his son and grandson. The clan held land in Stratherrick, east of Loch Ness, and gained territory in Strathspey when a Grant chief married the daughter of landowner Sir John Bisset.

A clear line of descent runs back from the current clan chief to Iain Grant, Sheriff of Inverness in 1434, who acquired lands in Kinveachy through marriage to the daughter of

▲ *The bridge at Grantown, which was built by the Grant laird in 1766.*

Gilbert of Glencairnie. Iain's younger son became Sir Duncan le Grant of Freuchie and his lands were made the barony of Freuchie in 1494. Sir James Grant built Castle Freuchie in 1536, while Sir Ludovic Grant, 8th Baron, made it the clan's principal residence in the 1690s and renamed it Castle Grant. In 1765 the architect John Adam enlarged the castle.

INTO BATTLE

In the Civil War the Grants fought in the Marquis of Montrose's Royalist army. After the Restoration Charles II (r.1660–85) planned to make Sir James, 7th Baron of Freuchie, the Earl of Strathspey, but the nobleman died

before he could be rewarded for his loyalty to the Stuart cause.

The Jacobite rebellions divided the clan. The Grants of Glenmoriston fought in the Jacobite ranks in 1689 at both Killiecrankie and Cromdale, in the second battle facing their own clansmen the Grants of Freuchie. The latter fought in support of William of Orange (1689–1702), who had been invited by James II's opponents to rule with his wife Mary, James's daughter. The Freuchie Grants' support for William and Mary brought Sir Ludovic, 8th Baron, a remarkable honour. In 1694 his lands were made a regality, giving him power to regulate commercial affairs and punish criminals on his own lands. Such was his position that he became known as the Highland King.

The Freuchie Grants supported the Government while the Glemoriston branch of the clan fought for Bonnie Prince Charlie at the battle of Prestonpans in 1745. When in 1746 the battle of Culloden put an end to Jacobite hopes the Glenmoriston Grants were severely punished: many were captured and sent into slavery in the West Indies.

▼ *The Grant of Ballindoch is based on the sett shown by James Logan in 1831.*

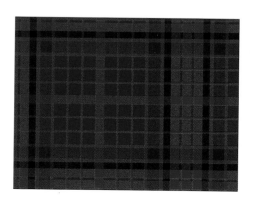

▼ *The Grant Hunting tartan was made by Wilson's of Bannockburn in 1819.*

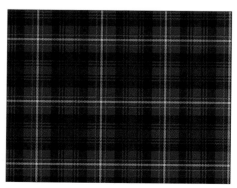

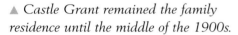
Castle Grant remained the family residence until the middle of the 1900s.

Together with the Campbells, Frasers and Munros, the Grants of Freuchie provided men for six Highland Independent Companies raised in 1725. In 1739 these were combined into the Government's 42nd Regiment, popularly known as the Black Watch. France's declaration of war in 1793 prompted Sir James Grant to raise a regiment of Grant Fencibles to defend the country. When it

▼ *The current chief, Lord Strathspey, authorized this official Grant tartan.*

appeared that the unit was to be posted overseas in 1795, the regiment mutinied at Dumfries and two men were shot as punishment.

In 1776 Sir James Grant founded the town of Grantown-on-Spey, which is now a Highland tourist resort.

LATER GRANTS

Some authorities claim that Ulysses S. Grant, general-in-chief of the Union forces during the US Civil War (1864–65) and later the 18th President of the United States, carried a piece of the Grant tartan with him throughout the war. His descent from the Grant clan cannot easily be traced although

▲ *Sir James Grant directs the Grant Fencibles in military manoeuvres.*

his family, which had been based in Devon before emigrating to North America, was proud of its Scottish roots. Other Grants of note include the Bloomsbury Group painter Duncan Grant and the film actor Hugh Grant, both descended from the Grants of Rothiemurcus, landowners in the region of Aviemore. Since 1817, the chiefs of clan Grant have held the title Baron Strathspey of Strathspey.

▼ *The Sobieskis showed the Grant of Rothiemurcus in* Vestiarum Scoticum.

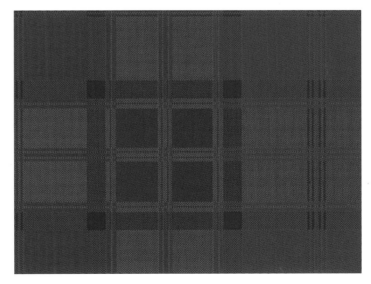

KENNEDY

The Kennedys rose to a position of dominance in the south-western lowlands of Scotland, along the shores of the Firth of Clyde, and married into the royal house of Stewart in the 15th century. The clan has significant connections with the United States.

According to most authorities the Kennedy name derives from the Gaelic *ceannaideach* ("ugly-headed"). However, some accounts say the name comes from Cunedda, a 5th-century ancestor who founded settlements in south-western Scotland. The Kennedys became a significant force in Carrick, Ayrshire, and during the reign of Scotland's William I (r.1165–1214) a Gilbert MacKennedy was witness to a document granting lands in Carrick to Melrose Abbey.

In the struggle for the Scottish crown after the abdication of John Balliol (r.1292–96), the Kennedys sided with the Bruce family against the Comyns, and later fought with Robert the Bruce (r.1306–29) for Scottish independence. John Kennedy of Dunure was named Baillie of Carrick in 1372 by the Bruce's grandson,

▼ *A darker Kennedy was printed in the French* Clans Originaux *(1880).*

▼ *This Kennedy clan tartan has been dated to around 1830.*

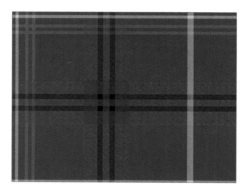

▲ *The 13th-century Dunure Castle was home to the Kennedys of Carrick.*

Robert II (r.1371–90), and two generations later the clan's status was sufficient for Sir James Kennedy to marry Robert III's daughter, Mary Stewart. Their son, Sir Gilbert, made Lord Kennedy in 1457, was a member of the Council of Regents during the

▼ *This Kennedy sett appeared in* Clans of the Scottish Highlands *(1847).*

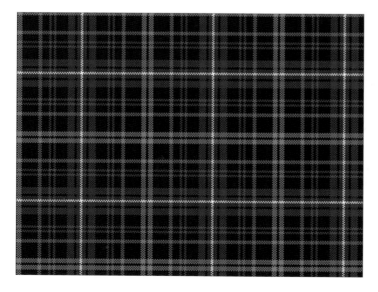

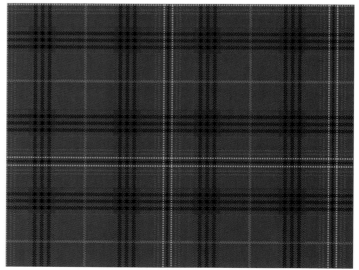

minority of James III (r.1460–88). Gilbert's brother James (d.1465), a leading churchman, courtier and statesman, was bishop of St Andrew's, guardian and tutor to James III, and for a period High Chancellor of Scotland. He founded St Salvator's College at St Andrews University in 1450 and built a magnificent tomb to his own memory in the college chapel.

POISONED IN A QUEEN'S SERVICE

Sir David Kennedy, 3rd Lord Kennedy and created Earl of Cassilis in 1509, was one of approximately 5000 Scots who died at the battle of Flodden in 1513. The 3rd Earl of Cassilis, Sir Gilbert, was made Lord High Treasurer in 1554. Four years later he was one of four commissioners sent to France to arrange the marriage of Mary, Queen of Scots, to the Dauphin, the son of François I. When he refused to accept that the Scottish crown should pass to a French heir, he was poisoned.

Quentin Kennedy, Abbot of Crossraguel, made his nephew John, 4th Earl, administrator of the abbey lands. When Quentin's successor, Allan Stewart, refused to sign the abbey

KENNEDYS IN AMERICA

Captain Archibald Kennedy, 11th Earl, a retired Royal Navy commander, settled in North America. He became a great landowner in New York, partly through his marriage to Anne, daughter of John Watts. Archibald lost all his property during the War of Independence (1775–81), and his New York residence, No 1 Broadway, was appropriated by George Washington.

Many other Kennedys left the Scottish lowlands to begin a new life in North America, particularly in the second half of the 19th century.

▲ *Archibald Kennedy, 11th Earl of Cassilis, was one of many Kennedys to thrive in North America.*

properties over to him, the earl tortured him on a spit over the fire at Dunure Castle. Although the abbot was saved by his Bargany relatives, the earl kept the lands.

LADY HAMILTON AND HER GIPSY LOVER

In 1649 the 6th Earl of Cassilis, another John, was made Lord Justice General of Scotland. A staunch Protestant, he supported the Parliamentary side against the Crown during the Civil War and sat in the House of Lords during Oliver Cromwell's Protectorate. His wife, Lady Jean Hamilton, had an affair

with Sir John Faa, which is commemorated in a ballad. According to the song, Faa carried her off with the help of a gipsy gang. The earl caught the fleeing group, hanged Faa from a tree in front of Lady Jean, then locked her up in Cassilis Castle.

Following the death of the heirless 8th Earl of Cassilis (yet another John), the Kennedy titles passed to the Kennedys of Culzean, descendants of the second son of Sir Gilbert, 3rd Earl. When Sir David Kennedy succeeded as 10th Earl in 1775, he hired the famous Scottish architect Robert Adam to design and build Culzean Castle on the ruins of a late 16th-century Kennedy stronghold on cliffs overlooking the Firth of Clyde. The castle is considered by many to be Adam's greatest work.

The 11th Earl's son, Archibald, 12th Earl, was made Marquis of Ailsa by William IV (r.1830–37), taking the name from the island of Ailsa Craig in the Firth of Clyde. The 5th Marquis gave Culzean Castle to the National Trust of Scotland in 1945 on condition that a top-floor apartment be kept as a Scottish home for General Dwight Eisenhower, in gratitude for his role in delivering an Allied victory at the close of the Second World War. Eisenhower made four visits to Culzean.

▼ *Sir David Kennedy was bankrupted by the magnificent redevelopment of Culzean Castle in the 18th century.*

MacDONALD

The ancient clan of MacDonald ruled with regal authority over vast territories in the southern Isles and western Highlands. At the height of their influence in the 15th century they challenged the power of the Scottish Crown itself. Legend claims that clan MacDonald is descended from Colla Uais, high king of Ireland and reputedly ruler of the Hebrides in the days before the Scots. According to historical records, however, the ancestor was Somerled, King of the Isles (d.1164), and the clan takes its name from Donald, Somerled's grandson, who inherited South Kintyre and Islay from his father Reginald in 1207.

Donald (d.1269) ruled with a firm hand for more than 60 years, but is said to have been so troubled by his many sins that he made a penitential pilgrimage to Rome. On his return he gave lands to the monastery at Saddel in Kintyre, where Somerled was buried. Donald was succeeded by Angus Mor MacDonald of the Isles, who in 1263 backed King Hakon of Norway's expedition against the Scottish king Alexander III.

Donald's grandson, Angus Og MacDonald, led his clan in support of Robert the Bruce and fought at the battle of Bannockburn in 1314. His reward from Robert was gifts of land in the western Highlands and in the islands. His son, John of Islay, 7th Lord of the Isles, married twice. Ranald, his son by his first wife, Amy MacRuairidh, heiress to the lordship of Garmoran, was ancestor of the MacDonalds of Clanranald, while Donald, his son by Margaret, daughter of Robert III, succeeded him as Lord of the Isles.

From Dunyvaig, his castle on Islay, Donald ruled the isles as a private kingdom. In 1411 he laid claim to the earldom of Ross, leading 6000 of his clan's fiercest fighters in an assault on Inverness and Aberdeen. They were joined by men of other Highland clans, including Mackintosh, MacLean, MacLeod, Cameron and clan Chattan. At the battle of Harlaw, near Aberdeen, they fought a bruising conflict against a Lowland army commanded by the Earl of Mar. The battle left 1000 clansmen and 600 Lowland fighters dead, and Donald was forced to retreat.

The independent power of the Lords of the Isles enjoyed a final flourish in the time of Donald's grandson John, 10th Lord, who established his own parliament at Ardtornish, on the Sound of Mull. In 1462 he formed an alliance with the English against the Scottish Crown but before the end of his chiefship James IV stripped him of his titles and lands. In time the MacDonalds accepted that they held their lands not as independent princes but under charter from the king.

MacDONALDS OF CLANRANALD

The ancestor of the Clanranald branch of the clan was Ranald, John of Islay's eldest son. Although he allowed the MacDonald chiefship to pass to his half-brother Donald, he did receive the bulk of the Garmoran lands from his mother, Amy MacRuairidh. Ranald's eldest son, Allan, followed his father as chief of the MacDonalds of Clanranald, while his second son, Donald, was the founder of the MacDonells of Glengarry.

The men of Clanranald killed their cruel 6th chief, Dugall, so his uncle,

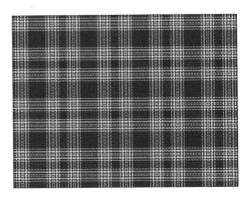

▲ *The MacDonald of the Isles first appeared in the* Vestiarum Scoticum.

▼ *This tartan is based on one worn in a portrait by the Lord of the Isles.*

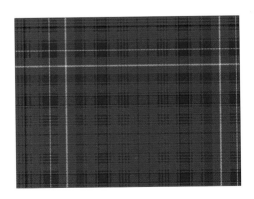

▲ *The MacDonald of Staffa tartan has been dated to the mid-19th century.*

▼ *The MacDonald of Sleat clan tartan derives from an 18th-century original.*

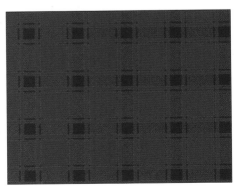

Alistair Allanson, took control. Following his death the chiefship was disputed by Alistair's son, John of Moydart, and Ranald Gallda, a brother of the 6th chief. Their disagreement came to a head in 1544 in the battle of Blarnaleine, at which Ranald was killed. John of Moydart established himself as Clanranald chief. His grandson Donald, 10th chief, was knighted by James VI.

The Clanranalds supported the Stuart kings, fighting under the Marquis of Montrose in 1644–45 during the Civil War and also at Sheriffmuir in the 1715 Jacobite rebellion, where Alan, 13th chief, was killed. In 1745 Ranald, 16th chief, fought in the cause of Bonnie Prince Charlie, but it was his son, "young Clanranald", who led the clan into the field.

MacDONALDS OF SLEAT
The Gaelic name of this branch of the clan is Clann Iisdein ("children of Hugh"). They are descended from Hugh, a younger son of Alexander, Earl of Ross and 3rd Lord of the Isles.

After the lordship of the Isles was forfeited in 1494, Hugh held his lands under charter from the Crown. In 1539 his son, Donald Gorm, tried to re-establish the MacDonalds' right to rule

▼ *The MacDonald of Glencoe tartan is a modern sett of uncertain origin.*

as Lords of the Isles, but was defeated and died. Among his descendants, Sir Donald MacDonald was made 1st Baronet of Sleat in 1625 and Sir Alexander MacDonald, 9th Baronet, was made Lord MacDonald in 1776. Today Lord MacDonald is recognized as chief of clan MacDonald. His seat is Armadale Castle on Skye.

MacDONALDS OF GLENCOE
In the wake of the failure of the 1689 Jacobite rebellion, clan chiefs were offered an amnesty on condition that they swore allegiance to William of Orange, but due to a series of mishaps the chief of the MacDonalds of

▲ *The MacDonalds' Dunyvaig Castle on Islay was probably built on the site of a Viking fort.*

Glencoe did not swear his oath in time, missing the deadline by a matter of days. A detachment from the Argyll regiment, under Captain Robert Campbell of Glenlyon, was despatched to make an example of the chief and his clan. On 15 February 1692, 38 men, women and children were slaughtered at Glencoe, while many survivors who fled to the hills died of cold.

▼ *The MacDonald is given in this or similar form by all early authorities.*

MacDONELL

The MacDonells, close kin of the MacDonald Lords of the Isles, backed their cousins in their 16th-century struggles with the Scottish Crown, but were fiercely supportive of the Stuart inheritance in the Civil War and the Jacobite rebellions of the 17th century.

The Glengarry and Keppoch branches of the MacDonalds spell the clan name MacDonell, which is a more accurate rendering of the Gaelic MacDhomhnuill ("son of Donald"). The Glengarry MacDonells are descended from Donald, the second son of Ranald, son of John of Islay.

Alistair MacDonell, 6th Lord of Glengarry, acquired lands in Lochalsh, Lochcarron and Lochbroom through marriage, but these were subject to prolonged and bloody feuding with the neighbouring Mackenzies of Kintail. By the early 17th century the MacDonells had been driven out of their Lochcarron lands, but in 1602 the chief, Angus MacDonell, led a raid on mainland Lochcarron from the island of Skye, burning houses and slaughtering the inhabitants. He loaded his boat with plunder, but the Mackenzies, in

▲ *Invergarry Castle was home to the MacDonell chief until 1746.*

small rowing boats, intercepted MacDonell at night in the waters that separate Skye from the mainland. In the ensuing panic the MacDonell boat overturned and many men were killed, including Angus. The survivors swam to Skye and escaped on foot, leaving their booty in the boat. The following year the MacDonells launched a fiercer raid; they burned an entire congregation of Mackenzies in the church of

Kilchrist, while the MacDonell piper marched around the building playing a spirited tune held dear to MacDonell hearts and later known as *Kilchrist*.

The lands of Glengarry were made a barony in 1627, under Donald MacDonell, 8th chief of Glengarry. Angus, 9th chief, was a staunch Royalist who during the Civil War fought under the Marquis of Montrose (1644–45) and in the battle of Worcester (1651).

▼ *A sample of the MacDonell of Glengarry has been dated to 1815–16.*

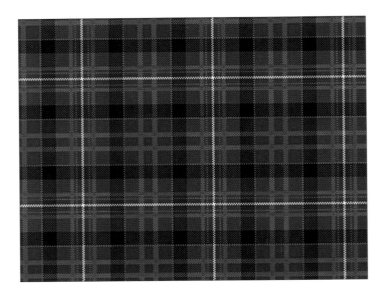

▼ *The red and green tartan is reserved for the MacDonells of Keppoch.*

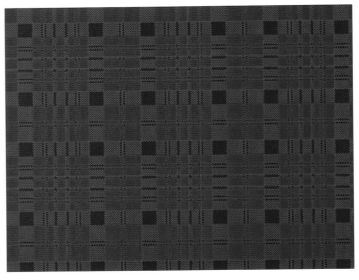

He lost his lands under Oliver Cromwell's protectorate (1649–60), but was compensated at the Restoration, when Charles II (r. 1660–85) made him Lord MacDonell and Aros. However, the peerage was limited to MacDonell and his male heirs, and as he had no eligible children it died with him in 1680.

Alistair MacDonell, 11th chief, fought in the Jacobite army at Sheriffmuir in 1715 and the following year was created a Jacobite peer as Lord MacDonell. Six hundred Glengarry MacDonells fought for Bonnie Prince Charlie, the Young Pretender, in the 1745 rebellion, and the family gave him refuge when he fled to their Invergarry seat after defeat at Culloden in 1746. The 13th chief had been captured before the uprising began and was imprisoned as a Jacobite in the Tower of London until 1747.

Sir James MacDonell, brother of Duncan, 14th chief of Glengarry, won glory for the clan at the battle of Waterloo in 1815. Alistair MacDonell, 15th chief, kept up a splendid public appearance, as he and his retainers always wore full Highland dress. A friend of the poet and novelist Sir Walter Scott, he was the inspiration for Fergus MacIvor in *Waverley* (1814). His son, Aeneas Ranaldson MacDonell, sold the Glengarry estate to the Marquis of Huntly and his sons emigrated to New Zealand, where they established a new base for the clan.

MacDONELLS OF KEPPOCH

The Keppoch MacDonells honour Alasdair Carrach MacDonell as their ancestor. He was the son of John MacDonald, 7th Lord of the Isles, by his marriage to Margaret, daughter of Robert II (r.1371–90). They supported their MacDonald kin's attempts to extend the powers of the Lordship of the Isles: Alistair of Keppoch fought alongside his brother Donald, 8th Lord of the Isles, at the battle of Harlaw in

▲ *A 19th-century MacDonell posed in clan tartan for Sir Henry Raeburn.*

1411; and Alistair's successor, Angus, fought alongside John, 10th Lord, in a 1452 uprising. As a result the Keppoch estates were forfeited and some of their Lochaber lands were given to the Mackintoshes, provoking feuding.

When John, 4th Lord of Keppoch, handed over a clan member to the chief of clan Chattan in the 16th century, he was deposed and succeeded by his cousin Donald Glas. In 1663 the seven murderers of Alistair, 12th chief, were apprehended and beheaded and their heads were washed at a well near Inverary before being presented to Lord MacDonell of Inverary. Known as the Well of the Heads, the spot is now marked by a statue.

Colonel MacDonell, 15th chief, fought in the Jacobite army at Sheriffmuir in 1715. His son Alistair, 16th Lord of Keppoch, was one of the first on to the field for Bonnie Prince Charlie in 1746 at Culloden, where he was killed.

MacGREGOR

The defiant MacGregors never allowed their clan to die out, despite suffering terrible losses during clashes with neighbouring Campbells and later being outlawed by James VI.

The MacGregors claim royal descent from Gregor, brother of Kenneth MacAlpin, the 9th-century king of the Scots and Picts, and their Gaelic motto is "*S Rioghail Mo Dhream*" ("Royal is my race"). Some accounts mention a MacGregor chief named Malcolm who fought for Robert the Bruce at the battle of Bannockburn in 1314 and later alongside the Bruce's brother Edward

in Ireland, but most historians identify the first chief as the 14th-century Gregor of the Golden Bridles. His son Iain Camm ("Ian One-eye"), 2nd chief, died around 1390.

Iain's sons founded the family's main branches: Patrick was ancestor of the MacGregors of Glenorchy and Strathfillan, Ian Dhu founded the MacGregors of Glenstrae, while a third, unidentified son gave rise to the MacGregors of Brackley and Glengyle.

CLASHES WITH THE CAMPBELLS

By the time of Iain Camm, the MacGregors were under pressure from the neighbouring Campbells. In the first quarter of the 14th century Robert the Bruce rewarded the Campbells' support of his claim to the throne with the barony of Loch Awe, which included MacGregor territory. The Campbells moved in and built the Castle of Kilchurn at the north end of Loch Awe. During the 15th century, the MacGregors lost all their lands except those in Glenstrae, which they held from the earls of Argyll. As a result they were increasingly driven to live beyond the law, plundering their neighbours' territory.

When Iain the Black of Glenstrae died without a male heir in 1519, Eian MacGregor succeeded as chief, supported by the Campbells because he had married the daughter of Sir Colin Campbell of Glenorchy. Eian was succeeded by his son Alistair. When Alistair died in the mid-16th century Sir Colin Campbell, who had purchased the superiority of the Glenstrae estates, refused to accept Gregor Roy MacGregor as the new Glenstrae MacGregor chief. Driven to assert his right with the sword, Gregor Roy fought the Campbells' authority for a

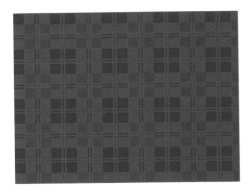

▲ *Some tartan authorities have traced this MacGregor sett back to 1750.*

▼ *This MacGregor is in the Cockburn Collection (c.1815) in Glasgow.*

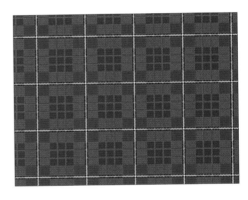

▲ *The MacGregor of Balquhidder was in Logan's* The Scottish Gael *(1831).*

▼ *The MacGregor of Glenstrae tartan also appeared in James Logan's book.*

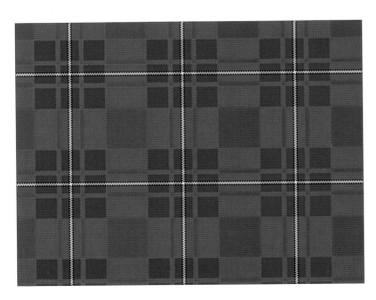

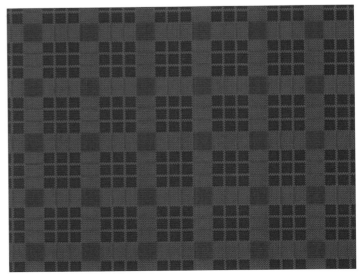

decade or more until he was captured and killed in 1570. His son Alistair took up the fight but the clan's defiance only provoked their enemies and the government to sterner reprisals.

A CLAN OUTLAWED AND HUNTED

In 1603 Alistair and his clansmen attacked and defeated the Colquhouns of Luss at Glenfruin by Loch Lomond. In response to this and other MacGregor raids, James VI outlawed the clan and banned the MacGregor name. MacGregors were also barred from carrying weapons and from meeting in groups of more than four at a time. The king's Privy Council gave the Earl of Argyll a warrant to hunt down MacGregors who violated these conditions with fire and sword. Many changed their names to Stewart, Graham, Drummond or even Campbell and dispersed across the Highlands to become, in the poet Sir Walter Scott's resonant phrase, "the children of the mist". The Earl of Argyll promised Alastair MacGregor safe passage to England but took him instead to Edinburgh, where he was hanged with the most loyal of his followers in January 1604.

Against all the odds the clan MacGregor survived. In 1644 a force of clansmen led by their chief Patrick MacGregor of Glenstrae enlisted with the Marquis of Montrose to fight in the Royalist cause. Following the Restoration of the monarchy in 1660, Charles II repealed the edicts outlawing the MacGregors, but these were re-imposed after William of Orange came to the throne as William III (r.1689–1702).

ROB ROY McGREGOR

In this period Rob Roy McGregor, son of Donald MacGregor of Glengyle and the daughter of William Campbell of Glenfalloch, began his notorious career as a cattle trader. After defaulting on

▲ *The Campbells built Kilchurn Castle on MacGregor lands in about 1420.*

debts and seeing his lands possessed by the Marquis of Montrose he became an outlaw and embarked on a long war of revenge against Montrose. In 1715 he joined the Earl of Mar's Jacobite army, but generally pursued his own interests. He died in 1734 and was buried in Balquhidder Church. He is celebrated in ballads and Sir Walter Scott's famous novel *Rob Roy* (1817).

A contingent of MacGregors fought in the Jacobite army for Bonnie Prince Charlie, taking part in the successful battle of Prestonpans in 1745 and his defeat at Culloden in 1746, after which they dispersed in the Highlands to avoid retribution.

OUTLAWS NO MORE

In 1774 the laws banning the MacGregor clan were finally repealed and clan members could again gather in numbers and use the name of their birth. John Murray of Lanrick, a general in the East India Company, was named as chief in a petition signed by more than 800 MacGregor clansmen. He was descended from John MacGregor of Glencarnock, who had changed his name to Murray under the name ban.

John Murray's son, Sir Evan MacGregor, succeeded him. During the visit of George IV to Scotland in 1822 Sir Evan proposed a toast to the king as "chief of chiefs" at an Edinburgh banquet. His descendants continue as clan MacGregor chiefs.

MACKENZIE

At the height of their power, early in the 17th century, the Mackenzies controlled territories that stretched right across northern Scotland, but their loyalty to the Stuart monarchs was to cost them dearly. Their fortunes never fully recovered from the destruction and bloodshed of the Jacobite era.

According to one tradition, the Mackenzies' ancestors were Irish settlers who came to Scotland in the 13th century. They fought in the service of Alexander III (r.1249–86) and were granted the territories of Kintail in Ross. Their Gaelic name – MacCoinneach ("son of the bright one") – may refer to Cernunnos, the Celtic god known as Lord of the Animals. Cernunnos is often shown with a stag's ears and antlers, and the shield of the Mackenzie chief shows the head of a stag.

In 1267 Kenneth Mackenzie and his clansmen were established around Loch Duich. They had blood links to the earls of Ross, being descended from a younger son of the Ross ancestor Gillean of the Aird. A 1362 charter of

▼ *The Mackenzie Bailey clan tartan was included in the Sobieskis'* Vestiarum Scoticum *(1842).*

▲ *A secret tunnel is said to run from beneath Dingwall Castle across the town of Dingwall to Tulloch Castle.*

David II confirmed the Mackenzies' rights to their Kintail possessions and described the Mackenzie chief Murdo as one of Gillean's descendants.

In the 15th century the MacDonald clan, self-styled Lords of the Isles, acquired the earldom of Ross through marriage. The Mackenzie lords supported the Scottish Crown in its struggles with the MacDonalds and other rebels and were rewarded for their loyalty with grants of land. The Mackenzies moved their clan seat eastward from Loch Duich to Kinellan, near Strathpeffer, and afterwards on to Brahan near Dingwall.

Kintail was made a barony in 1508. In 1513, Alasdair's grandson John led a Mackenzie force for James IV at Flodden and narrowly evaded capture. He and his men were also part of the 35,000-strong Scots army defeated by the English at the battle of Pinkie in 1547. His grandson, Colin, fought on the side of Mary, Queen of Scots, at the battle of Langside in 1568, after which defeat she fled to England. The following year Colin acknowledged her son James VI (r.1567–1625) as king and was pardoned.

Colin's son, Kenneth, was made Lord Mackenzie of Kintail in 1609. His son, also Colin, became Earl of Seaforth in 1623. His uncle Sir Rory Mackenzie married Margaret MacLeod, heiress of the MacLeods of Lewis, and was ancestor to the earls of Cromartie. He greatly extended an existing fortification near Strathpeffer to erect Castle Leod, now the clan Mackenzie seat.

▼ *This Mackenzie tartan had a military use – it was the one worn by the 72nd Seaforth Highlanders.*

Throughout the English Civil War and the Jacobite conflicts of the 17th and 18th centuries the Mackenzies supported the Stuarts, except at the very start when they moved against Montrose's Royalist army in 1644–45. This was because George, 2nd Earl of Seaforth, had signed the National Covenant in 1638, pledging to defend the Presbyterian Church. Following the execution of Charles I in 1649, however, Seaforth travelled to Holland to support the Prince of Wales's claim as Charles II.

Many Mackenzie clansmen fought with Charles at the battle of Worcester in 1651, which he lost to Oliver Cromwell. George Mackenzie's son, the 3rd Earl, fought on in Scotland but in January 1655 was forced to sign a treaty with Cromwell, whose army burned Mackenzie lands in Kintail, Loch Broom, Strathbran, Strathconan and Strathgarve.

In 1689 Kenneth Mackenzie, 4th Earl of Seaforth, joined the first Jacobite rebellion. He was jailed by William III, who also established a garrison at the Mackenzie clan seat of Brahan. On his release, Seaforth joined the exiled Stuart court in France, where he was made Marquis of Seaforth. His son William Mackenzie, 5th Earl, fought with his clansmen in the 1715 Jacobite rebellion and later, in 1719, at the battle of Glenshiel, where he was seriously injured by musket fire. His title was removed and his estates seized. George II's Government retributions – the burning of houses and lands – reduced many clansmen to extreme poverty, and William's son Kenneth did not lead his ravaged clan in the 1745 Jacobite rebellion. The Earl of Cromartie did fight, however, and lost his earldom as a result.

Kenneth's son, also Kenneth, bought the Mackenzie lands back from the Crown and in 1771 was restored to the earldom of Seaforth. Seven years later he raised 1000 clansmen to form the

72nd Regiment, Seaforth Highlanders, which fought in India, the Crimea, South Africa and Afghanistan. Colonel Francis Humberston Mackenzie raised the 78th Regiment, Seaforth Highlanders, which in 1881 was amalgamated with the 72nd. The Seaforth Highlanders later served with great distinction in both World Wars.

The Mackenzie tartan was designed for the use of the 72nd Regiment, Seaforth Highlanders.

The leadership of the clan passed to the earls of Cromartie, whose earldom was re-established in 1861. The current clan chief is John R. Mackenzie, 5th Earl of Cromartie.

NOTABLE MACKENZIES

In the latter part of the 18th century many Mackenzies travelled overseas. Alexander Mackenzie (1764–1820), a

▲ *A carved panel on the upper floor of Eilean Donan Castle preserves for posterity the names of its constables.*

fur trader-explorer, was the first European to encounter the Canadian waterway now known as the river Mackenzie. Another Alexander Mackenzie (1822–92), who emigrated to Canada in 1842, became leader of the Liberal Party from 1873 until 1880, and was Prime Minister of Canada (1873–78). Edinburgh lawyer and novelist Henry Mackenzie (1745–1831) wrote the influential book *The Man of Feeling* (1771). The novelist Compton Mackenzie (1883–1972) was the author of the fondly remembered *Whisky Galore* (1947); his earlier two-volume work, *Sinister Street* (1913–14), was an acknowledged influence on F. Scott Fitzgerald.

MacLEOD

For almost 800 years MacLeod chiefs have resided in Dunvegan Castle on the Isle of Skye. According to legend, a MacLeod ancestor wed a fairy princess here and fairy magic is available to MacLeods in their hour of need.

The MacLeod name comes from Leod, son of Olaf the Black (d.c. 1237), one of the last of the Norse kings of the Isle of Man and the North Isles. Having inherited Lewis and Harris and part of Skye, Leod increased his territories on Skye. He gained possession of Dunvegan Castle, still the chief's seat, by marrying the daughter and heir of Macrailt, the island's Norse steward.

The clan's two main branches are descended from Leod's sons. Tormod, the eldest son, founded the MacLeods of Harris and Dunvegan, also known

▼ *Dunvegan Castle, home to MacLeod lords for 800 years, is Britain's oldest continuously inhabited castle.*

as Siol Tormod ("race of Tormod"), whose chiefs carry the title MacLeod of MacLeod. Torquil founded the MacLeods of Lewis and Raasay, also known as Siol Torquil.

THE FAIRY FLAG

So handsome was Ian, 4th chief of the MacLeods of MacLeod, and so noble his bearing, he could have had the pick of any maiden for his wife. But no one attracted him until one day he was captivated by the beauty of a fairy princess. She fell in love with him, and despite the fact that he would die while she would live forever, she begged her father, the king of the fairies, for permission to marry. Reluctantly he agreed that she could spend a year and a day with Ian but must then return to her own folk.

The couple were married at Dunvegan Castle and lived happily for a year, during which she bore a bonny

baby boy. Before she left, the fairy princess made Ian promise never to leave their son alone or to allow him to cry, for the sound of his wails would cause her great suffering. One day the clan folk, wanting to cheer up their grief-stricken chief, persuaded him to dance some reels. When the nurse was tempted away to watch, the baby started to cry. Hearing his cries the fairy princess went to comfort him, wrapping her shawl around him before returning to her father's realm.

When the baby became a young man he told his father of his mother's visit. He also told him that if the clan were in danger, the chief should wave the shawl three times to summon the fairy army. The magic could be summoned three times only. MacLeod of MacLeod fixed the shawl to a staff like a flag, and twice since that day the chief has waved the Fairy Flag. When his clansmen were under attack and

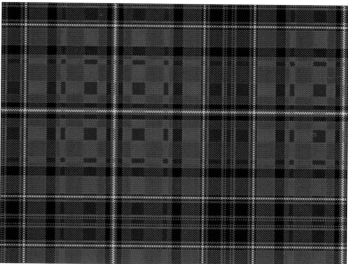

▲ *This tartan is derived from one worn by the MacLeod chief in the late 1700s.*

▼ *The MacLeod of Lewis tartan is in the* Vestiarum Scoticum *(1842).*

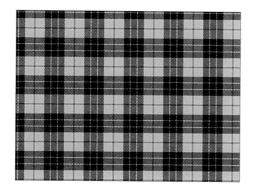

greatly outnumbered by MacDonalds the fairy magic made his army appear to swell in size, causing the MacDonalds to flee. On the second occasion the magic revived dead and dying cattle to feed MacLeod clansmen through a desperate winter. During the Second World War MacLeod of MacLeod was prepared to wave the Fairy Flag on the cliffs of Dover to repel a German sea invasion. The Flag is kept on display in Dunvegan Castle.

THE HUNCHBACK CHIEF

Alasdair Crotach ("Hunchback"), 8th MacLeod chief of Harris and Dunvegan, did a great deal to consolidate the clan's position. In 1542

he won legal possession of Trotternish, ending a long dispute with the MacDonalds of Sleat. He also built the celebrated Fairy Tower at Dunvegan Castle. He is said to have married the tenth daughter of the chief of clan Cameron after the first nine had refused him because of his deformed back. He rebuilt the 15th-century Church of St Clement at Rodel in Harris and was buried there in a magnificent wall-tomb.

Rory Mor, 16th chief, ended a long-running feud with the MacDonalds, extended Dunvegan Castle and was knighted by James VI (James I of England) in 1603. A medieval drinking horn named in Rory's honour is kept at Dunvegan Castle and each new clan chief is required to drink its contents – it holds a bottle and a half of claret – in one draught.

MACKENZIE LORDS

When Torquil MacLeod of Lewis died in 1597, possession of Lewis and the chiefship of this branch of the clan passed to his son-in-law Sir Rory Mackenzie of Cogeach. Sir Rory's descendants were the earls of Cromartie, who carried Lord MacLeod as a second title. Sir Rory's castle at Strathpeffer, now the seat of clan Mackenzie, bears the name Castle Leod. In 1777 Lord MacLeod, son of

▲ *In 1982 the MacLeod Red tartan was approved as the official clan sett.*

▼ *The MacLeod of Raasay tartan dates from the early 19th century.*

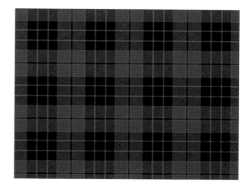

the Earl of Cromartie, raised the 73rd MacLeod's Highlanders, which saw service in India, and a regimental tartan was designed at this time.

After 1597 the male representatives of Tiol Torquil were the MacLeods of Raasay, who were descended from the 10th chief of Lewis. In 1988 their descendant Torquil Roderick MacLeod of Raasay was confirmed as chief of the MacLeod of Lewis branch, under MacLeod of MacLeod. He died in March 2001 and was succeeded by his son Torquil Donald as chief of the MacLeods of Lewis. The current chief of the main branch of the clan is John MacLeod of MacLeod, 29th chief, who lives in Dunvegan Castle.

MURRAY

In a proud history spanning more than 800 years, clan Murray provided leading figures in the Scottish struggle for independence and the Jacobite rebellions. Today the clan chief possesses, in the Atholl Highlanders, the only private army in the country.

The Murray name comes from the Pictish kingdom of Moireabh, or Moray. The clan's 12th-century ancestor is said to have been Freskin, who was granted the Moireabh territory by David I (r.1124–53); he may either have been a Flemish knight or a Pictish noble who won favour with David. His castle was at Duffus.

By the time of Freskin's grandson William the family was known as de Moravia. William de Moravia was Sheriff of Invernairn and two of his sons gave rise to the Murrays of Bothwell and the Murrays of Abercairny. In 1282 another son, also William, married Ada, the daughter of Malise, the Steward of Strathearn, and gained the lands of Tullibardine. He founded the house of Murray of Tullibardine, whose descendants became earls of Atholl.

▲ *The hilltop ruins of the former Murray stronghold at Duffus once supported a substantial stone tower.*

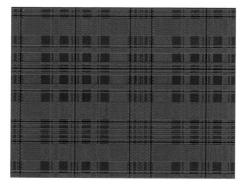

▲ *The Murray of Tullibardine clan tartan has been dated to at least 1794.*

MURRAYS OF BOTHWELL

The lords of Bothwell held positions of great significance in the 13th and 14th centuries. In 1255 Sir Walter Murray, Lord of Bothwell, was Regent of Scotland. His descendant Andrew was Governor of Scotland with William Wallace but died after the battle of Stirling Bridge in 1297. Andrew's son, 4th Lord, was Regent of Scotland in 1332. When Thomas Murray, 5th Lord, died in 1360, the Bothwell estates and name went to his son-in-law Archibald the Grim, 3rd Earl of Douglas.

▼ *The Murray of Atholl clan tartan is also known as the Atholl district sett.*

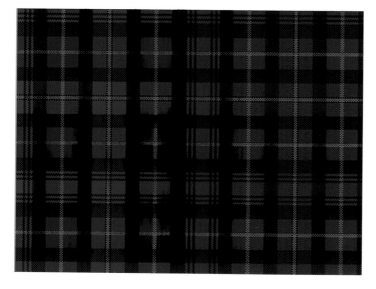

▼ *This sett is based on a tartan worn by a Murray in a portrait of 1670.*

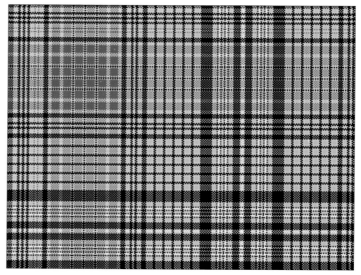

MURRAYS OF TULLIBARDINE

The possessions of this branch of the family were made a barony in 1443, in the time of Sir David Murray, 7th Lord of Tullibardine. His son was Sheriff of Perth and Keeper of Doune Castle. His descendant Sir John, 12th Lord, was a member of James VI's Privy Council; he was made Lord Murray in 1604 and Earl of Tullibardine in 1606. Sir John's son William, 2nd Earl, was made hereditary Sheriff of Perthshire. When he married Dorothea Stewart, daughter and heiress of John, 5th Earl of Atholl, he acquired the title and estates for his family.

A staunch Royalist during the Civil War, John, 2nd Murray Earl of Atholl, raised 1800 Murray men to fight under the Marquis of Montrose in 1644. In 1653 more than 2000 Murray men supported the Earl of Glencairn's Royalist army. The Cromwellian army captured Blair Castle, seat of the Murray earls of Atholl, in 1652 and held it for eight years. Following the Restoration of the monarchy, John was made Marquis of Atholl in 1676. He married Amelia Sophia Stanley, daughter of James, Earl of Stanley, a descendant of the Prince of Orange.

A CLAN DIVIDED

In 1703 the 2nd Marquis of Atholl was made Duke of Atholl. Because of his mother's connections he supported William of Orange, but his sons were

▼ *John Murray, 7th Duke of Atholl, rebuilt Blair Castle in 1869.*

ATHOLL HIGHLANDERS

Four Atholl regiments, totalling 1400 men, fought in the 1745 Jacobite rebellion. In 1777 Colonel James Murray raised the 1000-strong 77th Regiment of Foot, Atholl Highlanders, to serve in the War of American Independence. The war ended before they embarked so they were re-routed to Ireland. In 1842 Lord Glenlyon, later 6th Duke of Atholl, formed a 100-strong bodyguard for Queen Victoria when she visited Blair Castle. The Highlanders formed her permanent bodyguard two years later, and she arranged for the regiment to have its colours presented, making it the only private army in the country. Men of the Atholl Highlanders fought with the Scottish Horse Regiment in both World Wars.

▼ *The Duke of Atholl inspects the troops of the Atholl Highlanders.*

prominent in the Jacobite cause. William, Marquis of Tullibardine, fought for the Earl of Mar in the 1715 rebellion and in the Jacobite defeat at Glenshiel in 1719. He fled into exile but returned with Bonnie Prince Charlie. He signalled the start of the 1745 rebellion by unfurling the Prince's standard at Glenshiel. He sheltered the Prince at Blair Castle and fought for him at Culloden in 1746. William was captured at Loch Lomond and died in the Tower of London. Charles fought in the 1715 rebellion and another son, Lord George Murray, who also fought at Glenshiel, escaped to Holland where he died in 1760.

James, 2nd Duke of Atholl, inherited the titles of Baron of Strange and King of the Isle of Man through his mother. In 1765 the Government purchased the lordship of the Isle of Man for a kingly sum from John, 3rd Duke of Atholl. In 1828 the 4th Duke sold the family's remaining privileges and lands in the Isle of Man.

MURRAYS OF BALVAIRD AND STORMONT

This branch of the clan is descended from Patrick, a son of Sir David Murray, 6th Lord of Tullibardine. His descendants, the earls of Mansfield, built Scone Palace.

ROBERTSON

The Robertsons are known for their bravery in battle and love of the pipes and music. Alexander, their colourful chief at the time of the Jacobite rebellions, was the inspiration for one of Sir Walter Scott's literary characters.

The clan can trace its lineage back to Crinan, the 11th-century Lord of Atholl, who married a princess, the daughter of Malcolm II, and fathered a king, Duncan I. The clan's Gaelic name Clan Donnachaidh (pronounced "Donnakey"), or "sons of Duncan", refers to their chief Duncan, 5th Lord

▼ *The Robertson of Kindeace tartan, also known as the Hunting Robertson, is similar to the Murray of Atholl sett.*

of Glenorchie. Duncan led the clan in support of Robert the Bruce's struggle for Scottish independence and fought at the battle of Bannockburn in 1314.

The Robertson motto, "Glory is the reward of valour", could not be more apt, for the clan won enduring fame in 1437 when chief Robert Riabhach ("the Grizzled") tracked down and captured the murderers of James I of Scotland (r.1406–37); Sir Robert Graham and his conspirators were executed. Robert Riabhach's lands in Struan were made into a barony and the clan takes its name from him.

In 1636 the 11th Lord of Struan was succeeded by his infant grandson Alexander, whose uncle Donald, the

Tutor of Struan, took charge of the clan and raised a regiment of Robertsons to fight for the Royalist cause under the Marquis of Montrose in 1644–45. Alexander married twice and his second wife bore him two sons. The younger one, Donald, sought his fortune abroad and won great renown fighting under Peter the Great of Russia (r.1682–1725). The elder son, Alexander, studied to become a priest but succeeded as clan chief when both his father and his elder half-brother died in 1688.

▼ *The Robertson of Struan clan tartan was added to the collection of the Highland Society of London in c.1815.*

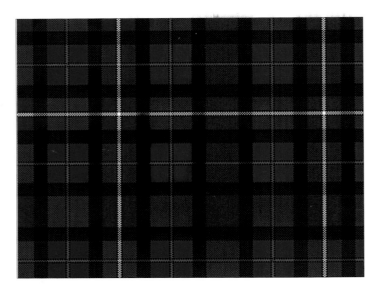

▼ *James Logan printed this Robertson tartan in* The Scottish Gael *(1831).*

▼ *This version of Robertson was produced by Wilson's of Bannockburn.*

▼ *This Robertson tartan is said to date to the era of the Jacobite rebellions.*

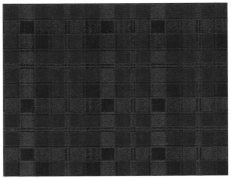

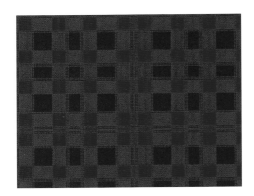

THE CLACH NA BRATACH

According to clan tradition, Duncan, 5th Lord of Glenorchie, dislodged a piece of rock crystal when he pulled his standard from the ground while on campaign. The remarkable stone, named the Clach na Bratach ("stone of colours"), changed and mingled colours when held up to the light. It was set in silver and kept safely by the clan chief, for it was believed to have magical powers to cure sickness in animals and humans. Whenever its power was required the chief washed it three times in spring water, which absorbed the curative properties. The stone was always carried into battle and tradition has it that on the eve of the battle of Sheriffmuir in 1715 it revealed a large flaw at its centre. If only this had been interpreted as a bad omen, the Jacobite forces might have withdrawn and been spared the defeat that cost so many Highlanders' lives. The stone is kept in the Robertson clan museum at Bruar Falls near Blair Atholl.

▼ *The Robertson clan has its own crystal ball in the Clach na Bratach.*

SUPPORTING THE JACOBITE CAUSE

Alexander was to win fame as "the poet-chief" and as a staunch Jacobite. On succeeding as chief he immediately followed Bonnie Dundee into the field in the cause of the exiled James II in 1689, but lost his title and estates when the uprising failed. Alexander went into exile in France with James II but returned to Scotland when Queen Anne granted an amnesty in 1703. In the 1715 rebellion he led 500 clansmen into battle under the Jacobite standard and was captured at Sheriffmuir. He escaped once again to France but returned when another amnesty was granted.

In the 1745 rebellion around 700 of his clan joined Bonnie Prince Charlie's cause, fighting in the Atholl Brigade, but Alexander, now aged around 75, was too old to fight. He died on 18 April 1749, without a lawful heir, after which a book of his poetry was published. He is said to have been the model for the Baron of Bradwardine in Scott's novel *Waverley* (1814).

In 1784 the barony and estate of Struan were restored to Colonel Alexander Robertson, a descendant of Duncan Mor, brother of the Tutor of Struan. George, the 18th chief, sold the barony in 1854. For some years after this the clan chiefs lived on their estates in Kingston, Jamaica, but subsequently settled in England where the current chief, Alexander Gilbert Haldane Robertson of Struan, lives.

MEN OF MUSIC AND LETTERS

Clan Robertson had a special connection to pipers and military music. According to clan legend, the well-known tune *The Lord of Struan's Salute*, also known as *The Coming of the Robertsons*, was passed down from the 14th century, when it was played as the clansmen marched to Bannockburn. General John Reid, a member of the Robertsons of Straloch, wrote the music for *The Garb of Old Gaul*, which became the Scots Guards' regimental slow march. On his death in 1807 he left money to endow the Chair of Music at Edinburgh University.

The celebrated Scottish historian William Robertson (1721–93), the author of *History of Scotland 1542–1603* (1759) and *History of Charles V* (1769), was Principal of Edinburgh University in the 1760s.

▼ *The Scots Guards march to the tune of a Robertson man, General John Reid.*

SCOTT

The Scotts rose to power in the volatile, often violent region of the English–Scottish Borders, where they proved themselves fierce raiders in clashes with neighbouring clans. Before going raiding or into battle they rallied at Bellendaine, a hill in the centre of their territory, and the cry "A Bellendaine" ("To Bellendaine") meant battle was close.

The Scotts' name is probably derived from that of the Scotti, a Celtic tribe from northern Ireland that settled in Argyllshire in the middle of the first millennium AD and founded the kingdom of Dalriada. The oldest documented ancestor, Uchtredus filius Scoti (Uchtred, the Scot's son), was named as a witness in the charter recording the foundation of Selkirk in 1120. The principal branches of the clan are descended from his sons: Richard founded the Scotts of Buccleuch, while Sir Michael founded the Scotts of Balweary.

Richard's descendant Sir Richard Scott married the heiress of the Lord of Murthockstone. He was ranger of

▲ *In the early 19th century the Scotts inherited Drumlanrig Castle, built in 1691 by the 1st Duke of Queensberry.*

▼ *Bowhill, near Selkirk, was dubbed "Sweet Bowhill" by Sir Walter Scott in* The Lay of the Last Minstrel.

Ettrick Forest and built a castle at Buccleuch. His son Sir Michael Scott, 2nd Lord of Buccleuch, supported Robert the Bruce's fight for an independent Scotland and fought valiantly in the face of crushing defeat at the battle of Halidon Hill in 1333. On a day when thousands of foot soldiers, 500 knights and 70 barons met their deaths, he was one of the few lords to survive. He was killed in battle at Durham in 1346.

Over the following 250 years the Scotts acquired many Border territories, and by the mid-15th century they were already established as one of the foremost clans of the area.

In 1606 Sir Michael's direct descendant Sir Walter Scott was created Lord Scott of Buccleuch and his son, another Walter, was made Earl of Buccleuch in 1619. His granddaughter Anne became Countess of Buccleuch following the untimely deaths of her father and elder sister. She married Charles II's illegitimate son James, Duke of Monmouth, in 1663 and the couple were made Duke and Duchess of Buccleuch on their wedding day. Monmouth attempted to raise a Protestant revolt against the Catholic regime of his uncle James VII (James II of England) but was defeated at the battle of Sedgemoor in 1685 and beheaded in the same year. As Anne had been created a duchess in her own right she

retained her title when her husband's was forfeited, and the lands and dukedom were inherited by her grandson Francis, 2nd Duke of Buccleuch. In 1810 the 3rd Duke inherited the title of Duke of Queensberry together with Drumlanrig Castle, both formerly possessions of the Douglas clan. The line continues to the present chief of clan Scott, John Montagu Douglas Scott, 9th Duke of Buccleuch and 11th Duke of Queensberry.

SCOTTS OF BALWEARY

In the late 12th and early 13th century Michael Scott of Balweary, great-grandson of Uchtred, was famous throughout Europe for his learning as a physician and mathematician. Reputed to be skilled in magic and the mysteries of astrology, he was also known as "the Wizard": it was said to be his magic that split the Eildon Hills in three places. He died in 1234. Following the accidental death of Alexander III (r.1249–86) another Sir Michael Scott of Balweary was sent to Norway to fetch the late king's granddaughter, Margaret, to the throne.

The line of the Scotts of Balweary finished in 1902 on the death of Sir William Scott, 7th Baronet of Ancrum.

▼ *The Scott Border clan tartan is very similar to Sir Walter Scott's sett.*

POET OF HIGHLAND TRADITIONS

The most celebrated Scott is without doubt the novelist, poet and historian Sir Walter Scott (1771–1832), 1st Baronet of Abbotsford. He was descended in the line of the Hepburne-Scotts from Walter Scott of Harden, a notorious cattle rustler of the 17th century. Another of Sir Walter's ancestors was William Scott of Harden, who after a botched cattle raid was forced to choose between the gallows and marriage to Agnes Murray of Elibank. This lady, known as Muckle-Mouthed Meg, had not managed to find a husband due to her rough looks.

Born and educated in Edinburgh, Sir Walter Scott drew great inspiration from the landscape, ballads and narratives of his clan's Border territories and

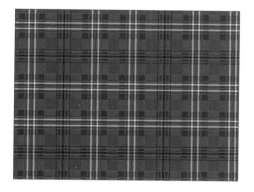

▲ *The Red Scott is probably the most popular tartan among clan members.*

▲ *Sir Walter Scott began work as an apprentice in his father's law office.*

did much to foster interest in the Highland clans' tartans and way of life. He began his literary career as a poet but moved on to writing historical novels, of which the first was *Waverley* (1814). He also wrote a history of Scotland from the Roman era to 1745 for his grandson, published under the title *The Tales of a Grandfather* (1827–29). A great number of the many Scott tartans in existence are associated with Sir Walter Scott.

▼ *This tartan, the Scott Green, was designed by Sir Walter Scott.*

STEWART

Clan Stewart rose to become the royal house of Stewart (or Stuart): rulers of Scotland and England in whose support many Scots fought and died during the 17th and 18th centuries. More than 50 tartans have been used by or made in honour of this great Celtic family.

The Stewarts' ancestor was Alan, a Celtic nobleman who was Seneschal (steward) of Dol in Britanny. His nephew Fitz-Flaald came to England with Henry I, William the Conqueror's son, and was appointed Sheriff of Shropshire. Fitz-Flaald's son Walter came to Scotland when David I returned home to become king in 1124. Walter was granted lands in East Lothian and Renfrewshire and became Steward of Scotland, a position Malcolm IV made hereditary for his descendants in 1157. The clan takes its name from the word "steward".

Walter, 6th High Steward, led part of Robert the Bruce's army at the battle of Bannockburn in 1314 and married the Bruce's daughter Marjory. Their son became Robert II (r.1371–90) on the death of his uncle David II (r.1329–71). He was the first of the line of Stewarts who occupied the Scottish and then the English throne from Robert II to Queen Anne.

The variant Stuart spelling of the family name was used in France, where Mary, Queen of Scots, lived for two years following her marriage to the Dauphin in 1558. After her return to Scotland, it was used as an alternative to the Scottish spelling.

In addition to the royal house of Stewart, other branches of the family also rose to prominence in the Highlands. Among these were the Stewarts of Appin and the Stewarts of Atholl, both branches preferring the original spelling of the name.

STEWARTS OF APPIN

The Stewarts of Appin were descended from Sir James Stewart of Pierston, grandson of the 4th High Steward, who was killed alongside thousands of his countrymen at the battle of Halidon Hill in 1333. His grandson Sir John Stewart of Innermeath married the daughter and co-heiress of the Lord of Lorne so their son Robert became Lord of Lorne and Innermeath. Robert's grandson, 1st Lord of Appin, was succeeded by Duncan, 2nd Lord of Appin, who was appointed Chamberlain of the Isles by James IV.

The Stewarts of Appin fought in the cause of their royal kinsmen during the Civil War and the Jacobite rebellions. In 1645 Duncan Stewart, 7th Lord of Appin, led Stewarts in the Royalist army of the Marquis of Montrose at Inverlochy and elsewhere. His lands and title were forfeited by the Cromwellian Government after the defeat of the Royalist cause, but were returned following the Restoration of the monarchy in 1660. In the 1715 Jacobite rebellion Robert Stewart, 8th chief, led 400 Appin clansmen in support of the Old Pretender in his unsuccessful claim to the British throne. Thirty years later 300 Appin men fought for his son, the Young Pretender (Bonnie Prince Charlie), in his equally unsuccessful bid for the British throne.

The Appin Stewarts were long-term enemies of the Campbells so when Colin Roy Campbell was killed in Appin in 1752 his clan demanded revenge. James Stewart of the Glens was hanged for the murder but was widely believed to be innocent. He was the last person to die in the Highlands as a result of a clan feud. Dugald, 9th chief of this branch, sold off the Appin estates in 1765.

▼ *James Charles Stuart acceded to the Scottish throne aged 13 months; at 37, he became King James I of England.*

ROYAL HOUSE OF STEWART
Robert II (r.1371–90)
Robert III (r.1390–1406)
James I (r.1406–37)
James II (r.1437–60)
James III (r.1460–88)
James IV (r.1488–1513)
James V (r.1513–42)
Mary, Queen of Scots (r.1542–67)
James VI of Scotland (r.1567–1625)
  and James I of England
  (r.1603–25)
Charles I (r.1625–49)
Charles II (r.1660–85)
James VII and James II of England
  (r.1685–88)
William and Mary (r.1689–94)
Anne (r.1702–14)

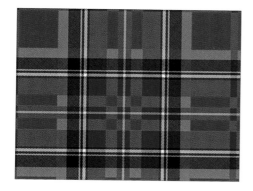

▲ *The Stewart of Galloway tartan was produced by Wilson's of Bannockburn.*

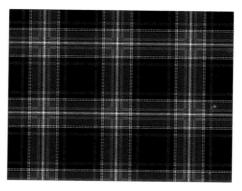

▲ *This variant is known as the Stewart black ground clan tartan.*

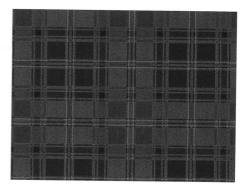

▲ *The Stewart of Appin tartan is similar to that of clan MacColl.*

▲ *The Stewart of Atholl tartan was reproduced by D.W. Stewart in his* Old and Rare Scottish Tartans *(1893).*

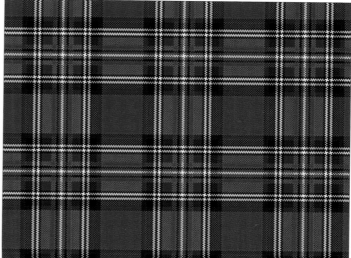

▲ *The Royal Stewart tartan was first published by James Logan in his book* The Scottish Gael *of 1831.*

STEWARTS OF ATHOLL

This branch of the family is descended from Alexander Stewart, Earl of Buchan and fourth son of Robert II. In a dispute with the Bishop of Moray he burned down the cathedral of Elgin and town of Forres, earning himself the nickname the Wolf of Badenoch. One of his illegitimate sons, James Stewart, built a castle at Garth in the late 14th century. The line descended down to General David Stewart of Garth, an officer in the 42nd Regiment, popularly known as the Black Watch. He published *Sketches of the Character, Manners, and Present State of the Highlanders of Scotland, with details of the Military services of the Highland Regiments* (1822), a two-volume work that proved very popular in England.

The Stewarts of Atholl could call 1000 men into the field and were renowned for their opposition to the royal houses of Orange and Hanover. As many as 1500 Atholl men fought under Bonnie Dundee in the 1689 Jacobite uprising, while in 1746 the Atholl Stewarts were again out in force at Culloden, alongside the Camerons in the Jacobite army's right wing.

STEWART TARTANS

The clan tartan is a dark design known as Stewart Ancient. The Stewarts of Atholl and the Stewarts of Appin each have their own tartan. The Stewart of Atholl tartan is derived from a tartan worn by the Stewart men of Atholl at the battle of Culloden. The green Hunting Stewart is distinguished by an asymmetrical pattern. It may once have been a general tartan worn by huntsmen of any family rather than one specific to the Stewart clan.

The best known of the Stewart tartans is the Royal Stewart. Dating from about 1800, it is worn by the regimental pipers of the Scots Guards and is often referred to simply as the Royal Tartan. George IV wore it on his state visit to Edinburgh in 1822, and it is the personal tartan of Elizabeth II. Just as clansmen can wear their chief's tartan, so any subject of the Queen has the right to wear the Royal Stewart sett.

FAMILIES AND ASSOCIATED CLANS

MANY OF THE SMALLER CLANS AND FAMILIES MADE A MAJOR CONTRIBUTION TO THE DEVELOPMENT OF THE SCOTTISH NATION. TODAY, MEMBERS OF THESE FAMILIES HONOUR THEIR RENOWNED ANCESTORS BY WEARING CLAN COLOURS WITH PRIDE.

ABERCROMBIE–ARBUTHNOTT

The Abercrombie tartan was one of the 55 designs listed by James Logan in his 1831 collection, *The Scottish Gael*. The Anderson tartan survives in many variant forms that ring subtle changes on its distinguished pattern.

ABERCROMBIE

The family's name derives from the parish of Abercrombie, in Fife. An early ancestor, William de Abercromby, paid homage to England's Edward I in 1296. When William's line ended in the 17th century, the chiefship transferred to the Abercrombies of Birkenbog, Banffshire.

Alexander Abercromby of Birkenbog was made Baronet of Nova Scotia in 1637. His kinsman Sir Ralph Abercromby, a celebrated military figure of the 18th century, fought in both the Seven Years War and the War with Revolutionary France. He was mortally wounded in 1801 while leading the Royal Highlanders against Napoleon Bonaparte's army in Egypt. His widow was made Baroness Abercromby of Aboukir and Tullibody, while his brother Robert commanded the British Army in India and served as Governor of Bombay. On his return to Scotland Robert was made Governor of Edinburgh Castle in 1801.

Previous pages: Ben Loyal.

▼ *Wilson's of Bannockburn listed the Abercrombie tartan from 1819.*

AGNEW

The Agnews may be descended from Norman knights who arrived in England in 1066 and found their way, via Ireland, to Lowland Scotland in the 12th century, their name deriving from the d'Agneaux barony in France. In 1190 William des Aigneau witnessed a charter of Ranulf de Soulis for Jedburgh Abbey. An alternative theory is that the Agnews' ancestors were the Ulster O'Gnimh family, who were bards to the powerful O'Neils of Antrim. If accurate, this would give the Agnews common ancestry with the Scottish MacDonald and MacDonell clans through Somerled, the 12th-century King of the Isles.

The first prominent clan members were the Lochnaw Agnews, hereditary sheriffs of Galloway from 1363. Andrew Agnew was made Constable of Lochnaw in 1426 and hereditary sheriff of Wigtown in 1451. Sir Patrick Agnew, 7th Sheriff of Wigtown, was made a Baronet of Nova Scotia in 1629. In the 1745 Jacobite rebellion Sir Andrew Agnew, 5th baronet, fought on the Hanoverian side, defending Blair Castle for almost a fortnight with a garrison of 270 against a much larger force. The Agnews' ancestral castle, mostly dating from the 16th century, stands beside the waters of Lochnaw.

▼ *The Agnews may have Irish origins; many settled in Ulster after 1600.*

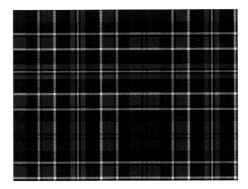

▲ *The motto of the Allison family is Vincit veritas – "Truth conquers".*

ALLISON

A branch of the MacDonald or MacAlister clans, the Allison name may derive from "son of Alice", "son of Ellis" or "son of Alister"; in documents it is also found as Allinson and Ellison. It first appeared in Scotland in the mid-13th century – more than a hundred years before Alison was used as a woman's first name – in the region of Loch Laggan, Glen Spean. In 1296 Patrick Alissone of Berwick signed the oath of allegiance to Edward I of England. In some accounts the clan is descended from the sons of Alexander MacAlister of Loup (Argyllshire), who settled in Lanarkshire under the name Allison at the time of Robert the Bruce (r.1306–29). Among documented clan members are Peter Alesoun, witness to a 1490 legal document in Brechin, and James Allasone, an official in Renfrew in 1688.

ANDERSON

The Anglicized form of "son of Andrew", referring to Scotland's patron saint, was used in Lowland Scotland, while MacAndrew was more common in the Highlands, and the MacAndrews were members of clan Chattan.

Andersons were established in Dowhill from 1540, and their cousins were known in Banffshire and

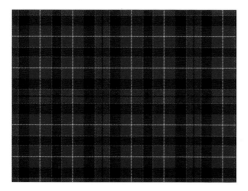

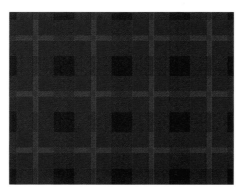

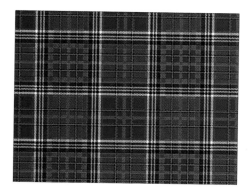

▲ *The elegant Anderson tartan dates back at least to the early 19th century.*

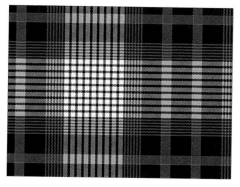

▲ *The Angus tartan can be worn by anyone linked to the Angus region.*

▲ *The Arbuthnott tartan, registered in 1962, is based on the Black Watch sett.*

Strathdon. In 1670 Iain beag MacAindrea despatched with arrows an entire party of cattle rustlers led by MacDonell of Achluachrach. The historian and antiquary James Anderson (1662–1728) made an important collection of Scottish seals and documents of historical interest. John Anderson (1726–96), professor of Oriental Languages and Natural Philosophy at Glasgow University, erected the city's first lightning conductor. Elizabeth Garrett Anderson (1836–1917), Britain's first licensed female doctor in 1865, helped found the London School of Medicine and was elected the country's first woman mayor in 1908.

ANGUS

This family's tartan is associated with the Angus region of eastern Scotland, which in the 9th century was controlled by the Scots – Gaelic-speaking immigrants from Ireland who had founded the kingdom of Dalriada in western Scotland. Members of clan Angus traditionally claim descent from Oenghus, one of Dalriada's founders. The first recorded Earl of Angus was Gilchrist. According to one account, he married the sister of William I (r.1165–1214), but had her killed for adultery. The king banished him, but he was later pardoned and restored to his earldom. Gilchrist's son Gilibrede, 2nd Earl, fought alongside David I at the Battle of the Standard in 1138. The earldom of Angus was later bestowed on members of the Stewart and Douglas clans.

ARBUTHNOTT

The name Arbuthnott comes from the family's home in Kincardineshire. In about 1175 William I granted lands there to Osbert Olifard, who died on the Third Crusade (1189–92). His heir and brother Walter granted the lands to Hugh de Swinton, whose son Duncan took the name Arbuthnott. A local legend about Duncan's grandson, Hugh le Blond, who killed a dragon to save the queen's life, is the source of a ballad by Sir Walter Scott. In 1420 Hugh Arbuthnott began building a castle that was finished by his grandson Robert. In the English Civil War Sir Robert Arbuthnott sided with the Covenanters, and this resulted in the family estate being ravaged by Royalist troops in 1645. Over the years the lords of Arbuthnott transformed the 15th-century castle into the Georgian-fronted house that graces the clan's ancestral lands today.

▼ *On the eastern coast between the Dee and the Tay, the proud region of Angus was fiercely independent.*

ARMSTRONG–BORTHWICK

The Armstrongs, Baillies and Baxters may all take their name from the occupations or by-names of their distant ancestors, while – according to one theory – the members of Clan Baird are descended from poets (bards).

ARMSTRONG

This once fierce Borders tribe is said to be descended from Siward Digry ("sword strongarm"), an 11th-century Anglo-Danish nobleman, and the family motto is *Invictus maneo* ("I remain unbeaten"). In the 16th century the Armstrong chief could call on 3000 mounted warriors: seeing the clan as a threat, James V moved against them, ambushing and hanging John Armstrong of Gilnockie in 1530. In the 17th century the last Armstrong lord was hanged for cattle rustling and the family spread out from the Borders. At least two Armstrongs became intrepid adventurers: Sir Alexander Armstrong (1818–99) explored the Arctic and US astronaut Neil Armstrong (b.1930) took their tartan to the moon in 1969.

BAILLIE

The clan name may have come from the title "baillie", which was given to royal officers. Alternatively, it may derive from John Balliol (r.1292–96), many of whose kinsmen changed their

name to Baillie after his abdication. In 1358 Sir William Baillie was confirmed as owner of the Lamington lands in Lanarkshire. His brother Alexander was Constable of Inverness Castle. Notable descendants of the clan include Robert Baillie of Jerviswood, a Presbyterian who was found guilty of treason against Charles II and hanged on 24 December 1684 in Edinburgh.

A tartan was made by Wilson's of Bannockburn for the Baillie Fencibles, one of several regiments raised in the late 18th century to defend the realm against a possible French invasion.

▲ Inverness Castle was built in 1835 on the site of the earlier fortress once commanded by Alexander Baillie.

BAIRD

According to legend, the founder of the Baird clan was rewarded with lands and royal favour when he saved William I (r.1165–1214) from a wild boar. The Bairds seem to have taken their name from land in Lanarkshire where they settled, although some histories suggest they are named after Le Seigneur de Barde, a Norman knight in William the Conqueror's company. In 1178 Henry

▼ The Armstrongs claim descent from the Scottish monarch's armour-bearers.

▼ The Baillie Fencibles regiment, which wore this tartan, disbanded in 1802.

▼ The design of the Baird tartan was recorded for the first time in 1906.

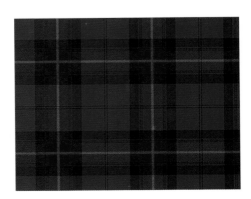
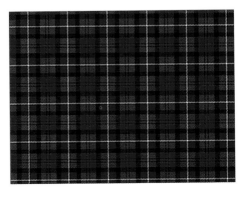
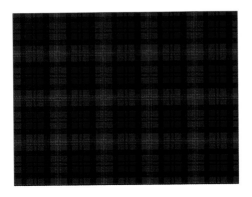

de Barde witnessed the king's charter concerning lands in Stirling. During the reign of Alexander III (1249–86) Richard Baird held lands at Meikle and Little Kyp, Lanarkshire, and early in the 14th century Robert Baird was granted the barony of Cambusnethan by Robert the Bruce.

The Bairds of Cambusnethan moved to Aberdeenshire and held lands at Auchmedden. Several Auchmedden Bairds were sheriffs of Aberdeen. An illustrious member of this branch was Sir David Baird (1757–1829), a leading general in the Napoleonic Wars, who defeated the Dutch to take the Cape of Good Hope in 1807. In 1926 John Logie Baird (1888–1946) pioneered television.

BARCLAY

The Barclays are descended from Roger de Berchelai, a Norman knight who came to England in the company of William the Conqueror and was granted lands in Gloucestershire. The name is said to be an Anglo-Saxon rendering of the French *beau* ("beautiful") and *lie* ("meadow"). The family became established in Scotland when Roger's son, John, was granted lands in Towie, Aberdeenshire, by Malcolm III (r.1058–93).

Many Barclays rose to positions of note. Sir Walter de Berkeley was Great Chamberlain of Scotland (1165–89). Colonel David Barclay of Urie, near

Stonehaven, converted to the Society of Friends (Quakers) and his son, Robert, published *Apology for the True Christian Divinity* (1678). An associate of the early Quakers George Fox and William Penn, he emigrated to North America in 1682, where he served as Governor of East New Jersey until 1688, before returning to Scotland. His London merchant son David founded Barclay's Bank in 1736. Two members of the Towie branch settled in Riga, on the Baltic Sea, as silk merchants in the 1620s. Their descendant, Field Marshal Michael Andreas Barclay de Tolly, commanded the Russian army, forcing Napoleon's retreat in 1812, for which service he was made a prince.

BAXTER

The family name derives from Middle English *bakstere* ("baker") and the clan may have become established in Angus as royal bakers at Forfar. Geffrie le Baxter of Forfar was a signatory of the 1296 oath of allegiance to England's Edward I. The Baxters of Kincaldrum used wealth created by their weaving business to patronize Dundee, donating Baxter Park and establishing a college that became Dundee University. The Baxters of Fochabers are processors and suppliers of soups and preserves. In Fife, Baxters can be traced back as far as the early 13th century, when Reginald Baxtar witnessed the gift of a church building at

Wemyss. The Baxters of Earlshall, Fife, erected an impressive castle near Leuchars. Baxters near Cupar, Fife, built Kilmaron Castle in 1820. West Scotland Baxters are generally seen as a sept or sub-group of clan MacMillan.

BORTHWICK

Early members of clan Borthwick, one of Scotland's oldest families, may have fought against Roman legionaries in the first century BC. The name comes from their Border territories along Borthwick Water. By tradition, the clan's ancestors include Saxon nobles who in 1067 travelled from England with Princess Margaret prior to her marriage to Malcolm III. In 1330 Sir William Borthwick accompanied Good Sir James Douglas on pilgrimage and, when Douglas was killed in Spain, Borthwick carried his body and the Bruce's heart back to Scotland.

Early in the 15th century Sir William Borthwick, Captain of Edinburgh Castle, held the Borthwick Water lands under charter. In the following years Borthwicks achieved great power as Lords of Parliament. In about 1430 Sir William's son, 1st Lord Borthwick, built the magnificent Borthwick Castle, south of Edinburgh, where Mary, Queen of Scots, took refuge in 1567. She was forced to flee in disguise and part of the castle is said to be haunted by the queen's ghost dressed as a boy.

▼ *The Barclay tartan was included in the Sobieskis'* Vestiarum Scoticum.

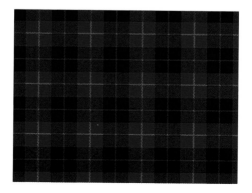

▼ *The Baxters share their motto,* Vincit veritas, *with the Allison family.*

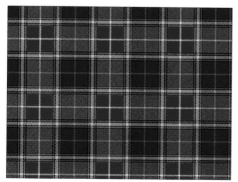

▼ *The Borthwicks' ancestral home was besieged by Cromwell in the Civil War.*

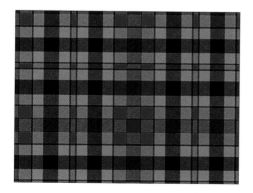

BOWIE–BURNETT

Tartan designs reflect blood ties. Because of family links, the Boyd sett contains elements derived from the Stewart of Bute and Hay tartans and the Buchan sett is similar to a district tartan worn by the Cummings.

BOWIE

The Bowies are seen as a sept, or sub-group, of the MacDonalds. Their name, found particularly in the islands of Bute, Uist and Jura and in Argyllshire, probably derives from Gaelic *buidhe* ("fair-haired"), although some accounts say it means "cowherd", from *bow*, meaning "cattle". In 1489 John Bowey held Dunbarton Castle in defiance of James IV's troops. In the reign of James VI (1567–1625) a Jerome Bowie was keeper of the king's wine cellar.

BOYD

According to tradition the Boyds are descended from Robert, nephew of Walter, Scotland's first High Steward

▼ *The isle of Bute is the ancestral home of Scotland's Stewart monarchs.*

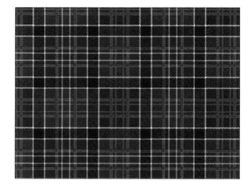

▲ *The name Bowie was common in Stirling in the 17th and 18th centuries.*

and ancestor to the Stewarts. The name is probably derived from the Gaelic for "fair-haired", although some authorities say it may have identified the clansmen as originating in the island of Bute, known as Bhoid in Gaelic.

Sir Robert Boyd served Robert the Bruce as a commander at the battle of Bannockburn in 1314, for which he received lands in Kilmarnock and Ayrshire. In the mid-15th century the family was elevated to the peerage and manoeuvred itself into a position of great power. After the accession of the young James III (r.1460–88) Robert, Lord Boyd of Kilmarnock, was one of the regents and became Great Chamberlain, while his brother, Sir Alexander, was one of the king's tutors. Robert's son Thomas was made Earl of

▼ *The Boyd tartan is based on one designed for Lord Kilmarnock in 1954.*

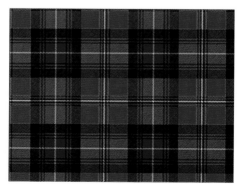

Arran and married the king's sister Mary. When the Boyds' enemies moved against them Lord Boyd escaped but Sir Alexander was executed for treason. The Earl of Arran, who was abroad at the time, settled into exile. The Boyds recovered royal favour under Mary, Queen of Scots (r.1542–67), and, after the Restoration of the monarchy in 1660, William, Lord Boyd, was made the Earl of Kilmarnock. In the 1745 rebellion the 4th Earl of Kilmarnock fought in the Jacobite cause and was captured and beheaded in London.

BRODIE

The Brodies are a family of ancient lineage, the name possibly deriving from the Pictish royal name of Brude. Malcolm was Thane of Brodie, near Forres in Morayshire, in the reign of Alexander III (r.1249–86), and his son Michael held the lands as Baron of Brodie under a 1311 charter of Robert the Bruce. In the 17th century Alexander Brodie of Brodie was one of the commissioners who visited Charles II in exile to discuss his return to Scotland; he also negotiated with Oliver Cromwell following the Royalists' defeat at the battle of Worcester in 1651. One of his kinsmen was the notorious Deacon William

▼ *Brodies wore a district sett before adopting this tartan in the 1820s.*

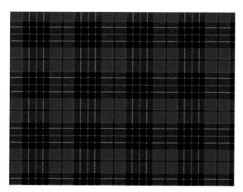

Brodie, who led a double life as a councillor by day and a criminal by night. Finally captured and hanged in 1788, the deacon is said to have inspired Robert-Louis Stevenson's chilling tale of a split personality, *The Strange Case of Dr Jekyll and Mr Hyde* (1886).

BUCHAN

The region of Buchan, in north-eastern Aberdeenshire, was one of seven Celtic sub-kingdoms ruled by *mormaers* (stewards). The earliest recorded family member is Ricardus de Buchan, clerk of the Aberdeen bishopric in 1207. The family was closely connected with the Comyns (Cummings), who by the 13th century had possession of the earldom of Buchan.

In the 15th century the Buchans of Auchmacoy rose to prominence as the main branch of the family. Thomas Buchan of Auchmacoy was a distinguished military figure in the late 17th century. He took command of the Jacobite forces after the death of Bonnie Dundee at the battle of Killiecrankie in 1689, after which he escaped into exile. He returned to fight again at Sheriffmuir in 1715.

In the 20th century, the popular novelist John Buchan published 50 books, including *The Thirty-nine Steps* (1915) and *Greenmantle* (1916). He served as Governor-General of Canada (1935–40) and was made 1st Baron Tweedsmuir of Elsfield.

▼ *Members of the Buchan family have worn this tartan since around 1965.*

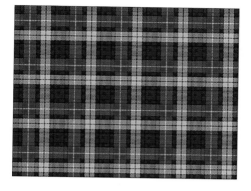

▲ *A version of Buchanan tartan was in James Logan's* The Scottish Gael.

BUCHANAN

The Buchanan clan claims descent from Anselan O'Kyan, an Irish chieftain who made the short voyage from Ireland to Argyll. Having helped Malcolm II (r.1005–34) defend western Scotland against the Norse, he received the lands of Buchanan to the east of Loch Lomond. Maurice of Buchanan held these lands, and the island of Clarinch on the loch, under a charter of 1282. Sir Alexander Buchanan fought for the French against Henry V of England at the battle of Beauge in Normandy in 1421. Having killed the Duke of Clarence, he grabbed his coronet as proof of the triumph, an act said to be the inspiration for the Buchanan crest – a hand holding a cap aloft. Sir Alexander was killed three years later at the battle of Verneuil in France and was succeeded as clan chief by his brother Walter.

In the late 17th century heavy debts forced the family to sell its lands to the Marquis of Montrose, whose descendants built Buchanan Castle. Among the clan's notable descendants was James Buchanan, 15th President of the United States (1857–61). The Buchanans may have lost their lands, but their clan society, founded in 1725 and the oldest of all the Highland societies, still has possession of the island of Clarinch. It holds a special place in the hearts of Buchanan clansmen, whose battle-cry was "Clarinch!"

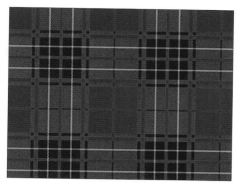

▲ *This Burnett tartan is an alternative to the Burnett of Leys family tartan.*

BURNETT

The Burnett clan is descended from the powerful Anglo-Saxon Burnard family, who accompanied Prince David when he travelled north to claim the Scottish throne as David I in 1124. Their name is probably derived from the Saxon *beornheard* ("fearless warrior"). They settled initially in Roxburghshire and in the 13th and 14th centuries made a number of grants to the monks of Melrose Abbey. For supporting Robert the Bruce (r.1306–29) Alexander Burnett received the barony of Tulliboyl in Kincardineshire, near Aberdeen, and territory in the Forest of Drum, as well as the jewel-encrusted ivory hunting horn now displayed at Crathes Castle. The Kincardineshire Burnetts became the principal branch of the family, known as the Burnetts of Leys. Sir Thomas Burnett of Leys, 1st Baronet of Nova Scotia, was related to and marched with the Marquis of Montrose in 1644–45. Major-General Sir James Burnett of Leys, 13th Baronet, fought with great valour in the First World War in the Gordon Highlanders and twice received the Distinguished Service Order (DSO).

The Burnetts' seat is Crathes Castle on the river Dee; it took more than 40 years to build, beginning in 1553, and is now kept by the National Trust for Scotland. The family shares its motto, *Virescit vulnere virtus* ("Courage flowers at a wound"), with the Stewarts.

BURNS–CLARK

Many family tartans sadly cannot be traced back beyond the late 19th century, but one of the Chisholm family setts can definitively be identified as the one worn by family heroine Mary Chisholm in a portrait of *c.*1800.

BURNS

In Scotland the Burns name is associated above all with the poet Robert Burns (1759–96), who was born to a farming family in Ayrshire. His lyrics on love, nature and peasant life won him the affection of his country and he is generally considered to be Scotland's national poet. His early verses were written while working as a farm labourer and although the success of his collection *Poems, Chiefly in the Scottish Dialect* (1786) opened the door to Edinburgh society he continued farming until he moved to Dumfries in 1791. Robert's name was initially spelled Burnes and a number of variations are found, including Burness and Burnis; all are probably derived from a place name linked to Old English *burna* ("brook") or the word "burnhouse" (the house by the brook). There is no recognized chief of clan Burns.

The Burns family tartan dates from about 1930–50, and a Robert Burns check and Burns Heritage check have also been issued.

▼ *Members of the Burns family can wear this 20th-century design.*

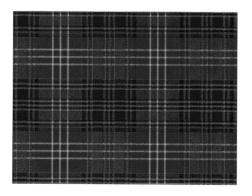

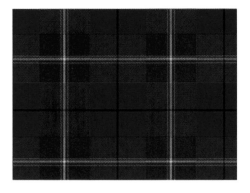

▲ *The Carmichael family's elegant tartan has been dated to around 1907.*

CARMICHAEL

The Carmichaels take their name from their Lanarkshire ancestral lands, which Sir John de Carmichael acquired in 1374. The Carmichael crest – an armoured hand clasping a shattered lance – commemorates a victory in 1421 at the battle of Beauge in Normandy, during which Sir John de Carmichael of Meadowflat rode against the Earl of Clarence and knocked him from his horse, breaking his own lance in the process. At the end of the 16th century another Sir John de Carmichael was appointed by James VI to several prominent positions. In 1647 the Carmichael chief was elevated to the peerage and in the 18th century a succession of Carmichaels, now titled the Earls of Hyndford, held positions of state and served with great distinction in the army.

CARNEGIE

The Carnegie name comes from the barony of Carnegie near Arbroath, which John de Balinhard acquired in 1358. Duthac de Carnegie added lands at Kinnaird, Forfarshire, in the early 15th century. Sir David Carnegie, Sheriff of Forfar, was made Lord Carnegie of Kinnaird in 1616 and Earl of Southesk in 1633. The Carnegie title and estates were forfeited to the

▲ *This is one of three tartans from which Carnegie kilts can be made.*

Crown after James, 5th Earl of Southesk, backed the Old Pretender to the British throne in the 1715 Jacobite rebellion. Title and lands were restored in 1855. The Dunfermline-born multi-millionaire and philanthropist Andrew Carnegie (1835–1919) emigrated with his parents to the United States in 1848. He built a vast steel empire, which he sold at great profit in 1901, enabling him to make donations totalling $350 million to worthy causes.

One of the Carnegie tartans is a variant of the MacDonell of Glengarry tartan said to have been worn by the 5th Earl in the 1715 Jacobite rebellion, with a yellow stripe replacing the white of the MacDonell of Glengarry sett.

CHISHOLM

The Chisholms trace the origin of their landholding to the gift made by a grateful king after clan members saved him from a wild boar, which figures in the clan crest. Originally Norman, the family took their name from their lands at Chieseholme, Roxburghshire, where they were established by about 1250. They settled further north when Robert de Chisholme was appointed Governor of Urquhart Castle by Loch Ness in 1359. His son Alexander acquired the Erchless lands through marriage, and these were made a

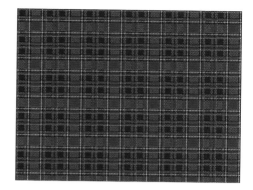

▲ *This is the Chisholm tartan worn by Mary Chisholm in a portrait.*

barony in the mid-16th century. The clansmen fought in the Jacobite cause in the 1715 and 1745 rebellions, but fewer than 50 survived the battle of Culloden in 1746. Following a drive by Ruaridh, 22nd chief, to raise rents, the mid-18th century saw major emigration of Chisholms to North America. Mary Chisholm, the daughter of Alexander, 23rd chief, supported the clansmen and became a family heroine. In a portrait dated to about 1800 she wears a Chisholm tartan that can, according to some authorities, be dated as far back as 1746. The dark red, white and green design is a variant of one of the MacIntosh tartans.

CHRISTIE

The Christie name is thought to be a diminutive of Christopher or Christian, although some authorities argue that it is derived from the Norse *trusty* ("swordsman"). Clan members were established in Stirlingshire and Fife by the mid-15th century, when John Christie was recorded as resident in Newburgh. James Christie of Perth became a friend of craftsmen and artists such as Thomas Chippendale and Thomas Gainsborough and established the famous art auction house, Christie's, in Pall Mall, London, in 1766. In the 19th century Thomas Christie of Lanarkshire served the Prince Regent as a doctor. Christies are identified as a sept of the Farquharsons.

CLARK

The clan's name derives from the Latin *clericus* ("clerk", "scribe" or "cleric") and its link with the Church meant that the name was common in many parts of Scotland. It is also spelled Clerk, Clerck or Klerck. In Gaelic it was Chleirich and descendants could be called Mac a'Chleirich ("son of the clerk"), which gave rise to the associated name McCleary, anglicized as Clarkson. There are particular links with the Camerons, MacPhersons and Mackintoshes. Clarks among the MacPhersons of Badenoch, who were members of clan Chattan, trace

▼ *An alternative form of the Christie tartan uses azure in place of blue.*

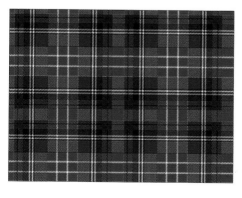

▲ *Sango Beach in Durness, where one of the branches of the Clark clan settled from the 17th century.*

their lineage to the 15th-century Gillemichael vic Chleric, personal attendant to Malcolm, 10th Mackintosh chief. Another branch of the family was resident in Durness from the 17th century.

Several Clarks made their mark overseas. In 1623 Richard Clark of Montrose was made vice-admiral in the Swedish navy. A Scot named George Clark settled in the north-west of Ohio in 1783.

▼ *The Clark tartan was worn both by clan members and men of the cloth.*

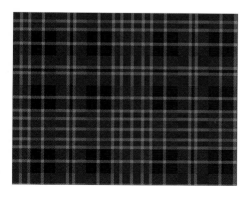

COCHRANE–CRAWFORD

A mistake in identification of the Cockburn tartan provides an insight into the way tartans have been wrongly named. In the early 19th century Lord Cockburn identified as a Cockburn sett a Mackenzie tartan worn by the regiment in which he served.

COCHRANE

The clan claims descent from a Viking warrior and won a reputation as the Fighting Cochranes. Their name may derive from the Gaelic word for "battle-cry", but is also linked to the name of their ancestral lands near Paisley, Renfrewshire, which was sometimes spelled Coueran or Coveran as well as Cochrane. The clan was settled in Renfrewshire by the 10th century, although its name is not recorded until 1262, when Waldev de Coveran witnessed a charter. William de Cochran held his lands under charter from

▼ *Glen Luss, to the west of Loch Lomond, is part of the ancestral lands of clan Colquhoun.*

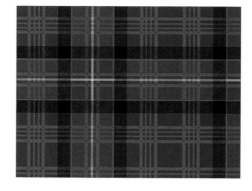

▲ *The design of this Cochrane tartan is derived from a Lochaber district sett.*

Robert II (r.1371–90). In 1638 the clan chief, another William, acquired the estate and 14th-century castle of Dundonald, Ayrshire. In 1669 the chief became the 1st Earl of Dundonald. His descendant Thomas, 10th Earl, was one of the greatest figures in British naval history, fighting in the Napoleonic Wars. He became an MP in 1806 but was barred from the Navy following a scandal engineered by his enemies. In 1817 he took command of the navy of Chile as the country struggled for inde-

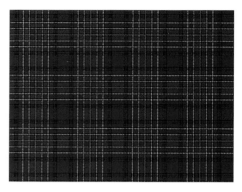

▲ *This Cockburn tartan uses blue rather than the normal green ground.*

pendence from Spain, and he later fought for Brazil, Peru and Greece in their wars of independence. The 14th Earl had a distinguished military career in the Second World War.

COCKBURN

Although the clan's badge shows a crowing cock and its motto is *Accendit cantu* ("He wakes us with his singing"), the name of this Borders clan appears to be either a corruption of the English name Colbrand or to be taken from the Cukoueburn, a Roxburghshire burn, or stream. The Cockburns were established in the Borders by the 13th century and Sir Pere de Cockburne was one of the landowners who signed allegiance to England's Edward I in 1296. In the early 14th century Sir Alexander de Cockburn acquired the Langton lands, in Berwickshire, through marriage. Sir Alexander was killed at the battle of Bannockburn in 1314; his grandson, also Alexander, was granted the barony of Carriden by David II in 1358 and became Keeper of the Great Seal (1389–96).

In 1815 Sir George Cockburn, an admiral in the British Navy, escorted the defeated Napoleon to exile on the island of St Helena. Sir Alexander Cockburn was Lord Chief Justice of England from 1874–80.

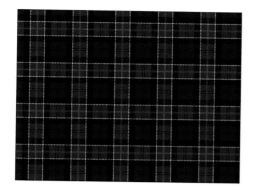

▲ *The Colquhoun appeared in the Highland Society collection in 1816.*

COLQUHOUN

The Colquhouns take their name from their lands on the western side of Loch Lomond and by tradition they were guardians of the crosier, or pastoral staff, of Kessog, a saint who lived on an island in the loch. In the time of Alexander II (r.1214–49) Malcolm, Earl of Lennox, granted the lands to Humphrey de Kilpatrick, whose son Ingram was the first to assume the name Colquhoun. The family acquired the lands of Luss by marriage in the reign of Robert II (r.1371–90) and in 1457 Sir John Colquhoun had the lands erected into the barony of Luss.

In 1602, after an attack on his lands by the MacGregors, Alexander Colquhoun of Luss was given a royal commission to pursue the men of that clan, but the following year the MacGregors massacred the Colquhouns at Glen Fruin. As a consequence, the MacGregor name was outlawed. A number of Colquhouns made a new life in North America, where the name is often spelled Calhoun. John Calhoun (1782–1850) was the US vice-President under Presidents Adams and Jackson.

CONNEL

The clan's name may derive from that of the Celtic mythological warrior-hero Conall Cernach ("victorious and strong as a wolf"). The name was popular in Ireland, and came to be used in

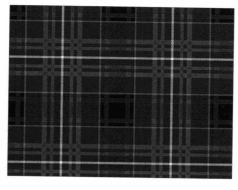

▲ *Connels can wear this MacConnel tartan, based on MacDonald Hunting.*

Scotland through the first missionaries. The Connel tartan bears a close resemblance to the Wallace sett published in the Sobieski Brothers' *Vestiarium Scoticum* (1842) and may be based on that design. However, the Connels, and the MacConnels, are regarded as a sept, or sub-group, of clan Donald rather than of the Wallaces.

CRANSTOUN

The family's badge depicts a crane holding a stone in its claw, while the name of its Midlothian lands appears to derive from the Anglo-Saxon words meaning "the place where cranes are seen". Elfrick de Cranstoun witnessed a charter of William I (r.1165–1214) to the monks at Holyrood Abbey, and Hugh de Cranstoun was among the Scottish landowners and churchmen who signed the 1296 oath of loyalty to Edward I of England. Thomas de

▼ *The* Vestiarum Scoticum *is the only known source for the Cranstoun sett.*

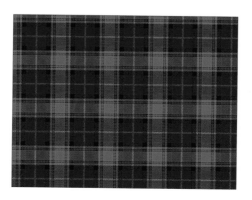

Cranston, ambassador to Scandinavia and England for James I, was made a warden of the Marches in 1459. William Cranstoun of Morristoun, a Captain of the King's Guards, was made Lord Cranstoun in 1609.

One branch of the family was established on Rhode Island, in North America, in the 17th century, where two of its sons, John and Samuel, served with distinction as governors.

CRAWFORD

The family, originally from Normandy, were by the late 12th century established in the region of Lanarkshire from which they take their name. A Galfridus de Crawford was recorded in 1179. In 1296 Sir Reginald Crawford was made Sheriff of Ayr. His brother, granted the lands of Auchinames by Robert the Bruce (r.1306–29), founded the Crawfords of Auchinames, regarded as the chief branch of the family. The brothers' nephew was the patriot William Wallace.

In the 15th century Sir Reginald's descendant, William Crawford of Craufurdland, won a reputation for bravery fighting for Charles VII of France, and died in 1513 fighting for James IV at the battle of Flodden. In the 20th century Hugh Crawford, 21st Lord of Auchinames, sold his estate and settled in Canada; the Crawfords of Craufurdland remain in possession of their ancestral lands.

▼ *The Crawford tartan was designed after 1739 and before 1842.*

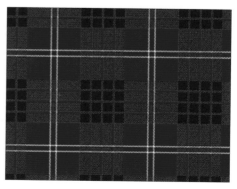

CUMMING–DUNBAR

D.W. Stewart's beautifully finished 1893 book, *Old and Rare Scottish Tartans*, contained a woven silk sample of each sett. The Davidson tartan reproduced opposite is the version used in Stewart's compilation.

CUMMING

This Norman family took their name from Comines, near Lisle in France. Robert de Comyn, a follower of William the Conqueror, was made Earl of Northumberland in 1069. His grandson William Comyn was granted land in Roxburghshire by David I (r.1124–53) and later became Chancellor of Scotland.

Through advantageous marriages, the family acquired the earldoms of Atholl and Buchan, Menteith and Monteith. By the early 14th century they were Scotland's most powerful family. This was changed, however, when Robert the Bruce moved decisively against the Badenoch branch of the family in order to safeguard his claim to the throne.

The Cummings of Altyre, who became clan chiefs, are descended from the brother of the 13th-century Sir John Comyn of Badenoch, the Black Comyn. The Altyre branch inherited the lands of Gordonstoun (now a public school) through marriage.

▼ *Wilson's of Bannockburn made this version of the Cumming from 1819.*

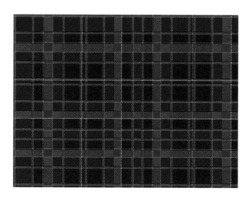

CUNNINGHAM

The family had settled in the Cunningham district of Ayrshire, from which they take their name, by the mid-12th century, when Wernibald, the first known chief, was granted Kilmaurs by the Constable of Scotland. The family's intriguing motto – "Over fork over" – refers to the time when a Cunningham ancestor, Malcolm, sheltered Malcolm III (r.1058–93) in a barn, hiding him under forkfuls of hay. Malcolm was well rewarded with lands. Harvey de Cunningham fought for Alexander III against the Norse at the

▼ *This version of the Cunningham, with black, dates from at least 1906.*

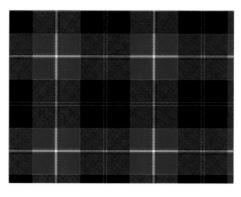

▲ *A monument marks the site of the 1263 battle of Largs, in which Harvey de Cunningham won royal favour.*

battle of Largs in 1263 and the following year was confirmed in possession of the Kilmaurs lands. His descendant, Sir Alexander Cunningham, was made Lord Kilmaurs in 1462 and Earl of Glencairn in 1488. Notable descendants include the historian Alexander Cunningham (1654–1737) and the poet Allan Cunningham (1784–1842).

The Cunningham tartan resembles the MacGregor sett and indeed Cunningham was one of the names adopted by clan MacGregor members when their own name was banned by royal decree.

DALZIEL

The family's name may derive from Gaelic *dailghil* ("the white valley"). The chief held the barony of Dalziel, or Dalzell, in Lanarkshire by the late 13th century. Sir Robert Dalziel was made Lord Dalziel in 1633 and Earl of Carnwath in 1649. The Dalziels of the Binns, a West Lothian estate, could

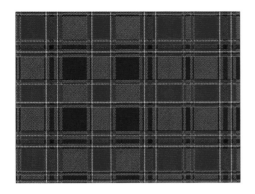

▲ *This Dalziel colouring is that given in Logan's* The Scottish Gael.

boast of their kinsman Sir Thomas Dalziel, a general of the Russian Tsar in 1655. Back in Scotland he was Commander-in-Chief of Charles II's army and defeated the Covenanters at the battle of Rullion Green in 1666. He raised the Royal Scots Greys regiment in 1681. In the industrial era the family name became that of a major steelworks in Motherwell. Dalzell Castle, which has a 15th-century keep, overlooks the river Clyde.

The Dalziel tartan resembles that of the Munro clan and was also used as the basis of a George IV (r.1820–30) tartan produced to commemorate the king's visit to Edinburgh in 1822.

DAVIDSON

Descended from the 14th-century nobleman David Dhu of Ivernahaven, the Davidsons were known as clan Dhai from his name. David Dhu was the son of Donald, grandson of the Red Comyn (ancestor of the Cumming clan), and Slane, daughter of clan Mackintosh's 6th chief. The Davidsons linked themselves to the clan Chattan confederation and fought alongside their Chattan allies in the battle of Invernahaven in 1370, when they were almost annihilated by Camerons. The clan was also established in Aberdeen, Perth and Dundee by about 1400. In this era, Sir Robert Davisoun, collector of royal taxes in Aberdeen, led a force of townsmen on the side of Alexander,

▲ *This Davidson tartan, from 1893, is similar to one of the Henderson setts.*

Earl of Mar, against a Highland force led by the MacDonalds in the ferocious but inconclusive battle of Harlaw in 1411. In the 19th century, Duncan Davidson, 2nd Lord of Tulloch, was an MP and Lord Lieutenant of Ross-shire; he often entertained Queen Victoria.

DRUMMOND

The Drummonds are named after Drymen, their Stirlingshire estates. They are said to be descended from Hungarian followers of Prince Edgar, who landed at Fife in 1067 when his ships were blown off course while fleeing William the Conqueror. The first known chief was Malcolm Beg ("little Malcolm"), who married the Earl of Lennox's daughter in the mid-13th century. His son Sir Malcolm was the first to take the name Drummond. In 1314 another Sir Malcolm de Drummond scattered the spikes on the

▼ *Clan Drummond members wore this sett to greet George IV in Edinburgh.*

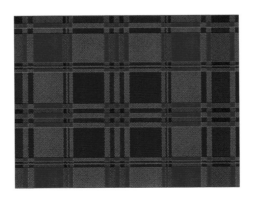

battlefield at Bannockburn that stopped the charge of the English cavalry. He was granted lands in Perthshire.

Bonnie Prince Charlie, the Young Pretender, is said to have worn a cloak made of the Drummond of Perth tartan when he led the 1745 Jacobite rebellion. Drummonds are known to have worn both Grant and Ogilvie tartans as well as their own.

DUNBAR

The Dunbars take their name from the strategically valuable family estate on the Scots/English border and claim descent from Crinan, father of Duncan I (r.1034–40). Duncan's nephew Gospatric was given the Dunbar lands by Malcolm III (r.1058–93), and his son, a witness to the foundation of Holyrood Abbey in 1128, was made Earl of Dunbar. Patrick, 8th Earl of Dunbar and Earl of March, was one of 13 claimants to the Scottish crown in 1291. In the 14th century the Dunbars were among the most powerful noblemen in Scotland, but in 1435 James I imprisoned George, 11th Earl, for treason and the earldom and estates were forfeited. The celebrated poet William Dunbar (*c.*1460–*c.*1530) was a member of James IV's household from 1500–13, while Gavin Dunbar was Lord High Chancellor under James V (r.1513–42). The clan chiefs, descendants of the Mochrum branch, live in the United States.

▼ *A Dunbar sett made by Wilson's in 1840 may have been a district tartan.*

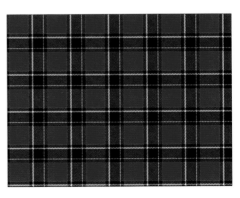

DUNCAN–ERSKINE

The green, black and blue background seen in the Dundas sett was typical of the Highland military tartans from which many Scottish clan tartans were derived. The Dyce sett uses the same colour scheme.

DUNCAN

The Duncan family are regarded as a sept or sub-group of the Robertson clan and share a common ancestry in Duncan the Fat, 5th Lord of Glenerochie, who fought for Scottish independence at Bannockburn in 1314. The Robertsons were known as clan Donnachaidh ("sons of Duncan") until the mid-15th century, when they took the name of their chief Robert Riabhach ("the Grizzled"). Duncans held the barony of Lundie and Gourdie estates in Forfarshire. Adam Duncan, a descendant of the Lundie Duncans, defeated the Dutch at the naval battle of Camperdown in 1797 and was made Viscount Duncan of Camperdown.

DUNDAS

The clan traces its ancestry back to Serle of Dundas in the reign of William I (r.1165–1214) and held lands in West Lothian. Sir Archibald Dundas, an ambassador for James III (r.1460–88), received the island of Inchgarvie in the Firth of Forth from James IV

▲ *The Dundas tartan is illustrated in the Sobieskis'* Vestiarum Scoticum.

(r.1488–1513). When the restrictions imposed on Highland clans following the 1745 Jacobite rebellion were eased in the 1780s, Henry Dundas, 1st Viscount Melville, oversaw the lifting of the ban on wearing tartan and the restoration of certain forfeited estates. Begun in 1424, Dundas Castle was the family's undoing and in 1875 most of their estates had to be sold to cover overspending on its improvement. In the early 19th century Sir David Dundas was Commander-in-Chief of the British Army.

DYCE

The Dyce family, who held land close to Aberdeen, were associated with the local Skene clan and can be traced back to 1467, when the earliest known ancestor, John de Diss, was a burgess of Aberdeen. The name had many variant spellings, including Dyess, Dyos and Dias. Among distinguished descendants who made their mark in the arts was the Edinburgh-born man of letters Alexander Dyce (1798–1869), who edited the works of Christopher Marlowe, John Webster, Thomas More and John Skelton and produced a celebrated nine-volume edition of Shakespeare. The Aberdeen-born painter and art education pioneer William Dyce (1806–64) studied in

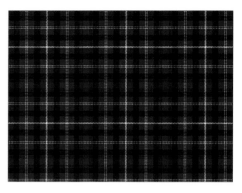

▲ *The Dyce sett is found in Whyte's 1906 collection of Scottish tartans.*

Edinburgh, London and Rome and was elected to the Royal Academy in 1848. A forerunner of the Pre-Raphaelites, he painted a series of frescoes in the Houses of Parliament in Westminster.

ELLIOT

This Border clan claims to have started out in Angus, but moved to Teviotdale during the reign of Robert the Bruce (r.1306–29). Robert Elliot of Redheugh, 10th chief, is documented in 1476 and another Robert, 13th chief, fought and died at the battle of Flodden in 1513. His son, also Robert, was, like many Elliot chiefs in this era, Captain of Hermitage Castle, south of Hawick. In later years a number of Elliots served the British Empire with great distinction. Sir Gilbert Elliot of

▼ *Elliots have an unusual sett and are said to have an independent character.*

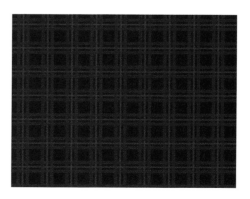

▼ *This Duncan tartan has Leslie links, so is also known as "Leslie of Wardis".*

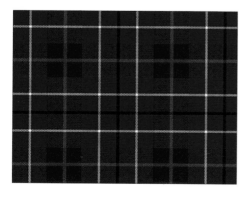

Minto was a diplomat in Vienna and Governor-General of India (1807–13); he was created 1st Earl of Minto. Another Gilbert, 4th Earl, served in the Scots Guards, worked in newspapers in the 1870s, then became Governor-General of Canada (1898–1905) and Viceroy of India (1905–10).

The Elliot tartan has a unique maroon and blue colouring. It was first recorded in Whyte's book *The Tartans of the Clans and Septs of Scotland* in 1906.

ELPHINSTONE

The Elphinstones take their name from their lands near Edinburgh in East Lothian, where they were settled by about 1235. They later acquired lands at Airth in Stirlingshire through marriage. Sir Henry Elphinstone, created Baron Elphinstone in 1509, died at the battle of Flodden in 1513. William

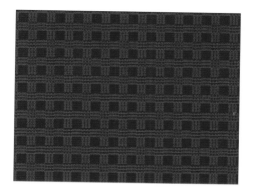

▲ *The Elphinstone tartan is similar to one of the Montgomerie family setts.*

Elphinstone became Bishop of Aberdeen in 1483 and Chancellor of Scotland in 1488; he served as an ambassador for James III and James IV. He also founded St Mary's College (later King's College) in Aberdeen. John Elphinstone, 2nd Baron Balmerino, was President of the Scottish Parliament in 1641.

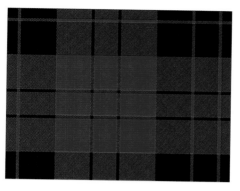

▲ *This version of the Erskine tartan may date back as far as 1830.*

The Elphinstone tartan resembles the tartans of clan Montgomerie, one of which has been dated by some authorities to the early 18th century. It was first documented in 1842, in the Sobieski Brothers' *Vestiarum Scoticum*.

ERSKINE

Henry de Erskine was Baron of Erskine in Renfrewshire in the early 13th century, and his descendants married into both the Bruce and Stewart families. Under David II (r.1329–71) Sir Robert de Erskine was made Constable of Stirling Castle and was created Lord Erskine. The Erskines were appointed as guardians to James IV and Mary, Queen of Scots (r.1542–67), and Mary made John, 6th Lord Erskine, Earl of Mar in 1565. The family also acquired the earldom of Kellie in 1619, and the chief still takes the title Earl of Mar and Kellie.

Another John, 6th Earl of Mar, raised the Old Pretender's standard at the battle of Braemar in 1715 and led a 10,000-strong Jacobite force against the Government army commanded by the Duke of Argyll at the battle of Sheriffmuir in the same year. The battle was not decisive and the Earl fled to France; his estates and title were forfeited until 1824.

◀ *Kellie Castle in Fife was built by the Oliphants, but the 5th Lord Oliphant sold the estate to the Erskines in 1613.*

FARQUHARSON–GOW

The Farquharson sett is well-documented: it was in James Logan's *The Scottish Gael* (1831) and in the books of Wilson's of Bannockburn from 1819, and 18th-century samples were displayed in an exhibition of Highland tartans in Inverness in 1930.

FARQUHARSON

The Farquharsons identify Farquhar, son of Alexander Ciar (Shaw) of Rothiemurchus in the early 16th century, as their earliest ancestor, which makes them members of clan Chattan. Farquhar's son Donald acquired Invercauld lands through marriage and Donald's son Finlay Mor, the royal standard-bearer at the battle of Pinkie in 1547, was the 1st Farquharson lord of Invercauld. The family's Gaelic name, Clann Fhionnlaigh ("sons of Finlay"), identifies them as descendants of Finlay Mor. John Farquharson, 3rd Lord of Inverey, dubbed the Black Colonel, fought with the Jacobite hero Bonnie Dundee in 1689; his exploits were the subject of many ballads. In the 1715 rebellion John Farquharson of Invercauld led 140 clansmen in support of the Jacobites, but was captured at Preston. Francis Farquharson of Monaltrie led 300 clansmen at Culloden in 1746. The family motto is "By fidelity and fortitude".

▼ *Samples of the Farquharson tartan have been dated to 1774.*

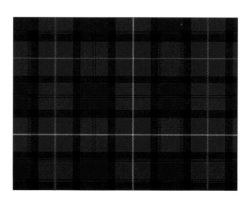

FLETCHER

The Fletchers are descended from arrow-makers who followed the clans they served; the name comes from the French *fléchier* ("maker of arrows"). Fletchers in Glenlyon, Perthshire, followed the MacGregors, and Fletchers are said to have once saved the outlaw Rob Roy MacGregor. Fletchers claim

▼ *The Fletcher of Saltoun was worn by Fletchers from all over Scotland.*

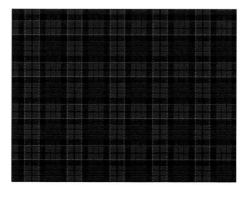

▲ *Mist wreathes the valley of Tulla, at Achallader, where the Fletcher clan preceded the Campbells.*

to have been the first inhabitants of Glenorchy and made their home for generations at Achallader on Loch Tulla. The family saying goes: "It was the Fletchers who first lit fires to boil their water in Glenorchy." But they were driven out by Campbells, some going to Jura and Islay and others overseas. By the early 18th century one branch of the clan was established at Dunans in Cowal. The Fletchers of Innerpeffer in Angus purchased the Saltoun estate in East Lothian in 1643. Among their sons was the politician Andrew Fletcher (1653–1716), a fierce opponent of the 1707 Act of Union.

The Fletchers of Dunans today have their own tartan, distinct from the commonly worn Fletcher of Saltoun.

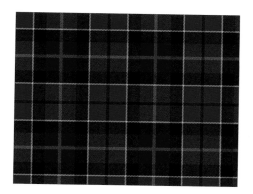

▲ *The Forsyth is like the Leslie sett, in which white lines replace the yellow.*

▲ *Wilson's of Bannockburn listed this Galbraith sett as "Hunter" in 1819.*

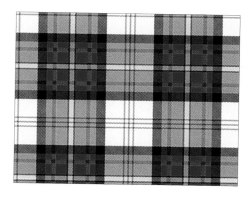

▲ *Dress tartans – like this Gillies dress sett – typically have a white ground.*

FORSYTH

The family name may derive from the Gaelic *fearsithe* ("man of peace"), but in some accounts the Forsyths are descended from a Norman family named de Fronsoc, who came to England in the mid-13th century in the entourage of Eleanor de Provence, Henry III's bride. Robert de Forsyth was a Scottish signatory of the 1296 oath of allegiance to Edward I of England, but his son Osbert fought with Robert the Bruce (r.1306–29) and was later granted the territories of Sauchie in Stirlingshire.

James Forsyth of Nydie married the great-granddaughter of James III (r.1460–88) and their descendants acquired lands in the vicinity of the Palace of Falkland. William Forsyth (1737–1804), an authority on the cultivation of fruit trees, worked as Chief Superintendent of the Royal Gardens at Kensington and St James's Palace in London. The *Forsythia* genus of plants is named in his honour.

GALBRAITH

The Galbraiths' name derives from Gaelic for "son of the Briton", and the clansmen were probably initially from Strathclyde, where the Britons had a kingdom from the 6th century AD. In the 12th and early 13th centuries Galbraiths had close connections to the earls of Lennox. In 1255 Sir William Galbraith was a co-Regent of Scotland during the minority of Alexander III. His son, Sir Arthur Galbraith, married a daughter of Sir James Douglas and fought valiantly alongside Robert the Bruce (r.1306–29) in the struggle for Scottish independence. The family fell from glory and lost their lands in the mid-17th century when Robert Galbraith, their lawless 17th chief, fled to Ireland.

Variously listed as a Hunter sett or a Russell sett in the pattern books of Wilson's of Bannockburn, the Galbraith tartan was identified as such by the Highland Society of London. It is the chosen tartan of the United States Air Force pipe band.

GILLIES

The earliest known representative of this family is Gillise, who was witness to a royal charter in about 1128. A quarter of a century later his son Uhtred was a landowner in Lothian. People bearing the Gillies name may be descended from churchmen, for it derives from the Gaelic for "servant of Jesus". Most authorities regard the family as a sept of clan Macpherson, whose name means "son of the parson" and which was itself part of the clan Chattan confederation. Surviving records suggest the Gillies lived in largest numbers in the Hebrides and in Badenoch. Modern members of the family have four dress tartans as well as two clan tartans to choose from.

GOW

The Gow name comes from the Gaelic *gobhan* ("blacksmith") and Gows plied their trade, making weapons and horseshoes, all over Scotland. They are linked to the MacGowans and regarded as a sept of clan MacPherson. The Gow tartan is based on the pattern of a pair of knee-length trousers worn by the celebrated Perthshire-born fiddler Niel Gow (1727–1807) in a portrait by Sir Henry Raeburn. Gow was a self-taught violinist who achieved fame as a performer of reels and – with his sons William, John and Andrew – as a publisher of Scots dance music. Niel's father was a plaid weaver and may have designed the cloth that became the family tartan. Another of Niel's sons, Nathaniel, was a highly regarded composer of airs and reels. Nathaniel's son, Niel the Younger, was known for his song *Flora Macdonald's Lament*.

▼ *The sett worn by fiddler Niel Gow was used as the basis for later designs.*

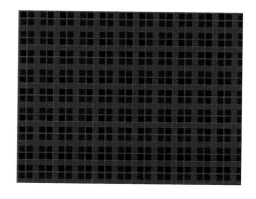

GUNN–HAY

Old designs are often the basis of new. An old Hannay kilt found in a family chest was given to John Hannay, tartan collector and designer, who used it as the basis of a new design that was manufactured in the 1950s.

GUNN

The Gunns claim descent from Gunni, a Norse chieftain whose wife Ragnhild inherited Caithness territories in the late 1100s. George Gunn, the first documented clan chief, was coroner of Caithness in about 1450. The family motto, "Either peace or war", and their badge, showing a hand holding a sword, are entirely appropriate for a clan that won a fearsome reputation for settling differences on the battlefield. They often raided the lands of the Keiths of Ackergill and in the 15th century a champions' battle was arranged to end the long-standing feud. The two sides agreed on 12 horses each but when the Keiths cunningly mounted two warriors per steed, the Gunns were overwhelmed. In the 17th century Sir William Gunn, of the Braemore branch, fought in the Swedish army for Charles I, then in the forces of the Holy Roman Empire.

The clan tartan was first recorded in James Logan's *The Scottish Gael*, published in 1831.

▼ *The Gunn tartan is sometimes made with black replacing the blue stripes.*

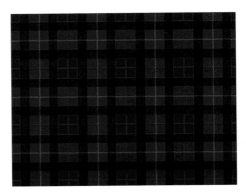

GUTHRIE

The name of the Angus barony of Guthrie may be derived from that of Guthrum, a Norse prince. The family appear to have bought their lands from the Abbey of Arbroath, which had been given the territory of Gutherin in about 1180 by William I, the Lion. In 1299 the Lord of Guthrie travelled to France to ask the Scottish patriot William Wallace to return to Scotland. Sir David Guthrie, Sheriff of Forfar, rose to become Lord Treasurer from 1461–67 and erected the magnificent Guthrie Castle near Friockheim, east of Forfar. He became Lord Chief Justice of Scotland in 1473. His son Sir Alexander Guthrie was killed at the battle of Flodden in 1513. Andrew Guthrie fought under the royalist Marquis of Montrose at Philiphaugh in 1645 but was captured and executed the following year. James Guthrie, a church minister, was arrested and beheaded in 1661 after preaching sermons that attacked Charles II's religious policy.

HAIG

According to clan tradition the Haigs are descended from Druskine, the 9th-century Pictish king. A more certain ancestor, however, is Petrus de Haga, the Norman nobleman who acquired

▼ *Guthries are proud of their ancestral home, a haunted castle built in 1468.*

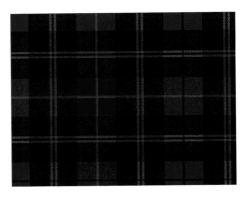

▲ *Haigs can choose between this tartan and a black-and-white check sett.*

the Haigs' ancestral lands of Bemersyde in Roxburghshire through marriage and witnessed a charter to Dryburgh Monastery in the late 12th century. The Haig chiefs were firm patriots who fought for Scottish independence with William Wallace and Robert the Bruce; the 6th lord was just 17 years old when he took part in the battle of Bannockburn in 1314. In 1545 Gilbert Haig captured the English commander Lord Evers in the battle of Ancrum Moor near Jedburgh, and in the First World War Douglas Haig, 1st Earl of Bemersyde (1861–1928), commanded the British Expeditionary Forces. Haigs also achieved distinction off the battlefield: in the early 17th century William Haig, 19th Lord, was King's Solicitor for Scotland under James VI.

HAMILTON

The Hamiltons descended from Walter Fitz Gilbert of Hambledon, a Norman lord, who held lands in Renfrewshire at the close of the 13th century. Robert the Bruce granted him further possessions, including the Cadzow estate in Lanarkshire, where the family built Cadzow Castle. By the late 15th century the Hamiltons were close to the Scottish throne. In 1474 James, 1st Lord Hamilton, married James III's daughter Mary. Their son James, Earl

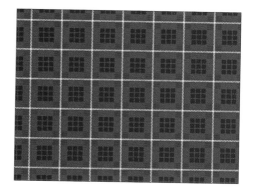

▲ *In the* Vestiarum Scoticum *the Hamilton tartan had dark blue stripes.*

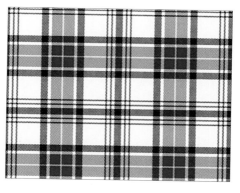

▲ *The bold Hannay sett has a white ground like a traditional dress tartan.*

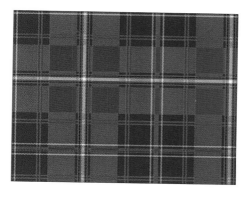

▲ *The Hay tartan is another first seen in the* Vestiarum Scoticum *(1842).*

of Arran, was Regent of Scotland in 1517 during the minority of James V. The earl's son, James, 2nd Earl of Arran, was also Regent in 1542 and was named Guardian to the young Mary, Queen of Scots. John, 4th Earl of Arran, was Chancellor of Scotland and was made Marquis of Hamilton in 1599. His grandson James, made Duke of Hamilton in 1643, was captured at Preston in 1648 and beheaded in London the following year. His brother, 2nd Duke of Hamilton, died fighting for Charles II at Worcester in 1651.

HANNAY

The Hannays came originally from the Celtic princedom of Galloway in south-western Scotland. Gilbert de Hannethe signed the 1296 oath of allegiance to Edward I of England, and around this time the family gained lands at Sorbie. In the 14th century the family's fortunes suffered when they backed their kinsman John Balliol, rather than Robert the Bruce, in the contest for the Scottish crown. The Hannays of Sorbie were outlawed and brought to ruin following a feud with the Murrays of Broughton in the early 17th century. The Hannays of Kirkdale became the clan chiefs. A celebrated son of the clan was James Hannay, Dean of St Giles in Edinburgh, whose attempt to read the new Episcopal church services in July 1637 succeeded in provoking a riot in the congregation.

Many Lowland families use a black and white check similar to the Hannay sett as the basis for their tartan. Collector and designer John Hannay added a red line to the ancient design for his version of the Hannay tartan.

HAY

The Hays are descended from Norman princes who came to England in 1066 with William the Conqueror. By about 1178 William de Haya, cupbearer to Malcolm IV, had possession of the clan's ancestral lands at Errol in Perthshire. His valiant kinsman Sir Gilbert Hay, 5th Lord of Erroll, won the trust of Robert the Bruce during his war for an independent Scotland and was appointed hereditary Lord High Constable of Scotland in 1314. Sir

Thomas Hay, 7th Baron of Erroll, married into the Stewart family when he wed Elizabeth, daughter of Robert II. William Hay was created Earl of Erroll in 1452. Staunch supporters of the Stuart kings, the clansmen fought in the Jacobite rebellions of 1715 and 1745. During George IV's visit to Edinburgh in 1822, William George, 18th Earl of Erroll, fulfilled his duties as Lord High Constable conscientiously, spending a fortune that almost ruined the family. William Hay, 19th Earl, worked tirelessly to improve the conditions of his clansmen. He founded the fishing village of Port Erroll in eastern Aberdeenshire.

▼ *Picturesque Glen Trool lies in the Hannay homeland of Galloway.*

HENDERSON–INNES

The Innes family have made major contributions to our knowledge of tartan. Sir Thomas Innes of Learney wrote *Tartans of the Clans and Families of Scotland* and was Lord Lyon (chief herald in Scotland) in 1945–69. His son Malcolm Innes was Lord Lyon from 1982–2001.

HENDERSON

There are three apparently distinct branches of this family, based in geographically distant parts of Scotland. The Hendersons of Glencoe claim to be descended from Big Henry, a partly mythologized Pictish chieftain and son of King Nectan. Subsumed into the MacDonalds of Glencoe, they formed the MacDonald chief's bodyguard. Their Gaelic name, Maceanruig, is sometimes translated as Mackendrick. In the Borders Hendersons held lands

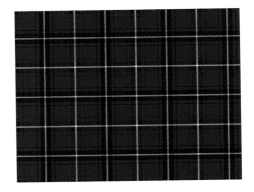

▲ *This Henderson tartan is known as the Henderson Mackendrick.*

and built a mansion at Fordell in Fife. James Henderson, who rose to become Lord Advocate in the late 15th century, and Alexander Henderson, who helped to draft the National Covenant in 1638, were sons of this branch. The Caithness Hendersons were descended from Hendry, a son of George Gunn.

The Henderson tartan resembles that of the Davidsons, who were part of the clan Chattan confederation. Both were first documented in 1906.

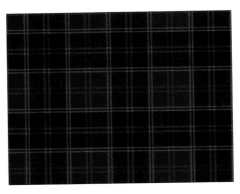

▲ *The Home tartan shares its scheme (design) with the Grey Douglas sett.*

HOME

This powerful Borders clan took its name, pronounced "Hume", from their Berwickshire lands, whose title seems to have derived from the Gaelic *uaimh* ("cave"). They trace their descent to the Saxon nobleman Cospatrick, Earl of Dunbar. The first Home name was that of Aldan de Home about 1170. Sir Alexander Home of Dunglass, a distinguished soldier who fought at the battle of Homildon in 1402, was killed in action at Verneuil, France, in 1424. His grandson, another Sir Alexander, was made Lord Home in 1473. His descendant Alexander, 6th Lord Home, was a favourite of James VI and was made Earl of Home in 1605. The Homes fought in the Jacobite cause in the 1715 and 1745 rebellions.

Prominent clansmen include the philosopher David Hume (1711–76), one of many who changed the spelling of the name to reflect its pronunciation, and Sir Alec Douglas Home (1903–95), UK Prime Minister 1963–64, who was made a life peer as Lord Home of the Hirsel.

HOPE

The first recorded family member was John de Hop, who signed the 1296 oath of allegiance to Edward I of England. John de Hope, ancestor of the

▼ *Fordell Castle, built by James Henderson in 1511, was later sold. It was restored in the 20th century.*

family's main branch, came to Edinburgh in 1537 from France with Madeleine de Valois, James V's first wife. In 1560 his son Edward was appointed a commissioner for Edinburgh in the Church of Scotland's first General Assembly. His grandson, Sir Thomas Hope (c.1580–1646), was Lord Advocate, a member of the Privy Council and Baronet of Nova Scotia (1628), and helped draft the 1638 National Covenant. He purchased an estate at Craighall, Fife, and his direct descendants, the Hopes of Craighall, are chiefs of the Hope family today. One of his sons acquired land in Hopetoun, Fife, and his grandson Charles was made Earl of Hopetoun in 1703. Hopetoun House was designed by the great Fife-born architect Robert Adam (1728–92). John Adrian Hope, 7th Earl of Hopetoun, was Lord Chamberlain from 1898–1900 and was made Marquis of Linlithgow in 1902.

HUNTER

The family's main branch traces its ancestry to the Duke of Normandy's huntsmen, who came to England with William the Conqueror and then travelled to Scotland in the retinue of David I (r.1124–53). Their Ayrshire lands were called Hunter's Toune (modern Hunterston). In the 13th century the lords built Hunterston Castle at the mouth of the river Clyde. Legend has it that the hunters made their longbows from the wood of an ancient yew that still stands in the castle's walled garden. William Hunter, probably the 10th Lord, held the lands under charter from Robert II in 1374.

In the following century members of the family were appointed to a hereditary position as Keeper of the Royal Forests of Little Cumbrae – an island in the Firth of Clyde – and Arran.

Robert Hunter, a grandson of the 20th Lord, held office as Governor of Virginia in 1697 and of New York from 1710–19.

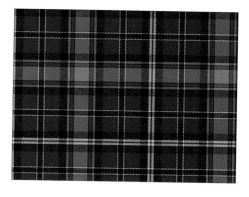

▲ *This version of the distinctive Hope tartan was first recorded in 1880.*

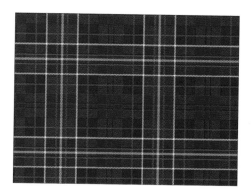

▼ *The official Hunter clan tartan is known as the Hunter of Hunterston.*

INGLIS

The family name means "Englishman" and was common in the Scots/English Borders. The clan ancestors were either English refugees fleeing William the Conqueror in the 11th century or Anglo-Norman noblemen who accompanied Prince David north when he claimed the Scottish throne in 1124. A prominent son of the clan was John Inglis (1810–91), who rose to become Lord Justice-General of Scotland. He was made Lord Glencorse in 1867 and became Chancellor of Edinburgh University in 1869.

The Inglis tartan appears to be a version of the sett worn by clan MacIntyre, which was based primarily at Loch Etive and in Argyll. The earliest known version of the Inglis dates from the mid-20th century. It was labelled "MacIntyre or Inglis" by the collector James MacKinlay.

▲ *In the Inglis sett yellow lines replace the green lines of the similar MacIntyre.*

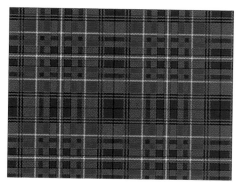

▼ *This Innes tartan is worn by members of the Innes clan from Moray.*

INNES

The Innes family take their name from the barony of Innes in Morayshire, granted to the Flemish lord Berowald by Malcolm IV in 1160. Berowald's grandson Walter took the name Innes in 1226 when Alexander II confirmed the clan's possession of these lands. The 11th Lord fought at the battle of Brechin in 1452 and was Sheriff of Moray. He founded Greyfriars, a Franciscan monastery in Elgin. His son Sir James, 12th chief, served as armourbearer to James III and in 1490 played host with great pomp to James IV at Innes Castle. Sir Robert's younger son Walter founded the Innes of Innermarkie, who became baronets of Balveny in 1628.

Another branch of the family descended from Walter built Coxton Tower in about 1574 and became baronets of Coxton in 1686.

IRVINE–KILGOUR

The colours of the family tartan grace reunions of Scottish clan members all over the world. Members of the Kilgour clan, for example, must be enlivened by the bright family tartan at meetings in northern Australia.

IRVINE

The Irvines claim descent from Scotland's early Celtic kings, although the name appears to derive from an English name, Erewine. By the time of Robert the Bruce (r.1306–29) they were settled in Dumfriesshire; William de Irwin, who served the Bruce as armour-bearer and secretary, was granted the royal forest of Drum in Aberdeenshire. Alexander, 10th Lord and Sheriff of Aberdeen, supported Charles I (r.1625–49) and in his time the family castle at Drum was besieged, occupied and stripped of valuables by anti-royalist forces. The 14th Lord fought in the Jacobite cause at Sheriffmuir in 1715 and his kinsmen also supported Bonnie Prince Charlie in the 1745 rebellion. After defeat at Culloden in 1746 the lord avoided capture by hiding in a secret place in Drum Castle.

Notable sons of the clan include the American author Washington Irving (1783–1859), whose forebears were from Orkney, and Sir Robert Irvine,

▼ *Tartan collector James MacKinlay dated the Irvine sett to 1889.*

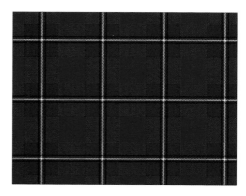

▲ *This is the Jardine Family tartan; there is another for the Castlemilk branch.*

a direct descendant of the early Dumfriesshire Irvines and captain of the liner *Queen Mary*, which was launched in 1934.

JARDINE

The name Jardine may derive from the French *jardin* ("garden"). Jardine ancestors came to England with William the Conqueror in 1066, went on to Scotland in the time of David I (r.1124–53) and settled at Applegirth, Dumfriesshire, in the 14th century. Sir Alexander Jardine was made Baronet of Nova Scotia in 1672. Legend has it that late in the 17th century the family was forced to abandon its Spedlings Tower stronghold by the ghost of a miller who had starved to death in the dungeon. They built Jardine Hall.

In the 18th century the Reverend John Jardine, a prominent literary figure, was one of the founders of *The Edinburgh Review*. In the 19th century Dr William Jardine, an East India Company surgeon, co-founded the trading house Jardine Matheson with fellow Scot James Matheson.

JOHNSTONE

This powerful Borders clan traces its name back to the 12th-century John Johnstone, father of Gilbert. In 1296 another John Johnstone, a Dumfries

landowner, swore allegiance to Edward I of England. His kinsman Adam Johnstone, lord in about 1410, fought at the battle of Sark in 1448. A 1608 attempt to reconcile a long feud between the Johnstones and the Maxwells ended in the death of the Johnstone lord at the hand of the 9th Lord Maxwell. Charles I (r.1625–49) made James Johnstone Lord Johnstone of Lochwood in 1633 and he became Earl of Hartfell in 1643. He fought in the king's cause during the Civil War and was captured at the battle of Philiphaugh in 1645. He survived the war to become Earl of Annandale and Hartfell in 1662. His descendant William was made Marquis of Annandale in 1701.

KEITH

A Norman knight named Hervey held the lands of Keith, in Lothian, under an 1150 charter from David I, and his son was made Great Marischal of Scotland in 1176. Sir Robert de Keith received the royal woodland of Halforest in Aberdeenshire from his friend Robert the Bruce (r.1306–29). In 1458 Sir William, 3rd Lord Keith, rose to become Earl Marischal. It is said that in the time of William, 3rd Earl, the family estates were so extensive that he could pass from Berwick to John

▼ *The Johnstone clan tartan has been dated to the early 19th century.*

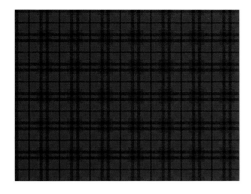

▲ *The Keith tartan was reproduced in silk in D.W. Stewart's 1893 book.*

O'Groats eating and sleeping always on his own lands. George, 4th Earl Marischal, was appointed ambassador to Denmark and founded Aberdeen's Marischal College in 1593. George, 10th Earl Marischal and friend of Frederick the Great of Prussia, was deprived of his lands and titles in the aftermath of the failed 1745 Jacobite rebellion. His brother James served in the Prussian army and that of Peter the Great, for which he was decorated with the Russian Order of St Andrew.

▼ *Falkland Palace, where many Kilgours worked, boasts what may be the world's oldest tennis court.*

The Keith tartan was listed as "Austin" by Wilson's of Bannockburn in 1819, but it is identified as a Keith sett in D.W. Stewart's *Old and Rare Scottish Tartans* (1893).

KERR

The family name may come from the Gaelic *ciar* ("dark-complexioned") or Norse *kjrr* ("dweller in the marshes"). The first person documented with the name was John Ker of Swinhope in the reign of William I (r.1165–1214). The family's two principal branches, fierce rivals for many centuries, are said to be descended from two Anglo-Norman brothers, Ralph and John Kerr, who were settled at Roxburgh around 1330. Ralph was ancestor of the Kerrs of Ferniehurst while John's descendants were the Kerrs of Cessford. Sir Andrew Kerr of Ferniehurst defended his castle so stoutly against the English in 1523 that the besiegers reported it to be guarded by the devil himself. Mark Kerr of the Cessford line became Earl of Lothian in 1606. Sir Andrew Kerr of Ferniehurst became Lord Jedburgh in 1621 and his kinsmen became earls of Ancram and earls of Lothian. Another Ferniehurst family member, Robert

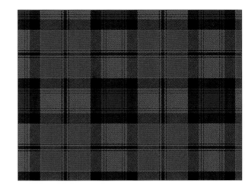

▲ *Members of the Kerr clan can also wear a blue and green "hunting tartan".*

Kerr, 1st Marquis of Lothian, was Scotland's Lord Justice General in the early 18th century.

KILGOUR

The name comes from the parish of Kilgour, near Falkland in Fife. Falkland Palace, a splendid Renaissance house (built 1501–41), was used as a hunting lodge by the Stewart monarchs and must have provided a livelihood for many early Kilgours; indeed the first Kilgour on record was Sir Thomas, a palace chaplain in about 1528. In the early 17th century another Kilgour churchman, John, was named as sacristan at Aberdeen Cathedral. The Kilgours are a sept of clan MacDuff, whose members were the earls of Fife. In the years of large-scale Scots emigration, northern Australia proved a haven for members of the Kilgour clan, and a river there bears the family name.

▼ *The Kilgour name is common in Fife and Aberdeen as well as in Australia.*

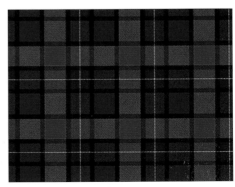

KINCAID–LENNOX

Many tartan designs were made only in the 19th century, although they were perhaps based on ancient originals. Sir Thomas Dick Lauder, a friend of the Sobieskis, may have created the Lauder shown in *Vestiarum Scoticum* (1842).

KINCAID

In 1238 the lands of Kincaid in Stirlingshire were held by Maldouen, 3rd Earl of Lennox, but towards the end of the 13th century they were acquired by a family that became known as Kincaid. In 1296 the clan's lord retook Edinburgh Castle from Edward I's English army and was rewarded by being made its constable. The Kincaid badge shows a raised arm above castle turrets and bears the motto "This I'll defend". From their Kincaid base the family expanded eastward, gaining Craiglockhart near Edinburgh through marriage and later adding Bantaskin near Falkirk, Blackness Castle near Linlithgow and Warriston (now an Edinburgh suburb).

At the start of the 17th century John Kincaid of Warriston was murdered by one of his grooms working in league with the lord's wife; both conspirators were put to death. The Kincaids were Royalists in the Civil War and later supported the exiled Stuarts. A number of Kincaids made a new life in North

America: David Kincaid in Virginia, after the failure of the 1715 Jacobite rebellion, and four sons of Alexander Kincaid, Lord Provost of Edinburgh, in Virginia after the 1745 rebellion.

KINNIESON

The Kinniesons were settled in Atholl before 1450. Their name is also spelled MacConach or Cuneison and means Conan's son, the Conan in question probably being a son of Henry, Earl of Atholl, named Conan of Glenerochy. John Cunysoun acquired the lands of Ardgery in 1474 and was Baron of Eddradoun. The clan is seen as a sept, or sub-group, of the MacFarlanes.

▼ *The name Kincaid may derive from Gaelic* ceann cadha *("steep place").*

▼ *The Kinnieson is similar to the MacFarlanes' black and white sett.*

▲ *Edinburgh Castle, once guarded by the Kincaids, dominates the city from its position on a rocky outcrop.*

LAMONT

The clan traces its descent from the O'Neill princes of Tyrone in Ireland, but its name is derived from the Norse *logmaor* ("giver of laws"), which in Gaelic was *ladhman*. On arrival in Scotland at the start of the 13th century, the family settled in Argyll. Soon after, Laumanus gave the church of Kilfinan and lands at Kilmun to the Paisley monks. Clan leadership passed from the first line of chiefs to their kinsmen at Inveryne, afterwards called Lamont of Lamont. They came into conflict with their ambitious neighbours, the Campbells, and in 1646 the Lamont lands were invaded and the castles at Ascog and Toward besieged. In a peace deal the Lamont chief Sir James sacrificed the castles to save his clansmen, but the Campbells reneged on the agreement, imprisoning Sir James for five years and slaughtering more than 200 Lamont men, women and children. The Lamonts never recovered parity with the Campbells. In 1893 the chief sold the remaining

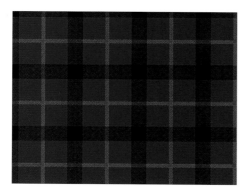

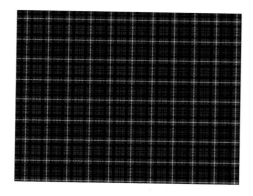

▲ *This tartan was approved by the Lamont chief in around 1816.*

▲ *This Lauder tartan was listed as No 48 in the Sobieskis' 1842 collection.*

deprived both of their chief William and his son and heir Alexander. A younger son, another William, succeeded as chief.

LENNOX

The Earls of Lennox were descended from the *mormaers* (ancient Celtic stewards) of Levenax, who governed lands in Dunbartonshire, Perthshire, Stirlingshire and Renfrewshire. Malcolm, 5th Earl, a staunch supporter of Robert the Bruce, invaded England with his clansmen and besieged Carlisle. In later years the Lennox title was attached to the Stewart family; in 1488 Sir John Stewart of Darnley was made Earl of Lennox (1st Earl in the new Stewart line) by James III. The 1st Earl was a member of the first Parliament of James IV (r.1488–1513). The 4th Earl's son Henry, Lord Darnley, married Mary, Queen of Scots (r.1542–67), and fathered James VI. James was heir to the title of earl, but bestowed it upon Esme Stuart, a grandson of the 3rd Stewart Earl of Lennox, in 1581. The title later came to Charles II, and he bestowed it upon his illegitimate son, Charles, whose title was Duke of Lennox and Richmond.

The Lennox sett was reproduced in D.W. Stewart's *Old and Rare Scottish Tartans* (1893) from a portrait, now lost, of the Countess of Lennox, wife of the 4th Earl in the latter part of the 16th century.

parts of the Lamont inheritance and settled in Australia.

The Lamonts' close proximity to the Campbells explains why the Lamont tartan is very similar to the sett known as Campbell of Argyll.

LAUDER

The clan is descended from a Norman lord, Sir Robert de Laudre, who came to Scotland in the reign of Malcolm III "Canmore" (r.1058–93) and received lands in Berwickshire to which he gave his name. His descendant, another Sir Robert, went with King William the Lion's brother, the Earl of Huntingdon, on the Third Crusade (1189–92).

In 1297 members of the Lauder family held the island known as the Bass on the Firth of Forth. Another Sir Robert de Laudre fought with Wallace in the Battle of Stirling Bridge in 1297. His son, yet another Sir Robert, was appointed Justiciar of the Lothians by Robert the Bruce (r.1306–29) and also became Governor of Berwick Castle and Chamberlain of Scotland. Sir Alan de Laudre was one of the party of knights who accompanied Good Sir James Douglas in his attempt to fulfil the Bruce's dying wish to have his embalmed heart carried to the Holy Land. Sir Alan fought with Douglas against the Moors in Spain.

In the 15th century William de Laudre was Bishop of Glasgow and also Lord Chancellor of Scotland.

LEASK

Most authorities identify William de Laskereske, who vowed allegiance to Edward I of England in 1296, as the first of the clan, but there is little agreement about the origin of the name. Some associate it with De Lesque in Normandy, others link it to the Anglo-Saxon word *lisse* ("happy") and others believe it derives from Gaelic *lasgair* ("brave"). The Leask possessions in Aberdeenshire were confirmed by a charter of David II around 1346.

In the mid-15th century James Leask, a younger son of the Aberdeenshire lord, moved to Orkney, where he founded a branch of the family. His grandson, Richard, founded another branch in Shetland. On 9 September 1513, when Scotland lost so many of her nobles on the disastrous field of Flodden, the Leasks were

▼ *The Leask tartan is a recent design approved in 1981.*

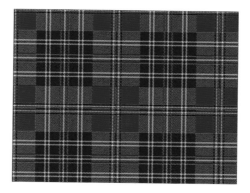

▼ *The Lennox tartan has venerable proof of the authenticity of its design.*

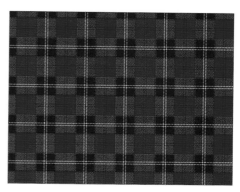

LESLIE–LUMSDEN

It is not usually easy to identify a tartan from its colour, because the shades used are left to the weaver's judgment. But the darkness of the Lindsay tartan means that the family allegiance of its wearers can be seen from a distance.

LESLIE

The Leslies are descended from Bartolf, a Flemish nobleman who followed Edgar the Aetheling, brother of Margaret, Malcolm III's queen, to Scotland in 1067. Bartolf became Governor of Edinburgh Castle and was granted lands in Aberdeenshire, Fife and Angus. During the 15th century George Leslie rose to prominence as Lord Leslie of Leven, later Earl of Rothes. Many Leslies were celebrated soldiers. In the 17th century Alexander Leslie won great repute fighting in the Thirty Years War for King Gustavus Adolphus of Sweden. On his return to Scotland he commanded the Covenanter Army in the Civil War and was made Earl of Leven in 1641. His kinsman David Leslie, also a Covenanter

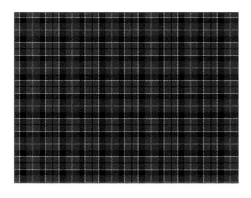

▲ *The Leslie tartan is said to be based on one worn by George, 14th Earl of Rothes (d.1841).*

general, was defeated by Cromwell at Dunbar in 1650 and imprisoned in the Tower of London. The 9th Earl of Rothes was Governor of Stirling Castle and commander in the Hanoverian army at Sheriffmuir in 1715.

LINDSAY

Baldric de Lindesay, a Norman knight of William the Conqueror, is the family ancestor. His descendant, Sir William de Lindsay, sat in Parliament in 1164 as Baron of Luffness, East Lothian, and held the lands of Crawford. In 1390 Sir David de

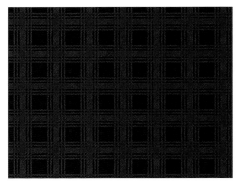

▲ *The Lindsay sett is similar to the Stewart of Atholl. A much brighter one, known as Chisholm Red, is also seen.*

Lindsay won great fame in a tournament attended by Richard II of England at London Bridge. He was made Earl of Crawford in 1398 and Lord High Admiral of Scotland in 1403. A later earl of Crawford, Ludovic Lindsay, fought at Marston Moor in 1644 and Philiphaugh in 1645 during the Civil War. The Balcarres branch of the family also fought with distinction in the war, and in 1651 Alexander Lindsay was made Earl of Balcarres. He became Governor of Edinburgh Castle and Secretary of State for Scotland. The two branches of the family were united and current clan chiefs are earls of both Crawford and Balcarres.

LIVINGSTONE

This proud family take their name from lands in West Lothian. They trace their ancestry to Leving, a Saxon lord who settled in Scotland during the reign of Edgar the Peaceable (r.1097–1107) and named his lands Levingestun. A Livingus, who may or may not have been his descendant, is known to have lived in the first half of the 12th century, and in 1296 Sir Archibald de Livingstone was among the knights who swore allegiance to Edward I of England. Sir Archibald's grandson, Sir William, fought with

▼ *The Lindsays acquired Edzell Castle through marriage in 1358.*

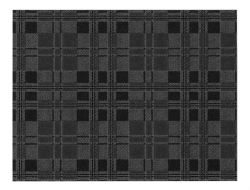

▲ *The Livingstone tartan is similar to the MacDonell of Keppoch sett.*

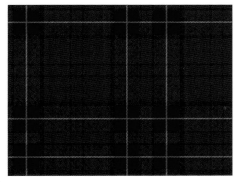

▲ *This Lockhart tartan is a modern design, created in 1996.*

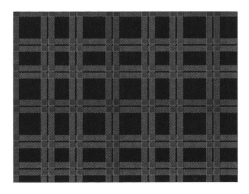

▲ *Wilson's of Bannockburn had two versions of Logan tartan in their books.*

David II in 1346, when he invaded England, and was granted the barony of Callendar in Stirlingshire. The family rose to a position of great power in the mid-15th century and in 1440 Sir Alexander Livingstone of Callendar took a leading role in the murder plot against William, Earl of Douglas, and his brother in the presence of the young James II at Edinburgh Castle. One of Sir Alexander's sons, Sir James, became Great Chamberlain of Scotland and Lord Livingstone in 1458.

Alexander Livingstone, 7th Lord Livingstone, became Earl of Linlithgow in 1600, but the family lost their titles after James, 4th Earl Linlithgow, took part in the 1715 Jacobite uprising. Dr David Livingstone, the 19th-century explorer of Africa, was descended from the "Highland Livingstones" of north-western Scotland.

LOCKHART

English refugees from William the Conqueror, the Locards had settled in Ayrshire and in the region of the Lee, Lanarkshire, by the 1100s. Sir Symon Locard, 2nd Lord of Lee, was a celebrated knight in Robert the Bruce's war of independence and rode with Good Sir James Douglas in 1330 in his attempt to carry the Bruce's embalmed heart to the Holy Land. Sir Symon carried the key to the silver casket it was carried in, and to honour this event the family changed their name to

Lockheart, included a heart in their badge and adopted the motto "I open locked hearts". Sir James died fighting the Moors in Spain before the party could reach the Holy Land. According to tradition, Sir Symon exchanged a prisoner for a stone said to have healing powers, which inspired Sir Walter Scott's 1825 novel *The Talisman*.

LOGAN

Two knights of this clan, Robert and Walter, accompanied Good Sir James Douglas to the Holy Land in 1330, but all three died fighting the Moors in Spain. There were two branches of the Logans: a Lowland one, originating in Galloway, and a Highland one from Drumderfit in Easter Ross, associated with the MacLennans. In the early 17th century Sir Robert Logan of Restalrig suffered the indignity of having his bones dug up and taken to Parliament as part of the proceeding of posthumously declaring him guilty of treason.

James Logan published his groundbreaking *The Scottish Gael* in 1831, containing valuable information on clan histories and customs gathered during a tour of the Highlands in 1826.

LUMSDEN

The family name comes from the manor of Lumisden in Coldingham, Berwickshire, one of several villages granted to the priory of Coldingham in 1098 by Edgar the Peaceable. The clan

founder was Adam de Lumisden, who, alongside his son Roger, signed the 1296 oath of allegiance to Edward I of England. The family acquired lands at Blanerne, where they had a fine castle, at Conlan in Fife and Cushnie in Aberdeenshire.

Many Lumsdens won renown on the battlefield, including three brothers who fought together in the army of King Gustav Adolphus of Sweden, around 1650, and returned to serve with the Covenanters in the Civil War. One of these, Sir James Lumsden of Innergellie, fought at Marston Moor in 1644 and Dunbar in 1650. Another, Robert of Mountquhanie, died defending Dundee. Andrew Lumsden of the family's Cushnie branch was secretary to Bonnie Prince Charlie during the 1745 rebellion and afterwards settled in Rome as Secretary of State for James, the Old Pretender.

▼ *Many brave family members wore the Lumsden tartan into battle.*

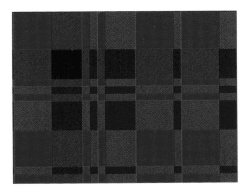

MacALISTER–MacBETH

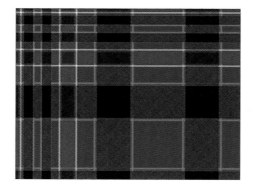

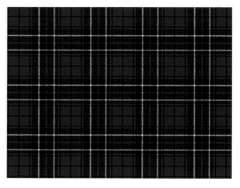

The unusual complexity of the MacAlister sett led some weavers in the past to take the option of shortening the pattern. This practice produced minor variations between different versions, which can be difficult to spot.

MacALISTER

The family, a branch of clan Donald, made their home in Kintyre. Chiefs and clansmen were known as MacAlisters of the Loup, from the Gaelic *lub* ("curve"), a reference to the curved shore that bounded their lands. They trace their descent as "sons of Alastair" from Alastair Mor, second son of Donald of Islay, Lord of the Isles, in the late 13th century. Ranald, son of Alexander, is recorded as clan chief in 1366. In 1481 Charles MacAlister was appointed Constable of Tarbert Castle and was granted extensive lands in Kintyre under charter from James III. His son John was the first clan chief to be called "of the Loup" in written records. In the 15th and 16th centuries

▼ *Loch Slapin on Skye, is part of the island realm of clan Donald and its MacAlpine offshoot.*

▲ *This version of the MacAlister sett is in Logan's* The Scottish Gael *(1831).*

clansmen spread to Bute and Arran and there was a branch at Glenbarr in Argyll. Alexander MacAlister, 8th Lord of Loup, supported the Jacobite cause, fighting at Killiecrankie in 1689 under Bonnie Dundee.

MacALPINE

The MacAlpines trace their line back to the birth of Scotland in the 9th century and sometimes claim to be the oldest Highland clan. Their ancestor is Alpin, a 9th-century king of Dalriada whose son, Kenneth MacAlpin, united the kingdoms of the Scots and the Picts. In about 1260 John MacAlpine

▲ *The MacAlpine tartan has a similar pattern to the Hunting MacLean sett.*

was witness to a charter of the Earl of Stratherne and in 1296 Monaghe fitz Alpyn swore allegiance to Edward I of England. The clan's traditional base is believed to have been Dunstaffnage, near Oban, Argyll, but the MacAlpines now have no lands or chief.

MacARTHUR

Some members of this ancient Argyll clan claim descent from a son of the legendary King Arthur. In the 14th century Robert the Bruce granted former MacDougall lands in mid-Argyll to Mac-ic-Artair, the MacArthur chief, as reward for his support in the war for Scottish independence.

The clan was dealt a major blow when its chief Iain was beheaded for treason by James I (r.1406–37). The

▼ *The MacArthur tartan is similar to the MacDonald, Lord of the Isles, sett.*

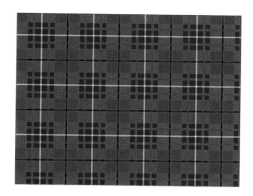

▲ *The MacAulay tartan reveals the clan's links to the MacGregors.*

MacArthur clansmen spread out in many directions. In Skye they established themselves as pipers to the MacDonalds of Sleat, while another branch of the family settled at Proaig, Islay, and served as armourers to the MacDonalds of Islay.

Following the failure of the 1745 Jacobite rebellion, in the late 18th and early 19th centuries many MacArthurs emigrated to North America, the West Indies and Australia. Celebrated clan sons include John MacArthur (d.1834), a pioneer of the wool industry in Australia, and General Douglas MacArthur (1880–1964), US military commander of the Southwest Pacific theatre during the Second World War. His grandfather arrived in the United States in about 1840.

MACAULAY

The MacAulays of Ardincaple, in Dunbartonshire, were closely associated with clan MacGregor and were vassals of the earls of Lennox. They took their original name from their family seat, but in the reign of James V (r.1513–42) Alexander, son of Aulay de Ardincaple, was the first to take the name MacAulay.

During the 17th century the extravagance of chief Aulay MacAulay and his descendants brought the family to a state of financial ruin. Another Aulay MacAulay, 12th chief, was obliged to sell the last of the family possessions

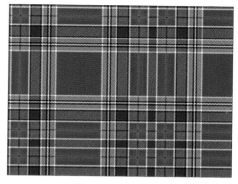

▲ *The MacBain tartan has many similarities to the Mackintosh sett.*

to the Campbell Duke of Argyll in about 1767.

The MacAulays of Lewis claim separate Norse descent, their name deriving from the Gaelic MacAmlaibh ("son of Olaf"). Their first recorded chief, around 1610, was the quick-tempered Donald Cam ("One-eye"). His son Angus fought in support of Charles I and was killed at the battle of Aldern in 1645. Angus's great-great-great-grandson was Thomas Babington MacAulay (1800–59), historian, poet and statesman, who was MP for Edinburgh (1830–56) and was made Lord MacAulay in 1857.

MACBAIN

The MacBains, whose name was often spelled MacBean, were members of clan Chattan who lived on the northern side of Loch Ness. They supported Robert the Bruce (r.1306–29) in his rise to power. Later they fought in the bloody but indecisive battle of Harlaw in 1411 as part of the 10,000-strong force of Donald, Lord of the Isles, against the Earl of Mar. The clan's 12th chief, Paul MacBean, sold many clan lands and possessions in 1685.

Following the failure of the 1715 Jacobite uprising many MacBain clansmen were sent to the plantations of South Carolina, Virginia and Maryland. Paul MacBean's grandson, Gillies Mor MacBean, fought with great valour at Culloden in 1746 and felled 14

Government troops before being killed. Sons of the clan went on to distinguish themselves in the army of the British Empire, fighting the Indian Mutiny in 1858 and against the Boers in 1881.

MACBETH

The name of this clan is forever associated with the murdering king of Shakespeare's tragedy, but in fact it means "son of Beathan", a Celtic forename derived from the word for "life". The historical Macbeth (r.1040–57) presided over a relatively peaceful era and towards the end of his reign made a pilgrimage to Rome. He was the son of Finlay, the Celtic *mormaer* (steward) of Moray, and Doada, daughter of Malcolm II, while his wife, Gruoch, was granddaughter of Kenneth III (d.1005). He had as good a claim to the throne as Duncan I (r.1034–40), whom he killed in battle. Macbeth died fighting the future king Malcolm III (r.1058–93), but was briefly succeeded by his stepson Lulach (r.1057–58).

Many forms of MacBeth and similar names were used interchangeably – including Bethune, Beaton and MacVeigh (because Gaelic *bh* could become "v") – so it is extremely difficult to trace the family's lineage. Many sons of the clan practised as physicians.

The MacBeth tartan appears to be derived from the Royal Stewart, but with a blue background rather than red with yellow edging.

▼ *The MacBeth clan tartan is also known as the Stewart Brydone.*

MacCALLUM–MacEWEN

The quest for historical authenticity can be difficult. D.W. Stewart, in *Old and Rare Scottish Tartans* (1893), reports that the MacCallums had a tartan made based on the recollections of old folk in their lands, but when they recovered an original tartan it was notably different from the new one.

MacCALLUM

The family name denotes a follower of St Columba (*c*.521–597), the Irish abbot who is credited with Scotland's conversion to Christianity. The MacCallums were established in Lorn, Argyllshire, by the end of the 13th century. In 1414 Ronald MacCallum of Corbarron was granted lands in Craignish and alongside Loch Avich, and was made hereditary constable of the castles at Craignish and Lochaffy. The family's main branch was in Poltalloch on the Bay of Craignish, and occupied lands acquired by Donald MacGillespie vic O'Challum in 1562. His descendant Zachary, 5th Lord of Poltalloch, inherited the estates of Corbarron. The 9th Lord of Poltalloch, Dugald MacCallum, changed his name to Malcolm, and his descendant John Wingfield Malcolm became Lord Malcolm of Poltalloch in 1896. The family home of this branch was the 11th-century Duntroon Castle.

▼ *This is the sett officially recognized as the MacCallum clan tartan.*

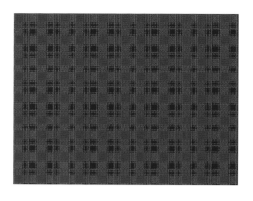

▲ *Wilson's of Bannockburn sold the MacColl tartan in 1797 as the "Bruce".*

MacCOLL

The MacColls originally settled on the banks of Loch Fyne. They were generally regarded as followers of the MacDonalds, who often used Coll as a forename, but were also associated with the Stewarts of Appin and the MacGregors. A feud with the MacPhersons led to a bloody encounter on the shores of Loch Garry in 1602 in which the clan was almost wiped out.

The Appin MacColls fought in the 1745 Jacobite rebellion in the Appin Regiment, and of 109 wounded or killed from that regiment, 33 were MacColls. A celebrated son was the Gaelic poet Evan MacColl (1808–98), who published *Clarsach nam Beann* (*Mountain Minstrel*) in 1838. He was born at Kenmore on Loch Fyne.

▼ *There are two rival MacDiarmid family tartans with similar colouring.*

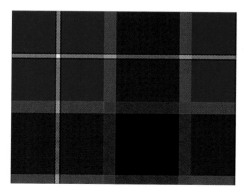

MacDIARMID

The MacDiarmids are a sept, or subgroup, of clan Campbell. The name means "son of Diarmid", a popular forename that belonged to an attendant of St Columba and was borne by no fewer than three heroes of Celtic mythology. There are many MacDiarmids in Argyll and the family lay claim to having been the original occupants of Glenlyon. MacDiarmids of Glenlyon were well represented in the Duke of Atholl's Fencibles, one of the regiments raised in the late 18th century to protect the country against possible invasion from France.

The tartan is not known before 1906, when it was published in H. Whyte's *The Tartans of the Clans and Septs of Scotland*.

MacDOUGALL

Dugall was the son of Somerled, King of the Isles (d.1164). After his father's death he ruled over the Hebridean islands of Coll, Jura, Lismore, Mull and Tiree, and on the mainland over much of Argyll. He and his immediate descendants were vassals of the King of Norway, but after King Haakon's defeat at the battle of Largs in 1263 Norway ceded control of the Hebrides to Scotland. In Argyll the MacDougalls were drawn into conflict with the

▼ *There are many extant variations of the complex MacDougall tartan.*

▲ *Early MacDougalls built the ancient castle of Coeffin on a crag overlooking the waves on the west side of Lismore.*

Campbells, leading to a fierce and bloody fight at the Path of Lorn in 1294. The MacDougalls were connected to the Comyns through marriage and so opposed Robert the Bruce. They lost a major battle at the Pass of Brander in Argyll in 1308 and had their lands forfeited. But after Ewen, 5th Lord of Lorn, married Joanna MacIssak, a granddaughter of the Bruce, David II restored most of the clan's mainland territories in 1344.

MacDUFF

The clan claims royal descent from King Dubh, or Duff (r.962–67), and had the right to enthrone the king at Scone and to lead the vanguard of the royal army. In addition, any MacDuff pursued for murder could claim sanctuary at the Cross of MacDuff, near Newburgh in Fife. MacDuff was the ancestral name of the Celtic earls of Fife, the first on record being Ethelred, son of Malcolm III (r.1058–93). The first known MacDuffs were the brothers Constantine and Gilliemichael

Mac-Duf, earls of Fife in the first part of David I's reign (r.1124–53). Their line appears to have ended in the early 1300s, but a century later David Duff of Banffshire claimed descent. His family rose in prestige and in 1759 William Duff was made Earl Fife and Viscount MacDuff. In 1889 Alexander, 6th Earl, married Louise, daughter of Edward, Prince of Wales, and was made Duke.

MacEWEN

The clan held land alongside Loch Fyne in Argyll, with a castle near Kilfinnan. The MacEwans were allies of the MacLachlans and MacNeills. In the early 15th century, following Sween

▼ *The width of the red and blue lines varies in different MacDuff versions.*

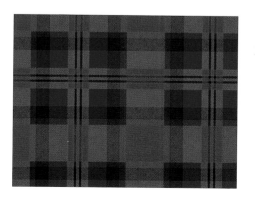

MacEwen's chiefship, their lands passed to the Campbells of Loch Awe.

Many Argyll MacEwens became dependants of the Campbells, whom they served as hereditary bards, while some lived as "broken", or clanless, men. The MacEwens who flourished at Bardrochat in Ayrshire from the 14th century onwards may have had no connection with the Argyll branch. Celebrated sons include Sir William MacEwen (1848–1924), who developed germ-free operating conditions.

The MacEwen tartan is similar to the Campbell of Loudoun sett, reflecting the clan's close association with the Campbells.

▼ *The MacEwen was reproduced in H. Whyte's book of 1906.*

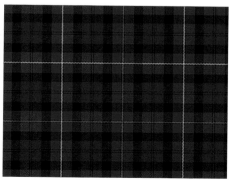

MacFADYEN–MacHARDIE

The tartans of the fierce MacFarlanes survive in a number of variants, including a plain black and white design also known as "Wallace dress". The MacFies, by contrast, have a single recently registered red, green and white tartan.

MacFADYEN

The MacFadyens are generally regarded as a sept, or sub-group, of the MacLaines of Lochbuie. Their name, sometimes given as MacFadzean, is derived from the Gaelic Macphaidin ("son of Little Pat") and was anglicized as Patonson. It was first recorded in 1304 when Malcolm Macpadene witnessed a charter covering the grant of lands at Achichendone in Kintyre. The

▼ *Victorian gentlemen display their clan colours: MacLachlan, Graham, MacFarlane and Colquhoun.*

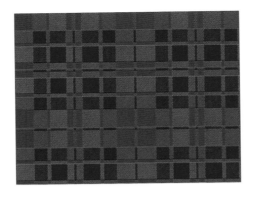

▲ *The MacFadyen tartan was the mark of a skilled craftsman in the Isles.*

clansmen claim to have been the first inhabitants of Lochbuie which, according to some accounts, they held under charter from John, 1st Lord of the Isles. Later they became wandering craftsmen, best known as goldsmiths on the island of Mull. Family branches were also established on Islay and Tiree.

▲ *This MacFarlane Dress tartan can be worn for dances and formal dinners.*

MacFARLANE

Famous for their bravery in battle, the warlike MacFarlanes were also notorious for feuding and cattle-rustling, to such an extent that the full moon under which rustlers operate became known as "MacFarlanes' lamp". They claim descent from Gilchrist, who in about 1230 inherited the Arrochar lands on Loch Lomond's west bank from his older brother Malduin, Earl of Lennox. The name is derived from MacPharlain, meaning "son of Bartholomew" (Parlan in Gaelic), taken from the 4th chief, Bartholomew.

At Flodden in 1513 the clansmen fought under their 11th chief, Sir John MacFarlane, and at the battle of Pinkie in 1547 they were led by their 13th chief, Duncan. Both chiefs were killed in battle. The clan also won great honour at the battle of Langside in 1568 and under the Marquis of Montrose at Inverlochy in 1645. Walter MacFarlane, 20th chief, was a notable scholar. He died childless in 1767 and most of the clan's Arrochar possessions were sold by his brother Andrew.

MacFIE

The MacFies of Colonsay derive their name from MacDuffie, in Gaelic MacDhuibhshith ("son of the dark fairy"), and are said to be descended

from a seal-woman who was forced to remain on the island. The name is also found as Macphee and Macafie. They were hereditary keepers of records for the Lords of the Isles, with whom their chief is said to have fought with great valour at Bannockburn in 1314.

In 1615 Malcolm MacFie of Colonsay fought alongside Sir James MacDonald of Islay when he rebelled against royal authority in the person of the Earl of Argyll, but they were betrayed and humbled. In the mid-17th century Colonsay passed into the MacDonalds' possession. Many MacFies became followers of the MacDonalds, while others settled in Cameron lands in Lochaber and in 1746 fought under Cameron of Lochiel at the battle of Culloden.

MACGILL

The MacGills are considered a sept or sub-group of the MacDonald clan. The name is taken to be a contraction of the Gaelic Mac an Ghoill ("son of the stranger", meaning Lowlander) and the family were known in Galloway, in south-western Scotland, before they settled on the island of Jura in the 18th century. One of the earliest records of the name is in 1231, when Maurice MacGeil witnessed a charter of the Earl of Leuenach to a church in Arbroath.

The tartan is known to have been worn on Jura before 1745, but was lost until a scrap was found in Kintyre.

▼ This sett was registered as the MacFie tartan by Lord Lyon in 1991.

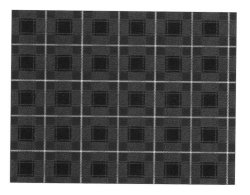

▲ The MacGill tartan is in the Scottish Tartan Society collection of 1930–50.

MACGILLIVRAY

The clan probably originally came from Scotland's west coast, perhaps from the island of Mull, where its members are known to have lived many centuries ago. It is likely they were churchmen, as their name means "son of the servant of judgment" and it is often found in church documents.

In about 1268 the MacGillivrays placed themselves under the protection of Farquhard, 5th Lord of Mackintosh, and became members of the clan Chattan confederation. In about 1500 the clansmen settled in Strathnairn at Dunmaglass, which became their base. Like other clan Chattan men, the MacGillivrays fought in the Jacobite cause in the 1715 and 1745 rebellions. After the failure of the latter, many emigrated to North America, where William MacGillivray became head of the Canadian Northwest Company.

▼ Wilson's of Bannockburn sold this MacGillivray tartan from 1819.

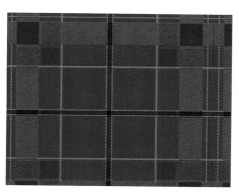

Back in Scotland, another William MacGillivray (1796–1851) was Professor of Natural History at Aberdeen University and published a magnificent five-volume *History of British Birds* (1837–52).

MACHARDIE

The MacHardie name probably comes from the Gaelic Mac Chardaidh ("son of the sloe"), and is a reference to the clan's Aberdeenshire lands. Another theory is that it derives from the French *hardi* meaning "bold", while other scholars believe it comes from the Pictish name Gartnaigh, which evolved over generations to MacCarday and then to MacHardie late in the 16th century. The clan was numerous in the Corgarff area of Strathdon, Aberdeenshire. The MacHardies of Strathdon attached themselves to clan Mackintosh and so were members of clan Chattan, while elsewhere MacHardies were followers of the Farquharsons. The name was first recorded in 1560, when the murderers of Thomas McChardy were brought to trial in Braemar, Aberdeenshire. In 1676 Donald McQhardies was listed as a Braemar court official, and in the same era John McArdie and Alexander MacKardie were extant in Invercauld. The name was also spelled Machardy, Macharday and McCardie. Many emigrated to North America, Australia, New Zealand and South Africa.

▼ The MacHardie has many similarities to the Farquharson tartan.

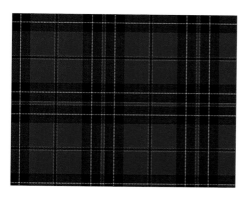

MacIAN–MACKAY

The MacInnes are a separate clan from the Innes of Moray, but the green MacInnes tartan has a similar structure to that of the red Innes tartan. Each clan wears the tartans of the other as "Dress" and "Hunting" variants.

MacIAN

Several families go under the name MacIan, which means "son of Ian, or John", and also appears as MacIain, MacKean and MacKain. Many of the families had links to the MacDonald clan. The MacIans of Ardnamurchan traced their ancestry to Eoin Sprangach, a 14th-century MacDonald chief, while the MacIains of Glencoe originated from the Glencoe branch of the MacDonalds and took their name from Iain Abrach, a son of the MacDonald chief Angus Og. The 12th chief of the Glencoe MacIans, Alasdair MacDonald, was killed with his MacDonald kinsmen in the Glencoe massacre of 1692.

A 17th-century MacKeane family made their name as merchants in Elgin. The MacIans also had links to the Gunn family, who originally came from the regions of Sutherland and Caithness. The first record of a MacIan tartan is in the Sobieski Brothers' *Vestiarum Scoticum* (1842), where it was listed under the name MacKeane.

▼ *MacIans wear this cloth to honour the death of their kinsman at Glencoe.*

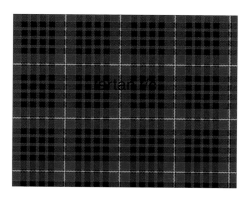

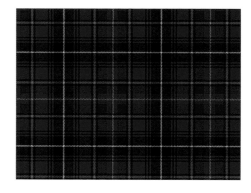

▲ *The MacInnes clan tartan was reproduced for the first time in 1908.*

MacINNES

Some authorities identify the MacInnes family as descendants of Oenghus, one of the founders of the kingdom of Dalriada, as their name is derived from the Gaelic MacAonghais ("son of Angus"). By the 13th century the MacInnes had established themselves in Morvern and Ardnamurchan in Argyllshire, said to have been a reward for stout military service to the MacDonalds. The last chief appears to have been killed in 1390, after which many clan members were subject to the Campbells of Craignish. One branch became hereditary constables of Kinlochaline Castle in Morvern, while members of another were hereditary archers for the MacKinnons of Skye. The family's principal badge has an arm holding a bow and the motto "By the grace of God and the king".

In later years MacInnes family members emigrated in great numbers and many are found today in New Zealand, the US, and especially Canada.

MacINROY

This Atholl family takes its name from its ancestor MacIainRuadh ("son of John the Red"), a member of the Robertsons of Straloch. They established themselves in the region of Dowally village and the Pass of

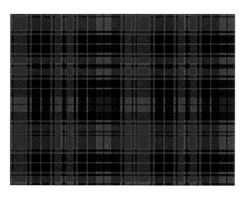

▲ *A MacInroy tartan was in existence by the early 19th century.*

Killiecrankie near Pitlochry in the 16th century and farmed there for generations. A small family, the MacInroys allied themselves with the Dukes of Atholl, as well as with the Stewarts and Fergussons. The main branch of the family was the MacInroys of Lude, near Pitlochry.

The MacInroy tartan was included in William and Andrew Smith's 19th-century *Authenticated Tartans of the Clans and Families of Scotland*.

MacINTYRE

According to family tradition the MacIntyres came originally from the Hebrides. In the 13th century they sailed from their ancestral home, carrying a white cow, and settled on the mainland at Glen Noe by Ben

▼ *A doublet made from MacIntyre tartan has been dated to 1800.*

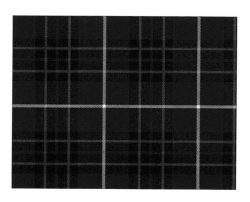

Cruachan. Their name comes from the Gaelic Mac anTsaoir ("son of the carpenter") and they are said to be descended from Macarill, a nephew of Somerled, Lord of the Isles in the mid-12th century. Macarill was nicknamed the Carpenter for his part in a scheme designed to win King Olav of Norway's daughter as a bride for his uncle. Having bored holes in the hull of one of Olav's ships, he would only fill them if the king consented to the wedding.

On the mainland the MacIntyres were hereditary foresters to the lords of Lorne. For many years they paid the Campbells of Glenorchy a symbolic rent of a white calf and a snowball for their Glen Noe lands. During the 18th century the rent was commuted to cash, then progressively raised. Donald, reckoned as 4th MacIntyre chief, could not pay so emigrated to Canada in 1783. His brother and successor, Captain Donald MacIntyre, tried but failed to make ends meet and the Glen Noe lands were lost in 1808.

▼ Following their motto, the Mackays ruled over these lands and waters in Strathnever "with a strong hand".

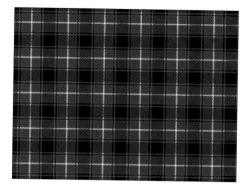

▲ The MacIver tartan was first printed in a 1953 book by Robert Bain.

MacIVER

Viking blood runs through MacIver veins and their name comes from the Gaelic MacIomhar ("son of Iver"), a common Norse forename. The family lands at Asknish and Glassary in Cowal are said to have been granted to Iver Crom, who in the 13th century fought for Alexander II against the clan's Norse kinsmen. Doenaldus MacYvar is mentioned in a 1219 agreement defining the boundary between Arbroath Abbey and the Kynblathmund barony.

In the 16th century the chiefs held positions of importance: Duncan MacIver of Asknish was Keeper of

Inveraray Castle in 1572 and Charles MacIver of Ballochyle was Chamberlain of Argyll in 1589. The MacIvers often intermarried with clan Campbell families, and their forfeited estates were restored in the late 17th century by the earls of Argyll on condition that they took the Campbell name. In the 20th century the MacIver Society, mindful of the family's motto, "I will never forget", set about restoring the clan's independent standing.

MACKAY

"Mackay country" is Strathnever in north-western Scotland. In some accounts the family, whose name comes from Gaelic MacAodh ("son of Hugh"), are descended from Aodh, brother of Alexander I (r.1107–24) and Abbot of Dunkeld.

In the early 15th century Angus Dubh Mackay, a powerful chieftain, could call on the support of 4000 men from his Strathnever territories. In about 1415 he married Elizabeth, a sister of Donald MacDonald, Lord of the Isles. The clan has a proud military tradition and its motto is "With a strong hand". Mackays made a name for themselves fighting in 17th-century continental Europe. At home, General Hugh Mackay of Scourie, who was defeated by Bonnie Dundee at Killicrankie in 1689, won a victory the following year over the Jacobites at the Haughs of Cromdale.

▼ This version of the Mackay tartan is often worn as the "Blue Mackay".

MacKELLAR–MacLACHLAN

The pattern books of Wilson's of Bannockburn make no mention of a MacKinlay tartan, but the surviving design is very similar to those produced by Wilson's for the Gordons, the MacLeods and the MacKenzies.

MacKELLAR

Established in Argyll by the 13th century, the MacKellars later spread out widely in Scotland and are now regarded as a sept of clan Campbell. The name is said to come from Gaelic MacEalair ("son of Hilary") and to be derived from that of St Hilary ("Hilarius" in Latin), the 4th-century bishop of Poitiers who wrote *De Trinitate*, a tract on the doctrine of the Trinity. The MacKellars' ancestors were probably known as Hilarius and this name is often found in early Scottish legal and territorial records.

MacKINLAY

The MacKinlays' name is from Gaelic MacFhionnlaigh ("son of Findlay"). Men of Lennox, MacKinlays claimed Findlay, son of Buchanan of Drumikill, as their ancestor. Some authorities, however, argue that the MacKinlays may have been connected to the Farquharsons of Braemar; they were also sons of Findlay, having descended from Findlay Mor, bearer of the royal

standard at the battle of Pinkie in 1547. But no documents show MacKinlays settled in the Braemar region. The clan has also been connected to the Stewarts of Appin and the Buchanans. William McKinley, the Ohio-born 25th President of the United States (1897–1901), was a clan descendant.

The MacKinlay sett is comparable to the Farquharson tartan, which has

▲ *The ruins of Castle Lachlan bear witness to the sufferings of the MacLachlans after the Jacobite defeat.*

additional yellow striping. Both are variants of the Black Watch tartan. The MacKinlay was identified as "Murray of Atholl" by James Logan, author of *The Scottish Gael* (1831).

MacKINNON

The MacKinnons are one of the clans of Siol Alpin ("race of Alpin") who claim descent from Kenneth MacAlpin (*c.*840–858). Their Gaelic name, MacFhionghuin, is said to derive from that of Fingon, great-grandson of King Kenneth. One branch of the family became hereditary abbots of Iona. John MacKinnon, the 9th chief and last of the hereditary abbots (d.*c.*1500), was also Bishop of the Isles. In the 14th century the clan sheltered Robert the Bruce on Arran, in reward for which

▼ *A MacKellar sett dating to 1930–50 is held by the Scottish Tartan Society.*

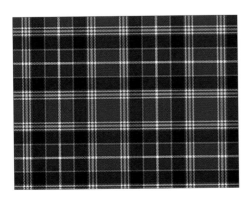

▼ *The MacKinlay tartan is essentially a "Black Watch" with added red lines.*

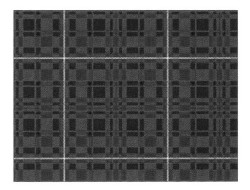

▲ *The MacKinnon tartan was certified as accurate by the clan chief in 1816.*

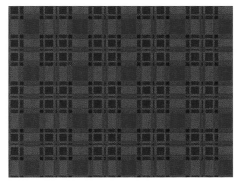

▲ *The Highland Society of London held this Mackintosh tartan in 1815.*

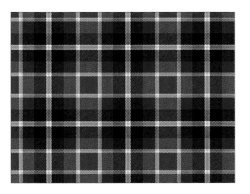

▲ *This version of the MacLachlan was in D.W. Stewart's collection of 1893.*

the chief later received lands on the island of Skye. Fittingly, the family motto is "Fortune assists the daring". The MacKinnons of Skye and Mull supported the Stuart kings in the 1715 and 1745 Jacobite rebellions. In the aftermath of defeat at Culloden in 1746, they hid Bonnie Prince Charlie in a cave; their chief, Iain Og, then carried the prince to Mallaig in his galley.

MACKINTOSH

The Mackintosh name comes from the Gaelic Mac anTosach ("son of the chief") and the clan claims its first chief in Shaw MacDuff, a son of Duncan, 3rd Earl of Fife. Shaw was Constable of Inverness Castle around 1160. His descendant Farquhar, 5th chief, supported Alexander III against Norway's King Haakon at the battle of Largs in 1263. Alexander's son Angus won the family its pre-eminent position in clan Chattan in 1291 by marrying Eva, only daughter and heiress of the Chattan chief Dougal Dal.

Malcolm, 10th chief (1430–64), presided over a great period in Mackintosh history when clan lands stretched from Petty all the way to Lochaber. The clansmen supported the Stuart cause in the Civil War and the Jacobite uprisings. Some 800 Mackintosh men fought in the Jacobite force in the 1715 rebellion and many were forcibly deported to North America in the wake of defeat. In the

1745 rebellion the Mackintosh chief, Angus, served in the Black Watch Regiment but his wife, Lady Anne, raised a force of clansmen to fight at Falkirk in 1746. She later received Bonnie Prince Charlie at Moy; the bed in which he slept is preserved in the family's Moy Hall, south of Inverness.

MACKIRDY

The family of MacKirdy, also spelled MacCurdy and McCurdy, is considered to be a sept of clan Stewart. They made their living from the sea, settling on the islands of Bute and Arran where they sought protection from the Stewarts of Bute. Their name may derive from Muirchertach, a Gaelic name indicating a sailor, although some accounts link it to King Myrkjartan, who features in Icelandic sagas. The first documented MacKirdy ancestor is Gilkrist Makurerdy, a landowner on Bute in the

▼ *The MacKirdy tartan is a design dating from the mid-20th century.*

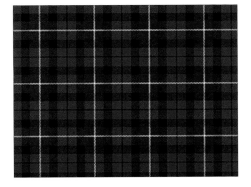

early 16th century. His contemporaries Finlay, John, Alexander and Donald Makurerdy are also recorded as landowners on the island. Donald MacKirdy is thought to have been the first to use this form of the name, around 1550.

MACLACHLAN

The MacLachlans claim descent from the MacLochlainns, a powerful Ulster family. In Scotland the clan's ancestor was Lachlan Mor, a 13th-century chief in the Loch Fyne area. Gillespie MacLachlan supported the cause of Robert the Bruce and attended his first parliament at St Andrews in 1308.

In the early 1400s the MacLachlan chiefs were documented as lords of Strathlachlan, lands which were made a barony in 1680. The family allied themselves to the Campbells of Argyll, the pre-eminent force in the region, and fought for them against the MacDonalds of Islay.

During the Civil War and the Jacobite rebellions the MacLachlans were staunch supporters of the Stuarts at the battle of Sheriffmuir in 1715 and at Culloden in 1746, where Lachlan Machlachlan, 17th chief and commissary-general on Bonnie Prince Charlie's staff, was killed. Castle Lachlan was destroyed in the retributions that followed that Jacobite defeat, but a new family seat was built nearby in the 19th century.

MacLaine of Lochbuie–MacMillan

D.W. Stewart, author of *Old and Rare Scottish Tartans* (1893), described the MacLaine of Lochbuie tartan as unique among traditional tartans because it contained so much blue. A red-based MacLaine tartan also survives.

MacLAINE OF LOCHBUIE

The family ancestor was Gilleathan na Tuaidh ("Gillean of the battleaxe"), the 13th-century warrior who fought in Alexander III's service at the battle of Largs in 1263. His grandson Malcolm fought at Bannockburn in 1314. Two of Malcolm's grandsons founded rival family branches: Eachann Reaganach ("Hector the stern") fathered the MacLaines of Lochbuie, while his brother, Lachlan Lubanach, was ancestor of the MacLeans of Duart. Hector's descendant John, 7th chief, won great acclaim by defeating an itinerant Italian swordsman. The clan fought in the Stuart cause in the Civil War and Hector MacLaine, 12th chief, triumphed for James VII at the battle of Knockbreck in 1689; he also fought later at Killiecrankie.

In 1773 John MacLaine, 17th chief, entertained Dr Johnson and James Boswell during their tour of the Hebrides; Boswell recorded the visit in his *Journal of a Tour to the Hebrides*, published in 1785.

▼ *The blue-based tartan of MacLaine of Lochbuie was first recorded in 1908.*

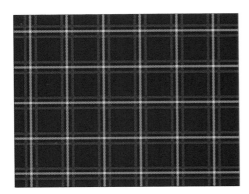

One version of the MacLaine of Lochbuie tartan can be found in the Cockburn Collection in Glasgow's Mitchell Library, so can be dated at least as far back as 1810, when the collection was made.

MacLAREN

The two distinct branches of this family hail from Balquhidder in Perthshire and from Argyllshire. The former are descended from Laurin, or Laurence, a 13th-century hereditary abbot of Achtow in Balquhidder. They suffered gravely at the hands of their neighbours, notably the Campbells and the MacGregors. MacLarens fought bravely during the Civil War in the Stuart cause. They also fought in the 1715 and 1745 Jacobite rebellions, and in the wake of defeat at Culloden in 1746 the family's Balquhidder estates were sacked by Hanoverian troops. Donald MacLaren survived as a fugitive until he was granted an amnesty in 1757.

The Argyllshire MacLarens claim descent from Lorn, of the 6th-century ruling house of Dalriada. They held the island of Tiree for many generations.

Wilson's of Bannockburn produced the tartan now known as MacLaren as the Regent tartan, but the name was changed after the Regency ended with the accession of George IV in 1820.

▼ *The MacLaren is like the Fergusson of Athol sett, but uses yellow for white.*

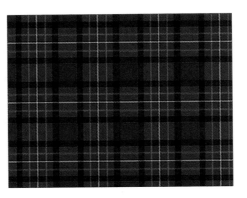

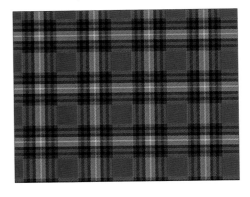

▲ *The MacLay is also called Livingstone because some MacLays used the name.*

MacLAY

Also known as McLea and McLeay, the MacLays are a sept of the Stewarts of Appin. The name appears to come from the Gaelic MacDhunnshleibhe ("son of Dunsleve", a forename indicating "a dweller on the brown hill"), though some say it means "the doctor's son", from the Gaelic *leche*: in some areas generations of MacLays served as surgeons and physicians. In the Lowland areas the name was often changed to Livingstone. The earliest known MacLay is probably James Mac Dunsleph, recorded in 1309 as a patriotic follower of Robert the Bruce. In 1504 a Kenzoch M'Coleif was in possession of lands in Strathconon and in 1509 Finla Makgillecallum Makcolluf and John Roy M'Culloiff were recorded as holding land from the chief of the Stewarts of Appin.

MacLEAN OF DUART

The MacLeans of Duart trace their bloodline back to Gillean of the Battleaxe, but this branch was founded by Lachlan Lubanach in the 14th century, when a leadership dispute split the family. Lachlan's son, known as Red Hector of the Battles, fought Sir Alexander Irvine of Drum in single combat at the battle of Harlaw in 1411; both warriors died of their

▲ *This MacLean of Duart tartan was reproduced by James Logan in 1831.*

wounds. In the late 1400s the family held the islands of Islay, Jura, Mull and Tiree, and parts of Argyllshire. They fought resolutely in the Stuart cause, running up debts that resulted in the loss of their family estates at Duart on Mull to the Campbells. The chief Sir Hector MacLean, a veteran of the 1715 Jacobite rebellion, was captured during the 1745 uprising and briefly imprisoned in the Tower of London before returning to the campaign. The MacLean chiefs regained possession of Duart in 1911 and rebuilt Duart Castle, their family seat on Mull.

MACLINTOCK

The MacLintocks may have begun as a priestly family. Their name comes from MacGhill'Fhionndaig ("son of Fintan's, or Findan's, servant"); a number of Celtic saints share the name Fintan, which is a diminutive of Finn. The

▼ *The MacLintock tartan can be traced back to the mid-20th century.*

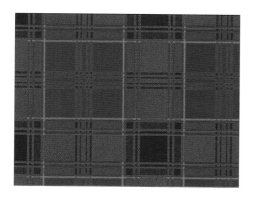

▲ *Robert the Bruce may have hidden close to Loch Arkaig when on the run.*

MacLintocks established themselves in Lorn and the region of Luss in about 1500. Their name is also spelled variously as MacClintock, MacClintick, MacLlandick, MacLlintog, MacLinden and even MacClinton, and was sometimes anglicized as Lindsay. The family is generally regarded as a sept, or subgroup, of clan MacDougall but sometimes also as a sept of the Colquhouns of Dunbartonshire, another clan with priestly origins. The first MacLintock on record is probably Duncan Megellentak, who was cited as witness in a 1549 document at Balquhidder, Perthshire.

MACMILLAN

The MacMillan family has a priestly origin, its name deriving from MacMhaoilein ("son of the bald or tonsured man"), and its motto is "I learn to help the unfortunate". The MacMillans were established at Loch Arkaig in Lochaber in the 13th century. Their chief Maolmuire sheltered Robert the Bruce when he was on the run in the Highlands, and the clan fought in the Bruce's victorious army at

Bannockburn in 1314. In about 1360 they acquired lands at Knapdale on the Argyll coast under charter from John of Islay, Lord of the Isles. The foremost branch of the family, the Knapdale MacMillans, built an imposing round tower near Castle Sween. In 1742 the MacMillans of Dunmore became chiefs. A company of MacMillans of Murlaggan fought for the Jacobite cause at Culloden in 1746 and, following defeat, were despatched to the Caribbean. Sons of clan MacMillan include the Dumfriesshire-born Kirkpatrick Macmillan, who invented the bicycle in 1839, and Harold Macmillan, who was British Prime Minister from 1957–63.

▼ *The MacMillan tartan has been worn by the clan since the early 1900s.*

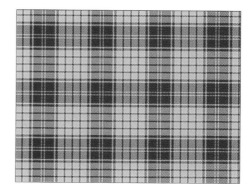

MacNAB–MacPHERSON

Several variants of the MacNab tartan were recorded in the early 19th century. Clan members are able to choose between the one recorded by James Logan in *The Scottish Gael* and a different sett printed at the time by Wilson's of Bannockburn.

MacNAB

The MacNabs held lands near Loch Tay in Perthshire alongside the river Dochart and had their family seat at Kinnell on the river's banks. They were descended from the hereditary abbots of Glendochart and Strathearn, their name coming from Gaelic Mac An Aba ("son of the abbot"). They were allied through marriage to Robert the Bruce's opponents the Comyns, and lost their lands when the Bruce established his position after victory at Bannockburn in 1314. Gilbert MacNab succeeded in making peace with the Bruce's son David II (r.1329–71) and in 1336 held the barony of Bovain, in Glendochart, under charter from the king.

In the Civil War era the clan's chief, "Smooth John" MacNab, had a number

▼ *The clifftop castle overlooks MacNab lands on the banks of the river Tay.*

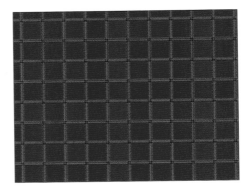

▲ *This MacNab was reproduced by Logan in* The Scottish Gael *(1831).*

of stirring adventures fighting in the royalist cause. Appointed to defend the Marquis of Montrose's castle, he was besieged there by General Lesley, but with his garrison fought free. He was captured and sentenced to death but escaped from Edinburgh on the eve of his execution and led 300 of his brave MacNabs to fight in the Battle of Worcester in 1651.

MacNAUGHTON

The MacNaughtons or MacNaghtens claim descent as "sons of Nechtan" from the Pictish royal house of Moray, in which there were several princes with the name Nechtan. The clan possessed land in Strathtay in the 1100s and in 1267 Gillichrist MacNachdan was recorded as Keeper of Frechelen Castle on an island in Loch Awe.

In the 14th century the clan paid dearly for not backing Robert the Bruce's claim to the Scottish throne, but by the time of Alexander MacNaughton (d.1515) the clan's fortunes had improved. John, 16th laird, fought in the army of Bonnie Dundee at Killiecrankie in 1689.

His son John, 17th laird, was involved in an escapade concerning his marriage, when he was tricked by the bride's father, Sir James Campbell of Ardkinglas, into marrying her less

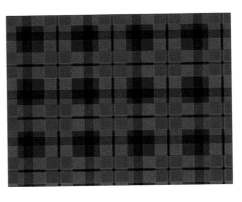

▲ *The MacNaughton tartan is similar to the cloth worn by the MacDuffs.*

attractive elder sister. The next day MacNaughton eloped with his beloved, the younger sister, but Campbell later succeeded in having MacNaughton condemned for incest and took possession of his estates, which had been forfeited following the clan's participation in the 1689 revolt. The chiefship was passed to an Irish branch of the family.

MacNEIL

The MacNeils are descendants of Irish kings. Niall, a scion of the Irish U'Neill dynasty who came to Barra in the Outer Hebrides around 1049, is held to be the clan's founder in Scotland. Tradition holds that Neil Og MacNeil, 6th chief, fought alongside Robert the Bruce at Bannockburn in 1314 and received territory in North Kintyre.

Gilleonan MacNeil, 9th laird, held Barra under charter from the MacDonald Lords of the Isles in 1427 and after the MacDonalds' lands were forfeited his descendant Gilleonan Mac Roderick MacNeil, 11th laird, was confirmed in possessions of the island by the Scottish Crown in 1495.

In the 16th century the MacNeil chiefs held powerful sway from Kismull Castle on Barra. Ruari "the Turbulent", 15th chief, launched raids on passing ships and was called to

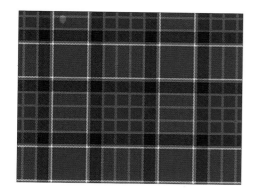

▲ *Wilson's of Bannockburn produced several versions of the MacNeil sett.*

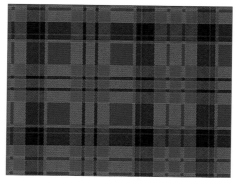

▲ *The MacNicol was reproduced by William and Andrew Smith in 1850.*

▲ *D.W. Stewart used this MacPherson in his* Old and Rare Scottish Tartans.

account for his actions by James VI. The family supported the Jacobite rebellions of the 17th and 18th centuries, then in 1838 General Roderick MacNeil, 21st chief, had to sell Barra. However, his descendant Robert Lister MacNeil, 25th chief, was able to regain possession of much of the island – including the imposing Kismull Castle – in 1937. One branch of the family were hereditary pipers to the MacLeans of Duart, and another held lands in Colonsay.

MacNICOL

The MacNicols flourished on Arran and Skye in the Western Isles and appear to be of Viking descent. Most authorities interpret their name as "son of Nicail" and identify the clan's founder as a Norse chief of that name who held sway on Lewis in the mid-13th century. Early in the following century John mac Nicail is on record as chief of the clan on Lewis, but the larger part of the clan's lands then passed to the MacLeods of Lewis, and the MacNicols settled at Scorrybreac on Skye. In later years the MacNicols aligned themselves with the MacDonalds of Sleat.

In the 1600s a number of MacNicols were Protestant ministers, and many anglicized their name as Nicolson. In the Jacobite rebellion of 1745–6, a company of MacNicols fought alongside the Stewarts of Appin at Culloden. A family by the name of Nicholson

established themselves in mainland Scotland and in 1980 the MacNicols and Nicholsons were recognized by the Lyon Court as separate clans. The MacNicols suffered in the Highland clearances and left Scorrybreac, but the clan has now regained possession of part of its ancestral lands.

MacPHAIL

There are several familes of this name, which means "son of Paul". One has long been associated with the Mackintoshes of clan Chattan and its members are said to have been followers of Angus Mackintosh, who married Eva, the heiress of clan Chattan, in 1291. They were later found in Inverarnie and Strathnairn. Many fought in the clan Chattan regiment in the 1715 Jacobite rebellion and were deported to North America following its defeat.

▼ *The MacPhail tartan was named and collected in the mid-20th century.*

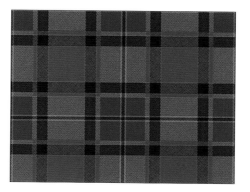

Some MacPhails were connected to clan Cameron in Lochaber in the 1500s; others settled in Sutherland and sought the protection of clan Mackay. Still others lived on Mull, and some in the Argyll region. The MacPhails anglicized their name to Polson.

MacPHERSON

The MacPhersons' name comes from Gaelic Mac-a-Phearsain ("son of the parson") and they trace their descent from a son of Muireach Cattenach, parson of Kingussie in Badenoch in the late 12th century. Muireach's son, Ewen Ban, had three sons – Kenneth, Iain and Gillies – and the clan is sometimes known as the "Clan of the Three Brothers".

The MacPhersons were part of the clan Chattan confederation. Duncan, 10th MacPherson chief, applied to the Lyon Court in 1672 to be recognized as chief of the whole Chattan confederation, but the Lord Lyon decreed that that honour had passed to the sons of Angus Mackintosh and Eva, Chattan heiress, who married in 1291.

In the late 1800s the clan lost its estates at Cluny-in-Badenoch through debt. A great many tartan setts are associated with the MacPherson name. One of these, once known as "the grey plaid of Badenoch" and later sold as "Hunting MacPherson", is based on a piece known to have been at Cluny-in-Badenoch in 1745.

MACQUARRIE–MACTHOMAS

MacRaes have a number of tartans to choose from. D.C. Stewart, author of *The Setts of the Scottish Tartans* (1950), thought that the count of one MacRae had been misquoted in earlier works, producing an "improbable" sett.

MACQUARRIE

The MacQuarries held part of the isle of Mull and Ulva, a small island off Mull, from at least the 15th century. Their name derives from the Gaelic first name Guaire ("noble"). The first family member on record is John MacQuarrie of Ulva, who was witness to a 1463 charter. Lachlan MacQuarrie, 16th Lord of Ulva, was chief when Dr Johnson and James Boswell visited in 1773 during their tour of the Hebrides. He sold the family property in 1778 and became an officer, at the advanced age of 63, in the Argyll Highlanders; he died in 1818, aged 103. His cousin, Major-General Lachlan MacQuarrie (1761–1824), fought in the British Army in North America, the West Indies and India. He became Governor of New South Wales, Australia (1809–21), overseeing large-scale development in the colony and setting up its first bank in 1817.

Several MacQuarrie tartans survive. One is a red-based sett very similar to the red MacDonald tartan.

▼ *The MacQuarrie tartan has been in collections since the early 19th century.*

MACQUEEN

There appear to have been two distinct families of MacQueen ancestors, one hailing from Argyll and Galloway, and one originating on the island of Skye. The former are descended from Suibhne, master of Castle Sween in Argyll in the 13th century, and were originally called MacShuibhne or MacSween. Members of the Skye branch share ancestry with the MacDonalds and came to the mainland with Mora MacDonald of Moidart, who married Malcolm, 10th Mackintosh chief, in about 1410. Their name means "sons of Sweyn" (a Norse first name) and they may originally have been MacSweyns. Their ancestor was Revan MacMulmor MacAngus so they were sometimes known as clan Revan. These MacQueens became established as the family's main branch, with lands at Corryborough on the river Findhorn, Inverness-shire. They fought with the Mackintoshes at the battle of Harlaw in 1411 and became important in the clan Chattan confederation. Some MacQueens remained at Garafad on Skye. Many of their descendants emigrated to begin a new life in North America in later years. Records indicate that a brave member of clan MacQueen killed the last wolf in Scotland around 1743.

▼ *The MacQueen combines the MacDonald and Mackintosh tartans.*

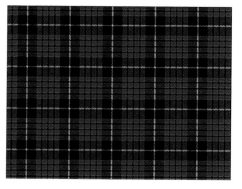

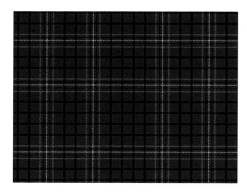

▲ *This MacRae tartan was reproduced by D.C. Stewart in 1950.*

MACRAE

Originally from the area of Beauly, the MacRaes established themselves in what became the clan lands at Kintail, beside Loch Duich in Ross-shire, in the 14th century. Their name appears to derive from the Gaelic MacRath ("son of grace") so they were probably churchmen. However, they were known as the Wild Macraes and fought so fiercely in the service of the Mackenzies of Kintail that they were nicknamed the Mackenzies' Coat-of-mail. MacRaes became hereditary constables of Eilean-Donan Castle and chamberlains of Kintail. They were staunch Jacobites and fought bravely at Sheriffmuir in 1715.

In the 17th century Duncan MacRae of Inverinate gathered the Gaelic poems preserved in the Fernaig manuscript. He kept such an impressive table that he was called Duncan of the Silver Cups. In the 1930s Lieutenant-Colonel John MacRae-Gilstrap of Balliemore restored Eilean-Donan while he was the castle's constable.

MACTAGGART

The family name comes from Gaelic Mac anT'sagairt ("son of the priest") and the MacTaggarts trace their descent from the colourful figure of Ferquhard Macintaggart. As Abbot of Applecross

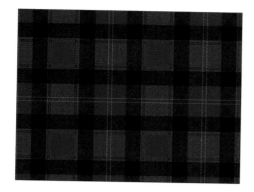

▲ *MacTaggarts can wear this tartan or a red, green and blue Ross clan tartan.*

Monastery in 1215, he was able to block a local revolt against the king's authority. He rounded up and beheaded the rebel leaders and then made a gift of their heads to Alexander II (r.1214–49), who rewarded him with a knighthood and later with the earldom of Ross. MacTaggarts were living in Dumfries in 1459 and the name was next recorded in 1583 when Walter McTagart and two followers faced arson charges. The family is considered a sept of clan Ross.

MacTAVISH

The name MacTavish means "son of Tammas" (a form of Thomas) and was anglicized as Thomson. In historical documents it is also spelled MacCamis, McKnavis and even MacAnish. From the 12th century onward the family held the lands of Dunardarie in Knapdale, Argyll. These lands were

▼ *The MacTavish tartan was included in this form in Whyte's book of 1906.*

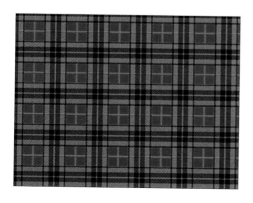

▲ *From the 1400s Glenshee was the adopted home of the MacThomas clan.*

adjacent to those of Campbell of Auchnabreck and the MacTavishes are generally regarded as a sept of clan Campbell, but they do have their own clan tartan. The clan did not fight in its own right in the 1745 Jacobite rebellion because the clan chief, Dugald MacTavish, was in prison. Nonetheless, the MacTavish clansmen fought in the Jacobite cause alongside the Mackintoshes and Frasers at Culloden in 1746. After the Jacobite defeat, many MacTavishes adopted the anglicized form of the name and emigrated to Ireland and North America.

The illustrated sett has been approved by Dugald MacTavish of Dunardry, the 26th and current chief, as the clan tartan.

MacTHOMAS

The family takes its name from Tomaidh Mor ("great Thomas"), great-grandson of William, 8th chief of clan Chattan. In the 15th century Thomas led a migration from the Chattan heartland of Badenoch to Glenshee in Perthshire, where his followers became known as MacThomas or McComie.

Iain, or John, McComie was chief in the Civil War era and fought bravely in Charles I's cause. When he took Aberdeen he captured Sir William Forbes of Craigievar, the Covenanter cavalry commander. He subsequently fell out with his Royalist allies and after the Restoration of the monarchy in 1660 he was ruined by fines. When McComie died in 1676 his sons were forced to sell the family lands. Many of the family moved on, settling in the Tay valley and in Angus and going by the name of Thomas or Thomson. In the 19th century clan descendant William McCombie of Tillifour helped to establish the celebrated Aberdeen-Angus crossbreed cattle.

▼ *The MacThomas clan society adopted this as the official tartan in 1975.*

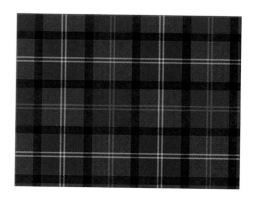

MacWHIRTER–MAXWELL

The information on clan tartans gathered in the 1820s by army clothier George Hunter has been of great value to subsequent generations. William and Andrew Smith were the first to make use of his findings, in a book of 1850.

MacWHIRTER

The MacWhirters are descended from a family of hereditary harp-players who appear to have originated in Ayrshire. Their name is a form of MacChruiter ("son of the harper"), which was anglicized to the name Harper. They are generally regarded as a sept of clan Buchanan but have their own clan tartan, which was included in William and Andrew Smith's early 19th-century work entitled *Authenticated Tartans of the Clans and Families of Scotland*.

MacWILLIAM

The MacWilliam name can be traced back to the 12th century in the Highlands. The oldest known MacWilliams were descendants of Duncan II, a son of Malcolm III (r.1058–93), who briefly ousted Donald III to rule for a few months before being murdered in November 1094. From their lands in Badenoch and Lochaber they tried repeatedly to regain the Scottish crown, but their chance was entirely extinguished in the early 13th century when the chief's only heir, his daughter, was brutally murdered by being dashed against Forfar market cross.

There were other MacWilliam families who were variously allied to the MacFarlanes and the Gunns. An associated family living in Glenlivet, named MacWillie, were followers of the MacPhersons, and a branch of the Robertson family of Pittagowan, Atholl, were also known as MacWilliam. Other variants of the name are Williamson, Wilson and Wylie.

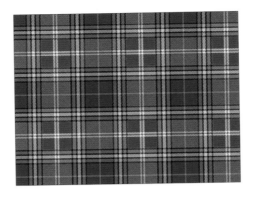

▲ *The MacWhirter tartan may have been among those found by Hunter.*

▼ *The MacWilliam is in the Scottish Tartans Society's collection (1930–50).*

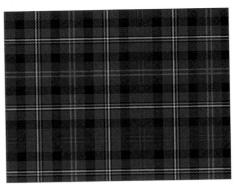

▲ *This Malcolm tartan is based on Wilson's of Bannockburn's 1847 books.*

▼ *The Countess of Mar chose this as "the proper tartan of the Tribe of Mar".*

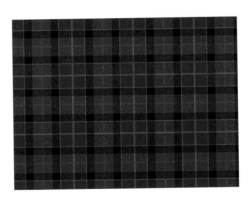

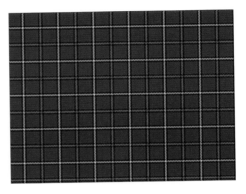

MALCOLM

The name is a form of MacCallum, which means a follower of St Columba (c.521–597), who from his base on Iona took a leading role with his devoted followers in spreading the Christian gospel in Scotland. The Malcolms were churchmen and their motto, appropriately enough, is *In ardua petit* ("He sets his aim at challenging things"). The form Malcolm was used in Dunbartonshire and Stirling from the 1300s onward. But it is not possible to identify separate histories for the names Malcolm and MacCallum since they were used interchangeably in Highland documents. The main MacCallum family held lands at Poltalloch, in Craignish, and from the 18th century Dugald

MacCallum chose to use the name Malcolm rather than MacCallum. Nevertheless, there are different setts recorded as Malcolm and MacCallum tartans. One of these, the Malcolm dress tartan, dating from the late 19th century, uses azure and gold to match colours in the family's coat of arms.

MAR

The region of Mar in Aberdeenshire was one of seven ancient Celtic provinces ruled by a *mormaer* (steward). The first to bear the title Earl of Mar was Rothri, who is named in an early 12th-century charter. His successor William, 5th Earl, was a Regent of Scotland around 1260, and toward the end of the 13th century the earl's daughter, Isabella of Mar, married into

▲ *The Maxwells may be named after this section of the River Tweed.*

the royal family when she became Robert the Bruce's wife. The family later intermarried with the Stewarts and subsequently both the reigning Stuart monarchs and the Erskine family, who traced descent from Isabella, laid claim to the earldom of Mar.

In 1565 Mary, Queen of Scots, made John, Lord Erskine, the 18th Earl of Mar. His descendant, another John Erskine, Earl of Mar, became Secretary of State for Scotland and is chiefly remembered as the leader of the Jacobite army in the unsuccessful rebellion of 1715.

The sett shown is known as the Mar district tartan and may be associated with the Skenes or the Duke of Fife.

MATHESON

The Mathesons appear to have Celtic ancestry, their name deriving from the Gaelic for "son of the bear" or "son of the heroes". The clan ancestors held lands at Kintail and Lochalsh from early times and later a branch of the family established itself at Shiness, Sutherland. The Mathesons of the Lochalsh area fought with Donald

MacDonald, 2nd Lord of the Isles, at the bruising battle of Harlaw in 1411 and their chief, Alastair, was arrested by James I and beheaded in Edinburgh in 1427. Alastair's son Iain, or John, married into the Mackenzie family and was Constable of Eilean Donan Castle. He was killed in 1539 defending the castle against an attack by the MacDonalds of Sleat.

Sir James Matheson, a descendant of the Sutherland branch, was a successful merchant who, with fellow Scot William Jardine, founded the trading house Jardine Matheson in Canton in 1832. Matheson later bought the island of Lewis and proved himself a model landowner, helping its inhabitants

▼ *This Matheson tartan is among those reproduced by James Logan in 1831.*

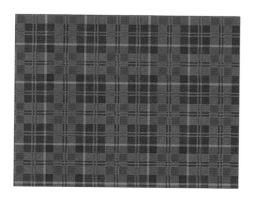

survive a severe famine. Descendants of the clan Matheson are found in numbers in the United States, Canada, New Zealand and Australia.

MAXWELL

The Maxwells' ancestors were Norman knights who came to England at the time of the Conquest in 1066 and later settled in Scotland. In some accounts the Maxwell name is derived from that of a fishing pool near Kelso on the river Tweed: it is called Maccus' Weil after a Saxon landowner in the Scottish–English Borders.

Sir John Maxwell (d.1241) was named Chamberlain of Scotland. His descendant, Sir Herbert, signed the oath of allegiance extracted from scores of Scottish landowners by Edward I of England in 1296, but Sir Herbert's son, Eustace, was active in Robert the Bruce's fight for Scottish independence and fought in the battle of Bannockburn in 1314. In 1440 another prominent family member named Sir Herbert was made Lord Maxwell and in about 1613 Robert, 8th Lord, was made Earl of Nithsdale. In the 18th century William, 5th Earl of Nithsdale, was an active Jacobite who made a remarkable escape from captivity. He was captured at Preston in 1715, thrown in the Tower of London and sentenced to death for treason but escaped on the eve of his execution, dressed as a woman, and fled to Rome.

▼ *The Maxwell tartan was printed in the* Vestiarum Scoticum *(1842).*

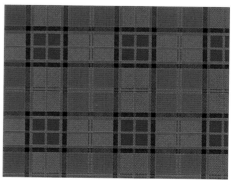

MELVILLE–MONCREIFFE

Tartans worn by Moncreiffe and Menzies clansmen have been dated to the early 1800s or even the late 1700s. By contrast the official Moffat tartan is a modern sett commissioned to celebrate the clan's revival from obscurity.

MELVILLE

The family name, which appears to derive from the barony of Malleville in Normandy, was known in Scotland by the reigns of Malcolm IV (r.1153–65) and William the Lion (r.1165–1214) when Galfridus de Malveill was named as a witness. In the same era a Richard Maluvell was captured with King William during the Scots' doomed invasion of Northumbria in 1174.

In the 16th century Robert, 1st Baron Melville of Monimail, was Mary, Queen of Scots', ambassador to England in 1562. His brother Sir James Melville was also a diplomat and wrote a well-known autobiography, *Memoir of My Own Life*, posthumously published in 1683. Celebrated Melvilles include Andrew Melville, who in 1574 succeeded John Knox as leader of the Scottish Reformed Church, and the New York-born novelist Herman Melville, author of *Moby Dick* (1851).

The tartan is similar to and often associated with the Oliphant pattern – both designs are sometimes listed as

▼ *This Melville tartan was listed by Wilson's of Bannockburn.*

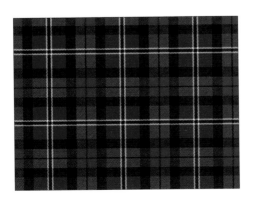

Oliphant and Melville. However, they were listed separately both by the Sobieski brothers in *Vestiarum Scoticum* and by Wilson's of Bannockburn.

MENZIES

The Menzies family hailed originally from Normandy, and appear to have drawn their name from Mesnières, near Rouen. They introduced the larch tree to Scotland, planting the first saplings on their Culdares estate in Atholl. Sir Robert de Meyneris was the first of the family to make a mark in public life, as chamberlain under Alexander II (r.1214–49). His son Alexander married the daughter of James, the High Steward. In the next generation,

▲ *The Menzies family made a lasting contribution to the Scottish landscape by introducing the larch tree.*

▼ *This design, one of many Menzies setts, was identified as the clan tartan by the chief in the early 1800s.*

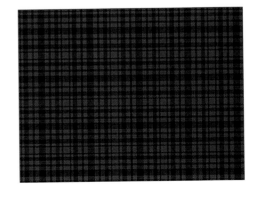

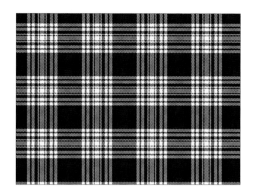

▲ *This variant Menzies tartan was reproduced by Robert Bain in 1953.*

▼ *Middletons can wear this family tartan or the Forbes clan tartan.*

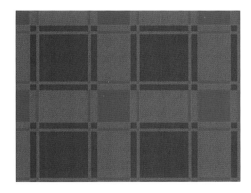

another Sir Robert demonstrated the family's commitment to an independent Scotland, fighting alongside Robert the Bruce, and received lands in Glendochart and Glenorchy.

The Menzies took the royalist side in the Civil War but fought on both sides in the 1689 uprising that ended after Bonnie Dundee's death at Killiecrankie. The clansmen fought for Bonnie Prince Charlie in the 1745 Jacobite rebellion and after the battle of Culloden in 1746 many of the defeated Jacobites took refuge on the family's Glen Lyon estates.

MIDDLETON
The family name derives from the location of its original lands, which were situated between two *touns* or farmsteads in Laurencekirk. The Middletons were known in Kincardineshire in the 13th century. In about 1230 Humfrey de Midilton was witness to a charter covering the gift of land to Arbroath Abbey, and in 1296 a kinsman of the same name was among the Scottish nobility who made an oath of allegiance to Edward I of England.

Little is known of the family's history for many years, but in the 17th century John, 1st Earl of Middleton, had a long and chequered career. He served first as a soldier in France, then as second-in-command in the Covenanter army and finally as Commander-in-Chief of Charles II's army in Scotland after 1660. After being accused of drunkenness, lustful behaviour and dishonesty he lived in disgraced retirement in England for some years before becoming Governor of Tangier. He died in exile in 1673. The family is sometimes identified as a sept of clan Forbes.

MOFFAT
This proud Border clan was known in Upper Annandale, Dumfriesshire, from the 11th–12th centuries. After the death of the chief in the 1560s, the Moffats were without a leader until in July 1983 Major Francis Moffat was accepted as chief in the Lyon Court. The family motto "I hope for better things" was borne out by the clan's recovery from four centuries without a leader.

The sett now identified as the Moffat family tartan was produced to mark the reinstatement of the chief. A second sett, which dates from at least the 1930s, is comparable to the Murray of Tullibardine tartan. By tradition, wearers of the Murray of Tullibardine design in the 18th century were signalling their support for the Jacobite cause of restoring the crown to the Catholic Stuart line.

MONCREIFFE
The Moncreiffes take their name from their lands in Perthshire, which Sir Matthew de Moncreiffe held under a

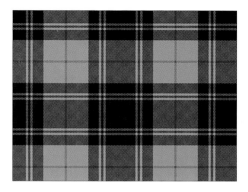

▲ *The Moffat family tartan, introduced in 1983, is based on the Douglas.*

▼ *This Moncreiffe sett was worn by tartan authority Sir Iain Moncreiffe.*

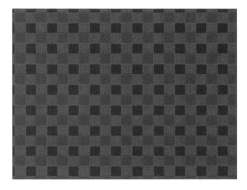

charter of 1248 from Alexander II. In the 15th century Malcolm Moncreiffe, 6th Lord, possessed the lands as the barony of Moncreiffe. Sir John Moncreiffe, 12th Lord, held the position of Sheriff of Perthshire and was made Baronet of Nova Scotia in 1626.

In the 20th century Sir Iain Moncreiffe (d.1985), a highly respected clan historian, established a line of descent for the family from a son of the 4th–5th century Irish High King, Niall of the Nine Hostages. The family had a longstanding association with the Murrays of Atholl. As a result the Moncreiffe clansmen often wore the Murray tartan, but Sir Iain established a red and green sett as the Moncreiffe tartan in 1974. The tartan, which dates to at least 1790, was formerly known as the MacLachlan, but was reassigned with the MacLachlan chief's permission.

MONTGOMERY–NAPIER

The Muir tartan is unusual in having three narrow red lines overlaid twice on each green square. This feature is also found in the Cochrane tartan. The Muir sett is found in *Land of the Scottish Gael* by John Ross (1930).

MONTGOMERY

The Montgomery ancestor, Roger de Montgomerie, was a governor of Normandy and a kinsman of William the Conqueror. He came to England in 1067 and was given the earldom of Arundel. His descendant Robert de Montgomerie is thought to have come to Scotland in the mid-12th century and acquired Eaglesham in Renfrewshire. His direct descendant, Sir John of Eaglesham, captured the English hero Sir Henry Percy, also known as Hotspur, at the battle of Otterburn in 1388 and used the ransom he received to build the castle of Polnoon. He acquired the barony of Eglinton and Ardrossan through marriage. His grandson, Alexander, was made Lord Montgomery in about 1440 and in 1507 his descendant Hugh, 2nd Lord Montgomery, was made Earl of Eglinton. In later years Archibald, 11th Earl, raised the 78th Highlanders and Archibald, 13th Earl, held the Eglinton Tournament of medieval-style jousting in 1839.

MORRISON

There are three distinct Morrison families, one in Aberdeenshire and two on the island of Lewis. Those who settled at Habost, on north-eastern Lewis, were descendants of the O'Muirgheasains, a family of hereditary bards originally from northern Ireland. Further south on Lewis, the Morrisons took their name from their shipwrecked ancestor MacGhille Mhoire ("St Mary's servant") who married an heiress of the Gow family. Their children were hereditary brieves, or lawmen, on Lewis. The Aberdeenshire Morrisons claim descent from Mauricius, a Norman knight. In the 16th century the southern Lewis Morrisons were drawn into feuds with the MacLeods and the MacAulays and eventually lost their lands.

The tartan identified as Morrison Ancient was based on a fragment of a sett discovered in a family Bible when a Morrison house on Lewis was cleared for demolition in the 1930s.

MOWAT

The Mowats settled in Scotland in the reign of David I (r.1124–53). Some accounts suggest they originated in Italy, others that they are descendants of Norman knights who settled in Wales before some of their number

moved further north. Their name derives from Norman *mont haut* ("tall mountain") and was often written in a Latinized form as de Monte Alto.

In the reign of William I (r.1165–1214) Sir William de Montealt was Lord of Ferne, Forfarshire, and in 1214 Richard de Montealto witnessed a document embodying a decision of the new king, Alexander II. In 1296 William de Monte Alto signed his allegiance to Edward I of England. The main branch of the family were the Mowats of Balquholly, Aberdeenshire, but confusingly they held estates with the same name, Balquholly, in Caithness. They also possessed estates in Shetland.

MUIR

The name Muir is thought to derive from the Gaelic *mor* ("big") or to have been given to people who lived near moorland. It was also spelled Moar, Moir, Moore or Mor. Among the family's early heroes were Sir Archibald Muir, who died defending Berwick against the army of Edward I of England in 1296; his son Sir William Muir, knighted by David II (r.1329–71); and Gilchrist More, who gained the family lands at Rowallan through marriage. In 1346 Elizabeth, daughter of Sir Adam Mure of Rowallan, married

▼ *The Sobieskis reproduced a slightly different Montgomery tartan in 1842.*

▼ *Tartan collector James MacKinlay dated the Morrison Ancient to 1745.*

▼ *This Mowat was reproduced in the French book* Clans Originaux *(1880).*

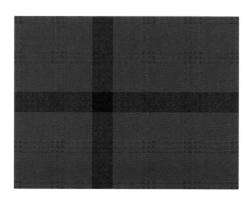

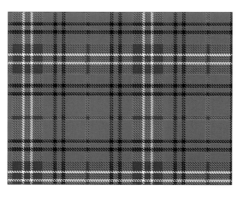

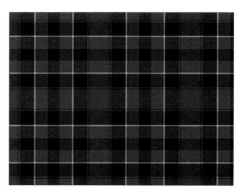

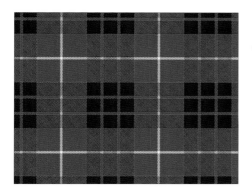

▲ *This Munro is in the Sobieskis'*
Vestiarum Scoticum of 1842.

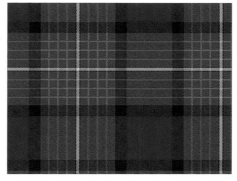

▲ *The Muir is in the collection of the*
Scottish Tartans Society (1930–50).

▲ *This is the form of the Napier tartan*
worn by modern members of the clan.

Robert Stewart, later Robert II, and although she died the following year the couple's son, John, succeeded as Robert III (r.1390–1406). Celebrated later holders of the name include the naturalist John Muir (1838–1914), who played a major role in the establishment of California's Sequoia and Yosemite National Parks, and the poet Edwin Muir (1887–1959).

MUNRO

The Munros held territories to the north of Cromarty Firth, where Hugh Munro of Foulis (d.1126) was the first chief. The family fought in Robert the Bruce's cause at Bannockburn in 1314 and against Edward III of England at Halidon Hill in 1333. Many Munro clansmen died with their chief, Robert, combating the 25,000-strong English army at the battle of Pinkie in 1547.

In the 17th-century Thirty Years War Robert Munro, nicknamed the Black Baron, was a commander in the service of the Protestant Gustavus Adolphus of Sweden, along with several other Munros. The Munros supported the Government against the Jacobites and in the 1745 rebellion their seat at Foulis Castle at Evanton in Ross-shire was ruined. It was restored in the late 19th century. In the US, James Munro (1758–1831) was the 5th President.

▶ *The memory of naturalist John Muir*
is honoured in his adopted California.

NAPIER

The Napiers were established on their estates at Kilmahew, Dunbartonshire, by the late 13th century, when John de Naper was named in a charter of Malcolm, Earl of Lennox. A fanciful account of the name's derivation claims the king announced a clan ancestor, Donald, such a champion as to have "nae peer" (no equal). Another explanation is that the name comes from the official in charge of napery (linen) in the royal household. Alexander Napier was provost of Edinburgh in the 15th century and established the Merchiston branch. His son, also Alexander, constructed Merchiston Tower in about 1460 and was Vice Admiral of Scotland. John Napier, 7th Lord of Merchiston, invented logarithms in 1614. His son, Archibald, became Lord Justice Clerk of Scotland and in 1627 was made Baron Napier of Merchiston. The family is a sept of the MacFarlanes, but the Napier tartan has most similarity with the MacDonald sett.

NESBITT–RAMSAY

The Raeburn tartan appeared for the first time in the trade lists of the company Ross's and Johnston's and cannot be traced in any collections. But clues to its origins may lie in its similarity to one of the MacLeod tartans.

NESBITT

The Border clan of the Nesbitts probably originated in Normandy, but its members were established in the Berwickshire family lands from which they took their name by the mid-12th century. In about 1160 William de Nesbite witnessed a charter from the Earl of Dunbar to the monks at Coldingham Priory, and Thomas Nisbet is recorded as Prior of Coldingham (1219–40). Nobles by the name of De

▼ *Coldingham Priory, associated with the Nesbitts, grew from a church founded in 1098 by Edgar, the king of the Scots.*

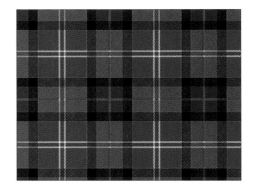

▲ *The colouring of the Nesbitt tartan is similar to that of the Munro.*

Nesbyth and also Nisbet swore the 1296 oath of allegiance extracted by Edward I of England from Scottish landowners and leading churchmen. Adam Nisbet of Nisbet held the estate of Knocklies under charter from Robert the Bruce (r.1306–29).

During the Civil War, Alexander Nesbit, Sheriff of Berwickshire, fought

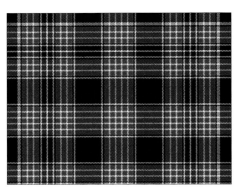

▲ *This Ogilvy tartan is an alternative to another, the Ogilvy of Airlie sett.*

with his sons in the cause of Charles I. One son, Philip – a general in the Marquis of Montrose's army – was executed after being captured at the battle of Philiphaugh in 1645. The author E. Nesbit (1858–1924) was a descendant.

OGILVY

The clan is descended from the Celtic rulers of Angus. Their ancestor was Gilbert, third son of Gillebride, Earl of Angus around 1170, who held the Ogilvy lands in Forfarshire under charter from William I. In the 14th and 15th centuries Gilbert's descendants were hereditary sheriffs of Angus. Sir Walter Ogilvy was appointed Lord High Treasurer in 1425 and was ambassador to England in 1430. His son, Sir John of Lintrathern, held Airlie Castle under charter in 1459 and his son Sir James was made Lord Ogilvy of Airlie in 1491.

Charles I made James, 8th Lord, Earl of Airlie in 1639. The family fought for the king in the Civil War and when the Covenanters burned Airlie Castle the event was commemorated in a ballad. The Airlie titles were forfeited, but the earldom was restored in 1826. The Ogilvys fought in the Jacobite cause in the rebellions of 1715 and 1745. Other branches of the family were earls of Findlater and Seafield.

OLIPHANT

The clan is descended from David de Olifard, a Norman knight who was granted lands in Roxburghshire by David I (r.1124–53). Sir Walter Oliphant of Aberdalgy married Elizabeth, Robert the Bruce's youngest daughter, acquiring the estate of Gask in Perthshire. Sir Laurence of Aberdalgy was made Lord Oliphant in 1458 by James II.

The Oliphants were staunch Jacobites. The 9th Lord Oliphant was jailed for his part in the 1689 campaign, but participated in the 1715 rebellion together with the Gask chief. The 10th Lord Oliphant fought in the 1745 rebellion and after the defeat at Culloden in 1746 escaped to France via Sweden. The poet Lady Nairne, a Gask Oliphant, wrote the celebrated ballads *Will Ye No' Come Back Again?* and *Charlie is My Darling.*

Both the Oliphant tartan and the Melville tartan are sometimes listed as "Oliphant and Melville": the designs are similar and there may have been inter-marriage between the families.

RAEBURN

The Raeburns take their name, which also appears as Rayburn and Reburn, from their Ayrshire lands. Known from about 1330, they are sometimes identified as a sept of clan Boyd.

The portrait painter Sir Henry Raeburn (1756–1823) is associated

▼ *This Oliphant tartan was recorded by the Sobieskis in their 1842 book.*

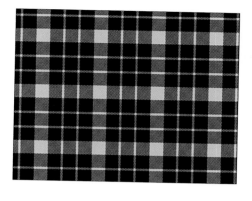

▲ *The Raeburn has thicker yellow stripes than a similar MacLeod tartan.*

with the history of tartan. In his time there was growing interest in traditional Highland dress and many of his subjects wore their family sett when posing. Some of his paintings provide valuable evidence for those seeking to establish the design of a family tartan. Unfortunately, there is no record of a Raeburn tartan before about 1930.

RAMSAY

The Ramsays' ancestor is the Norman knight Sir Symon de Ramsay, who in the 12th century was granted estates in Midlothian by David I. William de Ramsay swore allegiance to Edward I of England in 1296, but soon afterwards fought with Robert the Bruce and in 1320 signed the Declaration of Arbroath, the assertion of Scottish independence. Sir Alexander Ramsay defended Dunbar against an English attack in 1338 and was appointed Sheriff of Teviotdale in 1342. Shortly afterwards a rival knight captured him and left him to die of starvation in a dungeon. George Ramsay was made Lord Ramsay of Dalhousie in 1619 and his son William was Earl of Dalhousie in 1633. In later years Ramsays were prominent public servants: George, 9th Earl, was Governor of Canada (1819–28) while James, 10th Earl, was Governor-General of India (1847–56). Other notable Ramsays include the poet Allan Ramsay (1686–1758) and his painter son, also Allan (1713–84).

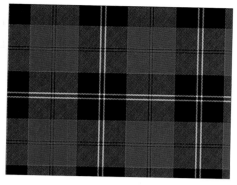

▲ *The Ramsay family tartan is another shown by the Sobieskis in 1842.*

The family tartan appears to be based on a MacGregor design. Ramsay was one of the names adopted by MacGregor clansmen after their own name was banned by royal decree in 1603. Ramsays also have the choice of a black and white dress tartan, a blue family tartan held in the collection of the Scottish Tartans Society and another red-based sett called the Ramsay of Dalhousie family tartan.

▼ *The Airlie Monument honours the 11th Earl of Airlie, an Ogilvy killed while fighting in South Africa in 1900.*

RANKIN–RUSSELL

Tartan historians often encounter false leads. A sample identified as "MacInroy" in a pattern book of Romanes and Patterson from the 1930s is in fact identical to the well-established Rattray of Lude family tartan.

RANKIN

The family name may have originated as a diminutive of the forenames Randolph or Reynard. A sept of clan MacLean, the Rankins were hereditary pipers first to the MacLean lords of Duart, then to the MacLeans of Coll. On Coll one of their number played to Dr Johnson and James Boswell during their 1773 travels, recorded by Boswell in *Journal of a Tour of the Hebrides* (1785). Perhaps the earliest Rankin on record is John Rankyne, burgess of Glasgow in 1456. Half a century later in Kilmarnock Peter Rankyne was cited as witness to a 1504 document.

The Rankin tartan has been known since 1882, but clansmen may also wear the MacLean of Duart tartan.

RATTRAY

Rattray Castle, in the clan's Perthshire estates, probably dates from the late 11th century, but the first recorded family member is the knight Alan de Rateriffe (d.1210), whose son Thomas was knighted by Alexander III and

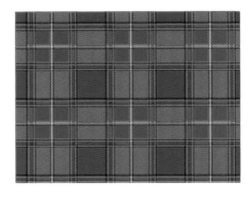

▲ *This Rattray tartan is similar to the one reserved for the Rattrays of Lude.*

gained lands at Glencavery and Kilcaldrum through marriage.

In the early 16th century the Earl of Atholl acquired the castle and much of the Rattray lands, partly through marriage and partly through force. Patrick Rattray erected a new stronghold, Craighall Castle, above the river Ericht but was killed in 1533 by the Earl of Atholl's men. The feud was ended when Atholl's niece Mary Stewart was married to Sylvester Rattray, and Charles II made the Rattray lands into the barony of Craighall-Rattray.

ROLLO

The Rollo family are documented in Scotland from 1141. They take their name from Erik Rollo, a Norman knight, who fought alongside his uncle

William the Conqueror in 1066. Rollo's kinsmen accompanied Prince David north when he claimed the Scottish throne in 1124.

In the 14th century John Rollo served as secretary to David, Earl of Strathearn, and was granted estates at Duncrub under charter from Robert II. William Rollo of Duncrub held the lands as a barony in 1511, and his descendant Sir Andrew Rollo of Duncrub was made Lord Rollo in 1651. One of Lord Rollo's sons, Sir William, proved himself an able lieutenant in the Marquis of Montrose's army, but was captured at Philiphaugh in 1645 and executed in Glasgow.

The family tartan was designed in 1946 and has some likeness to the sett worn by the Rollos' Perthshire neighbours the Campbells of Breadalbane.

ROSE

The Rose family took their name from their original home of Ros, near Caen in Normandy. They settled in southern England before moving to Scotland in the 13th century. Hugh de Ros was named as witness to a document marking the establishment of Beauly Priory in 1219. His son, whose landholdings were in Geddes, acquired lands at Kilravock (pronounced "Kilrock") when he married Sir Andrew de Bosco's

▼ *Variants of the Rankin tartan differ in the number and position of red lines.*

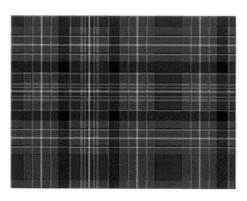

▼ *Lord Rollo commissioned the design of the Rollo family tartan in 1946.*

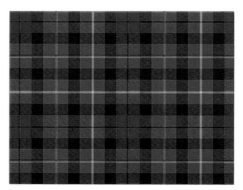

▼ *Author D.C. Stewart identified this Rose family sett as a dress tartan.*

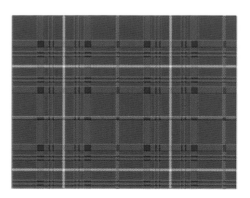

▲ *The Roses' 15th-century hilltop castle at Kilravock was remodelled in the 17th and 18th centuries.*

daughter Marie in about 1290. There the Rose family lived in a house overlooking the river Nairn until Hugh, 7th baron, began the construction of the castle in 1460. The family have lived in their castle ever since. Hugh held the barony of Kilravock under a 1474 charter from James III. In later years the castle had many distinguished visitors, including Mary, Queen of Scots (r.1542–67), James VI (r.1567–1625) and Bonnie Prince Charlie (1720–88).

ROSS

The family took their name from the province of Ross. The first recorded clan chief was Fearchar Mac an t'sagairt ("son of the priest"), who held the hereditary position of Abbot of Applecross around 1225. The Rosses fought fiercely for victory against the English at Bannockburn in 1314 and the Earl of Ross signed the Declaration of Arbroath in 1320. The last clan chief to hold the title of Earl of Ross was William, for after his death in 1372, without male heirs, the earldom passed out of the family. William's half-brother Hugh of Balnagowan took on the chiefship.

During the Civil War David, 12th chief, led a 1000-strong force of Rosses in the Royalist cause at the battle of Worcester in 1651; after their crushing defeat many were transported to North America. In the United States Colonel George Ross (1730–79) of the Continental Army signed the US Declaration of Independence in 1776. Elizabeth Ross (1752–1836), wife of Colonel George's nephew John, is said to have been the seamstress who designed the Stars and Stripes flag.

RUSSELL

The Russells were originally a Norman family and their name may derive from the Old French *rous* ("red") as applied to people with a reddish complexion. In about 1160 Walter Russell witnessed a charter concerning Paisley Abbey, while Robert Russel, a Berwickshire nobleman, signed the 1296 oath of allegiance to Edward I of England. A branch of the family at Aden, in Aberdeenshire, were descended from an Anglo-Norman knight named Rozel, or Russell, who settled in Scotland after fighting in the service of Edward III of England at the battle of Halidon Hill in 1333.

In the 18th century two Edinburgh Russells, Alexander and Patrick, travelled abroad to become well-known doctors – the first in London and the second in Italy.

The tartan shown was listed as Russell in the 1847 pattern book of Wilson's of Bannockburn, but in their 1819 book it was said to be a Hunter, while in the tartan collection of the Highland Society of London it was identified as a Galbraith sett.

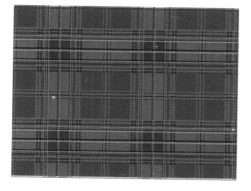

▲ *There are many unverified variants of this Ross family tartan.*

▼ *The US Air Force pipe band has worn the Russell as "Mitchell" tartan.*

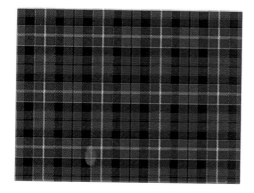

RUTHVEN–SINCLAIR

The Sinclair sett is one of several Scottish family tartans derived from garments worn in historical portraits. In this case the tartan is from a portrait of Alexander Sinclair, 13th Earl of Caithness (1790–1858).

RUTHVEN

The family's first chief was Sweyn Thorsson, a Norse nobleman who acquired lands in Ruthven, Angus, during the reign of William I (r.1165–1214). William Ruthven was made Lord Ruthven in 1488 and the family rose to a position of great power. They were also involved in a number of violent intrigues. Patrick, 3rd Lord, was an accomplice in the murder of David Rizzio, secretary to Mary, Queen of Scots, in 1566, and William, 4th Lord and Earl of Gowrie, took part in the "Ruthven raid" in 1582, which resulted in the imprisonment of the teenage James VI. Ruthvens were also embroiled in the 1600 "Gowrie conspiracy" to murder the king; as a result their name was banned, their lands forfeited and the earldom extinguished.

A 1641 Act allowed the Ruthvens of Ballindean to use their name again and rehabilitation was complete when Sir Alexander Ruthven of Freeland, Governor of Australia in 1935–6, was made Earl of Gowrie in 1945.

▲ *Ruthven Barracks, built following the 1715 uprising, were burned by Bonnie Prince Charlie's army in 1746.*

SCRYMGEOUR

The family name comes from the Old French word for a swordsman, *schyrmeshur*. In 1298 an Alexander Schyrmeshur was appointed Constable of Dundee Castle and given the lands of Upper Dudhope. Named royal standard-bearer, he fought alongside William Wallace at Falkirk.

In 1641 John, 11th Constable of Dundee, was made Viscount Dudhope, and his grandson, also John, became Earl of Dundee in 1660. Eight years later the Scrymgeour lands and titles were seized by the Duke of Lauderdale. Henry Scrymgeour regained the earldom of Dundee as 11th Earl in 1954. The tartan shown here was conceived by Donald C. Stewart, author of *Setts of the Scottish Tartans* (1950), and was chosen as the Scrymgeour tartan in the 1970s.

SEMPILL

Some authorities identify the family as Anglo-Norman, originating from Saint-Paul in Normandy. The Sempills had possession of their main estates at Elliotstoun in Renfrewshire by about 1350. The first recorded family

▼ *The Sobieskis were the first to identify a Ruthven tartan, in 1842.*

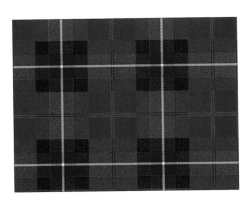

▼ *The Scrymgeours adopted their tartan after a clan gathering in 1971.*

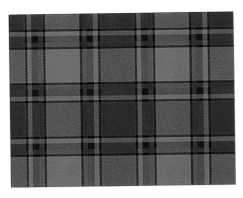

▼ *Family links explain the similarity of the Sempill tartan to that of Forbes.*

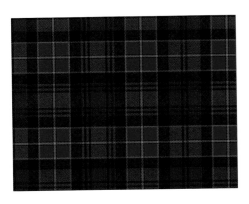

member in Scotland is Robert de Sempill, who witnessed a 1246 charter concerning Paisley Abbey. Later in the same century the family held the position of hereditary sheriff of Renfrew.

The Sempills fought alongside Robert the Bruce (r.1306–29) in the cause of Scottish independence. They fought at the battle of Sauchieburn in 1488, near Stirling, which led to the death of James III, and then with James IV at Flodden in 1513 against the English army. Following the 1745 rebellion the clan chief, Hugh, 12th Lord Sempill, fought in the Hanoverian army against the Jacobites at Culloden.

SETON

The family's earliest known ancestor in Scotland was Alexander de Seton who in about 1150 was named as a witness to a charter of David I and held the lands of Winton, Winchburgh and Seton. Having saved Robert the Bruce's life in the battle of Methven in 1306, Sir Christopher de Seton married the patriot's sister, Christina.

In the reign of James I William Seton was made Lord of Seton and Tranent. George, 5th Lord Seton, was Master of the Household for Mary, Queen of Scots (r.1542–67), and completed the Palace of Seton where he sheltered her in 1566. Two years later he helped her escape from Lochleven. His son Robert, 6th Lord, became Earl of Winton in 1600. Robert's son,

▼ *Setons can choose between this family sett and a green Hunting tartan.*

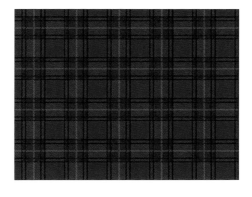

▲ *The Shaw clan tartan is based on the pattern worn by Fearcher Shaw.*

Alexander, made Lord Fyvie in 1597 and Earl of Dunfermline in 1605, became Chancellor of Scotland and completed the building of Fyvie Castle.

The Setons supported the Stuarts in the Jacobite era. James, 4th Earl of Dunfermline, commanded a troop of horse under Bonnie Dundee at Killiecrankie in 1689 and lost his property as a result. George, 5th Earl of Winton, was captured during the 1715 Jacobite rebellion but escaped from the Tower of London and fled to Rome.

SHAW

The Shaws were prominent members of the clan Chattan confederation. Their first chief, John, was a son of Angus, 6th Mackintosh chief, and Eva, daughter of Dougall Dall, 6th Chattan chief. Some accounts say John's son Shaw Bucktooth led the Chattan clansmen in the battle of the North Inch of Perth in 1396. Bucktooth's son James was killed in the ferocious battle of Harlaw in 1411. James's son Aedh, or Ay, settled at Tordarroch on the river Nairn and founded clan Ay.

Robert and Angus of Tordarroch led the clansmen in support of the Jacobites in the 1715 rebellion and after defeat at Preston both were jailed. Robert died as a result of his treatment, while Angus was despatched to Virginia. At this time the Shaw clan had already been without a chief for some 250 years and it did not acquire

one until Major C.J. Shaw of Tordarroch became chief in 1970.

Donald C. Stewart, author of *Setts of the Scottish Tartans* (1950), designed a Shaw of Tordarroch sett for the clan. Clansmen still also wear the Shaw clan tartan, based on the pattern shown in a drawing of Fearcher Shaw of the Black Watch regiment. Executed for mutiny in 1743, Shaw was regarded as a hero in the Highlands.

SINCLAIR

The Norman nobleman Woldernus, Count of St Clair, came to England with William the Conqueror in 1066. His descendants, who take their name from his Norman lands, had made their home in Scotland by about 1162, when Henry de St Clair held the estates of Herdmanston near Haddington under charter. His kinsman, Sir Henry St Clair of Rosslyn, was a supporter of Robert the Bruce and is remembered as "kind and true St Clair". His son William rode on pilgrimage with Good Sir James Douglas; the pair died in Spain fighting the Moors. Henry's great-grandson, another Henry, was Scotland's Lord High Admiral and discovered Greenland. Through his mother Isabel, a descendant of the Norse rulers of Orkney, he became Earl of Orkney. His grandson William was made Earl of Caithness in 1455 but under pressure from James III had to resign his claim to Orkney.

▼ *The Sinclair tartan is in the Cockburn Collection in Glasgow.*

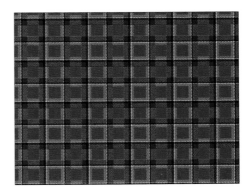

SKENE–TAYLOR

The Skene tartan survives in different versions in *The Costume of the Clans of the Scottish Highlands* (1845–7), in the pattern books of Wilson's of Bannockburn and in other sources. It is sometimes confused with the Logan.

SKENE

According to family legend, the Skenes are descended from a valiant son of Robertson of Struan who, armed only with a dagger, killed a wolf that was threatening the king. The grateful monarch rewarded the hero with lands west of Aberdeen, which he named after his dagger, or *sgian*.

The first documented family member is John de Skeen, who lived during the reign of Malcolm III (r.1058–93) and had his lands forfeited for supporting a rival of Edgar (r.1097–1107). The estates were restored by Alexander I in 1118. The Skenes were supporters of Robert the Bruce, who granted Robert Skene a charter for their lands in 1317. Later chiefs were killed fighting at Harlaw in 1411, Flodden in 1513 and Pinkie in 1547. In time the Skenes of Hallyards became the clan chiefs.

The historian William Forbes Skene wrote *The Highlanders of Scotland* and edited *Chronicles of the Picts and Scots*; in 1881 he was appointed Scotland's Historiographer Royal.

▼ *This Skene tartan is the one worn by family members today.*

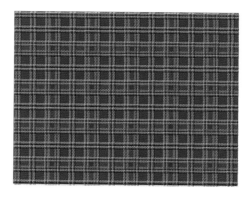

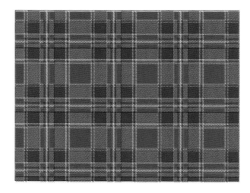

▲ *The Spens is similar to a Perthshire district tartan made by Wilson's.*

SPENS

The Spens family name comes from the title used in medieval households by larder keepers. The principal branch of the family, in Fife, claim descent from the MacDuff Earls of Fife; they were living at Lathallan in the 13th century. In 1296 Henry de Spens of Lathallan swore allegiance to Edward I of England and the family flourished under the protection of the earls of Fife until about 1430, when their estates were made into a barony held under charter from the Crown. In this era William of Lathallan acquired new possessions through his marriage to the daughter and heiress of Campbell of Glendouglas. One of his sons gave rise to the Spens of Kilspindie. Patrick Spens founded a family in France when he served there in about 1450.

In the early 17th century Sir James of Wormiston was James VI's ambassador to Denmark. Other branches of the family included those of Muirton in Fife and Bodham in Aberdeenshire.

STIRLING

The family had possession of their estates at Cawder during the reign of William I (r.1165–1214). In 1448 Lukas Stirling bought lands at Keir from George Leslie. Sir John Stirling of Keir was made Sheriff of Perth in 1516

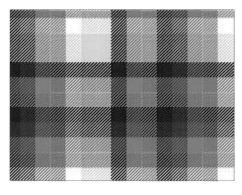

▲ *This is a modern district tartan made for Stirling Millennium Year.*

and his son, Sir James Stirling of Keir, married the heiress of the Cawder estate. Sir James's great-grandson, George Stirling, fought with the Marquis of Montrose when he was defeated at Philiphaugh in 1645. In the 18th century James Stirling had the Keir and Cawder estates forfeited for his part in the Jacobite rebellion, but they were later restored.

Other branches of the Stirlings include those at Glorat and Ardoch. Those at Fairburn are descended from members of clan MacGregor who adopted the Stirling name when their own was banned by James VI in 1603. A Stirling and Bannockburn tartan was produced by Wilson's of Bannockburn in the 19th century.

▼ *The Stirling and Bannockburn tartan was produced in honour of Scottish victories in 1297 and 1314.*

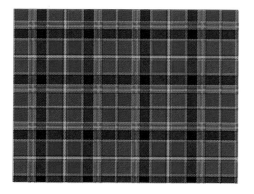

▶ *The Scottish Sutherlands host a gathering of clansmen from around the world each year at Dunrobin Castle.*

STURROCK

The Sturrocks were concentrated in rural areas in Angus and the name, the Gaelic word for a sheep or cattle farmer, is believed to have come from an occupational title. Laurence Sturrok, Vicar of Covil in 1453, is the first of the name to be recorded. He moved on to this position from one as a chaplain in Aberdeen.

SUTHERLAND

The family take their name from the Sutherland region in north-eastern Scotland. The Norwegian kings, who by the 10th century had possession of the islands and the mainland as far down as Inverness, knew this area as Sudrland ("southland").

The Sutherlands share an ancestor with the Murrays, for both trace their descent from Freskin, a Flemish mercenary who served the Normans. His grandson, Hugh, possessed large parts of Sutherland and his son, William, was made Earl of Sutherland in about 1235. Hugh's brother, also William, founded the Murray clan. In the 14th century two earls of Sutherland took royal brides: William, 5th Earl, married Robert the Bruce's daughter Margaret, while Robert, 6th Earl, married Robert III's niece. Robert later built Dunrobin

Castle. The family became dukes of Sutherland from 1833 and the 2nd Duke employed the Gothic Revival architect Sir Charles Barry (1795–1860), chief architect of the Houses of Parliament in Westminster, to transform the castle into a great palace.

TAYLOR

The Taylors are generally seen as a sept of clan Cameron. Clan tradition says they are descended from a mighty 16th-century warrior known as the Black Tailor of the Axe, the illegitimate son of Little Ewen, 14th chief of clan Cameron, and the daughter of the Lord of MacDonald. He was given his nick-

name because he was nursed by a tailor's wife and could not be matched when wielding his preferred weapon, the Lochaber axe. He is said to have taken command of the Cameron clan when the chief was a minor (1569–78). Many families across Scotland shared the name because of its occupational associations, and it is found in historical documents from about 1276, when Alexander le Tallur was recorded as a valet to Alexander III.

The Taylor tartan is comparable to the Hunting Cameron. It was designed in 1955 by Lieutenant-Colonel Iain Cameron Taylor. It is accepted as authentic by the Camerons of Lochiel.

▼ *Variants of the Sturrock tartan use blue where this design has black.*

▼ *This tartan dates to at least 1850 and is known as Sutherland Old.*

▼ *Taylors can also wear a fine Taylor Dress tartan on formal occasions.*

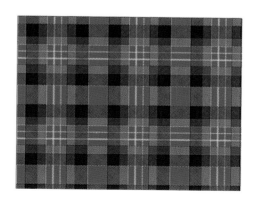

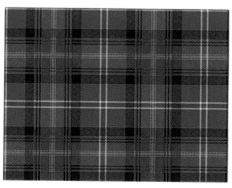

URQUHART–WOTHERSPOON

The Urquharts have one unique connection with tartan history. To add authenticity, the Sobieskis' *Vestiarum Scoticum* claimed to be based on a (forged) document supposedly written by Sir Richard Urquhart in 1721.

URQUHART

The Urquhart name appears to derive from Airchart, a place name. The earliest recorded ancestor is William de Urchard, who reputedly fought the English in Cromarty at the time of Sir William Wallace. Under David II (r.1329–71) the Urquharts were hereditary sheriffs of Cromarty and later constables of Urquhart Castle on Loch Ness. Thomas Urquhart of Cromarty allegedly fathered 25 sons, seven of whom died in a single day at the battle of Pinkie in 1547. His namesake, Sir Thomas Urquhart of Cromarty (1611–60), was a celebrated author

▼ *Urquhart Castle, long protected by the Urquhart constables, today stands in ruins on the shore of Loch Ness.*

and soldier who translated the works of the French satirist Rabelais. Captured by anti-Royalist forces at the battle of Worcester in 1651, he was released into exile where he died in 1660, reputedly choking with laughter when told of Charles II's Restoration. The Urquhart family seat is Castle Craig on the Cromarty Firth.

WALLACE

Fittingly for the family that produced the Scottish patriot Sir William Wallace (*c*.1270–1305), the Wallace motto is "For liberty". The family were originally Britons from the Strathclyde region and were established in Ayrshire and Renfrewshire in the 12th century. When William's father, Malcolm Wallace of Elderslie, in Renfrewshire, was executed after refusing to sign the 1296 oath of allegiance demanded by Edward I of England, he fled with his mother and embarked on his campaign of resistance. Following his victory over a larger English force at Stirling Bridge in 1297, he was made Guardian of

▲ *Logan recorded an Urquhart tartan with narrower red lines than these.*

▼ *The Sobieskis printed this version of Wallace in* Vestiarum Scoticum.

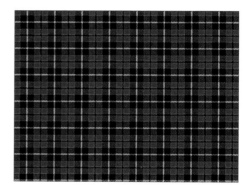

Scotland, but his star faded the following year when he was defeated by the English at Falkirk. He was betrayed, captured, and executed for treason in London on 23 August 1305.

Other branches of the family included the Wallaces of Craigie in Ayrshire, descended from William's uncle, Adam, 4th Lord of Riccarton, and those of Cairnhill. The Wallace clan tartan is one of those first recorded in the Sobieski brothers' *Vestiarum Scoticum* of 1842.

WEIR

The Weirs are descended from Norman followers of William the Conqueror and take their name from Vere in Normandy. The family were established in Scotland by 1174, when Radulphus,

or Ralph de Vere, was named as a prisoner captured at Alnwick with William I. In about 1180 he made a gift of land to the monks of Kelso Abbey. The Weirs established at Blackwood, Lanarkshire, claimed descent from this Ralph de Vere. In the 17th century, Major Thomas Weir of Kirktown, commander of the Edinburgh City Guard, was burned for witchcraft alongside his sister. A number of Highland MacNairs anglicized their name to Weir (the "mh" of the Gaelic form of the name, MacAmhaoir, is pronounced "v"). Weir was sometimes given as Vere or Wire.

Some clan members wear the Hope-Vere tartan. This family connection was made through the marriage in 1730 of Catherine, the daughter of Sir William Vere of Blackwood, to Charles, son of the Earl of Hopetoun.

WEMYSS
The Wemyss family take their name from their lands in Fife and trace descent to a younger son of a mid-12th-century MacDuff earl of Fife. The clan chief supported Robert the Bruce, as a result of which the English sacked Wemyss Castle. In the 16th century Sir John de Wemyss was a staunch supporter of Mary, Queen of Scots, and it was as his guest at the restored Wemyss Castle that Mary first met Henry, Lord Darnley, eventually her husband. Sir John Wemyss was made Lord Wemyss of Elcho in 1628 and became Earl of

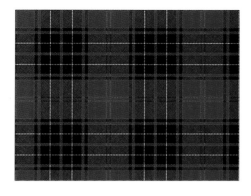

▲ *The Sobieskis'* Vestiarum Scoticum *is the source for the Wemyss tartan.*

Wemyss five years later. David, Lord Elcho, a son of the 4th Earl, commanded a troop of horse guards in Bonnie Prince Charlie's army in the 1745 Jacobite rebellion and escaped to France following the Jacobite defeat at Culloden in 1746.

WILSON
An anglicized form of MacWilliam, the Wilson name is common throughout Scotland, where it was known from the early 15th century. Wilsons in the Caithness area are associated with clan Gunn, for they trace their descent to a son of George Gunn, a mid-15th-century Caithness coroner. In other parts of Scotland some families are linked to clan Innes. Celebrated bearers of the name include the naturalist Alexander Wilson (1766–1813), who emigrated to the United States in 1794 and is remembered for his nine-volume

American Ornithology (1808–14). Woodrow Wilson (1856–1924), 28th US President, was the grandson of Scottish-Irish immigrants.

The record books of the tartan weavers Wilson's of Bannockburn (*c.*1750–1906) contain a wealth of information about clan tartans. The Wilson tartan was designed to mark the marriage of the founder's son William to Janet Paterson in 1780 and was originally called the Janet Wilson.

WOTHERSPOON
This name, from the Old English for "sheep pasture", was in use in Lowland Scotland in the 13th century. Roger Wythirspon, named in association with a grant of land in Renfrewshire at this time, may be the first family member on record. In the late 15th century James IV's fowler was named Widderspune and in 1546 an Archibald Wetherspune was vicar of Karridden. Two bearers of the name made their mark in North America. The Reverend John Witherspoon (1722–94), who became President of the College of New Jersey (Princeton) in 1768, was a member of the second Continental Congress in 1776 and signed the Declaration of Independence. General William Wallace Wotherspoon (1850–1921) managed the New York State system of canals. The family do not have a chief and their tartan was unknown before around 1930.

▼ *The Hope-Vere differs from this Weir tartan in having double thin blue lines.*

▼ *This Wilson has narrower green and broader blue than the "Janet Wilson".*

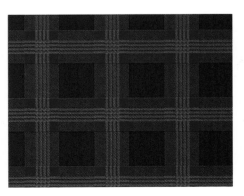

▼ *This Wotherspoon tartan has been dated to the 1940s.*

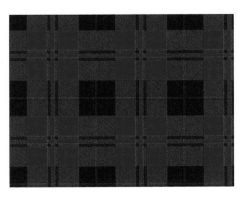

MODERN AND INTERNATIONAL TARTANS

MODERN TARTANS HAVE BEEN ISSUED FOR MANY DIVERSE REASONS, TO COMMEMORATE HISTORICAL EVENTS, TO PROMOTE THE NAMES OF CORPORATIONS OR SPORTS TEAMS AND TO RAISE MONEY FOR GOOD CAUSES. THIS IS A SELECTION OF JUST SOME OF THEM.

AMERICAN BICENTENNIAL–CORNISH FLAG

In recent years many national tartans have been produced for the descendants of 18th- and 19th-century Scottish émigrés. As a result places as diverse as Australia, Argentina and the Bahamas now have tartans. The issuing of commemorative tartans to mark national celebrations has also proved popular. These tend to fall out of use once the event is past, but the American Bicentennial was renamed the American (St Andrew's) and is still popular today. The recent surge of interest in tartan has prompted Scottish soccer teams, among others, to issue their own tartans.

AMERICAN BICENTENNIAL

The St Andrew's Society of Washington commissioned this tartan, designed by fellows of the Scottish Tartans Society, which was worn in celebration of the 1976 bicentenary of the US Declaration of Independence.

ARGENTINA

Designed in 1995 for the Argentinian St Andrew's Society of the river Plate, in honour of two Robertson brothers who oversaw a 19th-century emigration programme for Scots to Argentina, this tartan combines the colours of the Argentine and Scottish flags. Designer

Previous pages: Loch Arkaig

▼ *American Bicentennial, 1976.*

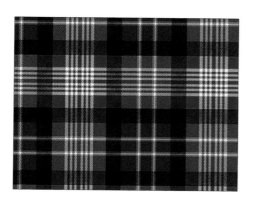

Edward MacRae based it on one of the clan Robertson tartans. Any Scot or person of Scottish descent living in Argentina is eligible to wear it.

AUBIGNY AULD ALLIANCE

Made in Scotland by MacNaughtons of Pitlochry for Aubigny-sur-Nère, Loire Valley, France, which has strong Scottish links, this design commemorates the "Auld Alliance" between Scots and French against their common foe, the English.

AUSTRALIAN NATIONAL

In this tartan designed by Betty Johnston of Canberra's House of Tartan, the green and yellow lines recall Australia's national colours while the blue and red refer to the Union Flag. The white lines stand for the stars of the Southern Cross constellation. Another tartan, the Australian, evoking the sandy browns used by Aboriginal artists, was designed by Melbourne architect John Reid in 1984.

BAHAMAS

This sett, designed by Gordon Rees, has been the official tartan of the Bahamas since 1966. The Bahamas were colonized by the British in the mid-17th century and early Scottish settlers included Forsythes, Malcolms, Thompsons and MacPhersons.

▼ *Australian National, 1984.*

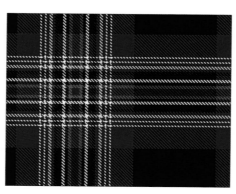

BRITISH COLUMBIA

The Quebec company Pik Mills produced this tartan in 1966 for British Columbia, Canada's westernmost province, to mark the 100th anniversary of its administrative unification with Vancouver Island.

CALIFORNIA

Designed in 1997, this sett was adopted as the official state tartan in 2001. It is similar to the clan Muir tartan in tribute to naturalist John Muir (1838–1914), who helped create the Yosemite and Sequoia National Parks.

CANADIAN CALEDONIAN

Made in 1939 by Cochrane and Macbeth of Vancouver, this tartan can be worn by all Scottish Canadians. Many Scots emigrated to Canada in the 19th century.

CANADIAN CENTENNIAL

Peter Bottomley designed this tartan in 1966 for the following year's 100th anniversary of the establishment of the Dominion of Canada in 1867.

CATALAN

Designed to mark the 1992 Olympic Games held in Barcelona, capital of the region of Catalonia in north-eastern Spain, this tartan is now used as a Catalan district tartan.

▼ *Bahamas, 1966.*

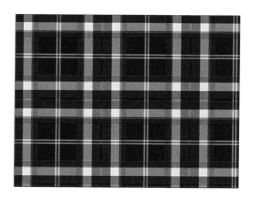

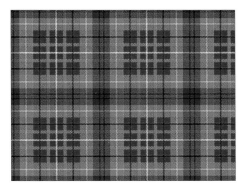

▲ *British Columbia, 1966.*

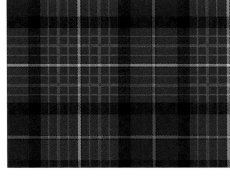

▲ *California, 1997.*

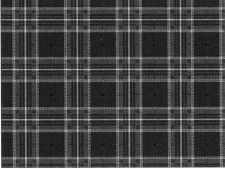

▲ *Canadian Caledonian, 1939.*

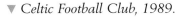

▼ *Celtic Football Club, 1989.*

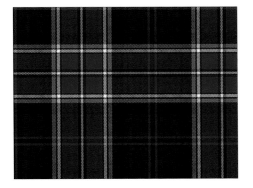

▲ *Canadian Centennial, 1966.*

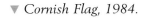

▼ *Cornish Flag, 1984.*

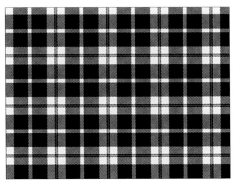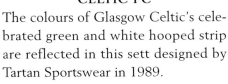

CELTIC FC

The colours of Glasgow Celtic's celebrated green and white hooped strip are reflected in this sett designed by Tartan Sportswear in 1989.

CHATTAHOOCHEE

Leah Robertson designed this tartan in 1994 to commemorate the "twinning" of the rivers Tweed (Scottish–English Borders) and Chattahoochee (Georgia/Florida).

CORK

This sett is one of a number of Irish county tartans manufactured by the House of Edgar, in Perth, during 1996.

CORNISH FLAG

This 1984 sett was originally known as the St Piran Tartan in honour of the patron of Cornish tin miners, a 5th-century Irish abbot. The design echoes the Cross of St Piran, which is often flown as a symbol of Cornish identity.

ABERDEEN FC

This Scottish soccer team has released three official tartans since 1990, all based on the colours of the team's home strip.

AMERICAN TARTAN

Created in 1975 in preparation for the following year's bicentenary of US independence, this can be worn by any American of Scottish descent.

ANNE ARUNDEL COUNTY

This tartan is used at the annual Highland Games run by the Anne Arundel County Scottish Festival in Maryland, USA. It was designed in 1998.

ARRAN

First produced in 1982 by MacNaughtons of Pitlochry, this modern district tartan is available in two versions, one in purple and red and the other in navy blue.

BEAUPORT

Anne-Marie Germain designed a sett in 1991 as a district tartan for Beauport, which lies north-east of Quebec City in Canada. It uses the colours of the town's coat of arms and has been approved as an official tartan for the area.

BERMUDA

The Scottish firm Peter MacArthur Ltd designed two Bermuda tartans in the 1960s for sale in the self-governing British colony of Bermuda.

CANADIAN IRISH REGIMENT

The 110th Irish Regiment of Canada was established in April 1914 and the tartan was probably designed around this time.

DIANA PRINCESS, MEMORIAL–FRANCONIAN

A number of tartans bear Princess Diana's name, including the Memorial sett and one issued in 1981 in honour of her marriage in Westminster Abbey to Prince Charles.

A very different woman with royal connections, Flora MacDonald has also had several tartans issued in her name. This daughter of a Scottish farmer helped Bonnie Prince Charlie escape from the English after the battle of Culloden in 1746 by disguising him as an Irish maid. Although Charles did escape, Flora was caught by the English and jailed in the Tower of London. She married after her pardon in 1747, and emigrated to North Carolina with her husband in 1774. When he was captured fighting against the English in the American War of Independence she returned to Scotland, where he eventually rejoined her.

▲ *Diana Princess, Memorial, 1997.*

▼ *Dunedin, New Zealand, 1988.*

DIANA PRINCESS, MEMORIAL
Tartan manufacturer Lochcarron of Scotland launched this tartan in 1997 to honour Princess Diana's memory and generate funds for her charities. The pattern was based on the Royal Stewart clan tartan, using colours inspired by Diana's life and character.

DONEGAL
This is one of a group of Irish county tartans that were issued during 1996 by House of Edgar, a Scottish firm. County Donegal, in the north-west of the Irish Republic, has a windswept, rugged coastline.

DUBLIN
This is one of the county setts issued by Scotland's House of Edgar in 1996. Dublin, the Irish Republic's capital, is also the chief town of County Dublin.

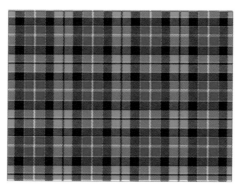

▲ *Dutch, 1965.*

▼ *Essex County, Canada, 1983.*

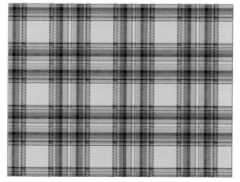

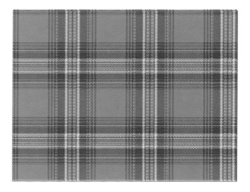

▲ *Edinburgh '86.*

DUNEDIN, FLORIDA
Dunedin lies close to Tampa on the Gulf coast. The city's name, like that of its New Zealand counterpart, is from the Gaelic name for Edinburgh, Dun Eideann ("hill fortress"). William L. Matthews designed a district tartan for Dunedin in 1986. He based his design on the Edinburgh district tartan.

DUNEDIN, NEW ZEALAND
Scottish heritage is proudly celebrated in Dunedin, in the eastern coastal region of New Zealand's South Island. The city has its own whisky distillery and kilt shop and is sometimes hailed as the "Edinburgh of the South". This regional tartan was made in 1988 to celebrate the arrival of the first Free Church of Scotland settlers in the area, who landed on 23 March 1848 after a 116-day voyage from the old country.

DUTCH
John Cargill based his design on the Mackay tartan because that clan had close links with the Netherlands. This tartan can be worn by any Dutch person with Scottish ancestry.

EDINBURGH '86
This sett was designed for the parade uniform of the Scottish athletes and officials at the 1986 Commonwealth Games, held in Edinburgh. The colours

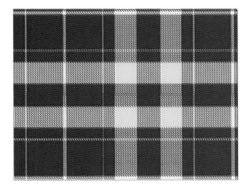

▲ *European Union, 1998.*

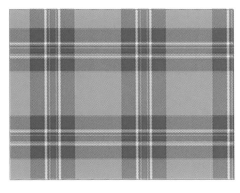

▲ *Federal Bureau of Investigation.*

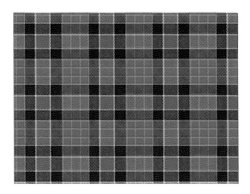

▲ *Flora MacDonald Portrait.*

have symbolic meaning: white for the running track lanes, red for the winners' tape and blue for the Scottish flag.

ESSEX COUNTY
This Canadian district tartan for Essex County, Ontario, was designed in 1983 by Edyth Baker and approved as the county's official tartan the following year. The yellow represents cereal crops and the red represents tomatoes, both of which are grown in abundance throughout the region.

EUROPEAN UNION
Designed by William D. Chalmers in 1998, this tartan can be worn by any European Union citizen who has Scottish ancestry. Its colours echo those of the Scottish and the EU flags.

FALKIRK
The local authorities in Falkirk, halfway between Edinburgh and Glasgow, held a competition in 1990 for a district tar-

tan. James McGeorge designed the winning sett.

FEDERAL BUREAU OF INVESTIGATION
The FBI pipe band wears this corporate tartan, designed and produced by Thomas Gordon & Sons of Glasgow. Designer Douglas Gillies based the sett on the Earl of St Andrews tartan, but added a red stripe to the design.

FITZPATRICK
An ancient Irish family, the Fitzpatricks or "sons of Patrick" have cousins of similar name – the original Gaelic Mac Giolla Phádraig was anglicized either as Fitzpatrick or Kilpatrick. The tartan was included in the 1880 book *Clans Originaux*, which contained a number of Irish setts alongside Scottish ones.

FLORA MACDONALD PORTRAIT
This tartan is taken from a portrait of

Flora MacDonald now hanging in Fort William Museum. Flora was a member of the MacDonalds of Clanranald. Her father Ranald lived at Milton on South Uist. She was one of the romatic heroes of the second Jacobite rebellion, and her name is forever linked with that of Bonnie Prince Charlie. She is immortalized in the popular song "Flora MacDonald's Lament" written by the violinist Niel Gow the Younger. Flora's name is a resonant one for a tartan as it conjures images of the old Highlands and recalls the many who died in the doomed but heroic Jacobite uprisings.

FRANCONIAN
This first German district tartan was commissioned by a group of whisky enthusiasts from Nuremberg. It takes its name from Franconia, an ancient district that now comprises the states of Bavaria, Hesse and Baden-Württemberg. The yellow lines refer to the whisky that inspired the group.

▼ *Falkirk, 1990.*

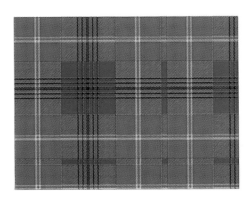

▼ *Fitzpatrick.*

▼ *Franconian.*

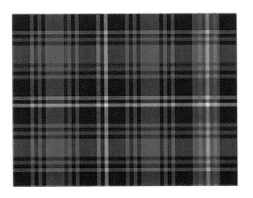

FREDERICTON–IRISH NATIONAL

It is not uncommon for "original" tartans to be used as the basis of modern designs. The originals may be representations found in paintings or engravings, or pieces of surviving tartan. One such remnant was a jacket worn by a soldier of a company of Caithness men massacred in 1612 on their way to fight as mercenaries in Sweden. As they marched through the valley of Gudbrandsdal in southern Norway, they were ambushed by locals who, perched on surrounding high land, hurled great boulders down at the trapped Scots.

Some recent setts have been developed in far less traditional ways. The Houston tartan, for example, was thought up by two geographically distant Houstons, one in Arkansas and one in New Zealand, communicating via email.

FREDERICTON
Dating from 1967, this district tartan celebrates the capital of New Brunswick province, Canada, named in 1785 after George III's son Frederick Augustus. The sett was made by a home-weaving group named the Loomcrofters.

GALICIA
The region of Galicia in north-western Spain has strong Celtic connections because some Celts migrated there in the 6th century when driven out of England by Anglo-Saxons. The colours in this district tartan derive from the Galician flag. The sett was woven by D.C. Dalgleish to an early 1990s design by Philip Smith.

GEORGIA
The Scottish Tartans Society made this sett in 1982 to celebrate the 250th anniversary of the state of Georgia, USA, named after George II, who in

▲ *Fredericton, 1967.*

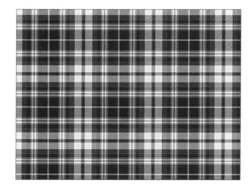

▼ *Georgia, 1982.*

1732 granted James Oglethorpe a charter to begin settlement. Highland soldiers were among the early settlers.

GERMAN NATIONAL
Any German with Scottish ancestry can wear this tartan, which was first produced in 1994. Its designer Douglas C. Ikelman, an American descended from German and Scottish emigrants, used elements from the tartans of his clan (Fraser) in the design.

GLASGOW RANGERS
Geoffrey (Tailor) Highland Crafts produced this sporting tartan, woven to a Chris Aitken design, in 1994. The sett reflects the colours of the football club's red-trimmed blue and white kit. By tradition, Rangers are a Protestant side, while their Glasgow rivals, Celtic, are Catholic.

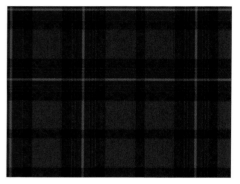

▲ *Gordonstoun, 1966*

▼ *Glasgow Rangers, 1994.*

GLENGARRY HIGHLAND GAMES
This Canadian corporate tartan was designed by Don Smith in 1998 to celebrate the 50th anniversary of the Glengarry Highland Games held in Maxville, Ontario, Canada. The tartan was registered in 1999 and was first woven in 1999–2000.

GORDONSTOUN
This is one of four registered tartans named for the celebrated independent boarding school established in 1934 by German educator Dr Kurt Hahn. In the 1960s Prince Charles attended the school, which is known for its enthusiastic application of the principle that tough living conditions and rigorous educational routines build character in young people. The school has been co-educational since 1972.

GUDBRANDSDALEN

Erik Poulsen of Norway presented this tartan to the Scottish Tartans Society in 1992, as part of a collection of intriguing Norwegian district setts. It honours Scottish soldiers ambushed and massacred by farmers in the valley of Gudbrandsdal, southern Norway, in 1612. The pattern was taken from a single jacket surviving the incident, an exact copy of which has been made.

GUELPH

The city of Guelph in Ontario, Canada, commissioned its own district tartan, which uses colours found in the Guelph coat of arms, in the 1990s. The city's university is a major centre of Scottish studies in Canada.

HOLYROOD

First made in 1977 to celebrate Elizabeth II's Silver Jubilee, this sett was renamed Holyrood after the Palace of Holyroodhouse in Edinburgh, the Queen's official residence in Scotland. The palace stands next to the remains of the Augustinian Abbey of Holyrood, founded in the 12th century.

HOUSTON

This tartan was jointly designed by New Zealander W.J. Houston and American J.P. Houston in 1994. The sett is intended for all those bearing the Scottish name Houston, which came originally from a Lanarkshire place name and is found in the Scottish historical record from the Middle Ages onwards.

HUDSON'S BAY COMPANY

Held by the Hudson's Bay Company of Canada, this tartan is based on an 18th-century piece believed to have belonged to Bonnie Prince Charlie. Formerly prominent in the Canadian fur trade and incorporated in 1670, the company is active in other commercial areas, with headquarters in Toronto. It also has a modern corporate tartan.

IDAHO CENTENNIAL

This sett was created to mark the 1990 centenary of Idaho's joining the Union and has been approved as the state's official tartan. Many Scottish immigrants settled in Idaho in the 1800s, and Scottish culture is popular there.

ILLINOIS ST ANDREW'S SOCIETY

The Illinois St Andrew's Society commissioned this tartan in 1990 to

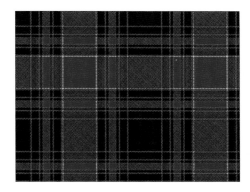

▲ *Gudbrandsdalen, 1992.*

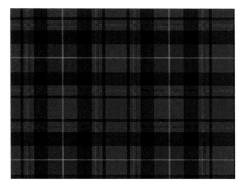

▲ *Hudson's Bay Company, 1700s.*

▼ *Idaho Centennial, 1990.*

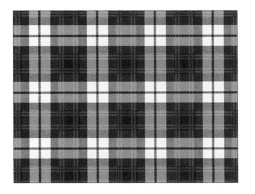

celebrate the 150th anniversary of its formation. Many Scottish settlers in North America established St Andrew's societies to preserve Scottish culture.

IRISH NATIONAL

This tartan can be worn by Irish expatriates or anyone with Irish ancestry. Designed by Scotland's House of Edgar to accompany its 1996 series of Irish county tartans, it uses the green and white of the Irish flag.

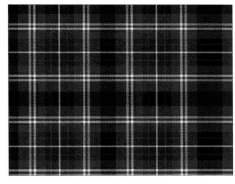

▲ *Guelph, 1990s.*

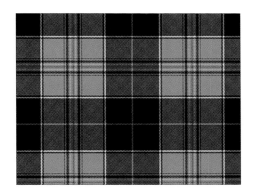

▲ *Holyrood, 1977.*

▼ *Irish National, 1996.*

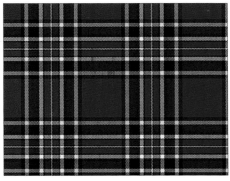

KATSUSHIKA–NEWFOUNDLAND

In Scotland most of the larger clans have separate tartans for different branches of the family, but very few groups of expatriate clan members have their own named sett. Unusually, the clan MacLeod members in California are able to wear their own sett, the MacLeod Californian. As an alternative to their clan tartan, other Scottish descendants in North America can usually choose a state or provincial one, as many US states and Canadian provinces have their own official tartans, which can be worn by anyone associated with the area.

KATSUSHIKA SCOTTISH COUNTRY DANCERS

This sett was designed for a Tokyo-based country dancing team in 1995. Some competitions require entrants to wear tartan so this team and their local rivals the Tokyo Bluebells commissioned their own setts. Both were designed by handweaver Donald Fraser.

LARGS

Sidney Samuels designed this 1981 sett in honour of the seaside Ayrshire town of Largs, site of a Scottish victory in 1263 over Norway's King Haakon that is often seen as marking the end of Viking control of Scotland. The event is celebrated each year with a festival that burns a replica Viking longboat.

LAVAL

The Tisserands de Laval (Weavers of Laval) produced this district sett in 1988, purple and blue being the official colours of Laval, Quebec's second largest city. The city also has a dress tartan, officially designated Tartan de la ville de Laval – Gala.

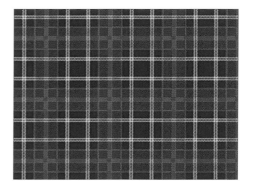

▲ *Katsushika Scottish Country Dancers, 1995.*

LEATHERNECK US MARINE CORPS

The US Marine Corps was founded in 1775 and its members were nicknamed the "Leathernecks" because their uniform in the 18th and 19th centuries included a distinctive leather neckpiece. The sett was designed by R.H. MacLeod and Bob Hall of the Scottish Tartans Society in the 1980s.

LOCH NESS

Kiltmakers of Inverness produced this trade tartan in 1983. Loch Ness is famous for the persistence of the story that a sea monster lives in its depths. The loch lies in the Great Glen, which cuts across the Highlands, and is 240m (788ft) deep and 36 kilometres (23 miles) long.

LOUISIANA

Anyone associated with the state of Louisiana can wear this tartan, which was adopted as an official state emblem in June 2001. It was designed by Joe McD. Campbell and its colours are said to represent Louisiana's environment and resources.

MacLEOD CALIFORNIAN

Frank Connonitto modelled this sett in the late 1980s on MacLeod of Harris and Baillie MacLeod tartans.

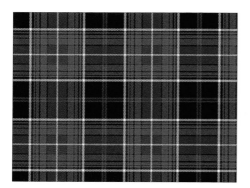

▲ *Largs, 1981.*

▼ *Laval, 1988.*

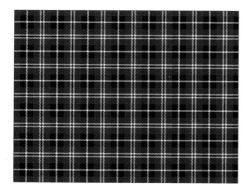

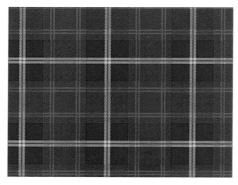

▲ *Leatherneck US Marine Corps.*

▼ *Loch Ness, 1983.*

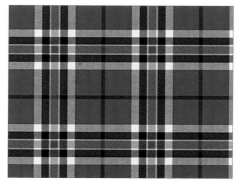

MAINE DIRIGO

Linda Clifford designed this sett for the St Andrew's Society of Maine, in New England. Another Maine tartan was designed in 1964 by Sol Gilis.

MANITOBA

Hugh Kirkwood Rankine designed this sett in 1962 in honour of Manitoba province in central Canada. The red squares in the design refer to the Red River Settlement which, together with the North West Company and Hudson's Bay Company trading posts, became the state capital of Winnipeg.

MANX NATIONAL

Patricia McQuaid designed this district sett for the Isle of Man after the idea of a national tartan was mooted in 1957. The Isle of Man lies in the Irish Sea, roughly halfway between Ireland and the north-west of England.

MAYO

The Scottish firm House of Edgar issued a series of trade district tartans, designed by Polly Wittering, for the counties of Ireland in 1996. County Mayo takes its name from the Irish Maigh Eo ("yew tree plain") and lies on the western coast of the Irish Republic.

NEW BRUNSWICK

This district tartan for the Canadian province of New Brunswick was commissioned by the press baron and politician Lord Beaverbrook in 1959. Beaverbrook was a native of Ontario and Chancellor of New Brunswick University (1947–53).

NEWFOUNDLAND

Louis Anderson designed this district sett for Newfoundland in 1972. The vast province contains over 16,000 kilometres (10,000 miles) of coastline and is known for the cod-fishing as well as its land-based industries of forestry and mining. The colours of the tartan were chosen to suggest these industries.

▲ *Louisiana, 2001.*

▼ *Maine Dirigo.*

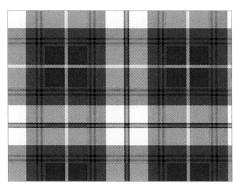

▲ *MacLeod Californian, 1980s.*

▼ *Mayo, 1996.*

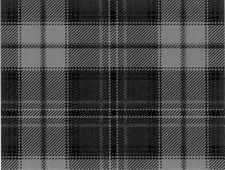

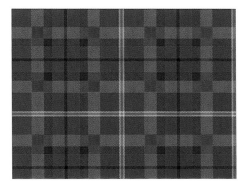

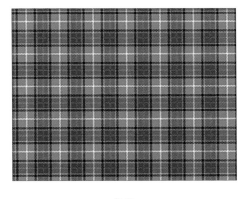

▲ *Manitoba, 1962.*

▼ *Manx National.*

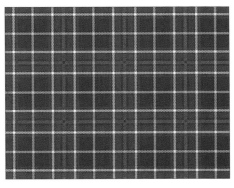

▲ *New Brunswick, 1959.*

▼ *Newfoundland, 1972.*

NEW HAMPSHIRE–ORDER OF THE HOLY SEPULCHRE

Some scholars believe that the Irish wore family tartans in much the same way as the Scots clansmen, but there is not enough evidence to be sure of this, even though a pair of tartan trousers dating from the late 1500s or early 1600s was dug up in Ireland in 1956. A number of Irish tartans were reproduced in *Clans Originaux*, published by Claude Fresklie in Paris in the 1880s, but there is some doubt as to the authenticity of these. Nevertheless Irish setts created as part of the recent renewed enthusiasm for tartans and family genealogy have been well received. Irish county tartans produced by the Scottish firm House of Edgar have been popular, as have tartans produced for those bearing the names of Ireland's great families of the past, such as the O'Neils, the O'Connors and the O'Briens.

NEW HAMPSHIRE

This sett was designed by Ralf Hartwell of Newton, New Hampshire, and was accredited as the official state tartan in 1995. The purple ground refers to the state's official flower (the purple lilac) and official bird (purple finch), while the black represents the granite of New Hampshire's mountains and the green of its forests.

NEW MEXICO

The red and yellow colours of the New Mexico flag are used in this sett, officially recognized as the state tartan. New Mexico joined the Union in 1912 as the 47th state.

NEW SOUTH WALES

Betty Johnston designed this tartan in 1998 as a charity fundraiser to help Australia's Motor Neurone Association and Cerebral Palsy Association. New South Wales lies in south-eastern Australia on the Pacific Coast. Sydney is the state capital.

NEW YORK FIREMEN'S PIPE BAND

This sett is essentially a regimental tartan created for a public service department. It was designed for the Emerald Society Bagpipe Band of the New York Fire Department by Grainger & Campbell of Glasgow in the 1960s.

NORTH VANCOUVER ISLAND

Anyone from Vancouver Island, British Columbia, Canada, can wear this district sett designed by Robert Fells in 1985 for the North Island Highlanders Pipe and Drum Band.

▲ *New Hampshire, 1995.*

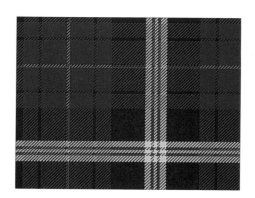

▼ *New Mexico.*

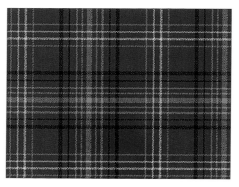

▲ *New South Wales, 1998.*

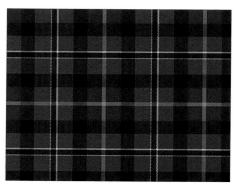

▼ *New York Firemen's Pipe Band, 1960s.*

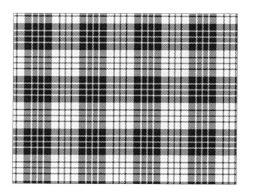

▲ *North Vancouver Island, 1985.*

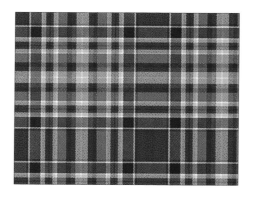

▼ *North West Mounted Police.*

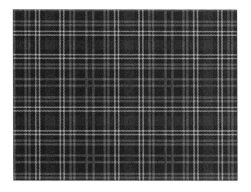

▲ *O'Brien.*

▲ *Ohio, 1984.*

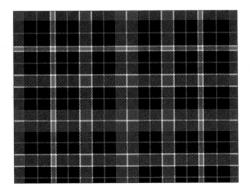

NEW ZEALAND

This sett was designed for the Piping and Dancing Association of New Zealand and is intended for use as a national tartan.

NORTH WEST TERRITORIES

Hugh Macpherson of Edinburgh designed this district sett for the vast region of northern Canada in 1969.

NOVA SCOTIA

The official tartan of Nova Scotia province in Canada was designed by Mrs Douglas Murray in 1953.

O'CONNOR

MacNaughtons of Pitlochry wove the tartan of this important Irish family. The main branch of the family claim descent from Conchobar, a 10th-century king of Connacht.

ONTARIO ENSIGN

The colours in this 1965 tartan are those of the coat of arms granted to the province in 1868 by Queen Victoria. Ontario, Canada's second largest province, has another district tartan named the Northern Ontario.

NORTH WEST MOUNTED POLICE

This is the name by which the Royal Canadian Mounted Police were known at their foundation in 1873, when they were formed to combat bootlegging. The colours of the tartan, made by the Sainthill-Levine company of Canada, echo those of their uniform.

O'BRIEN

This modern tartan, designed by the Australian Edward John O'Brien, commemorates the great Irish family descended from Brian Boru, High King of Ireland (r.1002–14).

OHIO

The Ohio state tartan, designed by Merry Jayne McMichael Fischbach, was approved on 29 March 1984. The blue represents the state's waterways, the white its cities and the red the state bird, the red cardinal. Ohio joined the Union in 1803 as the 17th state.

OKLAHOMA

This sett was adopted as the Oklahoma state tartan in 1999. It was designed by Jerrel Murray of the United Scottish Clans of Oklahoma, a charity that aims to promote Scottish Celtic culture in the state. Oklahoma joined the Union in 1907 as the 46th state.

O'NEIL

The tartan is intended for anyone who bears the name O'Neil. In Ireland the powerful Ui Neill (O'Neil) dynasty was descended from Niall of the Nine Hostages, High King of Ireland (r.AD379–405).

ORDER OF THE HOLY SEPULCHRE

This tartan was created in 1990 by Scotland's Ronald Kinsey for the Equestrian Order of the Holy Sepulchre of Jerusalem. Now involved in Christian work in Palestine, the chivalric order was established in

Jerusalem in the 11th century. The red evokes the crosses worn by Crusaders, while white and yellow are considered to be the colours of Jerusalem.

▼ *Oklahoma, 1999.*

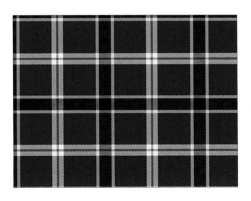

▼ *O'Neil.*

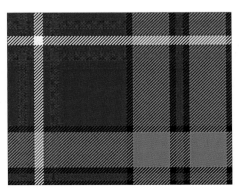

▼ *Order of the Holy Sepulchre, 1990.*

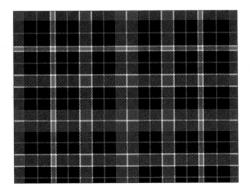

OTAGO PENINSULA–SALT LAKE CITY

Many modern tartans are designed and promoted to generate funds for charitable organizations. The St Columba tartan was created primarily as a means of raising money to repair the roof of St Columba's Church at Gruline, on the island of Mull, but it was also designed to honour the 1400th anniversary of St Columba's death on the island of Iona in June 597. The Irish-born abbot and missionary founded a church and monastery on Iona and with his followers brought the Christian gospel to Scotland.

Another fundraising sett was released in 1993 by the Royal and Ancient golf club at St Andrews, near Dundee, with the intention of generating the money needed to restore its older buildings. Similarly the Robert Burns, a simple checked tartan honouring one of Scotland's most celebrated sons, was produced in the 1950s as part of a fundraising drive for the Burns Society.

OTAGO PENINSULA
This tartan was designed by Vilma Nelson for the Otago Peninsula charitable trust, which manages a house and gardens in Dunedin on New Zealand's South Island. Vilma Nelson also designed an official district tartan for Otago as well as the Dunedin sett.

PAISLEY
Allan Drennan of Paisley, near Glasgow, won a tartan competition at Kelso Highland Show in 1952 with this sett. It has been used both as a district tartan for Paisley and a family tartan for people named Paisley. It deliberately touches on elements of the clan Donald (MacDonald) tartan.

POLARIS
A tartan designed for the Officers and men of the American Submarine base at the Holy Loch, Scotland, which makes Polaris submarine the first ship in history to have its own tartan. The idea was Captain Walter F. Schlech's, Commander of the squadron.

PORCUPINE
This tartan, first produced around 1956, is named after a mining district in Ontario that sprang up in the gold rush of the late 1890s. The weavers' guild in the area now produces the sett.

PRIDE OF SCOTLAND
This sett was produced by the Highland dress outfitters McCalls of Bridge Street, Aberdeen, in 1996 to a design by D.C. Dalgleish. It can be worn by anyone.

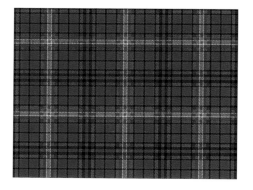

▲ *Otago Peninsula.*

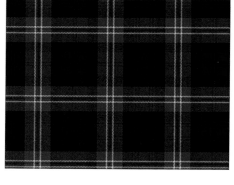

▲ *Polaris.*

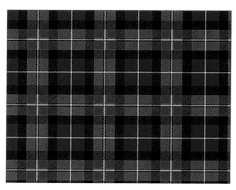

▲ *Pride of Scotland, 1996.*

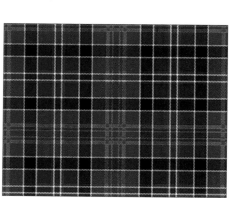

▼ *Paisley, 1952.*

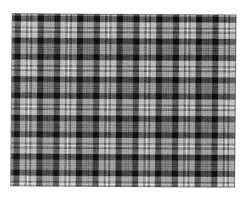

▼ *Porcupine, c.1956.*

▼ *Prince Edward Island, 1964.*

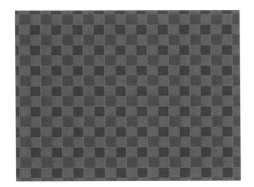

▲ *Robin Hood, 1819.*

▼ *Roscommon, 1996.*

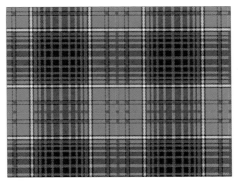

▲ *Royal Canadian Air Force, 1940s.*

▼ *Salt Lake City, 1996.*

SAINT COLUMBA
The historian and weaver Peter MacDonald created this Scottish fundraising tartan in 1997. It makes symbolic use of colour to celebrate the natural beauty of Iona, where the Irish missionary, St Columba, established his Christian monastery: dark blue represents the sea across which he sailed; pale blue the shallow coastal waters; cream its sandy bays; brown the lichen on the seashore rocks; green the island's hills; grey its rocks; and purple the wind-whipped heather.

SAINT LAWRENCE
The blue in this 1960s Canadian trade tartan represents the St Lawrence River, which runs 4000 kilometres (2500 miles) from its source in Minnesota through the Great Lakes to the Atlantic Ocean.

SALEM DANCERS
The Salem Scottish Dancers' Wee Blue tartan was commissioned by a group of highland dance enthusiasts in Salem, New Brunswick, Canada. The colouring picks up the blue and white of the Cross of St Andrew.

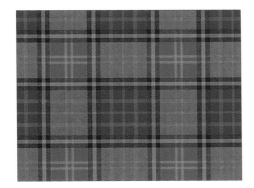

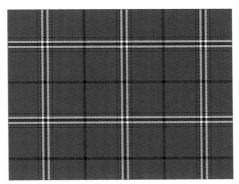

PRINCE EDWARD ISLAND
The tartan was created by Jean Reed in 1964 for Canada's smallest province. The reddish brown in the design is intended to suggest the colour of the island's soil and the white the surf that breaks on its beaches.

ROBIN HOOD
Wilson's of Bannockburn produced this tartan in 1819, when the tale of the English hero of Sherwood Forest was particularly in vogue, even in Scotland. It was later sold under the name Rob Roy in reference to the Scottish outlaw, Rob Roy MacGregor.

ROMSDAL
This district tartan was made for the Norwegian descendants of Scottish soldiers who survived the massacre at Gudbrandsdal in Norway in 1612. The soldiers had disembarked at Romsdal, and a keen interest in tartan continues in the area.

ROSCOMMON
This district tartan, released in 1996 by the House of Edgar, is named for the county of Roscommon in Connaught province of the Irish Republic.

ROYAL AND ANCIENT
The kiltmakers Kinloch Anderson created this sett in 1993 to raise money for restoration at the Royal and Ancient golf club in St Andrews. Its use is restricted to the members of the club. A separate district tartan, designed in 1930, is available for the townsfolk of St Andrews.

ROYAL CANADIAN AIR FORCE
The design of this sett is largely derived from the Anderson tartan, which uses a colour scheme (light blue, maroon and dark blue) that is appropriate for the Royal Canadian Air Force (RCAF). Loomcrofters of Gagetown, New Brunswick, produced the tartan in the 1940s.

SALT LAKE CITY
This district tartan celebrates Salt Lake City county in Utah. Its designer Richard David Barnes drew inspiration from the colours of the state university when creating the sett in 1996. Utah joined the Union in 1896.

▼ *Salem Dancers.*

SCOTLAND 2000–TEXAS BLUEBONNET

Scotland's accelerating development as a multicultural country has inspired some intriguing connections. In 1999 a Sikh, Sirdar Iqbal Singh, a retired property developer and energetic supporter of Scottish culture, who now lives in a castle at Lesmahagow, commissioned Lochcarron of Galashiels to make the Singh tartan. He saw the need for a Sikh tartan at a prize-giving at which many children were wearing family tartans, making the Sikh children look left out. In the same year A.J. Singh, another Scottish Sikh, had Kinloch Anderson design the Sikh tartan.

SCOTLAND 2000

This bright tartan was created by the Strathmore Woollen Company in 1999 to commemorate the new millennium and Scotland's developing position at a time of change.

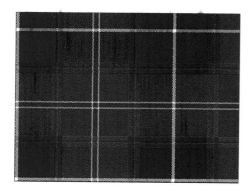

▲ *Scotland 2000, 1999.*

▼ *Scottish Knights Templar, 1998.*

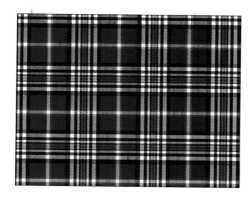

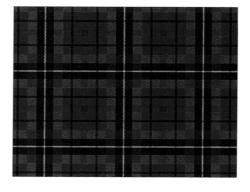

▲ *Scottish Parliament, 1998.*

▼ *Ship Hector, 1999.*

SCOTTISH KNIGHTS TEMPLAR

Stuart Davidson designed this tartan in 1998 to commemorate the Scottish branch of the Knights Templar, an order of monastic knights founded at the time of the Crusades.

SCOTTISH PARLIAMENT

This tartan, designed by Ronnie Hek, was released in 1998 to celebrate the referendum that approved the establishment of a Scottish Parliament.

SCOTT, SIR WALTER

According to Thomas Smibert in *The Clans of the Highlands of Scotland* (1850) Sir Walter Scott designed this tartan for his own use in 1822.

SEATTLE

Tomoko Edwards designed this district tartan in 1990 for Seattle, USA. Green

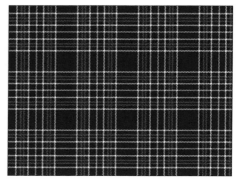

▲ *Seattle, 1990.*

▼ *Sir Walter Scott, 1822.*

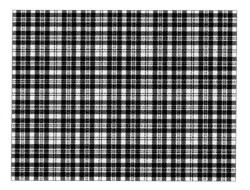

is for the Emerald city, gold for its sun, white for its snow-capped mountains, blue for the waters round the city, and pink for its rhododendrons.

SHIP HECTOR

As part of their millennium celebrations the people of Pictou, Nova Scotia, commissioned this tartan in honour of the good ship *Hector*, which safely carried Scottish emigrants there from Wester Ross in 1773.

SIKH

In 1999, when this sett was released, Sikhs were celebrating the tricentenary of their religion. A.J. Singh, who commissioned it, also wanted to mark the passage of 50 years since his family first came to Scotland. The tartan is for any Sikh and is available in the form of turbans as well as kilts.

SINGH

Iqbal Singh had this sett designed for Asians resident in or with links to Scotland. He was pictured wearing a kilt made from the tartan in an exhibition of miniature pictures by Sikh artists Amrit and Rabindra Singh at Edinburgh Royal Museum in 2000–1. The tartan's blue is a Singh family colour and the yellow is said to represent peace.

STONE OF DESTINY

The stone on which medieval Scottish kings were enthroned was taken from Scone to Westminster in 1296. When it was returned in 1996 Scotland's House of Edgar issued this commemorative tartan, which was designed by Polly Wittering.

TARA CLAUDE

Fresklie's publication *Clans Originaux* (1880) included this tartan but identified it as the Murphy family sett. It was later renamed Tara after a prehistoric ruin in County Meath, which is believed to have once been the home of the Irish high kings.

TARTAN ARMY

The sett was designed for use by Scotland's football fans by Keith Lumsden, who based it on the Royal Stewart tartan with Black Watch added as the background. The Scottish fans wore it to the 1998 World Cup in France, and since that time it has been adopted by followers of Scottish teams in other sports.

TEXAS BLUEBONNET

Designed by June MacRoberts in 1983, this tartan was used in 1986 for the 150th anniversary celebrations of the state's independence from Mexico. It was adopted as the official state tartan in 1989. The bluebonnet is the official state flower of Texas, where it grows wild in abundance.

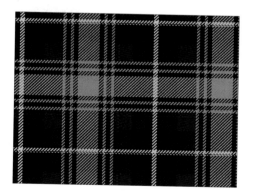

▲ *Sikh, 1999.*

▼ *Singh, 1999.*

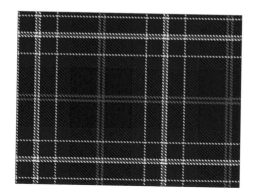

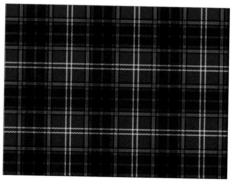

▲ *Stone of Destiny, 1996.*

▼ *Tartan Army, 1998.*

SALVATION ARMY

A blue, red and gold sett was designed by Captain H. Cooper for the celebrated Christian mission organization.

SPIRIT OF SCOTLAND

This universal tartan can be worn by people of any nationality or family.

SULTANATE OF OMAN

A brown, gold and blue regimental tartan was produced in the 1960s for the Sultanate of Oman Air Force (Juniors) Pipe Band.

SVANHOLM

This family tartan is intended for use by the members of the Swedish Svanholm family.

TASMANIAN

Isabella Lamont Shorrock designed a district tartan for the island state of Tasmania in Australia. It was approved as the state tartan in 1999.

TENNESSEE

The Tennessee state tartan was approved in 1999.

TIPPERARY

Scotland's House of Edgar released a distinctive red and green district tartan for County Tipperary in the south-west of the Irish Republic in 1996.

TOKYO BLUEBELLS

The Tokyo Bluebells Highland dancing team commissioned a corporate tartan.

TYRONE COUNTY

Tyrone in Ulster was one of the Irish counties provided with a district tartan designed by Polly Wittering for Scotland's House of Edgar in 1996.

ULSTER–YUKON

Scotland's links to the United States are extremely strong. Scots emigrated to North America in their thousands in the 18th and 19th centuries and many great figures in American history have been Scots or of Scottish descent. According to some sources, more than six out of ten US Presidents have had Scottish ancestry. The close links between the two countries have been celebrated by the release of the United States tartan. The authorities governing the Scottish tourist industry commissioned and released the tartan to promote visits to Scotland. As with a number of "universal" tartans that have been released in recent years, anyone can wear this tartan. Most universal setts are primarily aimed at the outfitters who specialize in hiring out Highland wear for weddings and other formal occasions. As it would be impossible for these firms to store kilts made up in all the many available family, district, corporate and national tartans, universal setts such as Pride of Scotland or, in the United States, the American tartan are available for hire.

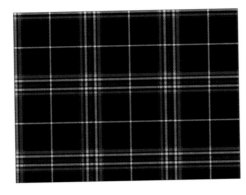

▲ *United States.*

▼ *Vancouver Centennial, 1986.*

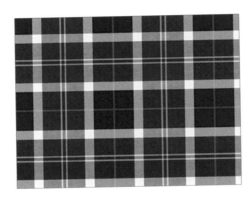

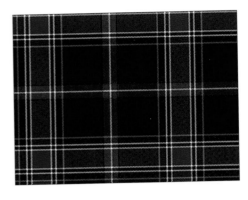

▲ *Victoria, 1998.*

▼ *Virginia Military Institute, 1996.*

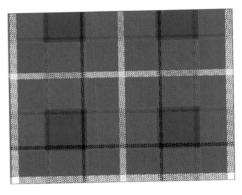

ULSTER

The modern district sett for Ulster is based on the remains of trousers dug up in 1956 at Flanders Townland in County Londonderry, Ulster, and dated to the 1500s or 1600s.

▼ *Ulster, registered 1950s.*

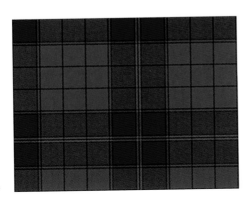

UNITED STATES

This tartan was released to promote visits to Scotland by American tourists and celebrate the close links between the United States and Scotland. Its designer, Malcolm Campbell, chose a colour scheme that echoed both the Cross of St Andrew and the Stars and Stripes.

UTAH CENTENNIAL

The state of Utah's official sett is based on the Logan clan tartan. Scottish emigrant Ephraim Logan settled in northern Utah and gave his name to the river Logan. Utah became the 45th state of the Union in 1896. The tartan was designed by Philip D. Smith, Jr.

VANCOUVER CENTENNIAL

This Canadian commemorative tartan honours the city of Vancouver in British Columbia. The tartan was released to celebrate the 100th anniversary of Vancouver's city status in 1886.

VERMONT

Andrew Elliot designed the Vermont state tartan in 1994. Vermont, in the north-eastern corner of the United States, was the 14th state of the Union when it joined in 1791. A number of Aberdeenshire Scottish immigrants settled in Vermont in the 18th and 19th centuries. The tartan's red and gold colours are those of the state flag.

VICTORIA

Betty Johnston created this sett in 1998 for Canberra's House of Tartan. The state of Victoria lies in south-eastern Australia. The pink line in the tartan is meant to suggest the state's official flower, the pink heath.

VIRGINIA MILITARY INSTITUTE

Two of the institute's cadets, Donald Fraser and Donnie Haseltine, designed this tartan in 1996. The state military college in Lexington, Virginia, was founded in 1839. It was destroyed by Union soldiers in 1864, but was afterwards rebuilt.

WASHINGTON

This is the official tartan of the US state of Washington, adopted in 1991. It was designed by Frank Cannonito and Margaret McLeod van Nus in 1989, to mark the 100th anniversary of the state joining the Union.

WATERFORD

County Waterford lies on the Irish Republic's south coast in the province of Munster. Polly Wittering designed this and a series of other Irish county tartans for Scotland's House of Edgar in 1996.

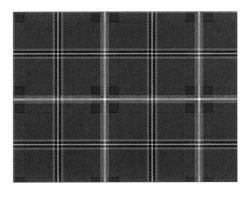

▲ *Washington, 1989.*

WELSH NATIONAL DISTRICT

This tartan, the Welsh National district sett, can be worn by anyone of Welsh extraction. It dates from 1993. A different green and red design by Ronnie Hek marks the establishment of the National Assembly for Wales in 1999.

WEST POINT

The official colours of the West Point military academy, properly known as the United States Military Academy, are yellow, grey and black and form the basis of its regimental tartan, designed by Kinloch Anderson in 1985. The academy, founded in 1802, is in Orange County, New York state.

WEXFORD COUNTY

Wexford lies in the south-eastern part of the Irish Republic. Its district tartan is one of a group released by the Scottish firm House of Edgar in 1996.

YORKSHIRE CCC

Amanda Hodgkinson designed this corporate tartan for the Yorkshire County Cricket Club, one of the leading lights of the English county game.

YUKON

Created by Janet Couture in 1965, this is the official tartan for the Yukon territory in Canada, home of the 1898 gold rush. Appropriately, gold colouring is a significant feature of the tartan.

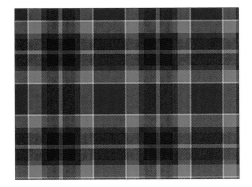

▲ *Waterford, 1996.*

▼ *Welsh National District, 1993.*

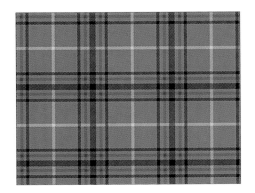

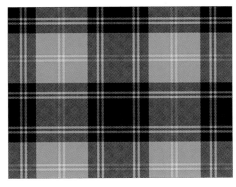

▲ *West Point, 1985.*

▼ *Wexford County, 1996.*

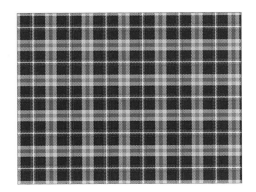

▲ *Yorkshire CCC.*

▼ *Yukon, 1965.*

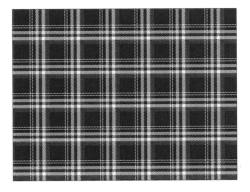

TARTAN INDEX

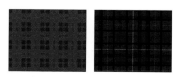

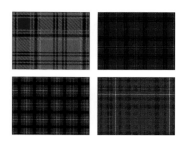

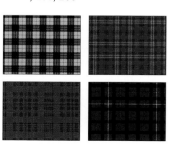

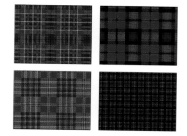

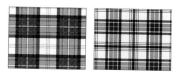

INDEX

ACKNOWLEDGEMENTS

The publishers wish to thank the following agencies for supplying images for the book: Aberdeen Art Gallery & Museums Collections: p27 *Baptism in Scotland* by John Phillip, AKG (London): pp 30t Anglo Saxon manuscript illumination, 37t *John Knox*, unsigned engraving, 44 *The Celebrated Battle of Culloden* by Grainger, 59 *Ossian's Dream* by Jean-Auguste-Dominique Ingres, 1813, 62 *The Arrival of George IV at Leith Harbour* by Thomas Butterworth, 64 *Sir Walter Scott* engraving by William Walker after painting by Henry Raeburn, 65t *Jeanie Deans and Queen Caroline* by Charles Robert Leslie, 74t, 87t *American War of Independence Advance of the American Troops* by Francois Godefroy, 106b *Capt Robert Gray's Ship "Columbia"* by Louis Dodd, 122b, 123t,
Alamy Images: p52b.
The Bridgeman Art Library: pp 1 & 206 *Four Gentlemen in Highland Dress* by Kenneth Macleay, 15 *Sir Mungo Murray* by John Michael Wright c1683, *Caledonians, or Picts*, engraving, English School 19th cent., 17t *Niel Gow* by Henry Raeburn, 1787, 26 *For Better of Worse – Rob Roy and the Baillie* by John Nicol, 1886, 30b *Mr Macready as Macbeth*, English School, 19th cent., 32bl *Robert the Bruce* from Seton's Armorial Crests, br *Baliol Doing Homage*, engraving, English School, 19th cent., 33b *The Death of John Comyn* by Felix Philippoteaux, 36b *Mary, Queen of Scots being led to Execution* by John Laslett Pott, 37b *James James VI of Scotland*, anon, 38t *The Beheading of King Charles I*, engraving, Dutch School, 1649, 40t *Kenneth Sutherland, 3rd Lord Duffus* by Richard Waitt, 40b *Portrait of a Jacobite Lady* by Cosmo Alexander, 44t *Prince Charles Edward Stuart Entering Edinburgh* by Thomas Duncan, 45l *Prince Charles at Holyrood*, 1833 by William Simson, 45r *Bonnie Prince Charlie in Hiding after the Battle of Culloden*, English School, 19th cent., 47t *Flora Macdonald*, 1747 by Richard Wilson, 48b *After Culloden: Rebel Hunting* by John Seymour Lucas, 53t *Lochaber No More*, 1883 by John Watson Nicol, 56 *Distraining for Rent* by Sir David Wilkie, 1815, 57b *The Last of the Clan* by Thomas Faed, 63b *The Entry of George IV into Edinburgh* by John Ewbank, 1822, 66t *George IV in Highland Dress* by Sir David Wilkie, 1830, 67 *Colonel Alistair Macdonell of Glengarry* by Henry Raeburn, 1812, 69b *Deer Stalking in the Highlands* by Sir Edwin Landseer, 76t *The Order of Release* by Sir John Everett Millais, 1853, 76b *The MacNab* by Henry Raeburn, 77 *The Highland Shepherd* by Rosa Bonheur, 79 *Scottish Settlers in North America* by Thomas Faed, 83tl *Gustavus Adolphus II*, German School, 19th cent., 86 *A Soldier of the 79th highlanders at Chobham Camp in 1853* by Eugene-Louis Lamb, 89 *Sir John Sinclair* by Henry Raeburn, 94b *Caesar Crossing the Rubicon*, French School, 15th century, 95t *Anecdote of the Bravery of the Scottish Piper* by Franz Joseph Manskirch, *A Military Review* by John Wilson Ewbank, 137tr *John Campbell, 3rd Earl of Breadalbane* by Charles Jervas 1708, 140t *Illustration to the Battle of Otterbourne* by Robert Burns, Anon, 145 *Battle of Culloden* printed by Laurie and Whittle 1797, 147bl *Portrait of Simon Fraser, Lord Lovat*, by William Hogarth 1746, 148 *Colonel William Gordon of Fyvie* by Pompeo Girolamo Batoni, 151b *Portrait of John Graham of Claverhouse*, English School 19th cent., 159 *Colonel Aistair Macdonell of Glengarry* by Henry Raeburn, 171t *Sir Walter Scott* by Francis Legatt Chantrey, 206b (see p 1), 224b, 225b, 227t, 228t, 231t, 232b.
Corbis: 85t, 132t, 133b, 137tl, 167t, 172.
Historic Scotland: p25 (all), 138bl.
Getty Images: p78.

Scotland In Focus: pp 2 & 161, 3, 4 (all), 7b, 8–9, 10–11 & 21, 12, 13 (all), 14mr &b, 17t, 19b, 20, 21 (all), 22 (all), 23b, 28t, 28b courtesy of D Corrance, 29t, 31 (all), 34–35 & 42b, 38b, 41t, 46b, 47b, 48t, 51br, 54-55 & 68t, 57t, 71bl, bm & br, 72br, 73t, 80-81, 83b courtesy of The Strathnaver Museum, 87b, 90t courtesy of the Stirling Museum, 96-97 & 104, 102t, 103tr &b, 107m, 108, 116 (all), 122t, 124 (all) & 125 courtesy of the Jakarta Highland Games Society, 127t, 128-129, 130-131, 133t, 134t, 138t, 139b, 140b, 143, 144t, 146 (all), 147br, 150, 152t, 153tr, 154t, 155b, 157t, 158t, 161, 162t. 163. 164, 166t, 167b, 169 (all), 170 (all), 174-175. 177b, 178t, 180bl, 183tr, 184b, 186t, 189b, 190t, 193b, 194b, 197b, 198t, 200b, 202b, 205t, 209b, 210t, 213t, 214b, 217t, 219t, 220t, 234-235. All tartan samples in the book were also supplied by Scotland in Focus.
Scottish Viewpoint: p63t.
Mary Evans Picture Library: pp 24, 39, 43, 51bl, 52t, 58b, 60, 61bl & br, 65b, 75t & b, 107tr, 134bl, 142t, 153tl, 223.
The National Archives: p134br.
National Library of Scotland: p36t, 42t, 70, 71t, 98 (all).
©The Trustees of the National Museums of Scotland: pp 7t, 14t, 18 (all), 19t, 29b, 66b, 68b, 69t, 88, 91b, 92, 93 all, 95b, 99b, 102bl & br, 103tl, 111tl, 114t & b.
The National Trust for Scotland: 155t,
Peter Newark's Military Pictures: pp 33t, 50, 58t, 84.
www.PerfectPhoto.CA/©Rob Van Nostrand: pp 51t, 53b.
The Royal Bank of Scotland: p49.
St Andrews Links www.standrews.org.uk: p118.
Topham Picture Library: p71bl, 82bl, 83tr, 99t, 100, 121bl, 123b, 126 (all), 127b.
Vinmag: 73b, 85b, 120 (all), 121t.

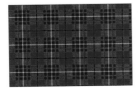 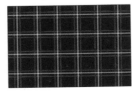